THE HISTORICAL AND CULTURAL ATLAS OF
AFRICAN AMERICANS

Macmillan Publishing Company
New York

Collier Macmillan Canada
Toronto

Maxwell Macmillan International
New York   Oxford   Singapore   Sydney

THE HISTORICAL AND CULTURAL ATLAS OF
AFRICAN AMERICANS

Molefi K. Asante
Mark T. Mattson

First Paperback Edition, 1992

Macmillan Publishing Company
866 Third Avenue, New York, N.Y. 10022

Collier Macmillan Canada, Inc.
1200 Eglinton Avenue East, Suite 200
Don Mills, Ontario M3C 3N1

Library of Congress Catalog Card Number: 90-46410

Printed in the United States of America

printing number
  2 3 4 5 6 7 8 9 10

Library of Congress Cataloging-in-Publication Data

Asante, Molefi K., 1942–
    The historical and cultural atlas of African Americans/
Molefi K. Asante, Mark T. Mattson.
        p.   cm.
    Includes bibliographical references and index.
    ISBN 0-02-897021-7
    1. Afro-Americans.   2. Afro-Americans—History
    3. Afro-Americans—History—Maps.
    I. Mattson, Mark T.   II. Title.
E185.A8   1991   973'.0496073—ac20   90-46410 CIP

Photo Credits   3 3090 01325 3341

A Pictorial History of the Negro in America, Langston Hughes and Milton Meltzer, 36
Lillian Anthony, 115
Bethune-Museum Archives, 105
Black Book, Middleton Harris, 63, 64, 94
Ebony Collection, 31, 38, 55, 82, 84
National Afrocentric Institute, 9
Stephen Shore, 4, 5
Bobby Seale, 124
Tafawa, 129
Temple University Archives, 102, 121, 146
Lincoln University, Special Collections, for all other photos

CONTENTS

PREFACE

African American culture has made enormous contributions to the cultures of the world. The impact is particularly significant in the American context because African American culture is a major component of what constitutes being American. In this regard, Africa in America has meant that America is more than a European nation or an African nation, it is a combination of these two important elements as well as many other cultural influences that provide the special character of the American nation. African-American culture is also African at its most elemental and fundamental level; from the construction of sentences to the choosing of music, the legacy and heritage of thousands of years of human response to the African environment impacts upon the 370 years of the African-American sojourn in North America. With this in mind we have combined our talents, Molefi Asante in African-American studies and Mark Mattson in cartography, to produce the first historical and cultural reference atlas of the African-American people.

The atlas will be a major reference work with interest for libraries, scholars, government workers, businesspeople, tourists, and individuals with an interest in presenting a portrait of the African-American community. The atlas is directed toward an American as well as a world audience. We wanted a book that would give individuals a spatial representation of some of the most important events, personalities, and facts about African Americans. It is the kind of atlas one would suggest to inquirers for information about the African-American population.

An atlas, however, is not an encyclopedia. One will not find *every* item of importance to African-American history included here. We have selected information, events, and personalities that represent the great expanse of the cultural spectrum. In this regard, we have been motivated by the desire to include the contributions of individuals and groups that have had an impact on the national and world character of the African-American people.

The fundamental purpose of the atlas is to provide detailed maps of information and events. As a reference work, this volume should be useful for those interested in a technical and historical guide to information. The reader should gain an appreciation of the historical and cultural origins of African Americans from the early chapters. We have tried to demonstrate that African Americans are not absolutely detached from the long history and cultural traditions of the continent of Africa itself.

Thus, we have carefully created maps and charts to give the reader a holistic view of the African-American people. In doing this, we have avoided a strict chronological order, preferring to interweave themes into certain broad time lines. Furthermore, we have painstakingly integrated the maps, statistical information, and cultural data into narrative segments which should be easy to follow. Of course, we have not repeated information found in the maps and charts in a word for word fashion. This type of redundancy served no purpose for this atlas and we avoided it as much as possible.

The atlas makes a head-on confrontation with several issues that have plagued African and African-American historiography. In the first place, we have used the term *African Americans* to refer to American citizens whose racial, cultural, or ethnic backgrounds are historically rooted in the African continent. Although nearly 75 percent of this population has racially or culturally plural backgrounds and more than 99 percent has ethnically plural backgrounds, we have followed the general practice in the United States of defining the African-American population by its African rather than European or Native American elements.

Historically, the leading African Americans, regardless of color or degree of non-African genes, have defined themselves in this manner since the seventeenth century. Had they defined themselves any other way it would not have mattered in a legal sense. Thus, in the United States the African population, with all of its mixture, has avoided the legal classifications of people by color as is found in Brazil and South Africa.

Using the new Afrocentric paradigm as a guide, we have attempted to view Africa holistically, that is, as one giant interrelated sector rather than as Sub-Saharan and north-of-the-Sahara Africa. Since the cultures of the continent have been flowing between regions for thousands of years we have tried to show the manner in which the African experience is similar in many places. The European Slave Trade, a principal part of the past 500 years of the African experience, contributed to the view of Africa as segmented and disjointed. Separate ethnic and linguistic experiences exist and are accounted for in the new paradigm but it also recognizes the similarity of myths, symbols, and cosmological orientations.

In choosing a structure for the first historical and cultural atlas of African Americans, we have utilized the Spirituals as reference points. No figures could be more significant or more appropriate in connection with African-American culture than these epic songs. They tell the story of Africans in America more poignantly than any prose. Consequently we have used them as keepers of the traditions.

The first chapter is "I Got My Religion from out of the Sun," and serves as the introductory chapter. It examines some of the ancient origins of the people who are now African Americans. Four hundred years ago there were no African Americans, only Africans with various ethnic names. This chapter looks at African origins of the human race as well as significant ancient historical sites. Chapter 2, "I Don't Care where You Bury My Body," is about adventure. Africans have migrated all over the earth, often by force but also because of the curiosity and spirit of adventure which often grabs human beings. The third chapter, "Dark Clouds A'Risin," discusses the beginnings of the slave trade which was to transport between 15 and 50 million Africans from the continent of Africa.

The title of the fourth chapter, "I Know de Udder Worl' is Not Like Dis," is a chapter which examines the nature of the Great Enslavement on the African population. The fifth chapter, "And Before I'd be a Slave," is a celebration of the resistance movement. The aim is to demonstrate the resistance in several areas of African American life. The Chapter 6,"All My Troubles Will Soon be Over With," shows the African American culture of resistance, the abolition movement, and the attack on the pro-slavery elements. In Chapter 7, "My Lord Gwineter to Rain Down Fire," we discuss the coming and prosecution of the Civil War. Chapter 8, "Swing Low, Sweet Chariot," is dedicated to the Reconstruction and the African American response to the white resistance to emancipation.

Chapter 9, "Now Ain't Them Hard Trials," is concerned with the wanton murder of African Americans during the late nineteenth and early twentieth centuries. Lynching became a national dis-

grace and Ida B. Wells Barnett was the leading voice of resistance. Chapter 10 is called "And Still We Rise" as a testament to the achievements of African Americans in many fields of endeavor. Chapter 11, "Great Day, Great Day, the Righteous Marching" discusses the Civil Rights Movement and the attendant political and organizational situations. Chapter 12, "Before This Time Another Year," is a portrait of the cultural and historical elements that have gone into the creation of a resilient culture. Chapter 13 "Didn't My Lord Deliver Daniel" presents data regarding employment, poverty, illiteracy, infant mortality, and the professions of African Americans.

Another feature of this atlas which should aid readers in understanding the persistence of certain themes, the similarity of adventures, and the appearance of particular responses to society are the biographical and thematic snapshots that are strategically placed to highlight given events and personalities. In general, the chapters are presented in chronological order. However, biographical and thematic snapshots which cross time lines might appear, for example, under a discussion of exploration. The aim of this feature is to provide the reader with an instant opportunity for comparison. We have deliberately not included snapshots in every section but have done so in those cases where we think it would make good sense.

Finally, we are in an extraordinary situation as authors. Our manuscript for the *Historical and Cultural Atlas of African Americans* was completed long before the data from the 1990 United States census count was processed. Thus, in chapter thirteen we had to rely upon data from the last completed census, 1980. While we apologize to our readers for any inconvenience this may cause, it could not be avoided given the

publication schedule of the atlas and the lack of completed census for 1990. We believe, however, that inasmuch as the data in chapter thirteen represent only a small portion of the information in the atlas, the reader will find that trends, themes, and events discussed in the other twelve chapters are basically unaffected by this use of data from the 1980 Census.

We recognize that no atlas can present a complete representation of a culture and ours is sure to fall short in many areas. The expert will undoubtedly discover omissions and commissions with which to disagree, but we hope that the manner in which we have treated the data, the maps, the photographs, and the charts will reflect not just accuracy but the love we have for such a noble subject.

ACKNOWLEDGMENTS

This book seeks to express the vitality and energy within the African-American community. We recognized very early that it would be impossible to capture the spirit of the historic African-American people without the contributions of many others. Chief among the scholars and writers who have informed our work in one way or another are Maulana Karenga, California State University—Northridge; Vincent Harding, Ilief Theological Seminary; St. Clair Drake, Professor Emeritus, Stanford; Lerone Bennett, *Ebony Magazine*; Ivan van Sertima, Rutgers University; John Hope Franklin, Professor Emeritus, Duke University; Sterling Stuckey, Northwestern University; Mary Berry, University of Pennsylvania; John Blassingame, Yale University; and John Henrik Clarke, Professor Emeritus, Hunter College. What we have received most from them is a sense of the magnitude of the African-American culture. Beyond the inspiration the works of these contemporaries have brought to our *Historical and Cultural Atlas of African Americans* is the tremendous intelligence with which they have worked in this field. They were preceded by Benjamin Quarles, Benjamin Brawley, William Wells Brown, Langston Hughes, Merle Epps, Carter G. Woodson, and W. E. B. DuBois. They, too, sang the complex songs and danced to the intricate rhythms of African-American culture. To both our contemporaries and our forerunners, we are grateful and forever indebted for understanding the vastness of this cultural and historical experience.

An undertaking such as this atlas is impossible without the assistance of many persons and institutions. Among the major resources which were made available to us and which we consulted were the Paley Library at Temple University, particularly its archival department; the Charles Blockson Afro-American Collection at Temple University; Lincoln University's Langston Hughes Library, Special Collections, the Schomburg Center for Research in Black Culture; the Institute for Afro American Culture in Los Angeles; and the newly formed Institute of the Black Peoples in Ouagadougou, Burkina Faso. Catherine Hooker at the Schomburg in New York and Lillian Anthony of the Afro-American Heritage Project in Louisville, Kentucky came through with some excellent ideas and suggestions at key moments. During the initial period of gathering maps, statistics, and photographs, we spent considerable time in archives, on the telephone and using facsimile machines—tracking down information. There were times when we had reached our mind's end regarding where to look for certain information for the atlas. We were fortunate to have Ella Forbes, Head of Special Collections, Lincoln University, and Pam Austin of the Temple University Archives, as ready sources of knowledge during these moments of impasse. They inevitably came through with bits of information and ideas that assisted in moving the project along. James Myers, Director of Libraries, Temple University, graciously made available a study room for the project.

The presence at Temple University of the nation's first doctoral program in African American Studies provided us the opportunity to work with many competent research assistants who made valuable contributions to the atlas. We owe a special thanks to five students, Karyn Lacy, Cecil Gray, Daniel Black, Rodney Patterson, and Eddie Glaude, who arrived on campus from Oberlin, Virginia, Clark-Atlanta, South Carolina, and Morehouse for the Temple experience and became part of our research team. Karyn Lacy particularly helped to keep track of materials and data during the early days of the project. Also we would like to thank Angelic Justin whose many trips to our library resulted in much useful information.

We have also benefitted from the intellectual ideas and encouragement advanced by H. Patrick Swygert, President, State University of New York at Albany, formerly the Executive Vice President of Temple University, and Peter Liacouras, President, Temple University; they represent the best tradition of administrators who are also scholars. We would like to acknowledge the support of the Department of African American Studies and the Department of Geography and Urban Studies. Those who had the opportunity to read various portions of the manuscript include C. Tsehloane Keto and Abu Abarry, Temple University, and Carol Blackshire, Ohio State University. Thanks goes to Stephen Shore and Scott Fort of the Cartographic Lab at Temple University, and to Yvonne Keck Holman, *Alternative Productions,* who was indispensable with her organizational skills, technical support, book design, and type composition. Nadia Kravchenko had the responsibility of decoding, actually deciphering, the many markings we first made on our word processors. Her work is impeccable.

Though it should be known, we should say explicitly that none of the people whom we have mentioned bear responsibility for anything which appears in this volume.

We thank Lloyd Chilton, Executive Editor at Macmillan, who visited us from time to time to make sure that our work habits and styles meshed. We thank him for both his insights and support. African fabrics were made available courtesy of LFS for Wonoo Ventures, Asante, Ghana; 1657 The Fairway, Jenkintown, PA 19046. Phototgraphs of these fabrics were taken by Stephen Shore.

Finally, we acknowledge each other for the wonderful joy of working together on a worthy project. We also say thanks to our families, with special attention given to our wives Kariamu and Cathy for their enduring understanding and love.

To the thousands who perished
in the Middle Passage

Wolof,
Senegal, Africa

"I GOT MY RELIGION FROM OUT OF THE SUN": AFRICAN ORIGINS 1

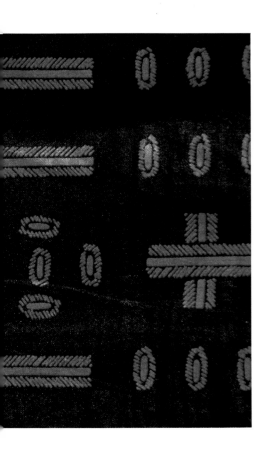

Africa is an incredibly diverse continent. As a geographical region it contains almost every type of topography found on the earth. There are deserts, the largest being the Sahara, but both the Kalahari and the Namib are formidable features of the continent's landscape. Rain forests exist where a day without rain is a phenomenal and momentous event. In such forests on the continent, more tropical plants, flowers, and herbs grow than in any other tropical area of the world except the Amazon Basin.

Rivers crisscross the vast surface of this second largest continent. The great Nile, mother of African civilization, has carried ideas, concepts, and people from near the Mountains of the Moon in Uganda-Zaire to the Mediterranean, the longest distance of any river, since time immemorial. The fabled Zaire (Congo) River, more massive than any river on earth, except the Amazon, is ten miles across in some places. Crossing the equator twice, a feat not achieved by any other river, the Zaire's volume is unaffected by the seasons. When the dry season exists in one part of the river the rainy season is occurring in the other and vice versa. The storied Niger, witness to caravans of faith, gold merchants, and ancient cities such as Timbuktu and Jenne, traverses the colorful and artistic West African region, while laying claim to its place as one of the most majestic rivers of the world.

The Zambezi, cutting through stones and forest, enters our consciousness as the source of Musi Wa Tunya, "The Smoke That Thunders" (Victoria Falls). A plaque at the falls says that David Livingstone, on seeing the Zambezi pound over the mile-wide cliff, once said "no more beautiful sight has ever been seen on earth."

There are lakes in profusion, most are natural, a few human-made and producing enormous supplies of electricity. The largest of these are the results of giant dams such as Akosombo in Ghana, Aswan in Egypt, Kariba in Zimbabwe-Zambia, and Cabora-Bassa in Mozambique.

Some lakes have produced strange chemical reactions, emitting gasses in the air, sometimes with deadly results as in the Cameroon. Lake Bosumturi in Ghana is a sacred lake dedicated to the deities. Its shape is almost a perfect 360°.

Mountains, brilliantly green at noon or azure in the dawn, snow-capped peaks at the equator or snow-dusted ranges in Lesotho or Morocco, are prominent on the continent.

Grasslands, called savannas, dominate in the west between the coast and the rain forest. Tall grasses have been used for centuries to make beautiful baskets and sleeping mats.

Africa's geographical and topographical diversity produces a variety of human responses to the environment. We see this diversity reflected in art, food, and the fabrics, such as *kente, bokolanfini, asoke, adinkra,* and *faso dan fani,* all harmonizing with the people, cultures, and environments of their origin. Archaeological and biological evidence point to an East African origin of the modern human as well as the earliest human society. Research by Louis Leakey and other anthropologists has established, in a series of impressive discoveries, that the oldest known human remains in the world are in East Africa. Indeed, Leakey's pioneering work in the Olduvai Gorge in Northern Tanzania, near Lake Rudolf in Kenya, and near the Omo River in Ethiopia has shown that hominids were using tools in this area more than 2 million years ago.

The early humans in East Africa were the first to use the hand-axe, although the name most often associated with the implements, Acheulian, refer to similar tools found in Western Europe. Anthropologists now know that the African sites in the Olduvai Gorge region have revealed the oldest tools known to humans.

Donald Johanson, an American paleo-anthropologist, contends that the skeleton known as Lucy, which he discovered in 1974 at Hadar, Ethiopia, and other fossilized bones found in both Ethiopia and Tanzania, belonged to a single hominid species called Australopithecus afarensis. According to Johanson, afarensis was the common ancestor of Australopithecines and humans. The date for these fossils was put at 3.5 million years ago, about 1.2 million years after the divergence of humans and apes. Hominid activity in the East African region predates any such activity in the world.

In the open African savannahs, early humans found adequate supplies of game animals and permanent quantities of water. The chill of the nights in the highlands of Africa probably led to

the next major technological achievement: the making and control of fire. About 60,000 years ago, African humans were using fire, an instrument for cooking and warmth. Thus, the adequacy of the food supply and the ability to make meat tender gave the early Africans a method for expanding the size of communities.

Climatic changes occurred over the long period of human evolution in Africa. Although the continent of Africa did not experience the massive Ice Ages which occurred in Europe, there was an appreciable effect on the African climate because of the vast ice caps at both the north and south poles. The Wurm Glaciation which covered Europe between 70,000 and 10,000 B.C.E. produced a cooler

and wetter Eastern Africa and a cooler and drier Western Africa. This condition altered the balance between the forest and savannah regions, making what are now forest regions more open and habitable by large groups of humans. Since humans had fire, the ability to capture and kill animals for food, the knowledge of plants and herbs, they were able to establish permanent homes and further increase the size and complexity of communities. Accordingly, the development of the Sangoan (named after the type-site at Sango Bay on Lake Victoria in Uganda) culture with its distinctive stone tools represents the most prevalent type of early human culture in Africa. Following the Sangoan culture

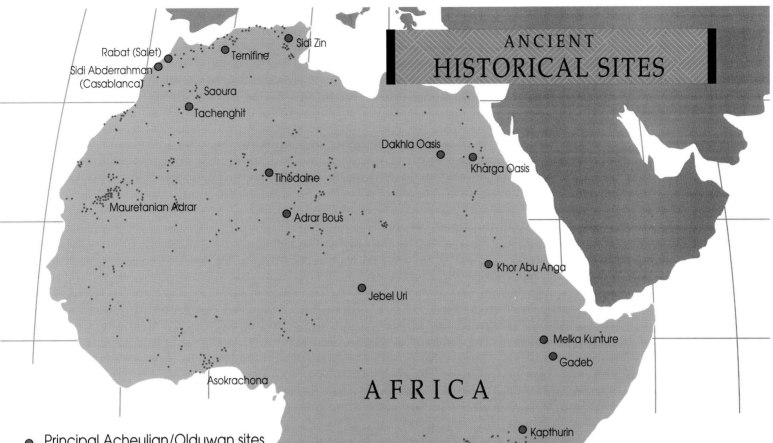

AFRICA

● Principal Acheulian/Olduwan sites

· Other recorded surface sites

was the Mousterian culture which evolved as a stone age culture between 35,000 and 8000 B.C.E.

One of the earliest examples of humans using stone to create instruments for calculation is the Isonghee abacus which was found in what is now the country of Zaire. According to experts, the Isonghee abacus is the oldest known human implement used for calculation. It is dated from approximately 6000 B.C.E.

Evidence of human societies has been shown to be rich in the central part of the African continent. Indeed, the ancient Egyptians claimed to have come from the Mountains of the Moon. The countries of Kenya, Zaire, Ethiopia, and Uganda are keys to history.

Ancient Historical Sites
Fabled cities of the fertile valleys of central and southern Africa as well as long-vanished towns and villages in the Sahara Desert speak of the richness of the human record on this continent.

Africa possesses the longest record of biological and cultural relics of early humans. Indeed, the Olduvai Gorge in Tanzania affords us a record of human biological and social evolution that is

not only a standard reference for the continent but has become, by virtue of the fullness of the record, a world standard.

Ancient tool-making sites have been found throughout Africa, many older than 1,500,000 years. Stone Age and Lower Paleolithic sites between 700,000 and 100,000 years old are numerous. Later, however, the emergence of other sites, particularly west and central African sites, represented increased in-migration from other African regions. Thus, sites established by 10,000 B.C.E., such as Tiemassas in Senegal; Yengema Cave in Sierra Leone; Adwuku in Ghana; Rim in Burkina Faso; Iwo Eleru, Jos, Ukpa, and Mejiro, near Old Oyo in Nigeria provide evidence of organized human activity and early technology. Although human activity and early social technology had occurred prior to this time, the record indicates a greater concentration of people and a wider variety of activities.

African rock paintings are older and more numerous than such paintings elsewhere. Most of the paintings and engravings occurred in areas where there were protective rock shelters, ledges, caves, or massive rock overhangs. Because of the protected nature of the rock painting sites, the naturalistic and schematic representations of the works are durable.

The African continent is rich in historical and cultural sites both prior to and subsequent to the pyramids, the oldest monumental constructions on the earth. Erected around 2500 B.C.E., the

Bamun Ancestral Figure, Cameroon

pyramids remain the most perfect example of African architectural antiquity. With the spread of human populations to west and central Africa as a result of numerous internal political and agricultural imperatives, large empires were welded together by outstanding military and political leaders. Many of these empires lasted into the twentieth century as fragmentary states within the more modern state structures established as a result of the colonial policies of the European nations. Even today, the Asante, Yoruba, Mossi, Lozi, Congo, and Fante nations exist as functional units within modern states.

West African Empires

The migration of people from Eastern African to the West African savannas occurred over thousands of years, accelerating from the third century B.C.E. to the tenth century A.D. The results of the movement of populations from various parts of East Africa are found in the dynamic civilizations that arose as a direct impact of the interaction between numerous empires and kingdoms. Among the names of civilizations that must be considered in connection with the rise of organized states in Central and West Africa are Nok, Ghana, Mali, Songhay, Mossi, and Kanem. Nok, which predates the Christian Era, is known primarily for its developed art. Mossi, Kanem, and other empires of the Sudanic belt have contributed to the richly textured history of the civilization of West Africa. However, Ghana, Mali, and Songhay are the best documented civilizations of the region.

Ghana

Ghana developed prior to the Islamic penetration of West Africa and shows highly developed artistic and governmental modes. Indeed, al-Bakri gave a good account of Ghana in 1067–1068. Already by this time, the empire was in decline, having arisen in 300 B.C.E. Nevertheless, al-Bakri said that the kingship was

derived from the matrilineal pattern, meaning that the king was the son of his predecessor's sister rather than the son of his predecessor. The king rules as an autocrat who communicated to his subjects through a mediator, much like the present okyeame in contemporary Ghana. The king was also the central figure in the religion of the people. Upon his death, his retainers were buried with him. According to al-Bakri, the king had an army of 200,000 men, of which 40,000 were archers. The economy of Ghana was based on gold which was controlled by the king. Numerous adventurers, writers, and scholars attested to the presence of a complex government in the region that stretched from the Atlantic Ocean on the West to the Niger River valleys on the East, the southern Sahara on the North to the Atlantic Ocean on the South. While not all areas in this region came under the direct control of the Ghana Empire, its influence was felt throughout the region through the control of both the gold and salt trades.

After the Almoravids, an army of blacks from Morocco, conquered Ghana in 1076, there was no longer a strong central government. Disorganized by constant internal battles and unable to find its former glory, the country fell prey to the Soninkes who defeated the Almoravids in 1087 and divided the land into several smaller states. By 1203, it was possible for Sumanguru, King of Sosso, to annex the now smaller Ghana territory to his own kingdom. However, in 1240, Sundiata, the legendary king of the Mandingo kingdom of Kankaba, vanquished the remnants of the Ghana empire and created the Empire of Mali.

Mali

The kingdom of Mali existed from the first century. Indeed the Mali Empire's history is the history of the famous Keita family of West Africa. This family ruled the empire for nearly thirteen centuries in one of the longest dynasties in world history. However, it was not until the rise of the Sundiata, the crippled military leader, that Mali burst upon the world scene as a mighty nation. In 1230, Sundiata ascended the throne left by his father, Nare Maghan I. He achieved quick, decisive victories over the enemies of Mali, organized the state to administer civil authority, and gave women powerful positions.

Military generals were made responsible for conquered regions. In the great epic of Sundiata by D. T. Niane we learn that laws and codes of conduct for the military leaders were put into force to provide proper guidance and protocol for the conduct of society. Everywhere in the empire, Sundiata and his story were repeated by griots who used the legend of the crippled military genius who became king, as an instrument of instruction. By the time he died in 1255, Sundiata had placed Mali in the annals of world history. It was an empire and a civilization equal to any in the world at that time. Sundiata was succeeded by kings with lesser political genius some of whom distinguished themselves in other ways. Responsible for sending long boats to the Americas, Abuba-kari I himself sailed to Mexico in 1312. Emperor Mansa Musa made a pilgrimage to Mecca in 1324 that impressed the world with his wealth. Mansa (King) Musa's entourage spent so much gold in Cairo that they left a legacy of inflation in the Egyptian capital.

Songhay

Songhay, emerging from the vassal state of Gao, succeeded the Mali Empire due to the consistent and intelligent military prowess and discipline of the army of Sunni Ali Ber, the last descendant of the dynasty established by Dia Assibia. In 1464, when he became sovereign of the Songhay state, Sunni Ali Ber defeated the Tuaregs at Timbuktu, captured the city and established himself as the most important West African leader. Sunni Ali Ber, the Great, extended his empire by controlling the Niger River with a navy of large boats

that patrolled both shores of the river. Refusing to accept Islam, Sunni Ali Ber advanced the traditional religions and cultures of the Sudanese people. His death in 1492 created a vacuum in the political life of the country. His son, Bakori Da'as, was unable to hold the empire together and was soon deposed by Mamadu Toure who ascended to the throne under the name Askia Muhammad and ruled from 1493 to 1529. During his reign, the University of Sankore reached its greatest heights as he restored the tradition of Islamic learning that had been discouraged under Sunni Ali Ber. The outstanding intellectual, Akmed Baba, the last chancellor of the university at Timbuktu, was credited with writing more than forty books on subjects as far ranging as logic, theology, ethics, mathematics, and rhetoric. He is considered one of the great intellectuals of the sixteenth century.

The major contribution of the reign of Askia Muhammad was the promotion of education and the advancement of science at the University of Sankore. He permitted scholars from Asia and Europe to come to Songhay to learn and teach at the principal centers of education: Gao, Jenne, and Timbuktu. Students studied law, rhetoric, grammar, literature, and medicine. Indeed, by the turn of the sixteenth century, the region was developing a literature fully its own based upon the traditional myths, beliefs, patterns of behavior, and philosophies of the West African people.

Muhammad had made all of this possible through expert institutionalization of banking systems and laws regulating the business of the empire. So successful did Songhay become under Askia Muhammad that other people envied the nation.

After the reign of Askia Muhammad, pushed from the throne by his son, the decline of Songhay set in. A period of decline followed by a period of rebuilding occurred until the empire was too weak to manage its internal affairs while trying to keep its external ene-

mies at bay. Various smaller states long accustomed to paying tribute to the Songhay Empire reneged on their obligations due to the weakness of of the empire. The struggles with its vassal states gave an opening for stronger nations to attack the mighty Songhay.

In 1591, the Moroccans crossed the desert with cannons in order to fight the army of the Songhay Empire. While most of the Moroccans died in the battle with Songhay, their cannons overpowered the army of Songhay which was still fighting with swords and spears. The technology of warfare in West Africa had now changed and this war was a prelude to the coming defeat

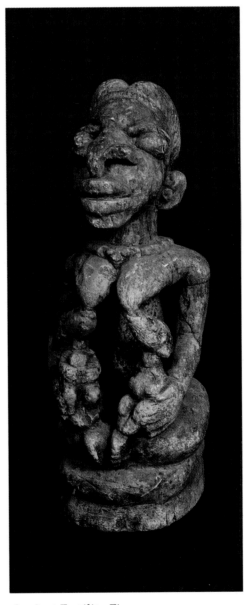

Ancient Fertility Figure,
Sierra Leone

of the African nations and empires by Europeans armed with the most modern weapons of warfare. The Mighty Golden Age of West Africa was over. It would be nearly four hundred years before Africa would regain some of its past glory. The intervening years meant the destruction of the centers of learning and power and threw Africa into political and social chaos. The eminent Senegalese scholar, Cheikh Anta Diop, was among the first scientists to explore the relationship of the ancient Kemetic civilization in what is now called Egypt to the West African empires and states. Diop found that the languages of more than twelve West African states could be traced directly to ancient Egypt. Thus, he had opened an entirely new field, linking all of Africa to its classical cultures in the Nile Valley. His dictum often repeated during his lifetime was: "Egypt is to

the rest of Africa as Greece is to the rest of Europe"(Diop 1974, xiv).

Cities long claimed by the marching sands of the Sahara Desert connected West African cities and villages to those farther east. Movements and migrations of people due to natural disasters (e.g., droughts, pestilence, and floods) or human catastrophes (e.g., war and internal conflicts) caused Africa to be a continent of powerful human interactions along the natural waterways such as the Niger, Nile, Zaire, and Zambezi rivers. The cities, especially along the Niger, created and kept in their trust the ancient memories of the societies of secrets. Along this river grew the towns that were to become famous in all of Africa. Caravans crossed the desert in the past from the banks of this river as they still do today. African Americans carry within them the heritage of these cities and caravans of the savanna.

Africa

The story of human societies in the western part of the African continent has not been fully documented in writing and yet the people convey as orature (i.e., proverbs, rituals, dramas, divinations, incantations, adages, myths, legends, and epics) the entire kaleidoscope of a creative and productive heritage inherited from the East and enriched in their Western experiences.

Here in the past millennia the great Lake Chad functioned as a laboratory for early shipbuilding and even today reveals the secrets of sail.

Here the River Niger, one of the four majestic rivers of Africa, roams through richly textured lands—the Sahel savannas, greens hills, and rain forests—as witness to the color and vibrancy of the region.

Here the names of history are studded like diamonds in our memories and remind us once more of the heritage of

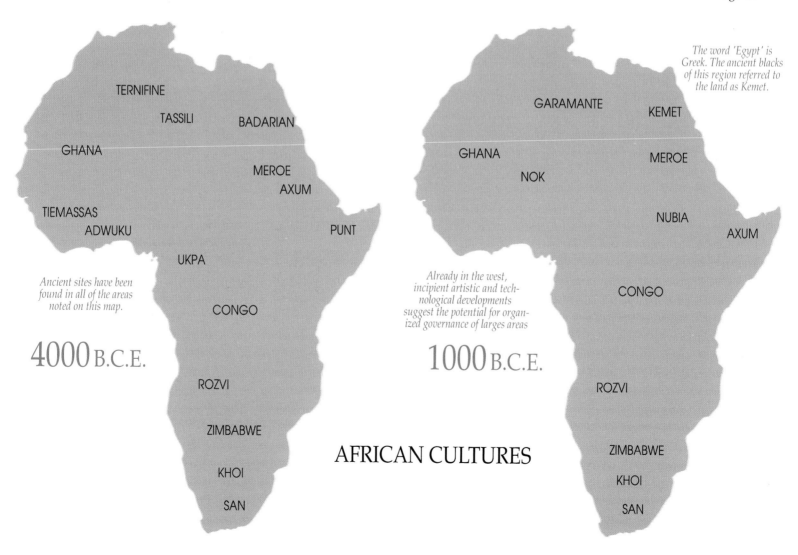

The word 'Egypt' is Greek. The ancient blacks of this region referred to the land as Kemet.

Ancient sites have been found in all of the areas noted on this map.

4000 B.C.E.

TERNIFINE

TASSILI   BADARIAN

GHANA

MEROE

AXUM

TIEMASSAS

ADWUKU   PUNT

UKPA

CONGO

ROZVI

ZIMBABWE

KHOI

SAN

Already in the west, incipient artistic and technological developments suggest the potential for organized governance of larges areas

1000 B.C.E.

GARAMANTE   KEMET

GHANA

NOK

MEROE

NUBIA

AXUM

CONGO

ROZVI

ZIMBABWE

KHOI

SAN

AFRICAN CULTURES

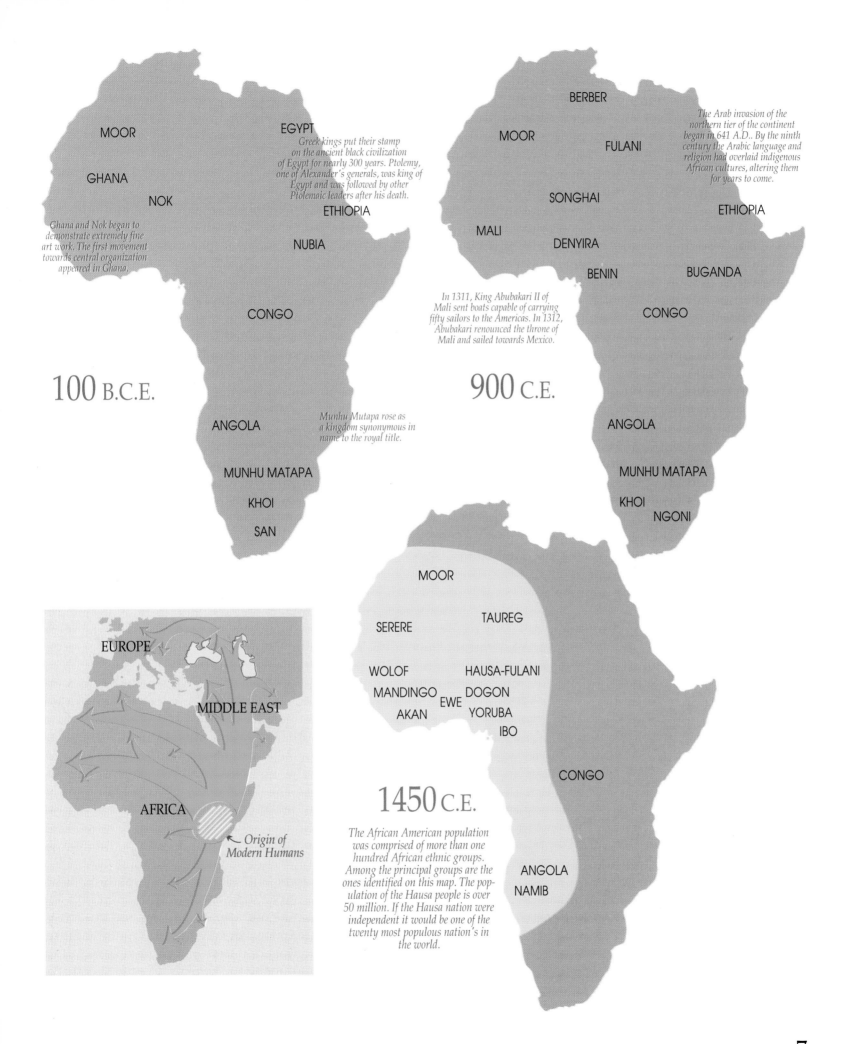

MOOR

EGYPT

GHANA

NOK

ETHIOPIA

NUBIA

CONGO

100 B.C.E.

ANGOLA

MUNHU MATAPA

KHOI

SAN

Greek kings put their stamp on the ancient black civilization of Egypt for nearly 300 years. Ptolemy, one of Alexander's generals, was king of Egypt and was followed by other Ptolemaic leaders after his death.

Ghana and Nok began to demonstrate extremely fine art work. The first movement towards central organization appeared in Ghana.

Munhu Mutapa rose as a kingdom synonymous in name to the royal title.

BERBER

MOOR

FULANI

SONGHAI

ETHIOPIA

MALI

DENYIRA

BENIN

BUGANDA

CONGO

900 C.E.

ANGOLA

MUNHU MATAPA

KHOI

NGONI

The Arab invasion of the northern tier of the continent began in 641 A.D.. By the ninth century the Arabic language and religion had overlaid indigenous African cultures, altering them for years to come.

In 1311, King Abubakari II of Mali sent boats capable of carrying fifty sailors to the Americas. In 1312, Abubakari renounced the throne of Mali and sailed towards Mexico.

MOOR

TAUREG

SERERE

WOLOF

HAUSA-FULANI

MANDINGO

DOGON

EWE

AKAN

YORUBA

IBO

CONGO

1450 C.E.

ANGOLA

NAMIB

The African American population was comprised of more than one hundred African ethnic groups. Among the principal groups are the ones identified on this map. The population of the Hausa people is over 50 million. If the Hausa nation were independent it would be one of the twenty most populous nation's in the world.

EUROPE

MIDDLE EAST

AFRICA

← *Origin of Modern Humans*

African Americans: Nok, Queen Amina of Zaria, Asantehene Osei Tutu, Ghana, Sundiata, Queen Nzingha, King Njoya, King Akwa, Okomfo Anokye, Yaa Asantewaa, King Odudua, Queen Idia, Abubakari, Mansa Musa, Timbuktu, Sankore, Nsibidi, Benin, Uthman dan Fodio, Gao, Jenne, Ouagadougou, Segu, Dogon, King Ansa, Touba, Keita, Mali, Shango, Oshun, Ogun, Kumasi, Agades, and thousands of other names of people, places, and ideas interconnected in the western region of Africa.

The empires of Ghana, Mali, and Songhay and the kingdoms of Benin, Asante, Oyo, Congo, and Angola left their political and cultural stamps as markers to greatness. From these political jurisdictions and their remnant political and military organizations came many of the Africans who were brought to the Americas. The ethnic names with which the Africans came included Mandingo, Fante, Ibo, Efik, Yoruba, Hausa, Serere, Wolof, Tuareg, Dan, Vai, Angola, Baule, Touculeur, Sherbro, Baga, Asante, Ga, Ewe, Fulani, Douala, and one hundred other names. In some cases, the entire ethnic group was wiped out in Africa by the European slave trade.

This vast region—containing more square miles of territory than the continental United States—was poised, by virtue of indigenous village industries and widespread trade networks, to make rapid advances in technical development. The appearance of Portuguese ships along the Moroccan, Mauritanian, and Senegambian coasts was to alter fundamentally the manner and rate of West Africa's technological advancement.

Estimates range from 15 to 50 million people uprooted because of the European slave trade. Millions more were dislocated on the continent, leaving broken bodies, spirits, and industries. There was nothing regular about what the scholar Dona Marimba Richards has called the *maafa*, the Great Disaster, in which Africa was literally robbed of its human and material wealth. When the trade ended it was as if a massive hand had indiscriminately plucked people from villages, towns, and cities. Hereditary kings and queens, princes and princesses, courtiers, okyeames, and queen mothers were faced with the indignity of having their titles stripped in the presence of their nations. Through-

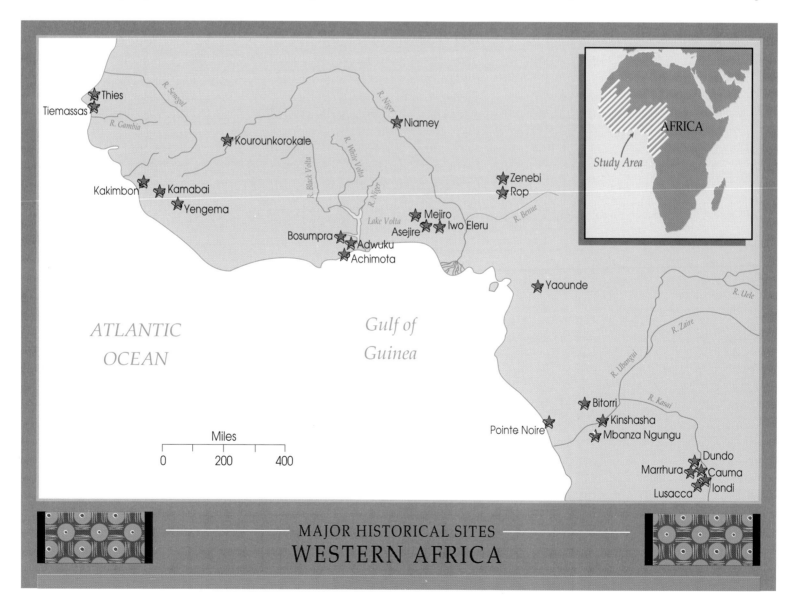

MAJOR HISTORICAL SITES
WESTERN AFRICA

out the huge continent, millions of Africans were in political, social, economic, and spiritual turmoil during the period of the Great Disaster. Wars were fought and captives taken on the basis of an entirely new ethic of warfare never before seen on the continent. The level of violence inflicted on historical enemies had rarely approached the level of slaughter that was brought in with the new European weapons. This was the mourning time for Africa. There were broad areas relatively emptied of people. Other areas lost artisans and still others were untouched by the trade. The millions of transported Africans, seariders who became landless in a strange land, recreated and re-formed Africa in thousands of farms, villages, and towns in the Americas and Caribbean. Langston Hughes, often called the "Poet of the African American People," summed up the pathos in the soul of African Americans in many of this poems. He was fond of using the river metaphor. Thus in one of his early poems he wrote, "I have known rivers, ancient dusky rivers and my soul has grown deep like the rivers." This metaphor is a mighty current running through the works of many African American authors as different as Mari Evans, Vincent Harding, and Houston Baker. It speaks to the enormity of the experience of being dislocated; it speaks to movement; it speaks to the variety of circumstances that engages the African. Whether it is the Mississippi, Ohio, Congo, Zaire, Nile, Niger, Zambezi, or Red River of Arkansas, the African knows rivers. They have carried the hearts and souls of the people from place to place.

Artists have enshrined the river in the African American culture. One sees it in the dance of Kariamu Welsh Asante or Alvin Ailey or Pearl Primus. It is the mother metaphor in the lyricism of Wynton Marsalis' horn or Michael Jackson's movements. John Coltrane and James Brown are connected by it; Aretha Franklin and Ruby Dee are sisters because of the river. In the end, it

must be viewed as it was, a mighty turbulent ocean.

African History and Culture

It is certainly true to say that there are many cultures in Africa but it is equally true to say that there is an African culture, just as one might speak of an Asian or a European culture. Variations in cultural and political styles, in religious and social institutions are found throughout the African continent. Yet the commonalities of the continent are plentiful. From music to dance, from foods to celebrations, from theological concepts to rituals, one finds great similarity. The enslaved ancestors of present day African Americans brought with them all of the abundantly complex rituals, symbols, and ideas of their large and diverse continent. West Africa represents the immediate ancestral home of the vast majority of African Americans. While it is true that Africans were enslaved in the Americas from East and Southern Africa as well as Madagascar, the principal areas of the European

Slave Trade were the regions adjoining the concavity of the African coast created by the Atlantic Ocean. The political institutions developed in the Senegal-Gambia region, the Niger River Valley, and the Zaire River basin were built on the foundations of cosmological and epistemological principles derived from the context of the people. They included systems of governance where the village constituted the key unit in the effective administration of law and rules. Numerous villages held together in confederation might constitute a large kingdom. Several kingdoms would become an empire. In every case, the organization was created out of the belief systems of the people. Most African empires had a hierarchical form of governance. The king stood at the top of the power structure. In all cases, however, the king was subject to the ancestral traditions. This meant that the king paid homage to those who had gone before him. He was the representative among the people of the distant power of the deities and the ancestors. In some instances, the king

Ancient Site, Egypt

could not rule alone. In those cases, he had advisers and councillors appointed by the king-makers who made the rules and laws governing the society. West African rulers typically related their prowess, courage, virility, wisdom, health, rhythm, and longevity to some primordial site of the nation.

In the myths of West African peoples one finds the names of Bosumpra, Yengema, Zenebi, Mbanza Ngungu—ancient African sites as animating forces in the philosophical and religious systems of the various states. All across the continent the integration of the historical sites with the special, primordial ancestors, is recognizable. In West Africa, this spirit is present every-

COLONIAL AFRICA

PRESENT DAY AFRICA

COUNTRIES GAINING
INDEPENDENCE

Before 1945

Between 1950 and 1960

In 1960

After 1960

Countries Fighting for
National Liberation

where. At the Berlin Conference of 1884–1885, Africa was balkanized in totally irrational ways as far as the interest of Africa was concerned. But for Europe the conference had worked out compromises to prevent European wars.

African Americans originated on a continent that is nearly four times the size of the United States excluding Alaska or three times the size of the United States including Alaska. Even Texas, legendary for its size, appears small when you view it in relationship to a country such as Sudan, Zaire, South Africa, or Tanzania. Of course, these are nations whereas Texas is a state. For comparison, consider the fact that Texas has 267,339 sq. miles while Sudan has 977,499 sq. miles; Zaire has 904,991 sq. miles; South Africa has 472,359 sq. miles; and Tanzania has 363,707 sq. miles.

Distances are very great on the continent. This makes travel and communication very difficult. The distance from Cairo to Capetown is approximately 5,000 miles; Dakar, Senegal to Mogadishu, Somalia is nearly 5,000 miles. It is possible for a person to travel 1,000 miles in Nigeria in order to reach the largest city, Lagos. One can be 800 miles from Dar es Salaam, the capital of Tanzania, and still be within the country. Similar distances occur in Zaire, Algeria, and Sudan. One of the most important challenges facing Africa is transportation.

During the periods of the slave trade and colonization, the lack of roads aided the African kingdoms in maintaining isolation from the coastal regions. However, the rudimentary system of highways built by the European powers in every nation made it easier to transport raw materials from the interior to the coast and for the white administrators to penetrate the interior with laws and ordinances.

The continent has virtually no major barriers to human movement. Relatively few internal barriers exist since most of the land consists of flat savanna or rolling plains. One might compare Africa to the American Midwest between the Rocky Mountains and the Alleghenies.

The huge Sahara is the most pronounced feature on the continent, roughly the size of the United States. But the desert is not so much a barrier as it is an obstacle that is overcome everyday in the lives of thousands of Africans who regularly traverse it. Camels from Libya, Algeria, Morocco, and Egypt went back and forth from Timbuktu, Katsina, and Ouagadougou. Salt, gold, ivory, gum arabic, spice, glassware, iron tools, and blankets were traded between these places. The Sahara trade was the source of much wealth for many of the African kings. They used the taxes from the permissions to travel to aid in the development of their state systems.

The second largest obstacle on the continent is the Congo (Zaire) Rain Forest. It is the most extensive area of swamps, forests, and dense vegetation on the continent. The Zaire River, after the Amazon, drains the largest area of any river in the world.

These factors and many others make the discussion of African Americans one of great complexity. Of course, it is simple to speak of the African Americans as those blacks who live in the United States or who were born in the Americas, North, Central, or South. But at a more profound level the question, Who are African Americans? must raise deeper reflections and require much more complex answers.

Most Americans, black or white, do not know the names of the African ethnic groups which comprise the African American population. Afterall, there were no such people as African Americans prior to the seventeenth century. Who, then, are African Americans?

In part, the answer to the question must be historical, that is, it must deal with origin and history on the African continent. One must consider the cultures and civilizations which constitute the African heritage: Egypt, Meroe, Ethiopia, Tichitt, Nok, Ghana, Kanem-Bornu, Carthage, Nubia, Katanga, Tekrur, Mali, Songhay, Hausa, Birgirmi, Wadai, Mossi, Fulani, Yoruba, Denkyira, Akwamu, Asante, Benin, Kongo, Luba, Kuba, Lunda, Angola, Munhu Matapa, Lozi, Bemba, Xhosa, Zulu, Basotho, Swahili, Buganda, Bunyoro, Galla, and Somali. Many additional and smaller cultures and civilizations exist and these made considerable contributions to human harmonization with the environment. Furthermore, members of the African American population normally are unable to identify, because of the disruption of enslavement, their African nation of origin. In this case, the entire continent becomes home to the African American who often chooses a particular cultural group or region because of the resonance one feels with that group.

Afrocentric scholars have begun to uncover much information about the African past. This work will link the African American more firmly to historical roots than most of the previous work has because its aim has been to dislocate.

The relocation of the African American in a world context has already begun in several places. One finds this attitude permeating the meeting of the Organization of African Unity. Documentaries for radio and television have been made situating African Americans in the larger African as well as American context.

All European ethnic groups have a heritage that extends prior to their arrival in America. No other ethnic group in the United States has been under such intense pressure to forget origin and cultural past as African Americans. Yet the relocation of African Americans in a psychological space that allows for joy and pride has already been successful.

Not since the abandonment of the name "African" in the nineteenth century by the most prominent blacks of the period has there been such a drastic return to Africa. It had always been correct. Now the literature reflects the attitudes of the people, that is, the literary people have begun to listen to the inner voices. The age of the African Methodist Episcopal Church, the African Free Society, the African Free School, and the African Benevolent Society was the age of outstanding men and women who understood that they were of African heritage although they lived in the United States. This was the eighteenth century. It would take the nineteenth century to assist in turning Africans away from themselves and into psychological confusion.

When the Colored Convention met in Philadelphia in 1817 to decide how to respond to the issue of sending Africans back to Africa, the seeds for future problems were created. Those seeds were sown when the speakers at the convention agreed that African Americans should refer to themselves, not as Africans, but as colored Americans.

This action predictably put a damper on anyone wanting to hold to traditions or to seek out African ancestry. When the leading citizens of the major urban centers called for a new policy they usually carried the day. This is precisely what happened in regard to the burning issue of "African" versus "Colored."

Sterling Stuckey has written perceptively about the culture of Africans during the enslavement, noting the continuity of ideas and ideals in the thinking of the early African Americans. The ancient kingdoms serve contemporary society by pointing to the sources of many ideas, customs, behaviors, and styles that live fully in the African American.

Munhu Matapa

The Munhu Matapa Empire began in the first century A.D. and lasted for fifteen hundred years in the area that is now the nation of Zimbabwe. Kings of the region were called Munhu Matapa and the empire took its name after them.

Shona and Lozi people, descendants of the ancient Munhu Matapa, are credited with the more than four hundred sites of stone ruins which were once flourishing villages found in South Central Africa. Stretching over Zimbabwe, Zambia, South Africa, and Mozambique, these ancient sites hold histories yet untold.

The largest of the sites is the Great Zimbabwe, literally "stone house," located in Southern Zimbabwe. There are two parts to the sites. One part is located on the top of a hill and the other larger area is located in the plains below. Both are extremely impressive and show excellent skill and artistry.

Made of the local granite, the huge stones which comprise the structures were expertly chiseled to fit without the use of any cementing element. The site atop the hill and the valley or plains site both display a dignity and strength that suggest nobility. In *Lost Cities of Africa* Basil Davidson wrote that, "Everywhere these structures are marked with an originality which seems to owe nothing to the rest of the world" (p. 247).

The ruler or Munhu Matapa was legendary in South Central Africa. Whenever a new Munhu Matapa rose to power he attempted to out-build the previous lord of the land. Indeed, at the height of its glory the ancient Zimbabwean kingdom traded with India, China, and the Arabs. There is no record of a European merchant or missionary reaching this empire. The deities, beliefs, and methods of civilization remained within the confines of the society itself. This was sufficient to make the empire respected by those who visited to trade.

Europeans who finally reached the site in the nineteenth century could not believe that Africans had erected it. They sought all kinds of excuses for the high quality of the work, the apparent organizational ability of the people, and the extent of their trade with the outside world. How could a people dominated by Europeans, a people despised by them, have created so a splendid civilization? This was to plague the white colonists' minds in Africa.

Jebel Uri

Under the Emperor Dunama Dibbalemi who ruled Kanem from 1210 to 1224, the Kanemic Empire stretched from the western banks of the Nile to an area just northeast of the Niger River. The successor kingdom to Kanem was the mighty Bornu, the remnants of which can be found in the present Nigerian sultanate of Bornu. Caravans from the Niger to the Nile and perhaps, as some authors claim, from the Niger to Somali, passed through the territory of the Kanem-Bornu Empire.

During the sixth century C.E., Nubian Christians were buffers between the kingdoms to the West and the Islamic invasions coming from the Northeast. It was not until the thirteenth century that the Nubians were finally conquered by Islamic culture. Evidences of their last stands are found in the ruins of churches that dot areas of Egypt, Chad, and Sudan.

The incredible ruins of Jebel Uri appear in this region. This ancient city with its nine-stepped auditorium to the cemetery of the long vanished Daju people is one of the largest ancient cities of Africa. The city was constructed of stone within a strong circular wall. From the size of this ancient community it is believed that a large population lived here for four or five centuries. Much like the architects of Great Zimbabwe, the builders of this city used no mortar. A mighty causeway of huge blocks of stone ascends to the top of the site. The earliest dates for the site suggest the time of Harkhuf, the traveler, around 2400 B.C.E.

West African Antiquity

Wahb ibn Munnabeh wrote of the migrations of African peoples from the east to the west and into the interior in 738 C.E. He spoke of the people of the Sudan as the Goran, the Zaghawa, the Habesha, the Copts, and the Berbers. In 947 C.E., the greatest geographer of the period, El Mas'udi, wrote in his book *Meadows of Gold and Mines of Gems*, that "the sons of Kush . . . traveled toward the west and crossed the Nile. There they separated. Some of them, the Nubians and the Beja and the Zanj, turned to the rightward, between the east and west; but the others, very numerous, marched toward the setting sun . . . ."

According to H. Lhote and other scholars, the Sahara has long been occupied by black people. In fact, Lhote reported that a painting in the Tassili area is similar to one of the same style found in Cote'd' Ivoire. The dessication of the Sahara forced Africans to move further west and south from the eastern area. We now know that human beings have probably lived in the West African region longer than thirty thousand years.

The records of antiquity in West Africa have become more numerous as scholars begin to investigate cultures that have occupied the savannas. Art historian Bernard Fagg reported that tiny fragments of charcoal from the Kanjeran pluvial produced an age of 39,000 years. Lhote has suggested that Africans invented portraiture art, painting men and women with sensitivity and realism as early as 3000 B.C.E.

The transformation of the world's power arrangements over the last five hundred years brought about major changes in international relationships. Africa became the favorite region for forced laborers and cheap raw materials. Seeking to expand its own power base, Europe found Africa a ready-made continent of economic opportunity.

Colonial interests of the European nations followed the early merchant and missionary inroads into the continent. The scramble, as it was called, for Africa was fed by the national desires of European states to reap the most benefit from a continent rendered too weak to defend itself by the tremendous upheavals from within and the avarice of nations from without. Like birds of prey, the colonial powers pounced upon any African state or kingdom that seemed to limp along in political disarray, economic disorganization, or worldly indifference to the European encroachments in the continent. European nations with fleets quickly outfitted them and headed for the coasts of Africa. The initial entry into Africa was for gold. Only when the Americas were being exploited did the need for laborers supersede the desire for gold. Not oil, but Africans were the original black gold.

Modern Divisions

Modern African states are the creations of boundaries established in the interest and for the benefit of colonial European powers. The borders of most states in Africa have no rational basis except that

they were set up in the various charters of the European nations. When the Berlin Conference of 1884–1885 was over, the African continent had been politically organized in the interest of Europe in ways which were to confirm the historical division of the continent created by the rise of the European slave trade itself.

Sensing the inherent weakness in an arbitrarily divided Africa, the most eminent African scholar of the twentieth century, Cheikh Anta Diop, called for the re-drawing of the boundaries of the continent to take advantage of natural and historical interests. In a similar vein, Molefi Kete Asante delivered a speech, to an international African conference in London in January 1987, later published as "Six State Continent" in the *African Concord*, in which he provided guidelines for re-drawing the continental boundaries. Kwame Nkrumah, the leading spirit for the development of the organization for African Unity initiated the call for a united Africa in the 1960s.

African Americans are largely descended from the western region of the continent. This area was much more accessible to Europeans seeking to transport Africans to the Americas. East coast and southern coast Africans had been taken by Arab and Portuguese slave traders to Asia and the Arabian peninsula. The Arabs under Tippu Tib continued their trade until the 1800s.

The anomalies produced by arbitrary division of the continent have resulted in tensions, disputed territories, political unrest, ethnic distrust, and frequent challenges to central governments. Thus, one finds Yoruba people in Nigeria and Benin; Mandingo people in Guinea, Senegal, Sierra Leone, and Mali; Akan people in Cote D'Ivoire and Ghana; and Ewe in Ghana and Togo. Consequently the borders of national states are often violated by individuals who are seeking to make contact with relatives and friends of the same ethnic groups. Divisions such as these did not exist during the European slave trade.

Europeans invaded or traded with unitary African states. For example, an agreement might be made between the Dutch and Fante nation or the English and Benin. The modern African National State is now laid over the traditional nations, often over several of them.

When the European slave trade began, the West African traditional nations and kingdoms were undergoing wide scale turbulence caused by inroads of Islam in the West. Already established in the arid regions of Mali, Senegal, and Mauretania, Islam pushed into the heart of the tropical forest region by converting many people of the present Guinea. The struggle against Islam weakened most nations and made those without Islamic allies easy prey for the superior weapons of the Europeans.

Striped Batakari,
Ghana, Africa

"I DON'T CARE WHERE YOU BURY MY BODY": THE TRANS-ATLANTIC JOURNEY

In 1311 and 1312, according to Al-Omari, the Malian prince Abubakari II, brother of Emperor Mansa Musa, sent shipping vessels across the west African sea (Atlantic Ocean). The historian and anthropologist, Ivan Van Sertima, in his book, *They Came Before Columbus,* tells us that Abubakari's fishing vessels landed in Mexico where the African settlers impacted on the local culture's language, rituals, myths, religions, and agriculture.

Other scholars have argued that Africans came to central America long before the fourteenth century. Indeed, evidences in the Mayan and Mexican forests of pyramids and large African sculptures (the Olmec heads) suggest an early African presence.

The Olmec civilization of Mexico, the first complex culture of the Americas, is thought to have been influenced by the classical African civilizations of Ethiopia, Kemet, and Meroe. The Olmec civilization flourished between 1200 and 400 B.C.E., when it fell into regional conflicts and finally became one of a series of smaller cultures of Mesoamerica.

The area of the culture was the southern Gulf Coast of Mexico where the Olmec economic, political, and social influence extended into the central Mexican highlands and southeast to the Pacific up to El Salvador and into other regions of Central America. Many later American civilizations trace their history to the Olmecs.

By 1200 B.C.E., Olmec civilization was fully developed at San Lorenzo, the earliest major ceremonial center. Later around 900 B.C.E., the power center of the civilization shifted to La Venta, where huge African heads of basalt have been found. Weighing several tons and resembling the faces and hairstyles of Africans of the same period of time, these heads lend support to the claims by Ivan Van Sertima and Michael Bradley that the Olmec civilization was the first civilization established by Africans outside of the continent of Africa.

The inspiration for the massive public works projects—clay building platforms and stone drainage systems—seem to be ancient Egyptian. Actually the large human heads and fine jade carvings suggest African influences at an early period. A further relationship to the classical African civilizations has been established through the similarity of the hieroglyphic systems of writing. The Nile Valley in Africa and the Mesoamerica region share several similarities, including the later development in the Americas of pyramids. Since there are no direct written records of the African origin of Olmec civilization, the arguments for African influences, substantial as they are, have been based upon the carved images of Africans, the similarity of cultural expressions, and as in the case of the Mali sailors, the presence of African customs, myths, and ceremonies in certain parts of Mexico.

However, the first African to enter what is now the United States of America was Estevanico. He entered the southwest as one of the principal explorers in a Spanish expedition. Estevanico's route covered a considerable part of the American southwest. After Estevanico, it seemed fashionable for Spanish, Italian, and Portuguese explorers especially to have African assistants along because of their prowess, courage, linguistic ability, and ingenuity.

Enough evidence exists to show that ancient Africans not only sailed to the Americas but were able to make boats that would take them across the oceans. However, it was as sailors and soldiers in European expeditions that Africans became known in more recent times.

The skill and courage of the African sailor was such that when European explorers sought to sail to unfamiliar lands they often relied upon Africans as navigators and ship hands. For example:

• Pedro Alonso Nino accompanied Columbus to the Americas.

• Alvarado, who is usually given credit in textbooks for his exploration of equatorial South America, was assisted by nearly two hundred African sailors, many of them veterans of several voyages to sea.

• In 1513, when Balboa reached the Pacific Ocean, thirty Africans looked upon the same scene as the Spaniard.

• The first wheat crop sowed in the "new world" was planted by an African with Hernando Cortes' expedition.

Unfortunately, many African explorers remain nameless because of three principal reasons: (1) they traveled under the flag of people other than their own nations; (2) the histories were written from the standpoint of the principal

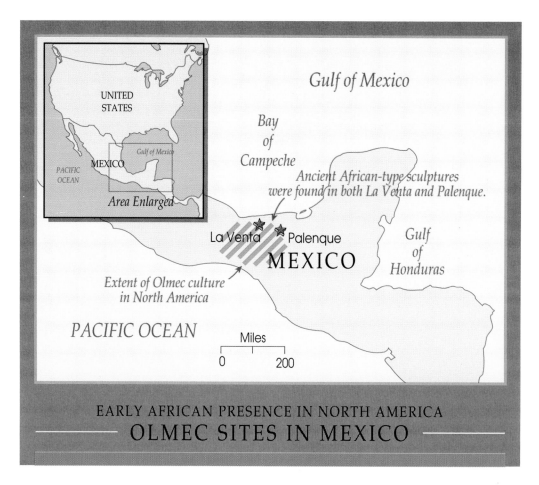

EARLY AFRICAN PRESENCE IN NORTH AMERICA
OLMEC SITES IN MEXICO

expedition leader; and (3) many Africans were conscripted as soldiers and servants to support the expeditions. The African explorers whose names we know, usually rose far beyond the station assigned to them. The list is impressive.

Estevan de Dorantes, often called Estevanico, "Little Steven" in Spanish, was born in Africa and became one of the greatest explorers of his day. Sold as a servant to the conquistador Andres Dorantes de Carranca, Estevan later joined him in 1527 in an expedition to the Americas under an experienced explorer named Panfilo de Narvaez.

In 1528, when the expedition of six hundred men entered Florida, Panfilo divided them into two groups. One group he led into the jungles of Florida, another group he directed to march towards the southwest to Mexico. The expedition was wiped out by sickness, native Americans defending their lands, and internal squabbles. The four who survived—Estevan, Andres Dorantes, Castillode Moldonado, and Alvar Nuniz (also known as Cabeza de

Vaca)—were captured by the Native Americans and made to work for them for six years. Escaping from the Native Americans, in 1539, Estevanico discovered the Zuni Pueblo. Attracted by the story of the seven cities of gold in the

Olmec Heads

African Builders of the New World

Time Period	Explorer	Accomplishment
1450–800 B.C.E.	Olmec (Nubian-Kemetic) Africans arrive in Central America (Mexico)	Trading, teaching, learning
1305–1312 C.E.	Abu Bakari II, the King of Mali, sends one fleet of ships and later leads another across what is now called the Atlantic Ocean	Exploration
1310–1491	Mandingo merchant explorers	Made over fifty trips to various Caribbean and Central and South American points including what is now called Panama, Honduras, and Haiti.
1492	Pedro Alonzo Nino	Piloted and navigated for Columbus.
1513	Nuflo de Olano	With Vasco Nunez de Balboa when Balboa claimed the "South Sea" for Spain. Olano and twenty-nine other Africans were with Balboa in the crossing of Panama.
1514	Group of Africans	With Pedrarias de Avila when he took the title of royal governor of a Spanish colony on the Isthmus of Panama.
1523	Group of Africans	With Pedro de Alvarado when Alvarado's expeditionary force entered Guatemala.
1527	Estevanico (Estebanico/Esteban; called Little Stephen)	Led Panfilo de Navaes' unsuccessful expedition from Spain to the southwest North America. Led three surviving Europeans on eight-year transcontinental journey from Florida through Texas and Northern Mexico to the Gulf of California and Mexico City.
1532	Twelve Africans	With Francisco de Montejo on his first campaign to the Yucatan Peninsula.
1539'	Group of Africans	With Desoto when he journeyed to the Mississippi River.
1539	Estavanico	Led expedition (which included Friar Marcos de Niza) giving Europeans their first contact with Arizona and the land of the Zuni people (now New Mexico)
1540	Group of Africans	With Francisco Vasques de Coronado when he entered the southwestern United States. They were looking for the city of gold—Cibola.
1565	Group of Africans	With explorers who founded St. Augustine, Florida.
1745	Jean Baptiste Pointe DuSable, the father of the city of Chicago	Born in St. Marc, St. Dominique (Haiti). Built the first permanent home on the northern bank of the Chicago River in 1779. Later established a thriving trading post which grew into the city of Chicago.
1781	Twenty-six Africans	Helped found Los Angeles, CA in the company of eighteen others
1798–1866	James Pierson Beckwourth	Born in Fredericksburg, VA. Explored western U. S. long before John Fremont. Assisted William Ashley of the Rocky Mountain Fur Co. until 1825. Served as chief scout for Fremont starting in 1848. Well liked by the Blackfoot and Crow nations, the Crow made him a chief (Bull's Robe). Discovered pass through Sierra Nevada Mts. in 1850 later used by wagon trains, pioneers, gold-seekers, and the Western Pacific Railway. The pass, a valley in Nevada, and a Methodist church in Denver, CO bear his name.
1810	Five Africans	With Lewis and Clarke expedition. One of the five, Rourk, was the group's scout, trapper, and trader.
1820	George Bonga	Opened a trading post on the northern Great Lakes. Married a Chippewa. A town in Cass County, MN bears his name.
1843	Jacob Dotson, Mifflin Gibbs, Andrew Jackson, and don Jesus Picos	With John Fremont. Dotson was a marksman and an expert with the lasso. He fought beside Fremont in the Mexican War and fought Kit Carson in the Bear Flag Party during the Civil War.
1848–1849	Mammy Pleasant	Helped build San Francisco, CA. Also aided Africans escaping slavery.
1909	Matthew Alexander Henson	Arrived at the North Pole; returned to carry Robert E. Peary physically to the North Pole.

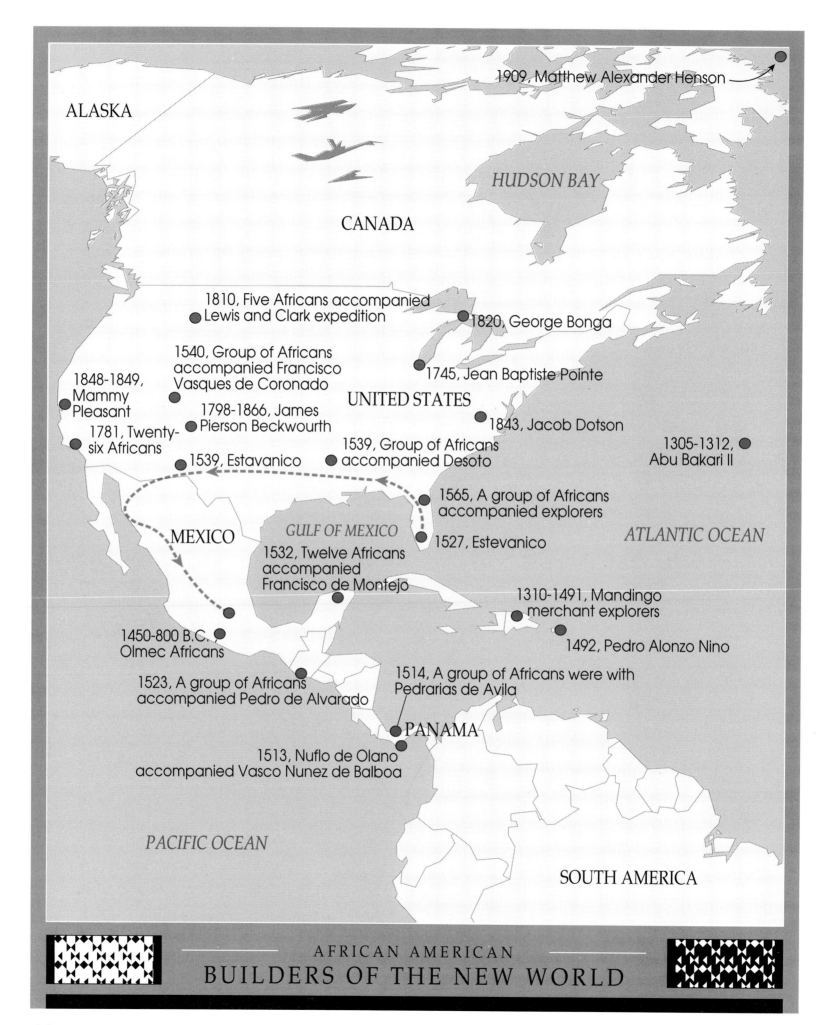

ALASKA

1909, Matthew Alexander Henson

HUDSON BAY

CANADA

1810, Five Africans accompanied Lewis and Clark expedition

1820, George Bonga

1540, Group of Africans accompanied Francisco Vasques de Coronado

1848-1849, Mammy Pleasant

1745, Jean Baptiste Pointe

UNITED STATES

1798-1866, James Pierson Beckwourth

1843, Jacob Dotson

1781, Twenty-six Africans

1539, Estavanico

1539, Group of Africans accompanied Desoto

1305-1312, Abu Bakari II

1565, A group of Africans accompanied explorers

MEXICO

GULF OF MEXICO

1527, Estevanico

ATLANTIC OCEAN

1532, Twelve Africans accompanied Francisco de Montejo

1450-800 B.C. Olmec Africans

1310-1491, Mandingo merchant explorers

1492, Pedro Alonzo Nino

1523, A group of Africans accompanied Pedro de Alvarado

1514, A group of Africans were with Pedrarias de Avila

PANAMA

1513, Nuflo de Olano accompanied Vasco Nunez de Balboa

PACIFIC OCEAN

SOUTH AMERICA

AFRICAN AMERICAN
BUILDERS OF THE NEW WORLD

southwest, Estevanico became a scout for an expedition led by one Father Marco. Traveling alone over vast reaches of the west, the African explorer sent messages to the main party by friendly Indians. The last message received from Estevanico was a huge cross—symbol of a great discovery. This message led the expedition to the Zuni Pueblo which Estevanico had thought was one of the legendary seven golden cities. When the main body of the expedition reached Zuni Pueblo, the Indians had already killed the explorer who had opened Arizona and New Mexico to Africa and Europe.

Africans in the New World

When Ibn Amir Hajib asked Emperor Kankan Musa of Mali about the navigation on the Atlantic Ocean, the king replied:

The monarch who preceded me would not believe that it was impossible to discover the limits of the neighboring sea. He wished to know. He persisted in his plan. He caused the equipping of two hundred ships and filled them with men, and of another such number that were filled with gold, water and food for two years. He said to the commanders: do not return until you have reached the end of the ocean, or when you have exhausted your food and water.

They went away and their absence was long: none came back, and their absence continued. Then a single ship returned. We asked the captain of their adventures and their news. He replied: Sultan, we sailed for a long while until we met with what seemed to be a river with a strong current flowing in the open sea. My ship was last. The others sailed on, but as each of them came to that place they did not come back nor did they reappear; and I do not know what became of them. As for me, I turned where I was and did not enter the current.

Ivan Van Sertima and Michael Bradley have demonstrated the presence of Africans in the Americas before Columbus. As we have seen, the African features on the sculpture at La Venta in

Mexico, are examples of that presence. There are also representations of Africans in the murals of the Temple of Warriors at Chichen Itza.

The migration of Africans from the Nile River valley to the Niger River area in West Africa was but the continuation of movement on the continent of Africa. The eastern cradle of Africa gave birth to numerous migrations. When the West Africans crossed the Atlantic (West African) Ocean they brought with them patterns and characteristics which had been found in East Africa as well. Bradley has shown in his book *The Black Discovery of America* (1981) that the West African culture is the proto-civilization for many of the cultures of the Americas. Whether one examines the bronze objects, portraiture in ceramics, weaving, dyeing, or mud-brick houses, one sees the relationship to the cultures of Mexico and the Andes. Since Nubians built large boats with sails as far back as 3100 B.C.E., it is logical that Africans who lived near the sea, either in the eastern or the western part of the continent, had that capability.

When Bartholomew Diaz and Vasco da Gama entered the Indian Ocean they found that Africans carried on an energetic trade from the Zambezi River eastward across the sea to China. When Columbus reached Cape Verde islands in the Atlantic Ocean he had been preceded by Mailian adventurers more than a century before. The records of these early mariners are found in the archaeological evidence in the Americas, the books by Moorish scholars, and the African plants, such as cotton and the pan-gourd, now found in the Americas.

Some African Adventurers in the American West

There is a long line of adventurers, cowboys, and trailblazers who added to the exploration of the American West. Some of the more colorful characters included Nat Love, the famous cowboy, and Isom Dart, who was considered one of the most feared men of his time. Both Love and Dart were known for their ability to hunt and track wild animals as well as for their skill with guns. Bill Pickett was

Crispus Attucks

A Typical Cowboy

an Oklahoma cowboy who became famous for inventing steer wrestling and popularized the sport as a performer with the 101 Wild West Show. Pickett was elected to the Cowboy Hall of Fame for his innovations in steer wrestling.

Perhaps one of the most exciting stories of an African adventurer in the West is that of Gobo Fango, a South African who went to Utah in 1861 with a white family named Talbot. According to the book *Our Pioneer Heritage* published in 1965 by the Daughters of Utah Pioneers, Gobo Fango was hidden under the skirt of one of the white women traveling in the party when a group of Confederate troops stopped them looking for Africans who had escaped from slavery. When the danger had passed, the young Gobo was taken to Grantsville, Utah. From there he was taken by Mary Anne Whitesides to Kaysville, Utah to assist in herding sheep. As a young boy, Gobo was given the responsibility of herding sheep on the plains. He learned the intricacies of tracking and rounding up sheep and became well known for his ability to survive in the outdoors. Often he went from ranch to ranch assisting in sheep-herding duties. He was able to make a living hiring himself out for extra money. Gobo was used for many chores by the family of Mary Ann Whitesides. Her husband, Edward Hunter, paid the previous "owner" of Gobo about thirty dollars a month until the end of the Civil War. Although Utah was not governed by the laws of the Confederacy, many sympathizers lived in the state. When the war was over, Edward Hunter began to pay Gobo the thirty dollars. This caused the previous "owner" to sue Hunter to no avail.

With his freedom, Gobo became famous as a sheep herder in the Oakley region of Utah. In 1880, he took Edward Hunter's sheep to the market in Oakley to run them on shares. A cattle war broke out and Gobo was shot by a man named Bedky who had pretended to be his friend. Gobo was badly injured but managed to crawl to the home of Walt Matthews. He was to live for only a few more days, but before his death he wrote a will leaving money for Mary Ann Whitesides and $500 to the Grantsville Relief Agency.

Throughout the towns, mountains, rivers, and passes of the American West, people celebrate the fact that Africans were early settlers and pioneers. The African American army private, George Washington, was responsible for persuading Billy the Kid to meet with Lew Wallace. Edward Booth was a pioneer in the gold fields of Alaska. Clara Brown lived in Central City, Colorado from 1859 to 1877. She had been born into slavery in Missouri. Clara Brown owned a laundry and gave much money to charity in Central City. When she died the town dedicated the Opera House to her honor.

The Conestoga wagon is well-known for having transported many travelers across the West. Independence, Missouri was one of the leading centers for the construction of the wagons. The city had become known for its Conestoga wagons because of the work of Hiram Young. He was the builder of the famous wagons upon which thousands of people depended.

Young employed more than fifty men

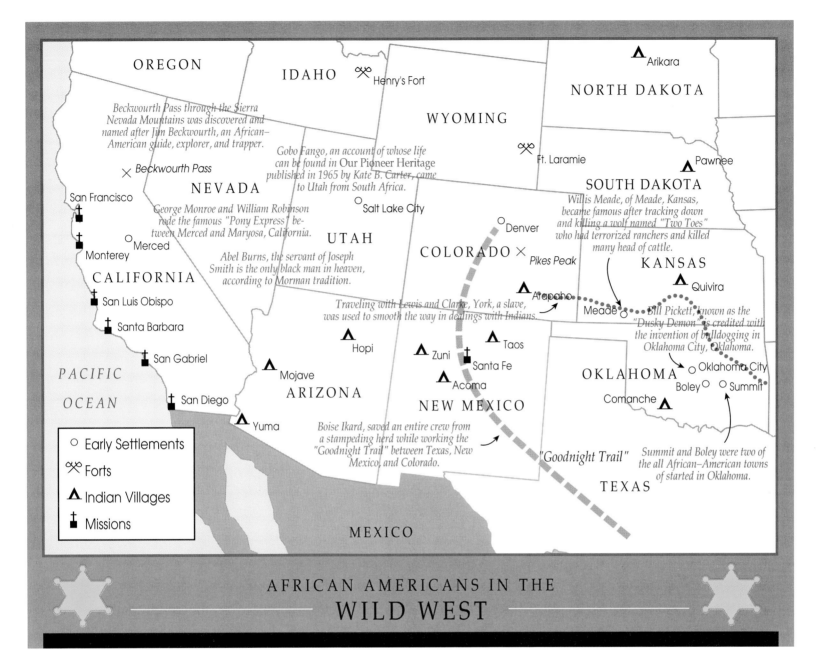

OREGON

IDAHO ⚔ Henry's Fort

NORTH DAKOTA ▲ Arikara

WYOMING

Beckwourth Pass through the Sierra Nevada Mountains was discovered and named after Jim Beckwourth, an African-American guide, explorer, and trapper.

× Beckwourth Pass

NEVADA

Gobo Fango, an account of whose life can be found in Our Pioneer Heritage published in 1965 by Kate B. Carter, came to Utah from South Africa.

⚔ Ft. Laramie

▲ Pawnee

San Francisco ✝

George Monroe and William Robinson rode the famous "Pony Express" between Merced and Maryosa, California.

○ Salt Lake City

SOUTH DAKOTA

Willis Meade, of Meade, Kansas, became famous after tracking down and killing a wolf named "Two Toes" who had terrorized ranchers and killed many head of cattle.

✝ Monterey ○ Merced

UTAH

○ Denver

CALIFORNIA

Abel Burns, the servant of Joseph Smith is the only black man in heaven, according to Morman tradition.

COLORADO × Pikes Peak

KANSAS

▲ San Luis Obispo

Traveling with Lewis and Clarke, York, a slave, was used to smooth the way in dealings with Indians.

▲ Arapaho •••• Meade ○

▲ Quivira

✝ Santa Barbara

▲ Hopi

▲ Zuni ✝ Santa Fe

▲ Taos

Bill Pickett, known as the "Dusky Demon" is credited with the invention of bulldogging in Oklahoma City, Oklahoma.

■ San Gabriel

PACIFIC OCEAN

▲ Mojave

ARIZONA

▲ Acoma

NEW MEXICO

OKLAHOMA ○ Oklahoma City

Boley ○ ○ Summit

✝ San Diego

▲ Yuma

Boise Ikard, saved an entire crew from a stampeding herd while working the "Goodnight Trail" between Texas, New Mexico, and Colorado.

Comanche ▲

"Goodnight Trail"

Summit and Boley were two of the all African-American towns of started in Oklahoma.

Legend	
○	Early Settlements
⚔	Forts
▲	Indian Villages
■	Missions

MEXICO

TEXAS

AFRICAN AMERICANS IN THE
WILD WEST

who operated the twenty-five forges in his smithy. His reputation was without peer as a builder of Conestogas. Many of the early settlers in the West would insist on using a Hiram Young carriage for transport. So important to the westward movement were Young's vehicles that cities and towns in Missouri got the recognition for being the places where the West truly began. This could certainly be said of Independence, Missouri, because of the work Young's smithy did in building the finest Conestogas around.

The tradition of adventurers, cowhands, and philanthropists came together in the finest examples of African American openness to difference and challenge in the

American West. This tradition did not end with the closing of the nineteenth century. A spirit of exploration and adventure led to Matthew Henson's trek with Admiral Robert E. Peary to the North Pole on April 6, 1909. Henson was the first man to walk on the North Pole. Peary could hardly walk because of frostbite and illness and Henson returned to carry him to the North Pole. The record of the exploits of the two men, one black and one white, in the Arctic Region is one of inspiration and victory. When Matthew Henson planted the flag of the United States of America at the North Pole, he was following in the path of many African explorers and adventurers before him, most of whom have remained anony

mous to history because their stories were never written.

The ascendancy of free spirits among African Americans was based upon the same kind of aspiration that captured the imagination of whites who set out to explore regions new to them. Thus, the early pioneers, cowboys, trail-blazers, scouts, and adventurers were curious about the world and wanted to increase their knowledge of it. Some among them were hunters and trappers, seeking to make a profit from their expertise. Others were seekers after gold in the mountains and valleys, but all were devoted to the free expression of their curiosity.

Ohene Kye, "The Kings Crown,"
Ghana, Africa

"DARK CLOUDS A'RISIN":
African Resistance To Enslavement

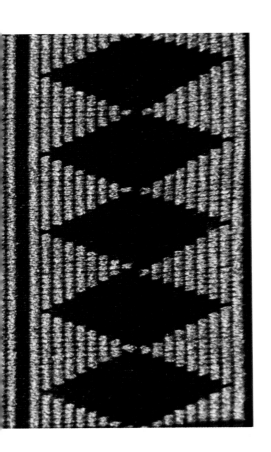

African resistance to foreign invasion was pervasive, aggressive, and continent-wide during the entire period of the slave trade. Every region was engaged in warfare against either Arab or European intruders who sought to exploit the human and natural resources of the continent.

The African people were not amused when they saw European nations competing to send missionaries, traders, and ambassadors to royal courts in an effort to obtain advantages over each other. As C. Tsehloane Keto puts it, "The history of Africa was being made by the masses of African people who saw the Europeans as interveners in the long history of Africa" (Keto 1989). The list of wars protecting the African homeland is long; the heroes and heroines who fought as patriots are now ancestral figures in various panoplies of recent deities throughout the continent. The wars for the control of the National Golden Stool between the Asante and the British, the wars to prevent expansion between the Zulu and the British, the Zulu and the Boers, the Yoruba wars, the Angolan resistance, the Baule resistance, the Shona Chimurenga wars, and the Benin wars were all fought for African honor. Nowhere in Africa did the Europeans enter uncontested once the people were aware of the potential disruptions.

Unfortunately, in most cases African awakening was too late.

Meeting in Berlin during the winter of 1884–1885 several European nations conferred on an agreement that divided the African continent amongst themselves. The major players were Britain, France, Portugal, and Belgium, although the Spanish and German nations were given power over significant African territories. Consultation with African people was nil.

Imposing political and military will on the African people through force of arms, the European nations succeeded in dominating most of Africa by 1900. Wars of resistance caused widespread destruction of life and property in every region. The Germans killed thousands of people in Namibia; the British shot on sight every African they encountered in the territory of Zimbabwe; the Portuguese murdered the royal families of Angola; and the French punished the resisters in Guinea and Mali.

Two principal factors most often led to the defeat of Africans: (1) a cultural factor, and (2) a military factor. According to the late Senegalese scholar Cheikh Anta Diop in his book *The Cultural Unity of Black Africa*, Africans have usually been xenophilic while Europeans have been xenophobic. The result is European aggression on people perceived to be weak. European adventurers often wrote in their diaries that Africans were childlike or Africans perceived Europeans as lost deities. Upon closer scrutiny what we see is a cultural misinterpretation. Numerous travelers into African territories were received with hospitality by kings and queens of the continent. Given passage through the various countries, Arab and European visitors often viewed Africans as naive. Openness to strangers rather than fear of strangers created the false impression that Africans did not care about the protection of their countries or their people.

African's lack of vigilance often allowed access to the resources and people of the continent. Thus, the cultural factor coupled with the military and technological inventions of warfare made Africa's struggle to protect itself unwinnable within the context of the times.

Asiento

So profitable was the European slave trade that the Roman Catholic Church entered the business as a grantor of commercial privilege to prevent Christian nations from engaging in fratricidal wars of access to the African coast. Usually the Pope signed an agreement with a slaving nation which ensured that nation's right to a specific region of Africa. A fee was paid to the church for this *asiento*. When there were competing claims to territory, the church could step in and determine which nation had the consent of the Church by virtue of the correct *asiento*. Since no European nation exercised complete hegemony over others, the Church became—and remained for several hundred years—the primary moral sanctioner for the brutal institution of slave trading.

The *Asiento* of 1713 between England and Spain granted England a monopoly of the Spanish colonial slave trade for thirty years. With the contract signed by the Pope, the kings of England and Spain were each to receive one-fourth of the profits of the trade. England advanced Spain 200,000 crowns for each

The Asiento
1713, March 26

The Asiento, or contract for allowing to the Subjects of Great Britain the Liberty of importing Negroes into the Spanish America. Signed by the Catholick King at Madrid, the 26th Day of March, 1713."

Art. `I. `First then to procure, by this means, a mutual and reciprocal advantage to the sovereigns and subjects of both crown, her British majesty does offer and undertake for the persons, whom she shall name and appoint, That they shall oblige and charge themselves with the bringing into the West-Indies of America, belonging to his catholick majesty, in the space of the said 30 years, to commence on the 1st day of May, 1713, and determine on the like day, which will be in the year 1743, viz. 144000 negroes, Piezas de India, of both sexes, and of all ages, at the rate of 4800 negroes, Piezas de India, in each of the said 30 years, with this condition, That the persons who shall go to the West-Indies to take care of the concerns of the asiento, shall avoid giving any offence, for in such case they shall be prosecuted and punished in the same manner, as they would have been in Spain, if the like misdemeanors had been committed there.`

Art. II. Asientists to pay a duty of 33 pieces of eight (`Escudos) for each Negro, which should include all duties.

Art. III. Asientists to advance to his Catholic Majesty 200,000 pieces of eight, which should be returned at the end of the first twenty years, . . .

[John Almon, *Treaties of Peace, Alliance, and Commerce between Great-Britain and other Powers* (London, 1772), I. 83–107]

African imported. The contract was ended in October, 1750.

Bartolome de Las Casas, who lived between 1474 and 1566, is considered the first proponent of using Africans as forced laborers in the Spanish colonies of America instead of Native Americans. He was one of the first missionaries to the Americas, arriving in Hispaniola in 1502, but was not formally ordained until 1512. His campaign to prevent the harsh treatment of the Native Americans culminated in his persuading the Spanish Crown and the Catholic Church to permit the importation of Africans to the region.

Monopolies of the trade changed hands between the leading slave powers: Portuguese, Dutch, French, and English. The European Slave Trade was the largest single employer in Holland and Portugal between 1500 and 1750. Thousands of individuals were employed in some aspect of the trade or a related industry. Millions of dollars in capital were placed at the disposal of the pioneering and adventuring slave captains.

Due to the intense competition in the business of trading in humans, the Portuguese, who had been the first Europeans in the trade, did not become one of the key nations in the later stages. Its power had run its own natural course.

By the middle of the sixteenth century the three biggest trading powers were England, Holland, and France. Spanish merchants had been effectively held out of the trade by the Papal arbitration of 1493 which allowed other nations to import Africans to Spanish territories in

After research by Joseph E. Harris

THE AFRICAN DISPERSION

the Americas. Portugal had not been permitted to license a company until 1692 when the Portuguese Company of Cacheo was allowed to compete in the slave business. Until then the Portuguese had been content on leaving the slave trade in the hands of merchants who proved ineffective against other nations. By the time the Portuguese Company of Cacheo entered as a regular slave trading company it could only gain the profits left over from the big three.

The Dutch had initiated their company in 1621, the Dutch West India Company, with the purpose of gaining control of the sea routes to the Americas. By the middle of the century, Dutch ships appeared in every port in the Americas.

The French transformed Rouen and some other Norman towns into centers for slave trading. In 1634, a group of Norman merchants had secured a patent from the government to begin the slave trade. However, other companies followed, including the French Company of the West Indies. France was having great difficulty competing with Holland and England until the establishment of the Royal Company of Senegal in 1673. This company gave France a foothold on the coast of Africa and made it a formidable trading nation. During the Seven Years' War with England and the American War of Independence, the African colonies of the two nations changed hands quite frequently. In the end, the French efforts at slave trading proved more profitable in areas where they did not have to compete with the English. Angola and Congo became regions of lively activity among French slavers.

England came to dominate the trade by aggressive attacks on other slave powers and intense competition for new regions. So successful were the English that long after the passing of Sir John Hawkins, the originator of the English slave trade in 1562, the English barons and imperial merchants had written the most daring story in the history of European slave trading. As John Hope

Franklin wrote in his book *From Slavery to Freedom*, the system for prosecuting the slave traffic was the product of English ingenuity.

The process of slave trading was not merely sailing to the African coast, securing a load of Africans, and sailing off again to the Americas. The ships spent considerable time on the African coast, capturing or negotiating for Africans to be sold into slavery. Wars of resistance at certain ports seemed constant. The crews of slave ships were often soldiers who fought against Africans kingdoms in order to stabilize the trade. Gaining enough Africans to make the negotiations profitable meant that some of the ships had to stop at several ports and engage in various kinds of force, pressure, and coercion for Africans.

European Slave Trade

The European Slave Trade overlapped and superseded the Arab Slave Trade on the African continent. From the fifteenth century until the last quarter of the twentieth century, Africa was in the vise of European colonial exploitation and domination; it has yet to overcome the powerful cultural and psychological impact of Europe. Evidence of the damage to the African image in the world as well as Africa's own image of itself has been seen in the way African history has been written. The negation of African achievements and accomplishments has largely been a product of the past five hundred years.

The achievements of Africa and Africans had been known to the Greeks, the Persians, and the Arabs. Historians and travelers from the Arab States had written of the riches of the various African kingdoms and empires in a matter-of-fact manner. For hundreds of years, caravans operated in the Sahara linking the savannas in the south with those in north as well as joining cities such as Gao, Jenne, Ouagadougou, Agades, and Tedmekka. Visitors to this region, Al Fazari, Al Yakubi, Al-Bakri, Al Omari, and Ibn Battuta recorded the

wealth of the West African empires from the eighth to the fourteenth centuries. Al Fazari wrote in the eighth century that the ancient kingdom of Ghana in the western part of the continent was a significant political and commercial entity. Nearly a century later, as reported by Al Yakubi, the evidence was still coming in that Ghana was a force to be considered in world civilization and that it had amassed its wealth from the gold mines in its territory. By 1067, Al Bakri could give the fullest picture of the Ghana empire ever given. In his record he described how the kingdom's capital was divided into two sections. The king and inhabitants occupied the central part of the town while the foreign merchants were given their own portion of the city. According to Al Bakri, the king was surrounded by governors and viziers and flanked by guards who held gold-handled swords. Gold seemed to have been everywhere in the kingdom of Ghana.

Al Omari saw the great wealth and power of Africa displayed in the reign of the Malian king, Mansa Musa, who journeyed to Mecca in 1324 with so much gold that he distributed it freely to officers of the local governments and various other officials in Mecca and Cairo.

Slavery in the American Colonies

Colony	Statutory Recognition
Virginia	1661
Massachusetts	1641
New York	1665
Maryland	1663–1664
Delaware	1721
New Jersey	1702
Pennsylvania	1700
Connecticut	1650
Rhode Island	1703
New Hampshire	1714
North Carolina	1715
South Carolina	1682
Georgia	1755

Thus, whether buying, selling, or gift giving, Mansa Musa made his presence indelible on the imagination of the people of Cairo as he passed through the city on his way to and from Mecca. Al Omari wrote that "the Sultan of this kingdom presides in his palace on a great balcony . . . flanked by elephant tusks . . . his arms stand near him, being all of gold. . . . Behind him there stand about a score of Turkish or other pages which are bought for him in Cairo. . . . One of them . . . holds a silk umbrella surmounted by a dome and a bird of gold" (Omari 1927).

The greatest traveler of the Middle Ages, Ibn Battuta visited several African kingdoms. An African of the Islamic faith, born in Tangiers, Ibn Bat-

tuta was a lawyer and scholar who traveled to places as distant as Samarkand, China, Sumatra, Crimea, and India during the fourteenth century. In the African country of Mali he observed a people who lived in complete security because injustice was rare. According to Ibn Battuta, "the Blacks are of all peoples those who most abhor injustice" (Battuta 1971).

Neither the scholars and travelers nor the African emperors could predict the fate that lay in store for the people of Western Africa a little less than one hundred years later when the Portuguese began their cruises down the coast of Africa. People from every major ethnic group of the western and southern coasts were brutally uprooted

and taken to the Americas and enslaved. Records show that when slavers came with their armies to invade the coast they encountered strong resistance from the Africans. In some cases, women and children took up swords and spears against the invaders; thus, the names of Nzingha and Yaa Asante-waa are forever in the annals of African resistance to enslavement.

The initiation of the European Slave Trade began the largest forced migration in the history of the world. Estimates of Africans removed from the continent range from 15 to 50 million from 1482 to 1888. No more tragic episode has ever been recorded in human history given its continuing impact on contemporary societies. In addition to the Africans

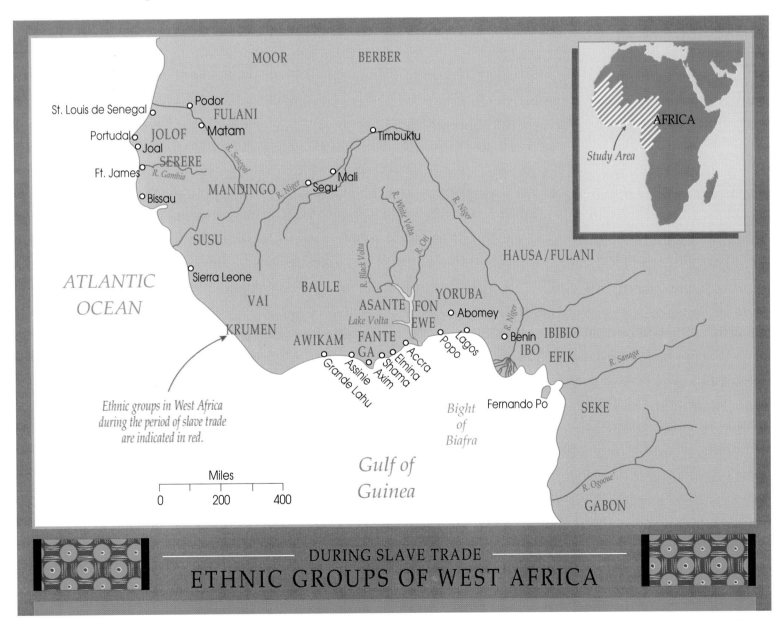

Ethnic groups in West Africa during the period of slave trade are indicated in red.

DURING SLAVE TRADE
ETHNIC GROUPS OF WEST AFRICA

taken from the continent, others were brutalized through warfare with the Europeans and subsequent warfare among Africans over the control of access to European goods. Long, forced marches from the interior to the coast, detention camp diseases, and the horrible Middle Passage across the Ocean to bondage, often killed one-third of the people captured by the enslavers. This brutish business depended upon force of arms, and Europeans ventured into Africa with their arms ready to snatch Africans from their villages. In addition to this practice, they turned to purchasing prisoners from African kings who were often lured by greed and intimidation into the transactions. However, the overwhelming majority of Africans taken from the continent had to be taken by force and were often held in fortresses until slave ships came. Almost every European nation had agents (called "factors") who "stocked" these fortresses (or "factories") with human beings. While such dehumanizing practices brought untold pain and suffering to Africans, the practices also meant that Europeans became numb to the brutality they caused. The guilt and distrust created over five centuries of enslavement and resistance to enslavement have persisted to the present era. As we shall see later, the infamous trade cast its shadow on every part of the modern world.

The European Slave Trade fueled the western economies for four centuries and turned Africa into a continent of spent energies. Entire nations were disrupted and more than one hundred small ethnic groups disappeared from the face of the earth in the great *maafa* of slave trading. Broken economies and shattered political orders littered the continent with dangerous tenants of once proud kingdoms and empires. In Europe, Portugal was first in the slave trade. The small Iberian nation was the leading seafaring country of the fifteenth century when Prince Henry, called the "Navigator," took an interest in the coast

of Africa. Arabs had occupied a portion of Africa since the seventh century and had participated in their own slave trade, transporting millions of Africans to various parts of the Arab world. However, under the leadership of Portugal and Spain, after the defeat of the Africanized Muslims, Europe struck its own chord for slavery. Every major European nation of the time became involved in the lucrative trade.

Portugal led the European nations in the infamous trade of Africans. Prince Henry sent Captain Gonzales to the coast of West Africa in 1441, where he captured three Africans who quickly offered ten other Africans as ransom. Gonzales accepted the trade and Africans were brought to Portugal as curiosities and presents. In 1444 Portugal began trading with the Guinea Coast. By 1482, Portugal had begun building El Mina in Ghana and King Ansa of the Fanti had granted the Portuguese the right to occupy the coast for gold trade. This soon became a major fortress for the European trade in human beings.

Spain joined Portugal in the European Enterprise in 1517; England in 1530 under William Hawkins and later his son, John, who began the trade in earnest when he went to Africa in 1562 with the good ship *Jesus*. In 1624, France joined the trade followed by Holland and Denmark.

The fact that the English were late in getting into the trade did not mean that they would be less determined to make their money in the market. The British entry into the slave trade led to conflict with the Dutch who commanded the premier position in the brutal business for most of the seventeenth century. The navigation ordinance enacted by the British in 1651 thrust England in direct confrontation with the Dutch. It took two wars for the British to succeed in taking control of the trade from the Dutch. Although Britain had granted rights to a special trading company in 1618, by 1662 other companies had received their charters. By 1698, the gov-

ernment had opened the trade to all British merchants who were capable of paying 10 percent duty on the English goods taken to Africa. So integral was the European slave trade to Britain that when it accepted the Peace of Utrecht in 1713, it also demanded to have a thirty-three-year exclusive right to transport Africans to the Spanish colonies in America.

The British trade with the coasts of West Africa principally involved the people of what is now Ghana, Nigeria, Benin, and the Cameroons, but it was by no means limited to these areas. Yoruba, Asante, Fante, Fon, Ijaw, Ibibio, Ibo, and Douala were a few of the nations decimated by the British slave trade. In the end, almost every African ethnic group along the West African coast had experienced the pain and fracturing of the British slave trade. As the major slaving power, Britain controlled access to the coasts for more than one hundred years. Other European nations took up any slack left by the British and consequently devastated entire ethnic groups.

The Trade Triangle
The European slave trade was more like a warped rectangle than the classic triangle depicted in American history books. This is particularly so in relationship to the Africans who eventually landed in the United States of America. The slave ships left *Europe*, traveled to *Africa* where they took on Africans, and sailed to the *West Indies* where Africans were "broken" and trained for enslavement, and then they were transported to the North and South *American* mainlands. Sometimes the "orientation" process took months and sometimes it took years. Of course, many Africans escaped and became Maroons; other were brought to the United States where they were given to "breakers" who tried to break their spirits. Some succeeded—others failed.

The trade in Africans disrupted the normal pattern of industrial and social development of the African continent, particularly the West African empires and nations. Actually, the period of the most intense trade in slave activity occurred just as the Songhay Kingdom was breaking up in the West African region. From about the third century B.C.E. to 1492, there was a solid period of growth, commerce, education, art, and science developing in the kingdoms of Ghana, Mali, and Songhay. (See maps of Ghana, Mali, Songhay). With the break-up of these savanna kingdoms due to internal struggles, Arab Islamic missionaries, and European traders, Africans were increasingly used in the slave economies of South and Central America and eventually North America.

Most of the leading European nations of the sixteenth century were involved in the trade in slaves. Entire European villages found their economic livelihood on the ravishing of African villages. Shipbuilders, sailors, money-lenders, out-fitters, mercenaries, and missionaries from Europe headed to Africa in order to partake of the huge profits that were to be derived from supplying Africans to European settlers in the Americas.

Portugal was the first nation to acquire the *asiento* (or license) to import four thousand Africans annually into the Spanish colonies in the Americas. The *asiento* was granted by King Charles V, who succeeded King Raymond and Queen Isabella

Captain Antonio Gonsalves of Portugal landed his ship near Cape Bojador in what is today the country of Senegal. Gonsalves' troops captured ten African villagers along with the cargo he had been ordered to obtain. The Africans were presented to Prince Henry as gifts. In turn, he presented a few of the Africans to the Pope of the Catholic Church, for which gift Prince Henry received from the Pope, without the African kings' knowledge, the "full possession" of Africa's coastal regions. By

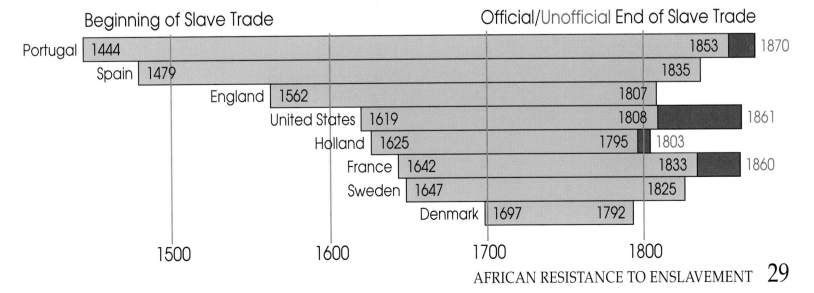

COUNTRIES INVOLVED IN THE EUROPEAN SLAVE TRADE

	Beginning of Slave Trade	Official/Unofficial End of Slave Trade	
Portugal	1444	1853	1870
Spain	1479	1835	
England	1562	1807	
United States	1619	1808	1861
Holland	1625	1795	1803
France	1642	1833	1860
Sweden	1647	1825	
Denmark	1697	1792	

1500   1600   1700   1800

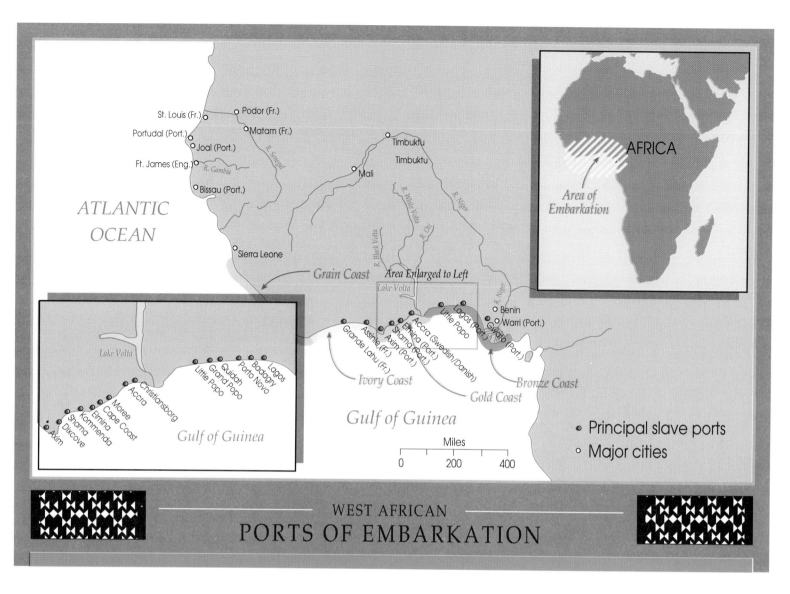

St. Louis (Fr.)
Podor (Fr.)
Portudal (Port.)
Matam (Fr.)
Joal (Port.)
Ft. James (Eng.)
R. Gambia
Bissau (Port.)
R. Senegal
Timbuktu
Timbuktu
Mali

ATLANTIC OCEAN

Sierra Leone

Grain Coast   Area Enlarged to Left

Lake Volta

Accra (Swedish/Danish)   Little Popo   Lagos (Port.)   Benin   Gwaro   Warri (Port.)
Elmina (Port.)
Assinie (Fr.)   Shama (Port.)   Axim (Port.)
Grande Lahu (Fr.)

R. Black Volta   *R. White Volta*   *R. Oti*   *R. Niger*

Ivory Coast   *Gold Coast*   *Bronze Coast*

Gulf of Guinea

AFRICA

Area of Embarkation

Lake Volta

Lagos
Badagry
Porto Novo
Grand Popo
Little Popo
Quidah
Christiansborg
Accra
Moree
Cape Coast
Kommenda
Elmina
Shama
Dixcove
Axim

Gulf of Guinea

Miles
0   200   400

- Principal slave ports
- Major cities

WEST AFRICAN
PORTS OF EMBARKATION

1481, with nothing more than the papal bull giving them what did not belong to them, the Portuguese had established the first European settlement in Africa at El Mina, The Mine, in what is now Ghana. With the advantage of heaven on their side the Portuguese dominated the gold, spice, and slave trade for nearly a century before other European nations were greatly involved. But the Portuguese importation of Africans was not only for the Americas; one thousand Africans were brought each year into Portugal itself for domestic use. In fact, the Portuguese population, it is claimed, gradually took on African characteristics as more and more Africans were absorbed. (*Ebony Pictorial History of Black America* 1971). Like Portugal, Spain also had a great influx of Africans. Many Africans of the Iberian Peninsula were

on voyages with explorers such as Columbus, De Soto, Cortez, Mendez, Pizarro, and Balboa. The Iberian monopoly was directly challenged by the Dutch, British, French, Swedes, Danes, and Prussians (Germans) by the beginning of the sixteenth century. While the Church may have given the Portuguese and the Spaniards a head start, technology and efficiency were to insure that the British would be leaders in the trade for the next few centuries. After a long struggle to acquire the coveted *asiento*, the British government finally succeeded in 1713 and quickly moved into the trade. Liverpool became the center of Britain's quest for black gold and numerous local industries grew up to support the trade. Already a ship-building center, Liverpool flourished as a city where the young British men could

easily lease a ship, hire a crew, or hire himself out to a ship, and go off to Africa in search of adventure and wealth through the trade. The British slave trade worked overtime to compete with the Portuguese, Spaniards, and Dutch: achieving between 1713 and 1793 the buying and selling of 308,000 individuals from Liverpool alone.

The European nations became very skillful in acquiring Africans for the slave trade. They would often dock their ships and make excursions into the interior of the continent from a "safe" fortress such as Cape Coast Castle or El Mina in search of unprotected Africans; they would purchase Africans who had been captured in war with another ethnic group; they would raid other European nations' holding centers for Africans; and they would attack unsuspecting African villages and towns with guns and cannons and take away men, women, and children. Marched in chains, often for great distances, the Africans were held in small cells until enough had been gathered to fill a cargo ship. Then they were placed on board and shipped to various parts of the world.

The staging areas were particularly horrifying. Hundreds of Africans together in chains—wailing—constantly discussing the fate of one's brother, children, husband, wife—trepidation and apprehension—drunken European sailors prone to violence and sexual assaults against men and women—and then the coming of the ships: despair.

The awesome "Middle Passage" would be talked about for generations. Africans who crossed without dying often wished they had died like nearly one half of those who boarded the ships in the coastal forts of Africa. The trip could take from five to eight weeks depending upon the winds. Although many people died while trying to escape perhaps more died from suffocating in the foul air of the ships' holds in which human beings were body to body often with less than eighteen inches between ceiling and floor, layers upon layers, to get as many people in the ship as possible. Defining the limits of the possible, the most efficient management of space, the most profitable arrangement of bodies became the constant talk of ship builders and slavers. (See detail of Ships.)

Estimates of the number of Africans who were forcefully uprooted from their homeland range between 20 million and 50 million during the middle of the fifteenth century to the middle of the nineteenth century. These estimates have to be based on the actual numbers of those who arrived in the Americas and, therefore, no one knows exactly how many Africans were taken from the continent.

Captives were shackled two by two on a ship. When the ship was ready to sail to the Americas with the human cargo on board, conditions turned to cruel and inhuman as Africans were forced to crouch in areas that were no more than four feet high. Only one entry led to the hold where the Africans were held shackled and crouched with their knees up to their chins. Few clothes were allotted to the captives and consisted mainly of cloths around their waists, whether men or women. To quench their thirsts the captives received a pint of water a day. In order to prevent serious circulation problems the slave captains made the Africans come on the deck and dance by the lash. Needless to say the Africans found this the greatest outrage and insult since dancing in African society was more than exercise. It was always a way to be in concert with ancestral spirits and national traditions.

Africans were often taken from several different ethnic communities and placed on the same ship which made physical assaults commonplace. In these cases the slavers would also have to take care that fights to settle ancient animosities did not occur. On the other hand, they were always afraid that Africans would organize insurrections on board the vessel. Caught between a desire to keep a full cargo for "sale" in the Indies or Americas and safety on the ships, white captains often killed weak Africans to place fear in the minds of others. But even so, Africans who survived the crossing carried with them the memory of the suffering as well as the victory of their fellows. The journey was a voyage of terror. They became witnesses to the long night of brutality visited upon their brothers and sisters and yet kept in their hearts the dream of freedom which never died.

The major European nations involved in the slave trade experienced internal economic growth as a direct result of the profits from the trade in Africans. The shipping industry, the munitions industry, the suppliers of rope and iron, and the food suppliers became wealthier because of the competition to outfit the ships in the Atlantic trade.

Africa's Underdevelopment

Walter Rodney has written in his major work, *How Europe Underdeveloped Africa,* that the European slave trade is responsible for stifling Africa's natural pattern of development. Evidence is shown in terms of the amount of natural and human resources taken out of the continent during the time of the slave trade and colonialism. Key contributors to the industrialization of Europe, even after the end of the slave trade, were often colonial officials serving in some capacity for the governments of Europe. For example, John Cadbury of Britain became wealthy and influential in the chocolate business as a direct result of his control over the cocoa board of West Africa. Instead of Africans controlling their own resources, whether diamonds, iron ore, gold, or ivory, other people had unlimited access to these resources. It would not be until the twentieth century that African nations would gain virtual independence and seek to control their own resources. This movement would usher in a new day of assessment in which the toll of the slave trade and the colonial experience would be determined.

Europe's eagerness to exploit the new economic opportunities was seen in the speed with which Pope Alexander VI made his international decree soon after Columbus' first voyage. The Pope, of Spanish heritage, declared that the world outside of Europe would be divided into two zones, one each on either side of a line running south to north 640 kilometers west of the Azores. The Papal Decree gave Spain all lands "discovered" in the western zone and Portugal all lands "discovered" in the eastern zone. An intense battle was set up over this line between the Spaniards and Portuguese. The Portuguese insisted that the line be moved 2,400 kilometers west of the Azores before they would sign it. The Spaniards finally agreed and the Treaty of Tordesillas of 1494 made it law between the two governments. Soon thereafter the Portuguese claimed all of Brazil which was now east of the line. When Pedro Alvares Cabral led his expedition to the Brazilian coast in 1500, he had acquired for Portugal the largest territory of the period.

Few nations outside of Spain and Portugal accepted the Treaty of Tordesillas as binding on them. In 1497, Giovanni Caboto, (John Cabot) had claimed Newfoundland for the English; in 1524, Giovanni de Verrazano charted the Atlantic coast from the Carolinas to Nova Scotia on behalf of the French; and ten years later Jacques Cartier, a Frenchman, made his journeys up the St. Lawrence River. For the most part, the Dutch, English, and French were content to share the commercial treasures of the Spanish finds. It was the full-fledged commercial activity in the newly occupied lands that would fuel the slave trade and make Africa the prime supplier of laborers for the many territories opened up by the Europeans in the sixteenth and seventeenth centuries.

The Structure of Dependency

The history of the colonization of the continent of Africa shows that the colonizing powers put into place a structure of dependency. It is this structure that remains in place in most African nations. From the beginning of the colonization scheme, Africa was placed in the role of supplier to the industrial engines of Europe. The decentered position of African states meant that Africa did not serve its own interests but the interests of the conquering powers of Europe. It is in this sense that Rodney speaks of the underdevelopment of Africa.

The structure of dependency is maintained by the colonizing powers controlling the industrial development of the colonies, forcing the colonies to accept an agricultural role, expropriating the material and human resources of the colonies for service in the colonial power sphere of influence. However, in order for the system to function, it is necessary for the colony to acquiesce in its own demise. Thus, the colonizing and conquering power cannot allow voices of resistance to the structural measures to be heard. Those voices must be stifled at all costs because once the people are aware of the manner in which they are oppressed and exploited, the possibility of revolt occurs. Such was the condition of Africa at the beginning of and during the slave trade.

Africans arriving in the Americas from the continent of Africa were placed in the system of exploitation that was to further underdevelop the continent itself. The need for more and more human and material resources to feed the capitalist engine was generated in large part by the effectiveness of the slavery system in stimulating development in the colonial power centers. Thus, the creation of the banking system, the backbone of the international trade in people and goods, was parallel to the rise of the slave trade itself. Contradictions were inherent in the nature of the system from the beginning. Inasmuch as the system of exploitation depended upon the agreement of the enslaved and colonized people, it would only be a matter of time when people would no longer accede to their humiliation and exploitation. When that time arrived, it would be the end of the system of exploitation by which human beings were dehumanized in order to serve the categories of existence created by force.

Dehumanization of the victims of slavery was necessary to maintain the structure of dependency. The structure depended on the colonizer as much as the colonized, that is, the colonizer had to believe in the process. If the colonizer developed a weakness for moral or ethical principles, or viewed the Africans as human beings entitled to the same rights and privileges as himself or herself, then the system of dependency could not go on existing. As the structure was designed, it meant that there could not be an appreciation for the African.

To view the African as human meant that the white man would have to redefine the structural relationship. That is particularly why the indoctrination normally given to sailors prior to sailing to the coast of Africa had a lot to do with the "savage" nature of the inhabitants of the coast of Africa. Furthermore, many people had been prepared by the writers, preachers, and political leaders of Europe to accept the dehumanization of Africans.

It is no wonder that the brutality meted out to Africans was so callous. When the leading intellectuals of Europe, including Georg Hegel, succeeded in creating an anti-African attitude, even the common Europeans came to despise and hate Africans without having ever met any.

In general, the population of the colonizing country did not care very much about the creation of this anti-African hysteria. They believed the stories they heard—many of the more fanciful stories were passed around from city to city and from country to country.

Obviously, semi-literate and illiterate whites visiting a strange land would see different customs and ceremonies with which they had no experience and make fantastic accounts of these events. Such would probably be true about visitors from Africa to Europe or Asia to Europe. But in the case of the European powers, these fanciful stories served the purpose of exploiting the culture and resources of the African people.

It was necessary for the European colonizing powers to retain control of this image because this image of Africa assisted in the underdevelopment of Africa. It allowed the colonizers to have faith in the mission of enslaving the African in a strange land. Without such faith, the tension in the system would be broken and the Europeans on the frontlines of the struggle to support the structure would cease to work for its maintenance.

The most extreme manifestation of the attack on the African was the physical abuse, even death inflicted upon those who resisted. There was nothing discreet about the process of dehumanization because the European involved in the process did not see it as necessary to be subtle—afterall, the African had been defined as sub-human. Thus, whatever the colonizer wanted to do was possible within the moral framework in which he operated.

One should not underestimate the psychological impact of this process on both the European and the African. The African was reduced to a thing, objectified in the worst possible manner, as brute strength, sex, emotion.

This arrangement was so successful that Africans began to use the same arguments for themselves as the Europeans had used. This was the ultimate victory in support of the structure of dependency. Africans had succumbed to the bombardment of ideas and concepts about themselves, brought by outsiders, that reduced them to objects within the social and cultural system of Europeans. When Africans no longer controlled the ability to define themselves, the victory of the structure of dependency was won by the colonizers.

Every African idea, object, ceremony, ritual, or invention had to be explained in the context of the savagery which had been constructed in the mind of Europeans. African art, taken from the continent by the hundreds of thousands of pieces, was interpreted in the light of this negative view of the people. Indeed, Africans participated in this process by being so psychologically destroyed that they often presented to the Europeans some of the most historical treasures of the land. But having been told over and over again that their religion was pagan, that their deities were nothing, that they were alone in the world, and could not do anything without the help of the Christianizing European, it was a small step to accepting dehumanization. So the psychological warfare on Africans, those enslaved and those colonized, was severe in the extreme.

The structure of dependency was put into place over the entire period of European contact with Africans. Walter Rodney is correct to assert that Africa's underdevelopment was directly responsible for European development. He believes that African industry, commerce, and institutional development could have evolved more naturally without the disruptive intervention of Europe. Every index of modernity, from the making of iron to taxation to support a central government, existed in West Africa long before the coming of the European. Evidence from the major savanna empires—Ghana, Mali, Songhay, Mossi, and Bornu—suggests that West Africa would have established unified central governments over vast territories had there not been the intervention of the slave trade.

The breakdown of ritual patterns, the political interference of slave traders—European and African, the murder of traditional priests, the imprisonment of kings and queens, the internecine battles over the slave trade, and the introduction of the gun conspired against African potential. Out of the ashes of slavery, disintegration, and colonization, Africa would find difficulty in molding a stable economy for the next four hundred years. Dependency on Europe would become the single most powerful motivator in African economies as the European colonizers turned the interests of Africa away from Africans.

Old Baule Cloth,
Cote D'Ivoire, Africa

"I KNOW DE UDDER WORL' IS NOT LIKE DIS": THE GREAT ENSLAVEMENT 4

Slavery was pre-eminently a social system because of the interlocking nature of its various parts: labor, etiquette, overseers, importation, brutality, politics, products, leisure, punishment, and profit. Africans and whites were caught in the locks of this system, bound by its grinding motion in a veritable wheel of hell.

This draconian system played out its singular role on individual plantations throughout the South, although the North had its share of plantations as well. Nevertheless, it was on the southern plantations where African labor tied together the entire system of slavery. The major crops of the southern plantations were tobacco (Virginia and North Carolina), cotton (South Carolina, Georgia, Alabama, Mississippi, Louisiana, and Texas), indigo (Georgia), and sugar cane (Florida, Georgia, and Louisiana).

The South, with its fertile soil and abundant sunshine, was the center of agriculture in the United States during the eighteenth and nineteenth centuries. Agriculture demanded lots of land and was labor intensive. Unlike the northern industrial cities, the agrarian South depended upon Africans for every aspect of the economic life of the region.

From the beginning of the nation, the Great Enslavement of the African was a thorny political problem as well as a major moral issue. When the first Constitutional Convention met in Philadelphia in 1787, many abolitionists thought that it would declare slavery ended. They had hoped that the men sitting in deliberative assembly during those fateful days would address the issue that had burned itself into the consciences of many people. This optimism was seldom rewarded. The Constitutional Convention put into law what would become the mode of operation in the country for the following decades, even beyond the Civil War. The northern lawmakers placated the southerners by granting them twenty more years to import Africans into slavery. In the future, many who understood the moral dilemma facing the nation would take the option of appeasing the elements that demanded gradualism in freedom and liberty to Africans. Fortunately, this pattern has been broken often enough to suggest that the will of the nation is more frequently dictated by those who believe in the social and economic dream of a united nation. Yet in the early days of the nation, whites wrestled with the question of liberty for Africans.

During the Constitutional Convention, another concession was made to the southern plantation owners. Article IV, Section 2 of the Constitution states that "No person held to service or labor in one State, under the laws thereof, escaping into another, shall . . . be discharged from such service or labor, but shall be delivered up on claim of the party to whom such service or labor may be due." Thus, Africans held in bondage against their wills were not safe and secure even if they were able to escape to the North. Some communities in the North, such as Gap, Pennsylvania, developed reputations as residences for noted slave-catchers. An African escaping to the North and coming through such a town or city could be captured, held in prison, and returned to the South. The danger of physical enslavement did not end with an escape; it followed the African to every city and town in the United States.

The Constitutional Convention also made the crucial compromise which ruled, in effect, that Africans were three-fifths of whites in political weight when it came to voting for political offices. The conventioneers set in motion the system for the political inferiority of Africans. Even the articulate Thomas Jefferson said, "As a property, they are lawfully vested and cannot be taken away." He had

Slave Ship

Slave Ship

not freed his hundred-odd slaves on his own plantation at Monticello, and did not believe that the Constitutional Convention should allow this issue to divide the deliberative body. Later, when the scientific genius Benjamin Banneker, who was born in 1731, wrote to him contesting his attitude about the races, Jefferson opted to stand behind the principles of white supremacy— believing as he expressed that the African was inferior to the white person.

Earlier in his life Thomas Jefferson had made several phillipics against slavery. Indeed during the deliberations on the Declaration of Independence he raised the possibility of prohibiting the slave trade, but felt that because it was sup-ported by the king of England, it would be difficult for the colonists to control the high seas. The Americans who favored slavery were against Jefferson's views because they knew that if an attack against the slave trade prevailed in the Declaration of Independence, it would mean further attacks on the institution after independence. Thus the Declaration was written and adopted with no mention of slavery. Once the idea of African inferiority had been accepted by omission in the Declaration of Independence and by compromise in the Constitution, it would take nearly seventy-five years to eradicate this negative view.

Very early in the colonies, certain cities and towns held special places in the minds of Africans. Among the towns that attracted large numbers of Africans because of their owners' business or occupations were the growing industrial towns of Boston, New York, Philadelphia, Baltimore, Charleston, and Richmond.

It was natural that these cities would also be the leaders in agitation for African rights and the establishment of institutions. Several of these cities became principal centers for antislavery propaganda and supporters of the political program of Africans in the North. They gave money and protection to African antislavery organizers.

Boston had been the leading seat of protest against the British and in that capacity had attracted the attention of its African residents. Crispus Attucks had been the first person to die in the Boston Massacre in March 1770. Subsequent Africans had fought in the American Revolution—more than 5,000 Africans fought the British. Among them, Peter Salem and Salem Poor, distinguished themselves for valor and courage. Both were excellent soldiers who made other Massachusetts recruits proud. In succeeding years, Boston became a major arena of African American protest. David Walker wrote his famous *Appeal to the Colored Citizens of the World* in 1829 while a resident of the city.

Philadelphia was also a major antislavery community. Its Quaker background gave it a sense of fairplay and justice that did not always appear in other cities. The Quakers had protested the enslavement of Africans since the 1787 rally against slavery. Africans in Philadelphia lead the way in creating institutions such as schools, churches, lodges, benevolent organizations, and literary societies. The African Methodist Episcopal Church was founded in Philadelphia in 1794.

The presence of Africans in the cities of the North meant immediate attention to the betterment of the condition of Africans. Prince Hall, the most success-

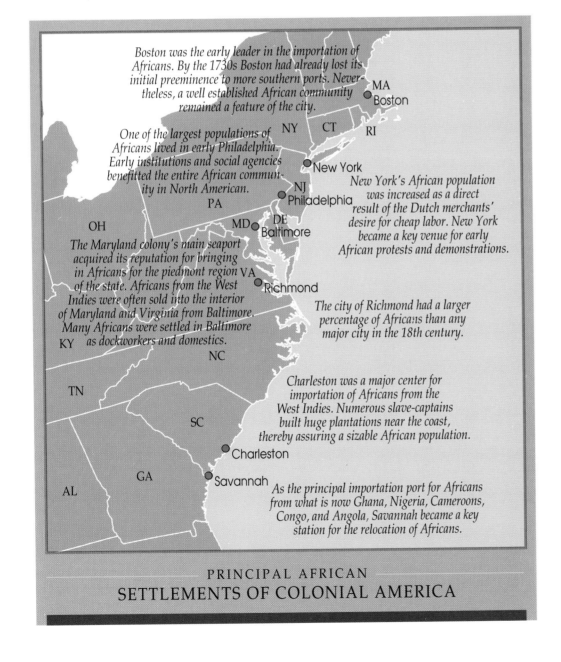

Boston was the early leader in the importation of Africans. By the 1730s Boston had already lost its initial preeminence to more southern ports. Nevertheless, a well established African community remained a feature of the city.

One of the largest populations of Africans lived in early Philadelphia. Early institutions and social agencies benefitted the entire African community in North American.

The Maryland colony's main seaport acquired its reputation for bringing in Africans for the piedmont region of the state. Africans from the West Indies were often sold into the interior of Maryland and Virginia from Baltimore. Many Africans were settled in Baltimore as dockworkers and domestics.

New York's African population was increased as a direct result of the Dutch merchants' desire for cheap labor. New York became a key venue for early African protests and demonstrations.

The city of Richmond had a larger percentage of Africans than any major city in the 18th century.

Charleston was a major center for importation of Africans from the West Indies. Numerous slave-captains built huge plantations near the coast, thereby assuring a sizable African population.

As the principal importation port for Africans from what is now Ghana, Nigeria, Cameroons, Congo, and Angola, Savannah became a key station for the relocation of Africans.

PRINCIPAL AFRICAN
SETTLEMENTS OF COLONIAL AMERICA

Phillis Wheatly

ful activist of his time, established the first Masonic lodge for Africans. Born in Barbados in 1748 he worked his way to Boston aboard a ship in 1765. He rose from obscurity to become a light for freedom in the colonies.

Hall led demonstrations and protests against the dismissal of African troops from the Continental Army. Under General George Washington's policy of black exclusion from the armed forces, Africans were denied the opportunity to fight until the protests by Hall and others caused a change in opinion. In one of the first petitions to a legislature in support of African rights, Prince Hall signed his name to indicate his support. The petition made the case that the petitioners had the same rights as the Americans claimed when they charged the British with unlawful trampling of their rights.

The most impressive achievement of this African was the founding of the first African Masonic Lodge, African Lodge No. 1, in Boston. He had asked to be initiated into a white Masonic lodge but was turned down by the white Americans. He sought out a British regiment encamped near Boston and asked the Masons in the regiment to initiate him and fourteen other Africans. The British Masons initiated him into a British mili-

tary lodge. After the British Army withdrew from the Boston area, Hall set up lodges in Philadelphia and Providence, Rhode Island.

Prince Hall's concern for his fellows did not stop with his establishment of the Masonic Temples, rather he continued his petitions on behalf of African people. Indeed, his petition to the Massachusetts legislature for the education of African children is remarkable for its clarity of purpose. The petition said in part, "We must fear for our rising offspring to see them in ignorance in a land of gospel light, when there is provision made for them as well as others and they cannot enjoy them, and no other reason can be given than that they are black." When Prince Hall died on November 4, 1807, he had become a wealthy and respected man throughout the Commonwealth of Massachusetts and other states. There are few African Americans who have accomplished as much as Prince Hall on behalf of the downtrodden. His work places him in the front ranks of those who have served the nation well.

The mid-eighteenth century was the period of Phillis Wheatley. Wheatley was born in Senegal around 1752 and arrived in Boston in 1761 on a slave ship. As a child of eight or nine years

old she was sold to a wealthy merchant and tailor named John Wheatley.

Phillis Wheatley was able to win acclaim and acceptance during the Revolutionary period. Her book, *Poems on Various Subjects, Religious and Moral*, was the first book by an African woman to be published in America and the second book to be written by a woman in America. She could not be called an activist or a radical; she did not use her talents to attack the system of slavery. However, what she did was significant because her works proved to some doubting whites that Africans could think and write. At a very early time in American history she gave the lie to the view that Africans had no mental or intellectual gifts. The fact that she was effective in the literary world, thought at the time to be outside the capability of Africans, makes her a figure of historic proportions.

The Wheatley family of Boston raised Phillis more like a daughter than a slave. They taught her how to read and write in English. She astonished the people of Boston by her ability to speak, write, and read in fluent English while she was still in her teen years. She wrote a blank verse eulogy about Harvard College as her first poem. Because she was such a novelty in the literary and intellectual

GANG OF 25 SEA ISLAND COTTON AND RICE NEGROES,

By LOUIS DE SAUSSURE.

On THURSDAY the 25th Sept., 1852, at 11 o'clock, A.M., will be sold at RYAN'S MART, in Chalmers Street, in the City of Charleston,

A prime gang of 25 Negroes, accustomed to the culture of Sea Island Cotton and Rice.

CONDITIONS.—One-half Cash, balance by Bond, bearing interest from day of sale, payable in one and two years, to be secured by a mortgage of the negroes and approved personal security. Purchasers to pay for papers.

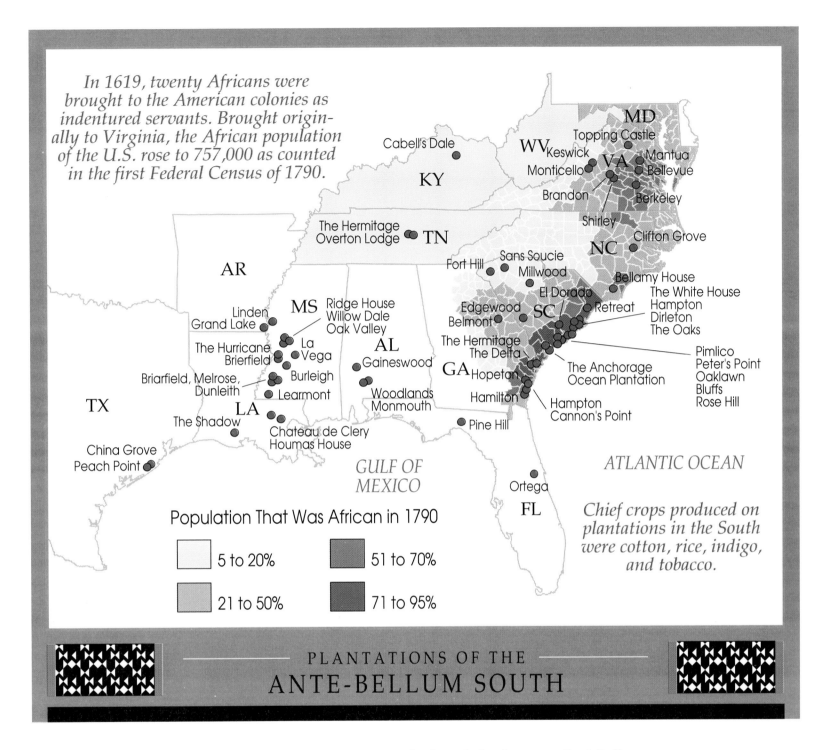

In 1619, twenty Africans were brought to the American colonies as indentured servants. Brought originally to Virginia, the African population of the U.S. rose to 757,000 as counted in the first Federal Census of 1790.

Cabell's Dale

MD
Topping Castle
WV
Keswick
Monticello
VA
Mantua
Bellevue
Brandon
Berkeley
Shirley
Clifton Grove
KY
NC
The Hermitage
Overton Lodge
TN
Fort Hill
Sans Soucie
Millwood
Bellamy House
AR
El Dorado
The White House
Edgewood
SC
Retreat
Hampton
Belmont
Dirleton
MS
Ridge House
The Oaks
Linden
Willow Dale
The Hermitage
Grand Lake
Oak Valley
The Delta
Pimlico
La
AL
Peter's Point
The Hurricane
Vega
Gaineswood
GA
The Anchorage
Oaklawn
Brierfield
Hopeton
Ocean Plantation
Bluffs
Briarfield, Melrose,
Burleigh
Rose Hill
Dunleith
Learmont
Hamilton
TX
LA
Woodlands
Hampton
The Shadow
Monmouth
Cannon's Point
Pine Hill
Chateau de Clery
China Grove
Houmas House
Peach Point

GULF OF
MEXICO

ATLANTIC OCEAN

Ortega
FL

Population That Was African in 1790

- 5 to 20%
- 21 to 50%
- 51 to 70%
- 71 to 95%

Chief crops produced on plantations in the South were cotton, rice, indigo, and tobacco.

PLANTATIONS OF THE
ANTE-BELLUM SOUTH

world, many white American and European people of literature heard about Wheatley and wanted to read what she had written or hear her speak. Even Voltaire wrote that Phillis Wheatley wrote "very good English verse." In 1773, she had the fortune to visit England where her volume of verse was published and she became almost immediately celebrated as an American phenomenon.

There is no militancy in Wheatley's poetry and she concentrates mostly on religious themes, praising, for example,

the circumstances that brought her in contact with the Christian religion. In addition to religion, she wrote about American patriots such as George Washington. When Washington was commissioned as Commander-in-Chief of the United States Military Forces in 1776, Phillis Wheatley wrote a poem expressing her genuine delight over the occasion in a tribute to the General. Washington wrote her a short note inviting her to visit him at his headquarters. She accepted and met the "father of the nation."

Paul Cuffe

Paul Cuffe was an original protester against the system of exploitation of Africans. He was born in 1759 on Cutterhunker, Massachusetts, an island near Bedford, Massachusetts. While he was still a teenager, Cuffe went to sea on a ship bound for the Gulf of Mexico. The name Cuffe is an anglicized version of the Akan name Kofi found among the Asante and Fanti people of West Africa. Determined to make a difference, Paul Cuffe decided to enter the business world.

RAFFLE

Mr. Joseph Jennings respectfully informs his friends and the public that, at the request of many acquaintances, he has been induced to purchase from Mr. Osborne, of Missouri, the celebrated

DARK BAY HORSE, "STAR,"

Aged five years, square trotter and warranted sound; with a new light Trotting Buggy and Harness; also, the dark, stout

MULATTO GIRL, "SARAH,"

Aged about twenty years, general house servant, valued at *nine hundred dollars*, and guaranteed, and

Will be Raffled for

At 4 o'clock P. M., February first, at the selection hotel of the subscribers. The above is as represented and those persons who may wish to engage in the usual practice of raffling, will, I assure them, be perfectly satisfied with their destiny in this affair.

The whole is valued at its just worth, fifteen hundred dollars; fifteen hundred

CHANCES AT ONE DOLLAR EACH.

The Raffle will be conducted by gentlemen selected by the interested subscribers present. Five nights will be allowed to complete the Raffle. BOTH OF THE ABOVE DESCRIBED CAN BE SEEN AT MY STORE, No. 78 Common St., second door from Camp, at from 9 o'clock A. M. to 2 P. M.
Highest throw to take the first choice; the lowest throw the remaining prize, and the fortunate winners will pay twenty dollars each for the refreshments furnished on the occasion.
N. B. No chances recognized unless paid for previous to the commencement.

JOSEPH JENNINGS.

himself. Paul Cuffe became a prosperous shipowner within a few years. He owned a small fleet of ships and a shipyard where he built and repaired his ships.

Captain Cuffe was not distracted by his wealth. He remained committed to his ideals and principles, believing that Africans were discriminated against and needed the support of the government. He was the wealthiest African in America during the 1790s. He built a school and opened it to anyone who wanted to learn. This was to be an example of what education ought to have been for all citizens. Cuffe's point was that education is valuable to all people and that no one should be denied the opportunity to learn.

Near the end of his life, Cuffe gave much attention to the colony of Sierra Leone. He furthered the cause of Africans who wanted to emigrate. He visited the colony himself and in 1815, two years before his death, he transported thirty-eight immigrants to Sierra Leone in West Africa at his own expense. Cuffe furnished the immigrants with all necessities for their new environment.

Africans in the English Colonies

The first recorded presence of Africans in the English colonies as indentured servants was 1619 in Jamestown. The Africans had been seized from a Spanish ship and brought to Virginia in a Dutch warship. This was to be the beginning of a long hard sojourn in North America for Africans. The Spanish and Portuguese had already supplied their earliest colonies with Africans from the east and west coasts of the continent of Africa.

The pattern of interracial interaction was established very early in Virginia. Initially there had been white indentured servants prior to the coming of Africans. For a brief time, both groups had served as indentured servants. Within a few years, the status of African had decreased and the relationship between the Africans and Europeans

When he was twenty-one years old, Cuffe was threatened with jail by the Massachusetts authorities for not paying his personal taxes. Cuffe took a direct position on the question of Africans paying taxes. He argued, as the Americans had argued, that there should be no taxation without representation. He wanted to be exempted from taxation. The tax collector did not accept Cuffe's logic and so the young Cuffe paid the nominal sum.

Angered by the incident and believing that Africans were exploited, Cuffe sent a petition to the Massachusetts legislature, appealing his case. He wrote

that blacks ought to be granted immunity from taxation since they had "no voice or influence in the election of those who tax us." Cuffe's case was argued in the legislature. When the appeal was finally decided, a law was passed granting Africans the same rights as other people in Massachusetts. The audacity of this young man caused his stature to rise in the black community. He was also recognized by the white community as a leader among Africans.

When his father died, Cuffe inherited some land which he promptly sold and bought a ship which he captained had been degraded to the point where only Africans were legally enslaved.

By the middle of the seventeenth century the condition of Africans as servants for life, or slaves, was clearly a part of the generally accepted codes in Virginia. In 1640, when three servants ran away and were captured, the penalties exacted showed unequal treatment. Each of the runaways received thirty lashes with the whip. The two white servants were required to give their masters an additional year of service and three years of service to the colony. On the other hand, the African servant was sentenced to servitude for life.

Throughout the seventeenth century, a century of transition for the business of slavery in America, the African was consistently valued more than the white in terms of wealth, thus indicating the change of status. The African could be held for life and was therefore more valuable as property than the white who remained essentially an indentured servant, normally serving no more than twenty-one years. Virginia court cases during the 1650s indicate that in the buying and selling of Africans servitude for life was usually mentioned. Furthermore, the status of life servitude was inherited by the children of the enslaved person.

Africans who entered the colonies after this period lacked indentures; they were enslaved for life. Africans indentured and freed earlier participated in fighting against these laws because some, like Richard Johnson, a carpenter, and Anthony Johnson, a landowner, had acquired black and white servants of their own.

The gradual legalization of slavery resulted in a psychological and cultural dislocation of Africans to rival the economic and physical dislocation. In 1661, the first legal reference to slavery is made in an act which decreed that if a white and black servant fled together, then the white was to make up the time missed by the black. A further indication of the growth of the legality of

slavery was that in 1662 the Virginia House of Burgesses reversed the long standing English common law that children followed the status of their fathers. Since the colony was seeing an increasing number of children who had white fathers and black mothers, the House of Burgesses passed a new law that said children would follow the status of their mothers, bond or free. Thus, the children of a free white father and an African

woman who was herself enslaved would be enslaved. The debates in the Virginia House of Burgesses expressed the moral agony that had afflicted some members of the society over the question of enslaving Christians in perpetuity. A number of the Africans had become Christians. How was a Christian to hold another Christian in perpetual bondage?

It had been a different story for the earlier white colonists. In effect, they

BY

HEWLETT & BRIGHT.

SALE OF

VALUABLE SLAVES,

(On account of departure)

The Owner of the following named and valuable Slaves, being on the eve of departure for Europe, will cause the same to be offered for sale, at the NEW EXCHANGE, corner of St. Louis and Chartres streets, on *Saturday,* May 16, at Twelve o'Clock, *viz.*

1. **SARAH,** a mulatress, aged 45 years, a good cook and accustomed to house work in general, is an excellent and faithful nurse for sick persons, and in every respect a first rate character.

2. **DENNIS,** her son, a mulatto, aged 24 years, a first rate cook and steward for a vessel, having been in that capacity for many years on board one of the Mobile packets; is strictly honest, temperate, and a first rate subject.

3. **CHOLE,** a mulatress, aged 36 years, she is, without exception, one of the most competent servants in the country, a first rate washer and ironer, does up lace, a good cook, and for a bachelor who wishes a house-keeper she would be invaluable; she is also a good ladies' maid, having travelled to the North in that capacity.

4. **FANNY,** her daughter, a mulatress, aged 16 years, speaks French and English, is a superior hair-dresser, (pupil of Guilliac,) a good seamstress and ladies' maid, is smart, intelligent, and a first rate character.

5. **DANDRIDGE,** a mulatoo, aged 26 years, a first rate dining-room servant, a good painter and rough carpenter, and has but few equals for honesty and sobriety.

6. **NANCY,** his wife, aged about 24 years, a confidential house servant, good seamstress, mantuamaker and tailoress, a good cook, washer and ironer, etc.

7. **MARY ANN,** her child, a creole, aged 7 years, speaks French and English, is smart, active and intelligent.

8. **FANNY or FRANCES,** a mulatress, aged 22 years, is a first rate washer and ironer, good cook and house servant, and has an excellent character.

9. **EMMA,** an orphan, aged 10 or 11 years, speaks French and English, has been in the country 7 years, has been accustomed to waiting on table, sewing etc.; is intelligent and active.

10. **FRANK,** a mulatto, aged about 32 years speaks French and English, is a first rate hostler and coachman, understands perfectly well the management of horses, and is, in every respect, a first rate character, with the exception that he will occasionally drink, though not an habitual drunkard.

☞ All the above named Slaves are acclimated and excellent subjects; they were purchased by their present vendor many years ago, and will, therefore, be severally warranted against all vices and maladies prescribed by law, save and except FRANK, who is fully guaranteed in every other respect but the one above mentioned.

TERMS:—One-half Cash, and the other half in notes at Six months, drawn and endorsed to the satisfaction of the Vendor, with special mortgage on the Slaves until final payment. The Acts of Sale to be passed before WILLIAM BOSWELL, *Notary Public,* at the expense of the Purchaser.

New-Orleans, May 13, 1835.

had enslaved Africans who had not signaled their acceptance of the Christian religion. So strong was the propaganda regarding the moral advantage to the Africans of being enslaved that the white colonists never considered the possibility of Africans becoming Christians. When the decision had to be taken, however, the Virginians came down on the side of their commercial and material interests. They enacted a law in 1667 which decreed that baptism does not alter the condition of bondage or freedom. The African was caught in the Great Enslavement and every law, code, and custom would be re-arranged if necessary to make the system function.

White servants still formed the mainstay of the farm labor force in 1671. The total population of Virginia at that time was 40,000. Of this total, there were 2,000 African slaves and 6,000 white servants. By the turn of the century African enslavement had taken precedence over white servitude.

Unlike Virginia and to some extent, Maryland, slavery in Carolina was expressly called for in the Fundamental

Constitutions of 1669. There was no period of uncertainty about the institution. Carolina engaged in the importation of Africans with a vengeance, opening up the great tobacco plantations to intensive farm labor. Georgia, founded in 1733, attempted to forego slavery. The proprietors thought that slavery was unsound on mercantilist grounds. By 1750, however, Georgia settlers were pressing for their own importation of Africans. South Carolina had demonstrated the feasibility of using African laborers in intensive agriculture.

Different colonies developed crops according to the capabilities of their soils. For example, Virginia, Maryland, and North Carolina were centers for the growing of tobacco. In South Carolina and Georgia, indigo and rice (and later, cotton) were the principal crops. South Carolina and Georgia had heavy concentrations of Africans along the low lying areas of the Atlantic sea coast. In fact, South Carolina had several counties that were dominated numerically by Africans during the eighteenth century.

In the southern colonies the large numbers of Africans created fear of insurrection and riot for the white population. Laws were passed with the intention of governing every aspect of the enslaved African's life. Among the more common regulations found in the plantation states were prohibition on Africans carrying

firearms, prohibition against Africans owning property, and the requirement that all Africans carry passes when they left the plantations. When South Carolina discovered insurrectionary activities in 1739 and again in 1740, the legislature tightened the codes controlling the sale of liquor to Africans and prevented Africans from assembling without permission of their owners.

The late-eighteenth century was a period of dramatic change in the status of Africans in America. Two unrelated events held sway over the future of the enslaved African in America. The first was the signing in 1787 in Philadelphia of the Constitution. The second was the development in 1793 of the cotton gin. Both events were to cast a damper on the antislavery movement.

There had been some relaxation of the stringencies of the slave system during the American preoccupation with the Revolutionary War. Some of the key leaders of the Revolution believed that it was inconsistent for the colonists to be fighting for their own freedom while maintaining the enslavement of Africans. Some blacks had fought in the Revolutionary War. The antislavery movement had been organized in 1775 and reorganized in 1787 with Benjamin Franklin as president. In New York, the Society for Promoting the Manumission of Slaves was established in 1785 with John Jay as president. Quite a number of Revolutionary era leaders sought to end slavery during this period of egalitarian spirit. But the Constitution was a certain stop to the movement.

Opposition to the slave trade and to slavery was raised at the Constitutional Convention but the strength of the slave states produced a compromise that was to eliminate any action which would lead to a quick end to slavery. Taking the doctrine of John Locke as their guide, the conventioneers chose to protect property rights, that is, the ownership of slaves, over the protection of human rights. The Constitution accepted and legitimized the enslavement of Africans. Three ominous clauses were entered into the Constitution with the effect of setting back the anti-slavery movement. An African was to be considered three-fifths of a white man for purposes of taxation and apportioning representation in the House of Representatives; the slave trade was allowed to continue until 1808; and states were bound to return fugitive slaves to their owners.

Eli Whitney is credited with inventing the cotton gin in 1793, although some believe that it was invented by an enslaved African who could not be cited for the invention as a slave. Whatever the case, the appearance of the cotton gin radically changed the fate of the African population. With the rise of industrialization in England and the new techniques in America, a whole new era dawned. Cotton had been domesticated first in Africa and later in Arabia and India, but with the invention of the cotton gin and the techniques for spinning and weaving which were developed in England, it became a rather inexpensive textile. The demand for African labor was almost insatiable. No longer would cotton be second or third to tobacco, rice, and indigo in the various regions of the south—cotton would be king.

The expansion of the use of Africans on farms and the serious interest in cotton were dramatic given the context. Now that a machine could separate the seeds from the lint, laborers could be used to plant and harvest more of the white gold. New lands were staked out and placed under cotton cultivation. Within ten years of the invention of the cotton gin, the numbers of Africans involved in cotton production had tripled. Georgia and South Carolina became the prime areas for cotton growing. In 1803, more than 20,000 Africans were imported from Africa to those states. The principal function of the enslaved Africans in those states was to grow and harvest cotton.

Although indigo, tobacco, rice, and later sugar cane were the major crops in the gulf states of Louisiana, Alabama, and Mississippi, after 1795 those regions eagerly accepted the cotton gin and became producers of cotton as well. The expansion of cotton production to more states meant a further increase in the number of Africans used in cotton production.

The Haitian Revolution

The French loss of Haiti to the Haitian revolutionaries was to have a major impact on slavery in the United States. When the two religious leaders, Bookman and a woman whose name now escapes history, met in the woods to plan the revolution against the French, they had no idea of the significance their actions would have for Africans in the United States. Activated in part by the French Revolution of 1789, the Haitian Revolution was centered on freedom from the control of the French elite in Haiti.

Toussaint L'Ouverture, the military leader of the Haitian Revolution, was able to wrest control of the island nation from the French Army. Defeated by the Africans of Haiti, Napoleon was forced to sell the Louisiana Territory to the United States in 1803.

The impact of the Haitian Revolution on the Africans in America was awesome. When word circulated that a black army had defeated the grand army of Napoleon, the African population was stunned. Never had they dreamed that it would be done in Haiti. Furthermore, the fact that the Haitians would now be in control of their own destinies was too much to imagine. DuBois had said, in effect, that L'Ouverture created a problem for the Western Hemisphere and caused France to sell the Louisiana Territory thus setting up the inevitable end of the slave trade by the United States in 1807. Therefore, the Haitian Revolution had both psychological and practical implications for Africans. In the first place, the overwhelming victory by Toussaint L'Ouverture's army meant that it was possible for Africans to be free. Secondly, the situation for Africans in the United States was stabilized in terms of the importation. The white settlers did not want to import trouble.

Actually the French refusal to extend to the Africans the rights that they had won during the French Revolution was the immediate reason for the revolts in Haiti. No similar uprising had occurred after the American Revolution because the Africans who had fought in the war believed that the Americans would grant freedom to the black population in keeping with the grand ideas of liberty and rights. However, in Haiti, the situation was different. The Africans greatly outnumbered the French in the colony producing a fear on the part of the French that they would be dominated by the Africans if they extended the rights of the French Revolution to them. In 1791 the African Haitians rose up and killed their white masters, resulting in the French Assembly withdrawing even the limited rights of the Africans. They also felt compelled to send soldiers from France to put down the disturbances. To gain some kind of acceptance among the people, the French issued a decree saying that all who supported the French government would be granted freedom.

Toussaint L'Ouverture was the dominant military presence on the island even with the French Army on patrol. An able soldier and an astute tactician,

L'Ouverture was able to elude capture by the French. When Napoleon tired of the fact that L'Ouverture was the one person who could prevent a French Empire in the Americas, he sent General Le Clerc with 25,000 troops to subdue the Haitians. Le Clerc's army was finally able to capture L'Ouverture, but they could not pacify the island.

Concern about Haiti filled the minds of most Americans. This was particularly true of the southerners. There was terror caused from the reports coming in from Haiti, each more frightening than the previous. Blacks were in revolt, they were ruthlessly killing their white masters, taking their land, and destroying their homes. Not even the war between the French and English could supersede the events of Haiti in the minds of the Americans.

South Carolina and Georgia, heavily dependent upon African labor, became timid in regards to importation of Africans. They wanted more enslaved persons to assist in running the farms but they were reluctant because of the situation in Haiti. No white person wanted to see the condition in Haiti become the condition in South Carolina. In 1792, the colony of South Carolina refused to allow Africans into the colony for two years. North Carolina passed a law to prevent further importation of Africans from the West Indies or Africa.

The Haitian Revolution did a lot to convince some whites that they were bringing into the country Africans who could create future revolts. In fact, the Meeting of Friends in New York and Pennsylvania asked Congress as early as 1790 to legislate against the slave trade. The activities of Toussaint L'Ouverture and his Haitian Army quickened the pace of the discussions about prevention of importation. Indeed, by 1794 a bill was passed seeking to prevent the slave trade between the United States and foreign ports and to prohibit the outfitting of foreign ships for the slave trade at United States ports. More than the elo-quence of the newly formed antislavery movement, it was the fear that the Haitians might spread their revolution to the southern states that brought about a lessening of support for the slave trade.

Another aspect of the enslavement business which caused considerable fear in the plantation south was the fugitive slave. Since the American Revolution, Africans had moved around from one place to another in search of safe havens. Indeed, even Caribbean Africans had escaped from the islands into the United States. With the escapees from plantations in the United States, the continued influx of Africans from the West Indies, the threat of violent uprisings grew increasingly more possible. Afterall, Haiti had shown that it was within the realm of Africans to ruthlessly overthrow their owners. Fugitives had to be controlled.

The Constitution had provided for the return of fugitives. This provision had not been effectively operationalized. The first fugitive slave law was passed in 1793. This law empowered the slave owner to travel to any state or region and seize an African who was claimed to be a chattel of the slave owner, carry the person before a magistrate, and obtain a warrant to remove the person from the state from which he or she had fled. The law did not provide trial by jury and allowed the African to be convicted on the oral testimony of the claimant or with an affidavit from a magistrate in the state from which the African was to have fled.

Numerous antislavery groups protested the passage of the law but the idea had already taken hold due to the fear that arose from the Haitian uprising. While the fugitive slave law of 1793 appeared on the books, it was a difficult law to enforce. Africans continued to escape and move around the country from state to state. Elaborate schemes were created to hide them from their pursuers.

The Louisiana Purchase was connect-ed with the Haitian Revolution in political, economic, and social ways. Sugar cane was now a fast growing crop in the region. Both the Spanish and French had begun to grow sugar cane for commercial reasons before the territory became a part of the United States. Many of the Africans brought into the Louisiana area had come from the Caribbean. The acquisition of the Louisiana territory by the French in 1800 created suspicion in the United States. When France sold the territory in 1803, as a direct result of the Haitian Revolution and the therefore the thwarting of the French Empire in the Americas, the western farmers in the United States gained greater and freer access to the mighty rivers of the area. Already by this time the number of Africans in the Louisiana territory was growing at a steady rate. Both the Spanish and French settlers had brought Africans in as slaves and there remained a strong contingent of these early Africans, often creolized, as the Americans took over the governance of the territory. New Orleans became the centerpiece of the territory. It was a combination of all of the influences in the area. Africans, French, Spanish, English, and Native Americans gave New Orleans a special place in American slave society. Africans, of course, were as elsewhere the laborers who fed the engine of New Orleans society.

An outbreak of slave revolts, caused in part by the lingering effects of the Haitian Revolution and excited by the masses of Africans who had come into the Louisiana territory from the Atlantic seaboard, created havoc in the social climate of the newly formed state. The biggest such revolt occurred in 1811, eight years after Napoleon sold the territory to the United States. Four hundred Africans in New Orleans rose up against ill-treatment and their enslavement. The federal government sent troops to New Orleans to quell the insurrection. Several dozen Africans were killed.

New Orleans also had a relatively

large population of persons of mixed racial ancestry who were the offspring of white men cohabiting with black women and in rare instances black men cohabiting with white women. These persons were usually treated by the law as all other blacks. In fact, as early as 1816, New Orleans passed an ordinance requiring separation of the races in public accommodations. Definitions of who was an African were a part of the legal exercises that brought the most debate about social styles in the southern states. Most state legislatures agreed that if a person had one drop of African blood then that person had to be defined as an African.

African Religion in New Orleans

The fundamental religious practices of the Africans in New Orleans in the early period were influenced by two elements: the Congo religions and the Yoruba religions. The Congo religions came from the African groups that were brought into Louisiana and Texas. The Yoruba religions were imported from Haiti and Cuba. Both of these religious influences played a major part in the development of the African American religious outlook in New Orleans, despite a heavy concentration of Catholicism. Indeed, Catholicism served the interests of the various African deities in New Orleans as it had done for Africans in Cuba, Brazil, and Haiti.

Yoruba beliefs came to dominate the religion of the Africans of New Orleans perhaps more than any other region of the country. Much like in Haiti, the religion was called Voodoo in New Orleans. In other places in the South the religion took on different names. It may be called Santeria, Obeah, Hoodoo, Myal, or Roots. The idea behind the religion is the same: the power of God is manifest in many different ways to alleviate human problems. Thus, there are more than four hundred *orishas*, deities of Yoruba religion.

The major powers used in the religion in New Orleans during the Great

Enslavement were Ogun, Shango, Ifa, Legba, Obatala, and Oshun. Ogun is the deity for ironworks and creativity; Shango is the deity for thunder and lightning and the elements; Ifa is the deity who knows the beginnings of knowledge and wisdom; Legba is the deity of uncertainty; Obatala is the deity of reproduction and fertility; and Oshun is the deity of the Oshun River. She is one of the many deities in female form.

New Orleans, from its inception, held a special place in African-American history. Under the southern skies of this city on the Mississippi River, Africans created song, practiced magic, rewrote religious catechisms, explored the limits of freedoms, and challenged the racial order.

In 1836, there were 855 free Africans in New Orleans. They owned 620 other Africans and paid taxes on property assessed at $2,462,470. Twenty-four years later, the free Africans in New Orleans had increased their property holdings to $15,000,000.

This was not merely a population concerned with material possessions. Spiritual matters were always on the minds of the Africans in New Orleans. The city was the center for numerous spiritual movements and leaders. Some of the spiritual leaders had small followings, a few had considerable influence throughout the city.

New Orleans hosted Madame Marie Laveau's religious regime in the nine-

---

Four Thieves Vinegar Spell of Marie Laveau

Marie Laveau was a Voodoo priestess of old New Orleans. Four Thieves Vinegar potion was used by her in ways she claimed would drive away ones enemies.

- *Smear the liquid on the doorknob of ones enemy. It is sure to be touched and its effects felt.*

- *Put a small amount of the potion in a bottle together with the enemy's name written on parchment paper. Throw the sealed bottle into the moving water of a stream or river. It draws the enemy with it as it floats away. He or she will want to move from their home immediately.*

Free Africans played a major role in New Orleans life. Free Africans were more numerous than often thought, and contributed to various American communities as artisans and artists. New Orleans was one of the most important centers for free Africans. Many had come to the city during the Haitian Revolution and they remained to become a sizable part of the population. Louisiana was the southern state with the largest free African population and New Orleans was the vanguard city in Louisiana.

teenth century. No person held such power over New Orleans as did the priestess of the African religions, Marie Laveau. She was charismatic and persuasive. Africans and whites came to her for advice. They sought Madame Laveau's wisdom on all matters of fate, fertility, love, wealth, death, impotence, enemies, and happiness. In the twentieth century, New Orleans was to become the home of jazz, but in the nineteenth century it was whatever music Madame Laveau chose to play.

Senufo Figures, "The Ancestors Will It So,"
Cote D'Ivoire, Africa

"AND BEFORE I'D BE A SLAVE": REMEMBERING AND ORGANIZING 5

The impact of enslavement on Africans was psychological, political, social, and economic. Torn from the continent of origin, Africans developed responses to the different environment which indicated resistance and accommodation experienced by those who have been unfairly discriminated. Both attitudes co-exist within the African American community as a result of the psychological dislocation often felt in a Eurocentric hegemonic culture. The psychological dislocation is perhaps as important a factor in African American history as physical dislocation was at one time. Continuation of the psychological dislocation is no longer dependent upon the actual physical removal of Africans from the continent. It is now the result of more than 370 years of a condition that the philosopher Maulana Karenga calls "the cultural crisis."

The first and second generations of Africans enslaved in America remembered or were told about Africa. They knew the names of rivers, towns, and mountains. They had at their disposal the rituals, ceremonies, dances, and music of their respective ethnic communities. They knew how to worship the deities and to give praise to the elders and ancestors in their own language. The loss of this sense of connectedness and the inevitable loss of self respect

drove Africans to the development of novel responses to the Great Enslavement, responses that never had to be made in Africa itself. Even those who had been fortunate enough to have been captured and made to serve in the employ of Africans still found the circumstances in America difficult beyond imagination. In order to secure psychological space and spiritual peace, the ability to create forms of resistance and accommodation that allowed them to reconstruct dignity within the confines of the slave situation was necessary.

These forms were expressed as music, speech, and dance. Using the Sunday morning church services that were eventually permitted, Africans combined all of the elements of resistance and accommodation, dance, music, and speech, into one festive occasion "in the name of the Lord." Taking the one day of rest to renew their spirits and to re-establish connections to the African deities through the medium of Christianity, the enslaved Africans gave permanence to a transmuted and transfigured social and cultural reality.

This was not a slave culture. It was the expression of African culture under duress. When the African musicians were prohibited from using drums, they expressed the percussive elements with sticks, cans, bottles, and even the human body as in hand-clapping or the hambone.

Yoruba, Asante, Mandinka, and Angola were different languages, yet the Africans were able to combine elements of these languages, mainly syntax, with lexical items from English to create a pidgin, and later a creolized language which gave them the ability to communicate with each other and the whites. In language as in music, Africans demonstrated a willingness to resist the enslavement through creative uses of structure and words.

Physical resistance was not out of the question. However, after petitions and demonstrations, many Africans felt that freedom was worth the threat of death. Thus, cultural resistance was only one method of attacking the enslavement.

Free Africans in the North (United States)

During and after the colonial period there were free Africans, indeed, some who had never been enslaved in North America, although their numbers were small and their power insignificant. John Hope Franklin reports that there were 59,000 free Africans in the United States in 1790. Of that total, 27,000 were in the North and 32,000 were in the South. By 1860, there were 488,000 free Africans, and 46 percent of them lived in the Atlantic South, and 44 percent lived in the industrial North. The remainder lived in the West or central states.

By 1860, the concentration of free Africans was in the following cities: Baltimore, Washington, Charleston, Mobile, and New Orleans in the southern region; Boston, New York, Cincinnati, and Philadelphia in the northern region. The largest concentrations were in Baltimore, 25,600; Philadelphia, 22,000; New York, 12,500; New Orleans, 10,600; and Charleston, 3,200. Isolated pockets of free Africans were found in places like Cass County, Michigan; Hammond County, Indiana; and Wilberforce, Ohio.

Soon after their arrival in America, the Africans organized churches and other institutions for social relations as well as spiritual comfort. The major church was the African Methodist Epis-

copal (A.M.E.) during the later eighteenth century. Other churches had been started and had disappeared.

The church represented the one institution in America where the African could conceivably keep council with the ancestors. It was a "place of refuge in a stormy time." Evidence exists of churches being set up in Petersburg, Virginia in 1776, in Richmond in 1780, and at Williamsburg in 1765.

In Georgia, as early as 1779, Africans set up their own churches after the War of Independence. George Liele, who had shown industry among the Africans in Savannah, Georgia, established a Baptist Church before finally settling in Jamaica. Andrew Bryan, Liele's assistant, continued to preach at the church in Savannah, urging both blacks and whites to treat others as they wished to be treated. Bryan was arrested and imprisoned after the Americans won the War of Independence, but his church, according to John Hope Franklin, became the nucleus of African Baptist churches, and probably influenced the religion of Africans in South Carolina.

However, it was in Philadelphia with the work of Richard Allen that the rise of the free churches truly began. Allen saved enough money to purchase himself from his Delaware slave owner in 1777. A year later he began to preach and win over many others to his denomination which at the time was the Methodist Church. In 1786, he moved to Philadelphia and proposed to establish a separate church, but the officials of St. George's Church where he occasionally preached refused to allow him to do so. Allen drew large numbers of Africans to hear him whenever he would preach but the officials of the church insisted on segregating the Africans from the rest of the church-goers. Allen knew that the time would soon come when Africans had to have their own place of worship. The time was hastened when officials of the church yanked Allen, Absalom Jones, and William White from their knees during prayer meeting. They left

and Richard Allen and Absalom Jones organized the famous Free African Society. Out of this organization Richard Allen was able to set up the Bethel African Methodist Episcopal Church in 1794.

Bethel was truly Mother Bethel. It quickly developed branches in Wilmington, Baltimore, Camden, and Norristown, Pennsylvania. By 1816, the churches under the leadership of men such as Daniel Coker, Morris Brown, and Nicholson Gilliard, were able to formalize themselves into a conference. Coker was elected bishop but resigned and Allen was elected to fill the place. By 1820 there were 4,000 African Methodists in Philadelphia and the church had spread to Pittsburgh in the west and Charleston in the south.

As in Philadelphia, Africans in New York and Boston were expressing an interest in their own churches at the turn of the century. The establishment of the African Methodist Episcopal Zion Church in New York in 1776 was led by Peter Williams, James Varick, George Collins, and Christopher Rush. They ordained themselves and by 1822 had elected their own bishop.

In Boston, the African population organized its own Baptist church under the leadership of Reverend Thomas Paul in 1908. Paul traveled to New York to assist in setting up the Abyssinian Baptist Church. Between Boston and Charleston, despite the intervening condition of the slave system, Africans set about establishing churches that reflected a desire for freedom from constraints imposed by the attitudes of whites.

The African American church as an independent organization did not develop in earnest until the eighteenth century, although Christianization had begun in the seventeenth century. Independent churches in the South did not appear in numbers until after the Civil War when recently-freed Africans began to assert their spirituality through the formal Christian church. Concurrent with the Christian church have always been the Hoodoo, Roots, and Cuba phenomena

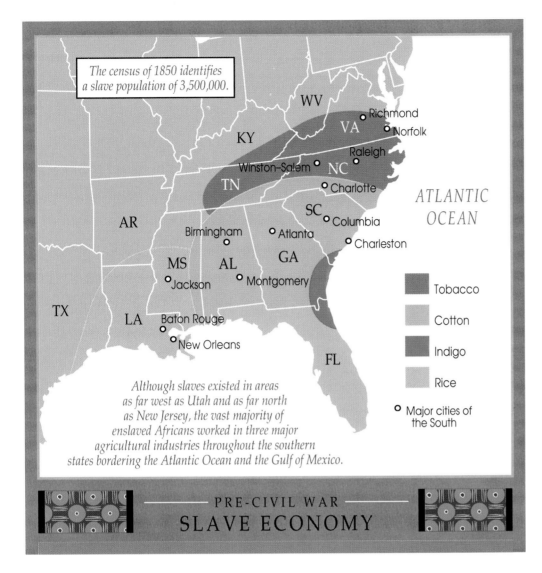

The census of 1850 identifies
a slave population of 3,500,000.

ATLANTIC
OCEAN

Tobacco

Cotton

Indigo

Rice

○ Major cities of
the South

Although slaves existed in areas
as far west as Utah and as far north
as New Jersey, the vast majority of
enslaved Africans worked in three major
agricultural industries throughout the southern
states bordering the Atlantic Ocean and the Gulf of Mexico.

PRE-CIVIL WAR
SLAVE ECONOMY

with elements in traditional African re-ligions. Strong semi-independent and independent churches reflected an ea-gerness for self-direction and leader-ship. These churches, mainly Baptist and Methodist became the leadership training institutions for the community. Early preachers also became the inter-preters of black social and political agendas, placing themselves between the white man and the membership. Forced by this position to assume a leadership role, the African American preacher often became the lead-off wit-ness against racism. By their tone and behavior, they taught their membership what and how to think on the leading social and political issues.

Richard Allen's break with the Methodist church in 1794 and Bishop George Stallings' break with the Cath-olic Church in 1989 represent the

motive force in the progressive African American church. Resistance to discri-mination coupled with a humanizing mission provides the best example of the African American church. Deter-mined to throw off the shackles of infe-rior treatment and secure independence from white conceptual hegemony, early Africans in America found religion a possible ally. Allen's establishment of the African Methodist Episcopal Church was a prime example of the will to freedom.

In 1777, Richard Allen had saved enough money to purchase his freedom from the Delaware family that enslaved him. When he moved to Philadelphia in 1786 he had already begun to conduct prayer meetings with Africans. Both whites and some Africans opposed his proposal to set up a separate church. Only when the presiders and officials at

St. George's Church decided to segre-gate him and the large number of Africans who came to hear him speak did Allen act on his previous inclina-tion—so he organized the A.M.E.

By 1816, the church had spread to towns in Maryland, Delaware, and New Jersey, as well as the Pennsylvania towns. Mother Bethel soon sent preach-ers as far south as Charleston and as far west as Pittsburgh.

New York followed Philadelphia in 1796, when Africans withdrew from the John Street Methodist Episcopal Church, and under Peter Williams' leadership, founded The African Methodist Episco-pal Zion Church. Unlike Richard Allen, who persuaded Bishop Asbury to ordain him, no white in New York would or-dain the A.M.E.Z. leadership. However, determined to succeed, they ordained themselves and the church was fully or-ganized by 1822.

Throughout the North, the pattern of separation from white congregations and establishment of black churches was the same. In 1809, Thomas Paul orga-nized an independent African Baptist Church in Boston. The indefatigable Reverend Paul also assisted in the orga-nization of the Abyssinian Baptist Church of New York during 1809.

Anxious to develop leadership and education, Africans found the church and some fraternal organizations to be excellent proving grounds. In March 1775, when a British lodge of freemasons attached to the British Army under Gen-eral Gage initiated fifteen Africans, in-cluding Prince Hall, they started a revo-lution. Many African groups were estab-lished in the larger cities to care for the social welfare of the growing popula-tions swelled by the influx of newly-ar-rived Africans from the West Indies as well as escaped Africans. Organizations such as the African Society (founded in Boston in 1796), the African Free School, and the African Benevolent Society are socially and historically connected to the themes of Bishop George Stallings in the twentieth century.

Richard Allen's spirit is the spirit of creativity, invention, resistance, redefinition, reconstruction, and restoration. The most honorable path in African American history has been this road to freedom—born of a commitment to the belief that Africans were as capable as any Americans despite the social, political, and economic attempts to deny this fact.

There would be throughout the history of African Americans men and women who challenged the stereotypes held by whites. They would be in every profession, live in every region of the country, and have many different political views. Yet the common goal would be to disprove the inferiority of the African.

Preachers were the first line of offense in the struggle for decency and respect. Early African preachers took to the pulpit as a justifiable avenue of protest, admonition, and indeed, if need be, insurrection. Many of the revolts in African American history were the work of preachers who had seen certain visions. Given permission to learn the Bible in order to preach to Africans, the preachers learned first of all the verses in the Bible that supported slave uprisings and revolts. Although the slave owners also had their verses and just as easily told the enslaved Africans that the "Lord wanted them to obey their masters," the preachers could teach the Africans that "to obey the devil is a sin against God."

Scientists also rose up to say with a collective voice, "And before I'd be a slave, I'll be dead and buried in my

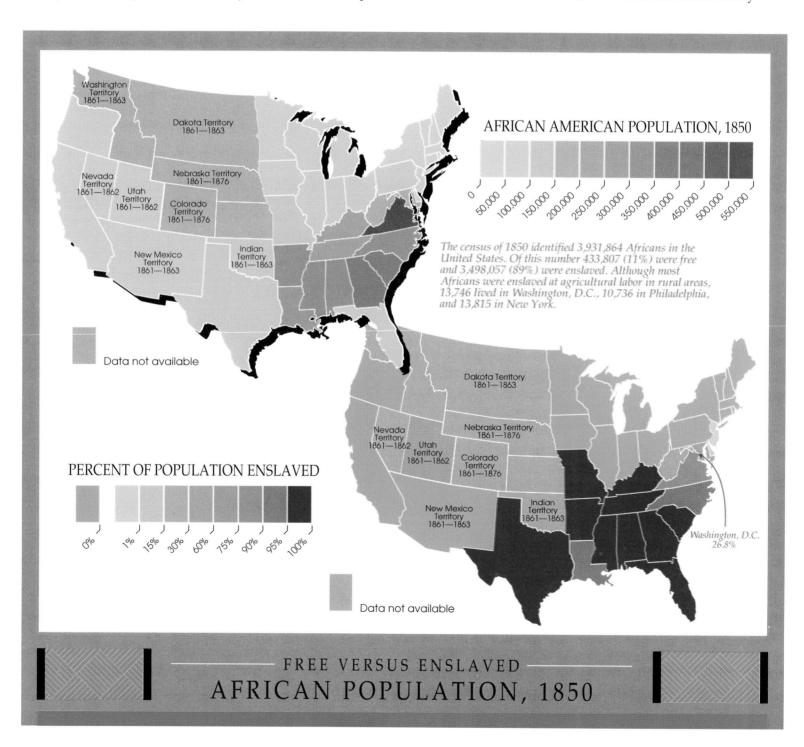

The census of 1850 identified 3,931,864 Africans in the United States. Of this number 433,807 (11%) were free and 3,498,057 (89%) were enslaved. Although most Africans were enslaved at agricultural labor in rural areas, 13,746 lived in Washington, D.C., 10,736 in Philadelphia, and 13,815 in New York.

AFRICAN AMERICAN POPULATION, 1850

PERCENT OF POPULATION ENSLAVED

Data not available

FREE VERSUS ENSLAVED
AFRICAN POPULATION, 1850

African American Occupations, 1890

	Both Sexes	Male	Female
Agricultural Pursuits	1,728,325	1,300,658	427,667
Domestic and Personal Service	956,754	450,765	505,989
Manufacturing and Mechanical Pursuits	208,374	181,415	26,959
Building Trades	42,692	42,667	25
Chemical and Allied Products	1,225	1,214	11
Clay Stone and Glass Products	12,245	12,210	35
Fishing and Mining	29,078	28,936	142
Food and Kindred Products	5,926	5,731	195
Iron, Steel, and Their Products	19,359	19,314	45
Leather and Finished Products	6,553	6,466	12
Liquor and Other Beverages	696	693	3
Lumber and Its Remanufactures	22,285	22,167	118
Metal and Metal Products			
Other Than Iron and Steel	1,442	1,428	14
Paper and Printing	1,290	1,177	113
Textiles	27,101	5,979	21,122
Miscellaneous Industries	65,757	39,579	26,173
Professional Service	33,994	25,170	8,824
Trade and Transportation	145,717	143,371	2,346

grave." They demonstrated by their productive and qualitative enterprises that Africans could do anything that was possible for others. Whether in nuclear fission, aeronautical engineering, biology, or agricultural chemistry, the record is the same when the African American is given an opportunity to pursue, to the fullest extent, his or her chosen field. The record is that slavery is not on the agenda of these scientists.

Preachers and scientists represent only two of the professions which have been involved in the resistance to cultural, physical, economic, and political enslavement of the African American community. Artists, particularly musicians, have done an incredible job of retaining or attempting to retain the African roots of cultural resistance. From break dancing to rap, from jazz to gospel, the cultural and psychological message is the same: resist domination. The reason that this attitude governs most of the thinking of African Americans is because the quest is always for liberation, for freedom from color and racial prejudice. There is no other American quest accepted so well by the African American people.

Freedpersons

Although the overwhelming majority of Africans in the United States were enslaved, there were free Africans from the beginning of the country. The categories of free Africans included those who were neither indentured nor enslaved, those who had escaped to freedom, those who had been manumitted by previous owners, and those who had purchased their own freedom. In the first class were individuals whose ancestors had descended from Africans who had entered the Americas in the sixteenth century with Spanish explorers and were not legally bound by Anglo-American enslavement. Many of these people, like most free Africans, had to constantly defend their right to be free. The second class included those who had successfully escaped and eluded capture or whose parents had done so. These individuals constituted a category of Africans in large towns and cities, both North and South, who were technically free but who were always in danger of being captured by slave hunters. The third class was comprised of Africans whose owners had freed them as a moral act, usually in their wills or on their deathbeds. Such Africans were able to live among enslaved Africans in the South or travel to the North. They usually took menial jobs, occasionally serving as overseers, or domestics in the towns. The fourth class of free Africans was characterized by determined and proud individuals who had purchased their freedom. Sometimes slave owners would give Africans the opportunity to work extra time to pay their purchase cost plus interest. Many did so and lived with great pride because of their achievement.

Although they could never be sure that they would not be challenged for their liberty, the majority of free Africans found gainful employment. The chief positions were in agricultural, manufacturing, and domestic work. While the North did not have as much agricultural work as the South, it was not without its share of farm work and need for farm laborers. Just as in the South, the majority of the free Africans worked on farms and as domestics. However, the Africans in the North owned his or her labor, while in the South the laborer was owned by the slave master. The freed person was at liberty unknown in the South.

Richard Allen

Richard Allen was born in Philadelphia in 1760. Allen was the founding bishop of the African Methodist Episcopal (A.M.E) Church. The A.M.E Church was the first major black institution in America, and Allen was the first major leader of African Americans in the United States. Born of slave parentage, he grew up in slavery in Delaware and became a zealous Methodist minister whose many converts included his master, who let him buy his freedom. Allen returned to Philadelphia around 1786, where he brought so many African Americans into St. George's Methodist Church that friction soon developed in the church between whites and blacks. He proposed a separate church for blacks and by 1787 had formed the Free African Society, one of the first official organizations of African Americans. It was dedicated to self-improvement and advancement. In the same year, whites segregated blacks by assigning them to the gallery at St. George's Church. Allen and Absalom Jones led an exodus of black parishioners from that church, and Jones and members of the Free African Society established St. Thomas's Free African Church within the Protestant Episcopal Church. Allen, in turn, formed the Bethel African Methodist Episcopal Church (Mother Bethel). Ordained a bishop in 1799, he gained complete independence for the control of his church in 1816.

James Forten

James Forten was born in Philadelphia in 1766. Like many of his contemporaries in Philadelphia, Forten was a sailor. He served aboard a privateer during the American Revolutionary War. When the war ended, Forten devoted considerable time to the betterment of the African race in Philadelphia and elsewhere. He was one of the signers of a petition asking Congress to modify the Fugitive Slave Act of 1793. Active throughout the city for the good of the entire community, Forten joined Richard Allen in 1814 to organize a force of 2,500 Africans to defend Philadelphia against the British forces.

Forten was committed to the idea that Africans in America who lived in the North were "colored citizens" and deserved as many rights and responsibilities as any other citizens of the United States. He was one of the leaders of a major meeting in 1817 to protest the American Colonization Society's scheme to send Africans back to Africa. This meeting, held at the Bethel African Methodist Episcopal Church in Philadel-phia, was attended by delegates from as far away as upstate New York. Forten chaired the meeting and assisted in writing the resolution which declared that the free blacks of the North were opposed to any attempt by the southern planters to send Africans back to Africa so as to separate them from their enslaved brothers and sisters.

The Church and the Professions

During the last half of the nineteenth century African Americans flocked to the churches. The end of the Civil War brought great activity on the part of several denominations which sought to exploit the newly found field of potential believers. Black church membership grew phenomenally; the Baptist Church alone gained 500,000 members by 1870. But growth was also recorded by the Methodist Episcopal Church which had divided into a northern and southern church over the slavery issue. The African Methodist Episcopal Church, one of two black controlled denominations at the time, increased its membership as well. It had gone underground in the South during the struggle to eliminate slavery. The other black denomination was the African Methodist Episcopal Zion Church. It increased its membership from 25,000 in 1860 to 200,000 in 1870.

The Catholic Church made its progress in the District of Columbia and the state of Louisiana. Father Patrick Healy and his natural brother James Augustine Healy were appointed to important posts in the Catholic Church. In 1873, Patrick Healy became president of Georgetown University in Washington and James Augustine Healy was appointed to the post of Bishop in 1875. He was later made an assistant to the papal office. The Church was not an avenue for professional growth.

Bishop Henry McNeal Turner

Bishop Henry M. Turner was born in Newberry Court-House, South Carolina on February 1, 1833. He was free born due to his mother's freedom. Her father of royal blood in Africa was never enslaved. He was brought to America and declared free. Therefore, Henry grew up amidst slavery but he was a free child. This did not make his life any easier as the whites that he worked for often had overseers who wanted to use him as a test case for the enslaved Africans. He was hired out to several places where he had to fight the overseers. He was determined that no white man lash would ever scar his back. He resented every attempt to whip him. One dream stood out in his mind as a child: to impart knowledge to his people. Against all of the odds for an African in the South, Turner learned to read. He was appointed in 1863 by President Lincoln as the first commissioned African chaplain in the army.

Benjamin Banneker

Benjamin Banneker was one of America's earliest scientists. He made a clock out of wooden parts while he was still a young man. It was the first wholly American-made clock in the country. His clock kept time accurately for twenty years.

Banneker, who was born in Ellicott, Maryland of a free mother, attended a private school until he received the equivalent of an eighth grade education. As a child he loved mathematics and soon published almanacs, mastered astronomy, and became a surveyor. Secretary of State Thomas Jefferson recommended Banneker to President George Washington for the post of surveyor along with Pierre L'Enfant and Andrew Allicott in laying out the nation's new capital in the District of Columbia. L'Enfant's resignation made Banneker a key figure in the planning process. He was the first African given a presidential appointment. On August 19, 1791 Banneker wrote Thomas Jefferson, sending him a copy of his annual almanac and disputing Jefferson's claim that Africans were inferior to whites.

The achievements of scientists such as Banneker would continue to refute the claims that Africans were less intelligent than whites. Banneker's accomplishments in the eighteenth century were to be followed by even greater technological and scientific work in the nineteenth and twentieth centuries. The scientific world recognized the contributions of individuals such as Katherine Johnson, Percy Julian, Lewis Latimer, Charles Drew, Ernest Just, Daniel Hale Williams, and George Washington Carver. Each in his or her own field made outstanding contributions to the advancement of American science. While these are the names that are most memorable, literally hundreds of men and women, under the worst of technological circumstances, succeeded in establishing a remarkable record for African Americans in medicine, biology, chemistry, agriculture, and technology.

Banneker's letter to Jefferson explaining his objection to Jefferson's view about the African race was exceptional because of the absence of an abundance of examples of achievement among the enslaved Africans of his day. However, since the time of Banneker, African American scientists have been in every field and discipline working for the advancement of the human race. By taking the initiative, these men and women have moved mountains of apathy to etch their names in the annals of history.

Henry Blair

Henry Blair was the first African to receive a patent for an invention in the United States. Blair was born in Maryland in 1804 and received a patent for a corn planting machine in 1834. Two years later he received a patent for a cotton planting machine. Blair was designated as "a colored man" in the official records. Since enslaved Africans could not receive patents it is most likely that Henry Blair was a free African.

George R. Carruthers

George R. Carruthers was one of the two naval researchers who helped to develop the Apollo 16 lunar surface ultraviolet camera/spectrograph, which was placed

on the moon in April 1972. Carruthers designed the instrument and William Conway adapted it for the Apollo mission.

Carruthers was born in Chicago in 1940 and made his own telescope at the age of ten. He is only one of dozens of creative African Americans who work for the space program of the United States. With a Ph.D. in physics from the University of Chicago, Carruthers was well qualified to receive the Exceptional Scientific Achievement medal from the National Aeronautical Space Agency, as he did in 1972.

Charles Richard Drew

Charles Drew was born in Washington in 1904. At his death in 1950 he was celebrated for his outstanding achievements in the field of blood research. He pioneered in the development of techniques for preserving blood, making it

possible to save thousands of lives of American and allied soldiers during the Second World War.

Drew attended Amherst College where he established a reputation as an athlete and a scholar. He received the Messman Trophy for bringing the most distinction to his college. Drew received his medical degree from McGill University in Toronto in 1933. He perfected the techniques for separating and preserving blood at McGill. He then went to Howard University to teach pathology. Believing that he needed to explore blood research more deeply, he enrolled in the doctoral program at Columbia University. His work on "banked blood" brought him to the attention of the British government who asked him to set up the first blood bank. He later directed the American Red Cross and became chief surgeon at Howard University.

Katherine Johnson

Katherine Johnson was born in West Virginia in 1918. She became well known for her work as an aerospace technologist while working at the National Aeronautics and Space Administration's Langley Research Center in Hampton, Virginia. Her research involved more sophisticated ways to track manned and unmanned space vehicles. She became an expert at analyzing data from the manned and unmanned moon missions.

Percy Julian

Percy Julian was born in Montgomery, Alabama in 1898. His major achievement was in the development of derivative drugs which aid in the treatment of arthritis. Julian attended Harvard and the University of Vienna. He taught at Fisk, Howard, and West Virginia State before deciding to concentrate on medical research. He worked first with soybeans and specialized in the production of sterols, thus enabling arthritis sufferers to be able to afford cortisone, a sterol derivative, more inexpensively. In 1935, Percy Julian synthesized the drug physostigmine which is used to treat glaucoma.

Samuel L. Kountz

Samuel L. Kountz was born in Lexa, Arkansas in 1931. Kountz was a brilliant surgeon who attended the University of Arkansas Medical School—he was the first black to enroll at the school. He was the international leader in performing kidney transplants during his life. He was responsible for more than 500 kidney transplants during the time he was head of surgery and chief of general surgery at Downstate Medical Center and Kings County Hospital Center, respectively. He also worked with other surgeons to develop the prototype of a machine that can preserve a kidney for 50 hours from the time it is taken from a donor to the time of transplanting. He contracted a strange illness while on a visit to South Africa in 1980. His illness was never diagnosed and he remained brain damaged until his death in 1981.

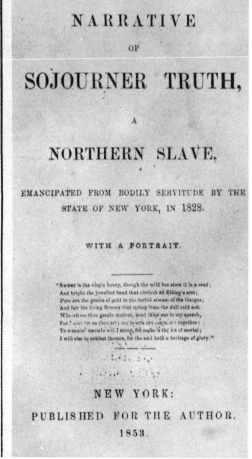

There were other scientists before Kountz, but none who achieved so much practical results in such a short period of time. Certainly Ernest Just who was born in Charleston, South Carolina in 1883 must be considered one of the first biologists, but Kountz became a legend during his brief career.

Amistad Mutiny

Cinque, an African, was seized and carried off to be sold into slavery in 1839. His father was a rice farmer from the Mende region of West Africa. The slave ship took Cinque to Cuba. In Havana, two Spaniards purchased fifty Africans, including Cinque, and placed them on a ship called the *Amistad* bound for Puerto Principe, Cuba. On board the ship with the Africans that had been purchased were the captain, two other enslaved Africans, and two whites serving as a crew.

When it was night, Cinque and other Africans surprised Captain Ferrer and the cook, killing both. In command of the ship, Cinque tied the owners of the cargo to the bridge and instructed them to steer the ship toward the African coast. The Spaniards guided the ship toward the United States, steering it north and west instead of east and south. For nearly two months the ship zig-zagged in the Atlantic Ocean. Ten Africans died before the *Amistad* finally reached Long Is-

Cinque

land, New York. They had been without adequate food and water for several days. In the New York waters the vessel was sighted by a United States Navy ship which sent a group of sailors aboard to investigate the character of the strange ship.

The Americans were shocked to find only Africans in charge of the ship. They ordered the Africans below deck at the point of pistols and took the ship to New London, Connecticut. When they arrived in New London, all of the Africans with the exception of three small girls were charged before the United States Circuit Court in New Haven with murder of the captain and mutiny aboard the *Amistad*. All of the Africans were imprisoned in anticipation of the trial.

None of the Africans in New Haven could understand the language which was spoken by the Africans who had captured the *Amistad*. Nevertheless, the Africans found many friends and supporters in the New Haven area. There were newspaper articles about them. The daring feat which they had accomplished was spoken of in the highest terms by students and faculty at Yale University as an example of the human spirit overcoming adversity. An Amistad Committee was also formed to raise money for the defense of the Africans. Lewis Tappan was a chief supporter of the Africans. In fact, the American Missionary Association was formed out of the Amistad Committee. The aim of the American Missionary Association was to combat "the sins of caste, polygamy, and slaveholding."

The fact that Africans lived in New Haven did not mean that the Africans in that area could understand other Africans. Since the continent has several hundred languages and the African American population was comprised of individuals whose descendants came from more than one hundred different ethnic/linguistic groups it was difficult to find someone who understood the Mende language. The language problem presented the court with extremely serious difficulties until a Yale professor,

Josiah Willard Gibbs, discovered a method for determining the exact language spoken by the Africans. He found a way to have them say the words for different numbers and then looked for Africans who understood those numbers. With this kind of research Gibbs was able to locate James Covey, a Mende sailor, who worked on a British ship in New York City. Covey was asked to serve as an interpreter for the Africans.

Once Covey began to interpret the information from the Africans, more details of the heroic story began to unfold. When Covey explained that Cinque told him that they had been kidnapped from their homes and taken to Cuba against their wills, the public sentiment, already pro-African, changed even more in their favor. The Abolitionists in Connecticut and New York rallied to their support claiming that since the Africans had been taken from their own lands without their consent they had a right to use any means necessary to obtain their freedom, just as other free men would do.

The case attracted national and international attention. There were many legal details and fine points of law to be decided in this case. Africans had mutinied and killed a white captain in international waters in order to free themselves from bondage and the vessel had been seized in the United States waters. The entire law class at Yale University was dismissed to attend the trial because the professors considered it to be the trial of the century.

When the trial began, Cinque testified in his own behalf. From his carriage and countenance, everyone could see that he was a man of considerable natural intelligence and dignity. He handled his testimony with deftness and eloquence. Covey, himself a Mende speaker, translated Cinque's words quickly, without hesitation. The Court ruled in favor of the Africans. However, the decision was appealed to the Supreme Court. Former President John Quincy Adams was emotionally moved by the plight of the Africans and undertook to argue their case before the Supreme Court. President Adams was convinced that the case should be decided in favor of the Africans. On March 9, 1841, President John Quincy Adams argued for eight and a half hours in support of the Africans. The Africans were freed. Later Adams would express his feeling that the practice of slavery had to be ended in the United States and that if it took everything that he could do, he would do it because the practice of judging some people to be slaves because of their color and some to be free because of theirs was intolerable and not within the bounds of human decency.

Before he left for Sierra Leone in 1842, Cinque and some of the other Africans who had led the mutiny learned a great deal in the United States. They learned to speak English, studied the laws and political systems of the New England states, and were regularly taken to the Christian churches in the area. When they left for Africa, they were accompanied by several missionaries who believed that Sierra Leone was a good place to establish a mission against the slave trade.

The *Amistad* affair had aroused so much controversy and interest in the United States because of the intensifying of the antislavery struggle. Already by the 1830s a number of functioning committees had been set up in the northern communities from Boston all the way to Philadelphia. New York had one of the more active chapters of the abolition movement and their sentiment, along with the intellectual community of Yale and other colleges, worked to create an environment favorable to a positive solution. Of course, the fact that the former President of the United States decided to argue the case for the Africans did not hurt. The entire incident and its resolution was a victory for the spirit of fairness in the courts.

Anthony Burns

Anthony Burns was arrested on May 24, 1854, and placed under guard in the federal jury room in a Boston court build-

ing. He was charged with being a runaway from enslavement. Burns' former owner, Charles Suttle of Alexandria, Virginia, wanted him back. When news that Burns had been arrested spread through the streets of Boston, many citizens jumped to defend him. In fact, three outstanding lawyers came to court the next morning to defend him. Charles M. Ellis, a member of the Boston Vigilance Committee, Richard Henry Dana, Jr., author of the book, *Two Years Before the Mast*, and Robert Morris, the most prominent African American attorney in Boston.

The famous Fanueil Hall was filled to capacity the next night to protest the capture of Burns. Among those in attendance were some of the historic names in the struggle to end slavery: Wendell Phillips and Theodore Parker.

A commotion was started in the Hall when a man shouted, "When we go from the cradle of liberty, let us go to the tomb of liberty—the courthouse!" The audience poured out into the streets and headed for Court Square. Already leading a group to the courthouse were Reverend Thomas Wentworth Higginson and Lewis Hayden. They had begun battering down the door of the courthouse to rescue Burns. Constables were inside the building with pistols and clubs. In the melee that followed, Reverend Higginson was killed and the military reinforcements came in to rout the abolitionists. The abolitionists had been unable to free Burns by force. They despaired that they would ever free him by legal means. Consequently, it was decided to raise the $1,200 needed to purchase his freedom. The United States Attorney refused to permit the transaction. He insisted that according to the Fugitive Slave Law, the escapee must be returned to the state from whence he had escaped.

When Burns came to trial, soldiers guarded every door. President Franklin Pierce wired the court to spare no expense in executing the law. After a week of testimony, Burns was ordered to return to slavery. More than twenty military units had been brought to Boston to see that he did not escape. More than 2,000 horsemen and

marines escorted him through a crowd of 50,000 supporters crying, "Shame!"

Nat Turner

Nat Turner is an epic figure alongside Frederick Douglass, Booker T. Washington, Martin Luther King, Harriet Tubman, Marcus Garvey, Malcolm X, and W. E. B. DuBois. His story is a central motif in African-American culture because around it revolved the pathos, the dreams, and the resistance to oppression that have characterized the African experience in America.

After considerable preparation and meditation, Nat Turner and his guerilla army began their campaign in 1831. Their intention was to free all slaves. Galvanized by his religious belief that he was to be the avenger for the sufferings of Africans, the messianic Turner left a path of blood through rural Virginia.

When Nat Turner was finally captured, the white population of the slave-holding states was stunned. They had never felt so completely vulnerable. New laws were enacted to tighten the already harsh regulations which restricted African movement and discussion. Turner was hanged for his involvement in the uprising. Rather than bringing an end to African revolts, the death of Nat Turner seemed to embolden other heroic figures.

The nineteenth century experienced the most widespread outbreak of resistance to white domination since it had begun in the fifteenth century. The list of African revolts included the eleven Asante wars, the Zulu wars, the revolts of Zeferina and Balaio in Brazil, and numerous other attacks on slavery and oppression. In this context, Nat Turner's rebellion was a testament to the courage and will of Africans in America to overthrow slavery. As such, it stands as an epic to resistance.

Turner's revolt was the culmination of a preparation that began soon after his birth on October 2, 1800. He was considered exceptionally precocious by his family. At twenty-one years of age, Turner ran away from his owner and, after staying away for a month, he returned voluntarily.

Important Events in Nat Turner's Life

1822   *Nat Turner sold to Thomas Moore when Samuel Turner died.*

1825   *Nat Turner's first religious vision. He begins to preach to those who would listen.*

1825   *Nat Turner baptized a white believer, Ethelred Brantley, who had declared himself a believer in Jesus Christ.*

1830   *Moved to the home of Joseph Travis when the widow of Thomas Moore married Travis.*

August 13, 1831   *A day-long atmospheric phenomenon in which the sun appeared bluish-green. Turner saw this as a sign from heaven.*

August 20, 1831   *Nat Turner asked two of his trusted friends, Henry and Hark, to meet him the following day to plan the revolt.*

August 21, 1831   *Hark, Henry, Nelson, Sam, Jack, and Will met in the morning at Cabin Pond to cook a pig and drink brandy. At 3:00 p.m. Nat Turner joined them and began planning the revolt.*

August 22, 1831   *The seven left about 2:00 a.m. to go to the Travis house where they were joined by Austin. Entering the house they killed Travis, his wife and child, and the two younger males, Putnam Moore and Joel Westbrook. They had committed their first act of rebellion against the evil system of slavery.*

August 22, 1831 (2:00 a.m. to dawn)   *The revolutionaries reached the house of Salathul Francis, whom they killed.*

August 22, 1831 (2:00 a.m. to dawn)   *The revolutionaries reached the home of Piety Reese whom they killed as well as her son, William. The farm overseer, James Barner, was severely wounded.*

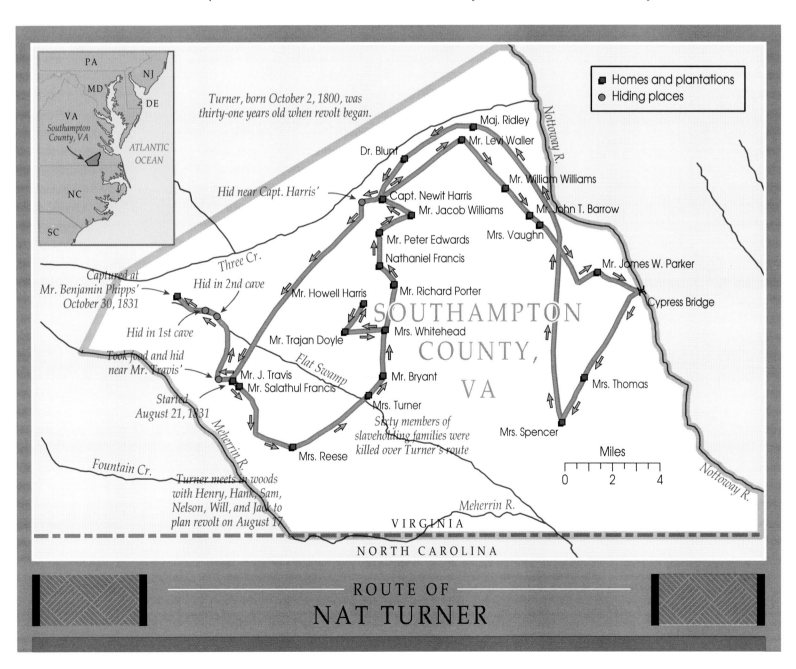

ROUTE OF
NAT TURNER

Nat Turner's Slave Revolt

August 22, 1831 (approximately 5:00 a.m.)
The revolutionaries visited the Wiley Francis house but after a confrontation with Francis' workers the men withdrew without violence.

August 22, 1831 (5:30 a.m.)
The revolutionaries reached Elizabeth Turner's house where they killed her, Mrs. Newsome, a neighbor, and the overseer, Hartwell Peebles.

August 22, 1831 (6:00 a.m.)
The revolutionaries divided: one unit on horseback (9 men) went to Mrs. Catherine Whitehead's house where they killed her, her mother, her son, four daughters, and a grandchild. One of the daughters, Margaret, was the only person Nat Turner admitted killing himself. The other unit (6 men) went on to Henry Bryant's home where they killed him, his wife, son, and his wife's mother.

August 22, 1831 (6:30 a.m.)
One unit of revolutionaries went to Richard Porter's house wherethey found no one home. They then went to Nathaniel Francis' house where they killed the over-seer, Henry Doyle, and two boys who were nephews of Francis. Mr. Francis and his mother were away at the time and Mrs. Francis was hidden in the attic by her own enslaved

Africans. The other unit of revolutionaries went to the home of Howell Harris. No one was at home but the group met and killed Trajan Doyle on the road outside the house.

August 22, 1831 (7:30 a.m.)
Some of the revolutionaries met and killed Mrs. John K. Williams and her child in the lane to the Francis' house.

August 22, 1831 (8:40 a.m.)
Nat Turner led a group of men to the home of Peter Edwards, which was found empty. About this time both units rejoined at the home of Captain John T. Barrow who was killed by the first unit to reach him. There were now more than forty armed and mounted African men in the revolutionary force. Word had obviously spread among the landowners that a revolt was occurring because increasingly the whites seemed alerted.

August 22, 1831 (9:00 a.m.)
The revolutionaries arrived at Newitt Harris' home to find the family had fled.

August 22, 1831 (9:15 a.m.)
The revolutionaries came to Levi Waller's home soon thereafter and killed Waller's wife and ten children in school at his house. Waller observed the attack from hiding and became later a principal prosecution witness in several trials.

August 22, 1831 (10:15 a.m.)
The revolutionaries went to the house of William Williams where they killed him, his wife, and two sons.

August 22, 1831 (11:00 a.m.)
The revolutionaries reached the house of Jacob Williams, where they killed his wife, three of their children, the wife of the plantation overseer, Mrs. Caswell Worrell, her two children, and a visitor, Edwin Drewry.

August 22, 1831 (noon)
The revolutionaries reached the house of Rebecca Vaughan where they killed her, her son, and her niece. At this point the revolutionary force had grown to sixty mounted and armed men. The decision was taken to march on the village of Jerusalem. Believing it was better to die than to live a slave, Turner persuaded the force to attack the village. However, they were met by an armed group of landowners who exchanged shots with them. No one was killed on either side, but the revolutionaries knew that they would face increasing resistance.

August 22, 1831 (2:00 p.m.)
Turner discovered that the main road to Jerusalem was guarded and attempted to cross into the village via a lower bridge. It, too, was guarded. The revolutionaries decided to redraw their strategy and took shelter near the Ridley house. Some men deserted the force, reducing Turner's number to about thirty men.

August 23, 1831 (daybreak)
Turner leads his force to the house of Dr. Simon Blunt. However, Blunt had given his enslaved Africans weapons and they fought a bitter battle against the revolutionaries. Men were killed on both sides and Turner's forces were reduced to about twenty-five men. Hark was wounded and captured.

August 23, 1831 (7:00 a.m.)
The revolutionaries met the armed landowners, whose force had now grown to more than one hundred men in a final battle. When the battle was over, most of the revolutionaries had escaped and several were killed, including Will.

August 23, 1831 (9:25 a.m.)
Nat Turner was alone, his men scattered or dead.

August 23–October 30, 1831
Nat Turner went underground to avoid detection. He hid in the vicinity of the Travis farm. A number of enslaved Africans gave him food. He managed to avoid the patrols and paddlerollers because of the support he received from people working on the farms. He changed his hiding place several times but was always in this same general area.

October 30, 1831 (noon)
Nat Turner was captured when his hiding area was discovered by a dog. He was taken to the Peter Edwards farm and held captive by Benjamin Phipps.

October 31, 1831 (noon)
Turner was surrendered to Edward Butts, the Deputy Sheriff of Southampton County, and put in the county jail.

November 1–3, 1831
Nat Turner is questioned by Thomas R. Gray in his cell. Gray claims that Turner dictated his "Confessions" during this time.

November 5, 1831
Nat Turner was tried in the Southampton County Court, found guilty, and sentenced to be executed.

November 11, 1831
At the age of 31, Nat Turner was hanged for leading the most serious African uprising in United States history. The severity of regulations governing the conduct of slaves was intensified beyond any degree known in prior years, so great was the white fear of an African uprising throughout the South. Nat Turner's name was whispered among blacks and whites in the immediate vicinity. The killing of Turner was meant to suggest to the African that death would be swift for anyone who attempted to overthrow their enslavement. Many enslaved mothers named their sons Moses while actually meaning Nat.

Abrewa Bim, "A Clever Elder,"
Ghana, Africa

"ALL MY TROUBLES WILL SOON BE OVER WITH": THE GATHERING OF FREEDOM FIGHTERS

During the 1830s Africans outnumbered whites in several cities such as Charleston, Savannah, New Orleans, and Richmond. Both Mobile and Norfolk were close to having black majorities. Thirty years later, in the 1860s, Africans were not a majority in any major city. The pace of white population growth was much faster due to immigration. Furthermore, few Africans were being brought into these areas. Whites had begun to sell as many Africans as they could to rural areas in order to prevent revolts, insurrections, and riots.

City life was politicizing for Africans because many free blacks lived in the urban areas. For example, out of the 18,000 Africans who lived in Baltimore in 1830, nearly 14,000 were free. By 1860, the free population was 25,000 out of 27,000. At the beginning of the Civil War, Baltimore was the fourth largest city in America and it had more free Africans than any other city.

There were several reasons for Baltimore's position in terms of free Africans. It was an active seaport, particularly engaged in commerce with cities farther South. This was not the same for New York or Philadelphia to the extent it was in Baltimore. The city was between the North and the South both in a geographical sense as well as

in a psychological sense. Africans from the Deep South could always find a ship going to Baltimore. Once an African was in Baltimore there were enough free Africans in the city to provide food, shelter, and advice. In time a strong antislavery spirit developed among the enslaved Africans in Baltimore. This was the city of Frederick Douglass and Harriet Tubman, among other famous leaders.

In the Deep South, New Orleans was the capital of free blacks. In 1830, it had 8,000 free persons out of 17,000 Africans; and in 1860, it was 10,600 free out of 24,000.

The first U.S. census was taken in 1790 and at that time free Africans constituted 8 percent of the African population in the nation. There were 59,000 free Africans out of 698,000 total. Seventy years later in 1860 there were 488,000 free Africans out of 3,953,000, or 12 percent.

Although the North took measures to end slavery in the 1780s there remained the fact that in 1790 there were more enslaved Africans in the northern states than free Africans. Indeed, more free Africans lived in the South than in the North. In 1790, 32,000 free Africans lived in the South compared to 27,000 in the North. Some 40,000 of the North's 67,000 Africans were enslaved.

In 1860 when slavery had been eliminated in the North, one still finds more free Africans in the South (250,000 to 238,000). The states with the largest numbers of free Africans in 1860 were Maryland (84,000), Virginia (58,000) and the northern state of Pennsylvania (56,000). Cities with the largest free African population in 1860 were:

Baltimore	25,600
Philadelphia	22,000
New York	12,500
New Orleans	10,600
Washington	9,200
Charleston	3,200

Restrictions on Free Africans

To be free did not mean that there were no restrictions on Africans. Severe codes were placed on free blacks to keep them in check. So called "slave codes" were drawn up to keep free Africans from socializing with enslaved Africans. Free Africans needed licenses to own guns for hunting. They could not have schools or hold meetings during the 1830s. Church services could only be held in the presence of a white adult. Movement was restricted to the county. Free Africans could vote in Maryland, Tennessee, and North Carolina but that right was abolished in 1810, 1834, and

1835, respectively. The fear of free Africans infected every security decision made in the South.

The historian John Hope Franklin has spoken of the Africans who were not enslaved as "Quasi-free," reflecting their dubious status within a racist society. They were always suspect and had to be vigilant in order to maintain their freedom.

The prohibition of slavery in certain Northern states and the constant influx of escaped Africans meant that the free population would increase with time. This increase in population did not bring with it much power of consequence nor any significant influence in the affairs of

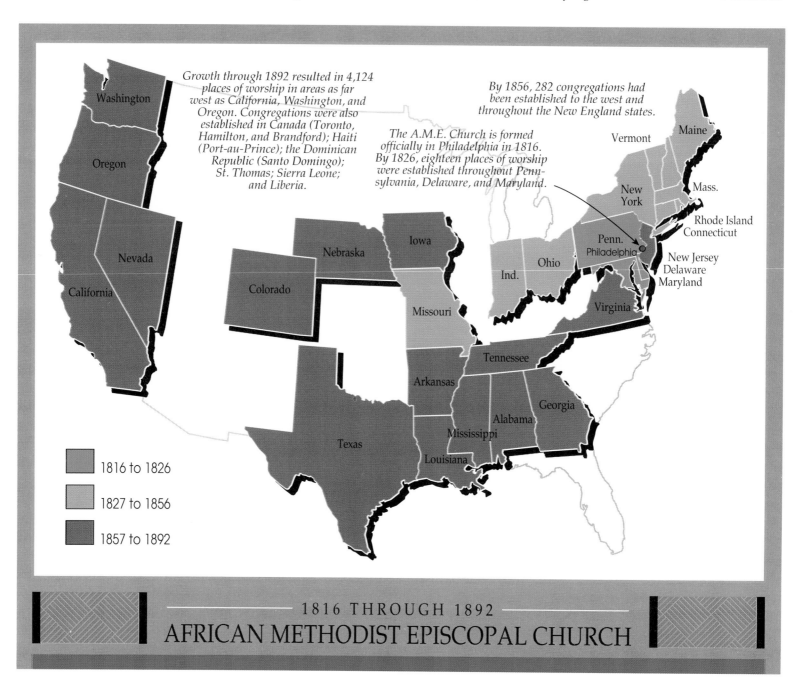

Growth through 1892 resulted in 4,124 places of worship in areas as far west as California, Washington, and Oregon. Congregations were also established in Canada (Toronto, Hamilton, and Brandford); Haiti (Port-au-Prince); the Dominican Republic (Santo Domingo); St. Thomas; Sierra Leone; and Liberia.

By 1856, 282 congregations had been established to the west and throughout the New England states.

The A.M.E. Church is formed officially in Philadelphia in 1816. By 1826, eighteen places of worship were established throughout Pennsylvania, Delaware, and Maryland.

1816 to 1826
1827 to 1856
1857 to 1892

1816 THROUGH 1892
AFRICAN METHODIST EPISCOPAL CHURCH

the states. On the other hand, the free Africans in the South proved to be a thorn in the side of the slavery system since they were symbols of the possibility of freedom for Africans. Whenever free Africans were able to successfully negotiate their livelihood, establish strong families, keep their farms prosperous within the context of the system, and demonstrate concern for their enslaved brothers and sisters, they proved that Africans could control their own lives and families. Such examples, however quietly they were lived, were dramatic within the environment of the South. Unlike the North which over time prohibited slavery, the South maintained the system until the end of the Civil War. Thus, many of the free Africans in the South existed because white slave owners often manumitted the Africans who worked for them. Some did this as an act of conscience. Religious conversion was frequently given as the reason for a change of heart. Others manumitted Africans who were their own children from slave mothers. Some slave owners, like John Randolph, who provided in 1833 for the freedom of 400 enslaved Africans on his plantation, made provisions through their wills for the release of their enslaved persons. There was no particular path to freedom in the slave South. The African who saved the Georgia state capitol from being burned to the ground was freed in 1834 by the state. Peter Chastang of Mobile was freed because of his valor and courage in the War of 1812.

James Pierson Beckwourth

James Pierson Beckwourth was born in Fredericksburg, Virginia on April 6, 1798. His father, who had fought in the Revolutionary War, moved the family westward when James was about eight years old. The succeeding years of his life proved to be historic because he became one of the best known trappers and mountain men of his day. Indeed, James Beckwourth became a leader among the Absaroka (Crow) people and

one of the most heroic figures of the nineteenth century.

James Beckwourth was sent to school in St. Louis. He studied for four years, which was a respectable time of study on the frontier unless one was going to become a preacher or lawyer. Apprenticed to a blacksmith, Beckwourth soon left this position and decided to travel to the lead mines for work. In a party of one hundred men and eight boats he struck out for Galena. Met by an army of Sac and Fox Peoples, the party had to

negotiate a treaty that would allow them to work the mines. In the meantime, Beckwourth became friendly with the Native Americans. They liked him and he liked them. After working for a while in the mines he traveled down the Mississippi to New Orleans.

At the age of twenty-five he signed on with the Ashley Rocky Mountain Fur Company in the fall of 1823. This was to be Beckwourth's ride to fame in the annals of American history. Alongside the experienced mountain man, Black

James Pierson Beckwourth

Harris, he rode ahead to buy horses from the Pawnee. The long trip to Pawnee territory undertaken in the middle of the winter nearly exhausted both Harris and Beckwourth before they were assisted by two Pawnees. When they returned to where they had left the Ashley party, the group had already gone ahead without them, thinking they were dead. Beckwourth stayed in the territory packing furs. Upon his return to St. Louis the following spring he met General Ashley, who was outfitting another group of trappers. He asked Beckwourth to join them and to carry about one thousand dollars in gold to one of the leaders of the group, Tom Fitzpatrick.

Soon Beckwourth became skilled in the culture of the Native Americans. The Absaroka People gave him the name White Handled Knife because of his bravery. When a fellow trapper named Greenword told a group of Absaroka People that Beckwourth had been born a Crow but was stolen in a raid by the Cheyenne when he was a boy, they believed the story because of Beckwourth's knowledge, bravery, and skill.

Captured by the Absaroka People while trapping beavers, Beckwourth was taken before Chief Black Lodge. When word got out that he was indeed an Absaroka himself, stolen from them as a baby, and as an adult had killed many Blackfeet, the enemy of the Absaroka, there was general rejoicing. Beckwourth married one of the daughters of Chief Black Lodge, Still Water. He was now given the Absaroka name, Morning Star. On several

Matthew A. Hensen

Isom Dart

Nat Love

occasions he demonstrated his bravery when the Absaroka engaged their enemy. After defeating so many enemies of the Absaroka, they gave him a name which meant respect and courage, Antelope. He later received many more names of honor from the Absaroka People.

Beckwourth took leave of the Absaroka Nation to work for the American Fur Company, started by John Jacob Astor. He then became a courier in New Mexico, and later joined the Gold Rush in California. In 1866 he was persuaded by the American government to return to the Absaroka to work out a treaty with them. When he returned the people met him with much praise and admiration. They pleaded with him to remain with them. His own son, Chief Black Panther, asked him to stay among the people. But Beckwourth told them that he could not remain with them since he had many attachments outside of the Nation. After a festive meal, Beckwourth died and was buried among the Absaroka. It has been surmised that because they loved him so much he was poisoned by the people to keep him from returning to the outside world.

The spirit of adventure is found throughout African American history. The examples of this adventurous spirit are numerous:

Waller Jackson was one of ten Africans to "round the Horn" in 1849 to prospect for gold near Downieville, California. The ninth and tenth Cavalry, African regiments formed from black Union troops, were sent to combat against the Apache and Cheyenne. The Cheyenne gave the African regiments the name "Buffalo Soldiers" because of their complexion and hair texture. Henry O. Flipper, the first African American graduate of West Point was the first black officer named to the 10th Cavalry. Allensworth, California, was founded by a famous African American soldier, jockey, and adventurer.

Charlotte Forten Grimke, born of wealthy free parents in Philadelphia, was one of the first persons to volun-

CAUTION!!

COLORED PEOPLE

OF BOSTON, ONE & ALL,

You are hereby respectfully CAUTIONED and advised, to avoid conversing with the

Watchmen and Police Officers of Boston,

For since the recent ORDER OF THE MAYOR & ALDERMEN, they are empowered to act as

KIDNAPPERS

AND

Slave Catchers,

And they have already been actually employed in KIDNAPPING, CATCHING, AND KEEPING SLAVES. Therefore, if you value your LIBERTY, and the *Welfare of the Fugitives* among you, Shun them in every possible manner, as so many *HOUNDS* on the track of the most unfortunate of your race.

Keep a Sharp Look Out for KIDNAPPERS, and have TOP EYE open.

APRIL 24, 1851.

THEODORE PARKER'S PLACARD

Placard written by Theodore Parker and printed and posted by the Vigilance Committee of Boston after the rendition of Thomas Sims to slavery in April 1851

teer to teach Africans in the South. Jean Baptiste Du Sable established a fur trading post around 1788 in the area that was to become the city of Chicago. The site where he constructed his log house is accepted as the original settlement of Chicago.

Henry Riding, an African pioneer in Iowa, was credited with stopping a railroad crew at gunpoint from laying tracks across his land. The company finally paid him $21,000. Isaiah Thornton Montgomery founded the town of

Mound Bayou in 1887 as a place where African Americans could obtain social, economic, and political rights in a racist South. George Washington Carver was born and raised in Diamond, Missouri. He was kidnapped when he was only six weeks old and ransomed for a horse valued at $300. Carver made his way through Minnesota, Kansas, and Iowa before he was asked to work at Tuskegee Institute by the famous Booker T. Washington in 1896. William Robinson and George Monroe worked for the famous pony express postal service carrying mail between St. Joseph, Missouri, and Sacramento. The riders, including Buffalo Bill Cody and Wild Bill Hickok, had only ten days for the trip.

The Pro-Slavery Position

The whites who believed in the system of slavery used five arguments to defend their position. They argued that Africans were biologically inferior to whites. Governors, state legislators, and even preachers articulated the view that it was necessary to have some one do menial jobs and that blacks were best qualified by biology to perform those services.

Their second argument was that Africans were intellectually inferior to whites and therefore most useful to serve, as Governor Hammond of South Carolina put it, "the mud-sill of society and political government."

In the third place, they argued, like George S. Sawyer, that Africans were incapable of throwing off "the chains of barbarism and brutality that have long bound down the nations of that race; or to rise above the common cloud of darkness that still broods over them."

A fourth point was that since Africans were heathens, it was necessary to enslave Africans to ensure that their souls would be saved and that they would be civilized. Thus, according to this doctrine, permanent enslavement was a good thing for the improvement of Africans.

The fifth point in support of slavery was that it had produced a unique civilization among the whites. The argument was meant to demonstrate that far from being a bad thing for whites, the slave system was good for whites because they had found time to spend on leisure activities that advanced culture. Each of these arguments was dissected and demolished by the abolitionists. In the end, slavery was shown to be brutal and unjustifiable.

The battle for the hearts and minds of the American people was fierce during the 1840s and 1850s. It did not always remain a battle of words. Many individuals who sought to protect Africans were beaten and killed. Some of the Northern whites who wrote editorials in support of abolition and against slavery had their newspaper offices bombed.

The Georgia legislature offered $4,000 for the capture of William Lloyd Garrison. Arthur Tappan had $12,000 on his head. Any person found with copies of David Walker's Appeal could be arrested and fined. Despite these attacks; the battle was won.

Abolitionists

Abolitionists such as Charles Remond, Frederick Douglass, Harriet Tubman, and Sojourner Truth were often joined by white antislavery leaders such as Elijah P. Lovejoy, Wendell Phillips, Lydia Maria Child, John Greenleaf Whittier, and William Lloyd Garrison.

Lovejoy was killed in Alton, Illinois, in 1837 by a white mob who did not like his antislavery articles. Phillips was one of the best orators of his day. He delivered hundreds of speeches against slavery. Whittier, a poet, wrote poems against the injustice and brutality of sepa-

---

NARRATIVE

OF THE

LIFE

OF

FREDERICK DOUGLASS,

AN

AMERICAN SLAVE.

WRITTEN BY HIMSELF.

BOSTON:
PUBLISHED AT THE ANTI-SLAVERY OFFICE,
No. 25 CORNHILL.
1846.

Charles Lenox Remond

The request which I would make of you is the request of suffering humanity—the observations I would direct to you are the observations of justice and of truth; and, such being the case, surely there is no Irishman, worthy the name, who will consider that my request is unreasonable, or my observations ill-timed or out of place. The request which I now make, and have often made, is, that those who hear me will forget complexion, and that when the hateful truth is naked to their ears, that slavery exists in America, they will be inclined to consider the subject not as one of color, but of kind—not as one, the merits of which are to be decided by the hue of the skin, but rather one the test whereof should be the nature and character of the being who is enslaved. Enough! he is a man, and so are ye.

rating children from parents. *The Farewell* and *The Slave Ships* are two of his best known works. Lydia Maria Child's *Appeal for that Class of Americans Called Africans* (1833) was the second most important book written against slavery in the United States. David Walker's *Appeal to the Colored Citizens of the World* had appeared in 1829.

Antislavery sentiments stretched from Virginia to Massachusetts and stirred the conscience of many people. The Quakers had held the first protest in 1789 in Philadelphia's Germantown section. Their spirit spread to other cities. Benjamin Lundy, a Quaker humanitarian who lived in Wheeling, Virginia, (now West Virginia) campaigned through his paper, *The Genius of Universal Emancipation*, for the liberation of the enslaved African. With a similar fervor and unselfishness, William Lloyd Garrison of Boston established *The Liberator* on January 1, 1831 to crusade against the evils of slavery. Garrison was one of Lundy's followers and a leader in agitation. Garrison wrote in the first issue of *The Liberator*: "I will be as harsh as truth and as uncompromising as justice. On this subject I do not wish to think or speak with moderation. . . . I am in earnest—I will not equivocate—I will not excuse—I will not retreat a single inch—and I will be heard!"

Denied the right of petition, and refused the use of the United States mail by President Andrew Jackson, the abolitionists, African and white, took to the platform with a vengeance. When the New England Anti-Slavery Society was formed in 1832 several Africans were prominent among the organizers. Charles Remond, son of a barber, would become the first popular spokesperson for the African community through his work with the New England Anti-Slavery Society. One year later in 1833, the American Anti-Slavery Society was formed and counted among its members most of the major African leaders for nearly half a century. It was not dissolved until 1870.

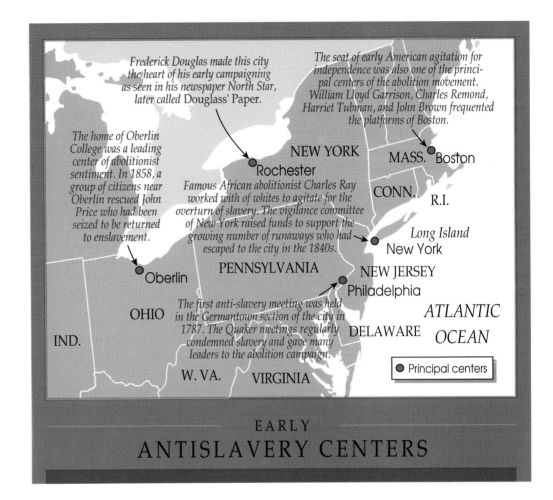

Frederick Douglas made this city the heart of his early campaigning as seen in his newspaper North Star, later called Douglass' Paper.

The seat of early American agitation for independence was also one of the principal centers of the abolition movement. William Lloyd Garrison, Charles Remond, Harriet Tubman, and John Brown frequented the platforms of Boston.

The home of Oberlin College was a leading center of abolitionist sentiment. In 1858, a group of citizens near Oberlin rescued John Price who had been seized to be returned to enslavement.

Famous African abolitionist Charles Ray worked with of whites to agitate for the overturn of slavery. The vigilance committee of New York raised funds to support the growing number of runaways who had escaped to the city in the 1840s.

The first anti-slavery meeting was held in the Germantown section of the city in 1787. The Quaker meetings regularly condemned slavery and gave many leaders to the abolition campaign.

● Principal centers

EARLY
ANTISLAVERY CENTERS

Frederick Douglass

Frederick Douglass, born in 1817, lived for ten years as a slave on a Maryland plantation before he was bought by a Baltimore shipbuilder. In the free time he could steal away from his work, Frederick taught himself to read. He escaped to freedom in 1838 and gave himself the name Douglas, adding an extra "s" after a character in the book *The Lady of the Lake*. Douglass had been in several fights with white overseers during his enslavement and had been severely flogged more than once. A precocious young man, he planned his escape with great care.

He lived at first in New Bedford, Connecticut. William Lloyd Garrison gave him some assistance with his education. An avid reader and a fine student of literature, Douglass soon became skilled enough to speak on the abolition of slavery.

In 1841 at an antislavery convention in Nantucket, Massachusetts, Douglass spoke with such eloquence and sincerity that he was immediately offered a job as an agent of the Massachusetts Antislavery Society. From that time until the outbreak of the Civil War, Douglass lectured in England and the United States. With one hundred fifty pounds raised by his new allies, Douglass purchased his freedom.

His career against every restraint on human beings was noble. He published two newspapers, *The North Star* and *Douglass' Paper*. Both were passionate instruments in the battle against slavery. Later in life he was appointed Recorder of Deeds in the District of Columbia and then Minister to Haiti.

Despite his many personal achievements in government service, editing newspapers and broadsides, public speaking and ceremonial oratory, statescraft and diplomacy, Douglass always felt that the nation never truly understood the deep hurt it had afflicted upon the African people during the Enslavement. He was one example of a former slave having accomplished against the odds.

Frederick Douglass

Douglass died in 1895, the year Booker T. Washington made his famous Atlanta Compromise speech. He was an international figure whose work for his own people inspired all people of all races and placed him in a uniquely significant historical position with respect to liberty.

Intensifying the Resistance

More than 100,000 slaves were lost to the South between 1810 and 1850 through the work of abolitionists and vigilance committees of the North and the determined, heroic efforts of the escaped Africans to remain free. It is

estimated that the total value of the "property" lost topped thirty million dollars and could have been as high as eighty million dollars.

It must be remembered that not all white southerners supported slavery. There was sentiment against it in almost every community, although this opposition rarely expressed itself in unpopular ways. As the South was not solid in its support of slavery, though nearly so, the North was not of a single mind either. In fact, George Whitefield, the famous hellfire evangelist, defended slavery. In Thomas Jefferson's *Notes on Virginia* he

had voiced the opinion that Africans were by nature inferior to whites. Other southerners took Jefferson's words to support their view of slavery.

The crucial decade of the 1850s brought sectional strife and strain that literally ripped the nation apart before a shot was fired. Lines had been drawn and sides had been taken. Pro-slavery leaders had become more aggressive in carrying their fight into the territory of the abolitionists. They had stepped up the pursuit of runaway Africans. They sought to strengthen their control over the thought of whites in the South while defending the system of slavery outside. Thus, they murdered whites in Georgia and South Carolina who had committed the crime of "mixing" with Africans. When Amos Dresser went to the South to sell Bibles and got caught by a mob who believed that he was stirring up trouble among Africans, he was condemned and then beaten publicly.

The discovery of gold in California and the westward movement of the population meant that the question of slavery in the new territories had to be discussed and decided. What was to be the policy in respect to the State of California? Several options were open to American legislators. They could exclude slavery from the entire area of new territories. They could let the people who populate the areas decide their own future. They could divide the new territories into slave and free. Others insisted that slavery could not be legally excluded from the territories. The antislavery forces began their own offensive. They outspoke and outwrote the South during this period.

The publication of *Uncle Tom's Cabin* in 1852 was a momentous event. Harriet Beecher Stowe's novel sold more than 300,000 copies in the first year. Orations from the book were given in public ceremonies and theatres put on dramatic productions of the work. Never had a book shown to such a wide audience the devastation of enslavement on human beings. Stowe's work detailed the cruelty of the slave owners and overseers in the most brutal form. The book provided a glimpse into the deprivations and pains of Africans under the system of the whip. No longer could the southern plantation owners or their defenders conceal the truth about the horrible institution which was a blight upon the land. Since most whites, even in the South, did not own slaves (although most supported the institution) they had rarely seen it shown in such graphic manner. The dehumanization of Africans by the white slave owners and overseers meant a greater dehumanization of the whites. This one book did more in 1852 to destroy the image of slavery as a necessary evil than all other books and articles combined. The southerners had been dealt a severe blow by *Uncle Tom's Cabin*.

Women of History

Sarah Allen, Missionary	1764–1849
Caroline Anderson, Doctor	1849–1919
Janie Barrett, Teacher	1870–1949
Matilda Beasley, Teacher	1834–1903
Ann Becraft, Teacher	1805–1833
Rosa Bowser, Teacher	1885–1931
Sue Brown, Organizer	1877–1941
Mary S. Cary, Abolitionist	1823–1893
Anna J. Cooper, Teacher	1858–1964
Anna Douglass, Abolitionist	na–1882
Susan Frazier, Organizer	1866–1901
Charlotte Grimke, Scholar	1834–1914
Emma Hackley, Artist	1877–1922
Alice D. Nelson, Author	1875–1935
Mary Patterson, Teacher	1840–1894
Mary Peake, Teacher	1823–1862
Frances Preston, Orator	1844–1929
Charlotta Pyles, Abolitionist	1806–1880
Susie Shorter, Writer	1859–1912
Georgia Simpson, Scholar	1866–1944
Amanda Smith, Missiona,	1836–1915
May Talbert, Reformer	1866–1923
Susan Vashon, Nurse	1838–1912
Josie .Washington, Organizer	1861–1949
Lulu Williams, Reformer	1874–1945

The Compromise of 1850, a temporary solution to the crisis of newly added territories, had left neither the North nor the South satisfied with the national situation over the question of slavery. The Compromise had allowed California to enter the nation as a free state; Texas to cede land to New Mexico, and be compensated; new territories to be set up without mention of slavery; creation of a tough fugitive slave law; and the prohibition of the slave trade in the District of Columbia.

When Stephen A. Douglas of Illinois introduced the Kansas–Nebraska Act of 1854 to the Senate, it signalled the end of the Compromise of 1850. It called for Kansas and Nebraska to decide the slavery issue themselves. Whigs, Free Soilers, and some Democrats who opposed the Act discussed a common strategy which led to the creation of the Republican Party.

The Women Fighters

When the final epic of the African American people is written, the role of women in the struggle for equality, dignity, and honor will be seen as a centerpiece of the drama. Never content to watch the battles from the sidelines, women have placed themselves in the thick of every contest for human rights ever fought on American soil. Indeed, these women have given the best accounting of themselves one could imagine. Perhaps the greatest African American to have lived is Harriet Tubman. No man nor woman has shown any greater commitment to freedom and self respect, to loyalty and work, to honor and courage, to love and faith, than Harriet Tubman.

Tubman was never alone in her hatred of slavery or in her willingness to die for freedom. Open the pages of any book on the African American experience and the names of women leap forward with clarity and definition: Sojourner Truth, Charlotte Forten Grimke, Charity Still, Cornelia Loney, Ann Maria Weems, Leah Green, Frances

Hilliard, Maria Jane Houston, Elizabeth Banks, Laura Lewis, Ellen Craft, Mary Shadd Cary, Diana Mills, Mary Cooper, Lydia Ann Johns, and thousands of others who campaigned actively against slavery and oppression by their own individual acts of courage or in preparing the way for others.

Women have contributed to every scene of the African American drama. From the very beginning when the slave ships left the shores of Africa, women demonstrated immense courage in the face of the most brutal and callous rage. When they could no longer take the abuse, some threw their children to the sea; others leaped to the sharks themselves. On board the ships, women led in the comforting of the sick, the care for the dying, and the affection for the parentless. Most of all, they saw visions, gave hope, and dreamed dreams which kept people alive.

Mary Ann Shadd Cary

Mary Ann Shadd Cary was the first black newspaperwoman in the United States. A fierce competitor, believing in her ability and possessing a grand sense of dignity, she became an outstanding educator, writer, lawyer, and antislavery abolitionist. Prior to the Civil War, she appeared on many platforms as a major speaker against the evils of slavery. Her lectures were received warmly because of the logic of her arguments. She was also one of the first women to openly speak up for women suffrage. When the Civil War began, Mary Ann Shadd volunteered as a recruiting officer and held the position of recruiting officer until the end of the war. When she died, she had achieved national recognition for her pioneering efforts as a newspaperperson and campaigner for human rights.

Shadd's example was to inspire a generation of young African American women to become involved in education and information distribution. In fact, of the many women to achieve distinction in this area, Ida B. Wells Barnett and

Mary McLeod Bethune became household names.

Mary McLeod Bethune

Mary McLeod Bethune's place in African American history is so monumental that to write of African Americans without her is to leave out a major chapter. Bethune was born on July 10, 1875 near the small town of Mayesville, South Carolina. Early in life she expressed a desire to be a teacher and spent seven years at the Scotia Seminary in North Carolina. Religion was central to her vision of progress in the African American community. She studied at the Moody Bible Institute in Chicago after leaving North Carolina. She wanted to

become a missionary. It was the good fortune of the African American community that her application to the Presbyterian Board of Missions in New York was turned down for an appointment to Africa. When she was unable to secure a post in Africa, she began teaching in the United States.

President Herbert Hoover asked her to come to Washington to attend the White House Conference on Child Health and Protection in 1930. President Franklin Roosevelt asked her to serve on the advisory board of the National Youth Administration (NYA). She was so successful at establishing the foundation of the NYA that President Roosevelt called upon her to set up an Office of Minority Affairs. This was the first time that an African American woman had been granted such a post. Her title was changed to Director of the Division of Negro Affairs.

Mary McLeod Bethune was one of the leading figures in the country in the 1930s and the only woman in the unofficial "shadow cabinet" set up by President Franklin Roosevelt. Always devoted to education, Mrs. Bethune founded her own school, the Daytona Educational and Industrial School for Negro Girls in 1904. In 1926 she oversaw its merger with the Cookman Institute, giving birth to the Bethune-Cookman Institute.

Mary McLeod Bethune died in 1955 at the age of 80. She had been drawn to the plight of the children of African American builders of the railroads in Florida in 1904, after her death the children of those children contributed a monument to her memory. It was the first monument to an African American or a woman ever built on pub-

lic lands in the United States. In her life and death, Bethune left a legacy of hope, challenge, faith, and racial dignity.

Sojourner Truth

Sojourner Truth was born about 1798 in Ulster County, New York, to parents who were enslaved. Her childhood experience living in the cold, wet cellar of the home of the family to which she and her parents belonged, left indelible impressions on her. She would later recount how her mother taught her the Lord's Prayer, and trust in God.

In 1827, New York granted legal emancipation to enslaved Africans but Sojourner's owner refused to release her. She escaped but was caught and would have been returned had not a friend agreed to pay for her services for the remainder of the year.

When she decided to leave New York for the lecture circuit she made a small bundle of her goods and told a friend that her name was no longer Isabella but Sojourner. She lectured everywhere she found people. Her wit and originality made her a very popular speaker. Sojourner also had the gift of song, and though she had little schooling, she commanded the attention of her audience by the force of her logic and the eloquence of her cadence. As to her name she said, "And the Lord gave me *Sojourner* because I was to travel up and down the land showing the people their sins and being a sign unto them. Afterwards I told the Lord I wanted another name, 'cause everybody else has two names, and the Lord gave me *Truth* because I was to declare the truth to the people."

She was buried in the Oak Hill Cemetery in Battle Creek, Michigan, where she settled after the Civil War. She died in 1883, she was 85 years old.

Ida B. Wells Barnett

When Sojourner Truth died, Ida B. Wells Barnett was a child of nineteen in Mississippi. She became the editor of the *Free Speech* newspaper in Memphis,

Sojourner Truth

Tennessee and led an energetic campaign against lynching. In 1895, her first pamphlet against lynching, *The Red Record,* was published. Several additional pamphlets were written by Barnett and distributed widely in America and Europe.

Barnett became chairperson of the Anti-Lynching Bureau of the National African Council, a post she held until she became the president of the Negro Fellowship League in 1908. She moved to Chicago in 1913 and remained active in human rights. In 1915 she was elected to the post of Vice President of the Chicago Equal Rights League, devoting most of her time to human rights until her death in 1931.

Mary Church Terrell

The life of Mary Church Terrell spanned an entire history of struggle. Born in 1863, the year of the Emancipation Proclamation, Terrell died in 1954, the year of the *Brown v. Topeka Board of Education* decision.

She was born in Memphis, Tennessee, but traveled throughout the world as an activist for African and women's rights. She graduated from Oberlin College and moved to Washington, DC where she was appointed to the school board in 1895. A year later, she became one of the founding members of the National Association of Colored Women.

From the various positions and platforms she occupied, she spoke out fervently against every form of discrimination and segregation. The laws in Washington made segregation legal until 1953. Mary Church Terrell led the campaign to integrate public facilities in the nation's capital. When the Supreme Court finally ruled that public accommodations had to be desegregated in Washington it was a victory for the many years of battle in which Mrs. Terrell had been engaged. Although Mary Church Terrell had been born of parents who had been enslaved, she never once believed that anyone could enslave her. She was a giant among giants.

Madame C. J. Walker

Born Sarah McWilliams in 1869 in the small town of Delta, Louisiana, the person who was to become the wealthiest woman of her race, was orphaned at seven. She was married at 14, and widowed at 20.

She traveled up river to St. Louis in order to begin life anew and make something out of herself. She secured a job in a laundry and worked to send her daughter to school. Soon after she arrived in St. Louis, she met and married Charles J. Walker. Using his initials, she became Madame C. J. Walker.

It was not long before her various formulas for beauty care began circulating in the African American community. Her innovations in hair-styling made her the virtual leader of African American hair fashions. By 1910, when she had moved to Indianapolis, she had developed an entire line of toiletries and cosmetics for the body and face. With the tremendous surge in African American interest in

beauty and fashion, due to the newly gained freedom to decide their own beauty styles, Madame C. J. Walker soon set up Walker beauty parlors across the nation. The results of this activity made her a millionaire. Before her death in 1919 she had become well-known for her philanthropy to African American institutions. Her gifts to the National Association for the Advancement of Colored People, the Young Men Christian Association of St. Louis, Tuskegee Institute, and Mary McLeod Bethune's original school for girls, were significant and instructional. Her will required that two-thirds of the profits of her company should be distributed to organizations that worked to improve the welfare of the community.

Rosa Parks

The name Rosa Parks is inextricably connected to the Civil Rights Movement. She gave no resounding speeches, led no massive demonstrations against the citadels of segregation, wrote no petitions, and

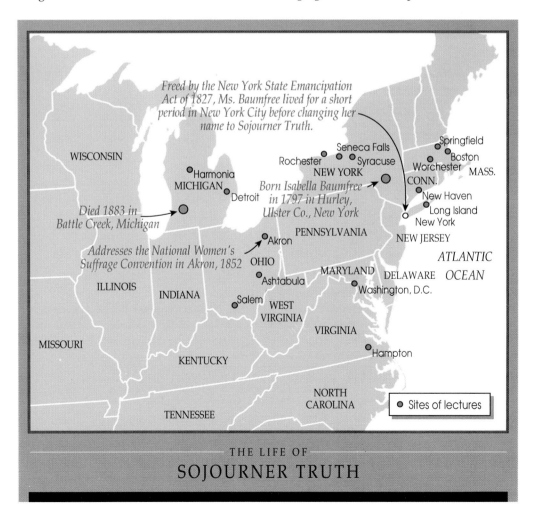

Freed by the New York State Emancipation Act of 1827, Ms. Baumfree lived for a short period in New York City before changing her name to Sojourner Truth.

Born Isabella Baumfree in 1797 in Hurley, Ulster Co., New York

Died 1883 in Battle Creek, Michigan

Addresses the National Women's Suffrage Convention in Akron, 1852

● Sites of lectures

THE LIFE OF
SOJOURNER TRUTH

argued no particular points of law. What she did was simple and electrifying.

On December 1, 1955, Rosa Parks took a public bus in Montgomery, Alabama, that was to land her in history as one of the most inspirational leaders of all time. She had entered the bus on her way home just as other passengers had crowded onto the bus. When the bus was filled to capacity, the white bus driver looked back and saw that Rosa Parks was seated in the "white" section of the bus while a white man was standing. As he had probably done many times without incident, the bus driver ordered Mrs. Parks to the rear of the bus. As far as he was concerned, she was breaking the law by sitting where only whites were allowed to sit.

Rosa Parks refused to move and allow the white man to take her seat. Her feet were tired and her soul said she should not move. She remained in her seat. The bus driver was annoyed. He stopped the bus and called the police. They came and arrested Rosa Parks for refusing to give up her seat. She was jailed and brought to trial. This incident caused the entire African American community to rise up as it had never done in any city. No black person rode the Montgomery buses. The boycott which was to be felt around the world was now on. Rosa Parks' courage and fortitude had sparked a movement. The names of the players would rewrite the history of America because of her action. Martin Luther King, Jr. and Attorney Fred Gray, two young, recent college graduates from northern schools, would join Rosa Parks in the noble cause.

The leadership positions of African American women have often been achieved with great opposition from men. Yet the record is clear that the women who have succeeded in establishing themselves in history by virtue of their works, have been among the most honored and distinguished African Americans.

Harriet Tubman

Harriet Tubman, fighter, comforter, confidante, nurse, and hero is without com-

parison in word or deed.

Harriet Tubman's name is synonymous with the famed escape route called "The Underground Railroad." Born in 1820 in Dorchester County, Maryland, she succeeded in escaping from slavery in 1848. Her life as a slave had been difficult, filled with hard work, severe punishment, harassment, verbal abuse, and little joy. Harriet left two brothers and her husband, John Tubman. He had taken money she had saved to purchase her freedom and then had threatened to report her escape attempt to her owner.

Tubman's freedom placed a heavy burden on her because she believed it was necessary to assist others in their escape attempts. Nineteen times between 1849–1859 she went south of the Mason-Dixon Line to bring Africans to the North. Slaveholders offered $40,000 for her capture. Never captured, Harriet Tubman became one of the leading spirits of the abolition movement. Her hatred of slavery had led her to recruit soldiers for John Brown's raid on Harper's Ferry. Tubman thought of John Brown as a more important emancipator than President Lincoln. During the Civil War she joined the Union Army as a nurse, spy, and scout, applying much of her knowledge of people, places, and terrain.

Two years after the war John Tubman died, and in 1869, Harriet Tubman married Nelson Davis, a Civil War veteran. The remainder of her life was spent in poverty. Although Sarah Bradford wrote and published Tubman's biography and Tubman was able to use some of the money to ease her financial burden, the government did not give her a pension until thirty years after the war. She was awarded $20 per month as a pension. With this money Harriet Tubman ran the Harriet Tubman Home in Auburn, New York, where she died in March, 1913.

Underground Railroad

The "Underground Railroad" is the name given to the various means by which some Northerners, black and white, assisted fugitives in finding safe places.

By the system, Benjamin Brawley says "thousands of people were enabled to get to Canada." The most favored routes were through Ohio and Pennsylvania since the Quaker influence in these two states was very strong and the Quakers had shown an early moral inclination to assist enslaved Africans in escaping bondage.

While admittedly various "stations" were established to aid fugitives, the great majority of Africans used their own ingenuity to find their way to safety. This is so despite the fact that Harriet Tubman made nineteen trips to the South to "steal away" 300 enslaved Africans or that Levi Coffin received nearly one hundred slaves per year at his house or that Thomas Garrett is said to have assisted 2,700 slaves in their search for freedom.

Harriet Tubman

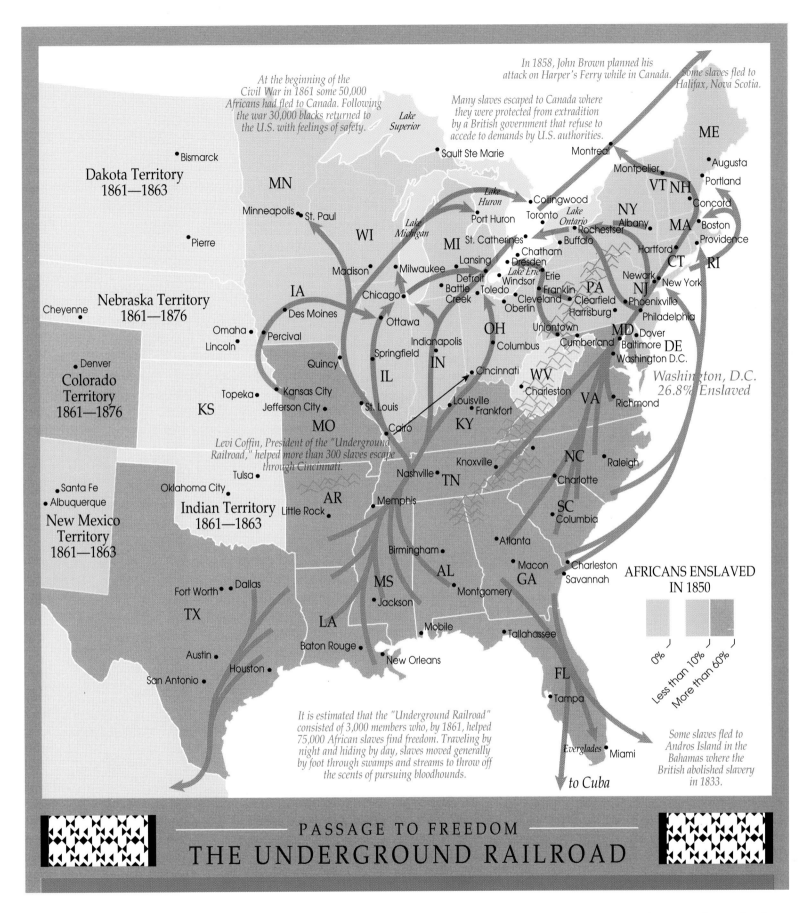

PASSAGE TO FREEDOM
THE UNDERGROUND RAILROAD

The truth is that the South was without sharp boundaries and in places it was an open sieve where thousands of runaways crossed over and made it to the North. The Mason and Dixon Line became the standard boundary between the slave-holding and relatively free states. It was in actuality the boundary between Pennsylvania and Maryland which had been drawn by two English surveyors in 1763–1767 to settle a dispute between the Penn and Baltimore families. However, the actual boundary between the slave and free states also followed the Ohio River to the Mississippi and with the exception of Missouri, the 36°30' established by the Missouri Compromise of 1820.

Most Africans who found their way North to freedom did so on the basis of their own intelligence and wit. They were not given maps, food, clothing, nor friendship. Thousands of these lone and unknown individuals, tired of slavery, organized their own liberation in spite of close supervision by plantation overseers. These unsung heroines and heroes of liberty constituted the largest number of escaping slaves.

Slave escapes have been romanticized because of the famous series of safe houses and way stations that constituted what was called the Underground Railroad. Harriet Tubman who rescued 300 Africans from slavery on nineteen trips to the South was the most knowledgeable conductor on the Underground Railroad. Known for her directness, courage, and leadership, she once pointed a gun at an African reluctant to follow her to freedom and said, "Before I'd see you a slave I'll see you dead and buried in your grave." The man followed her.

Harrowing escapes and daring disguises made eloquent testimonies for inspiration. In quaint shanty communities, when the day's work was completed, Africans often gathered to tell the stories of how someone had learned that someone else had "overcome" slavery and eluded the slave owners.

There was no more revolutionary act a slave could make than taking herself or himself out of the economic system. It meant that the slaveowner was deprived of labor and property, neither of which the African believed the whites rightly owned. Escape routes, though often improvised by virtue of the many individual efforts, became indelibly engraved in African history because of constant retelling once the people reached freedom.

William Still's great book, *The Underground Railroad*, did as much as the actual exploits of the escaped Africans to impress the idea of the underground railroad in the minds of the American people. The book was first published in 1872 and was an account of facts, authentic narratives, letters, and other reports of hardships, hair-breadth escapes, and death struggles of the slaves in their efforts for freedom from the horrible bondage.

William Still was for many years one of the principal people connected to the vigilance committee in Philadelphia. He was chairman of the Philadelphia Branch of the Underground Railroad. In that capacity he was personally involved with the attempts of many people to escape and to change their identities. The antislavery meeting in Philadelphia asked him in resolution form to record his reminiscences and the experiences he had relating to the underground railroad. Still wrote his book in response to that direct request from the society.

In January 1872, he wrote that his book included interesting narratives of the escapes of "many men, women and children, from the prison-house of bondage; from cities and plantations; from rice swamps and cotton fields; from kitchens and mechanic shops; from

Dred Scott

Border States and Gulf States; from cruel masters and mild masters; some guided by the north star alone, penniless, braving the perils of land and sea, eluding the keen scent of the blood-hound as well as the more dangerous pursuit of the savage slave-hunter; some from secluded dens and caves of the earth, where for months and years they had been hidden away waiting for the chance to escape; from mountains and swamps, where indescribable suffering from hunger and other privations had patiently been endured."

The escaping African used every bit of ingenuity at his or her disposal. Despite the limited knowledge they often had of the world, they created a system of escape mechanisms that were used by others familiar with the circumstances of slavery. In instances where the enslaved African had responsibility for shipping, they would often box themselves and ship themselves. Whatever was useful for escaping enslavement was used.

Dred Scott

In 1834, a white army officer by the name of Emerson stationed in Missouri decided to move to Illinois. He took with him an enslaved African, Dred Scott. Two years later, he moved to Minnesota, again taking Dred Scott with him. In 1838, the white man moved back to Missouri with Dred Scott.

By this time Scott began to raise questions about the legality of his situation. Slavery was illegal in Illinois and Minnesota was a free territory. Scott wanted to know if his residence outside of a slave state made him a free person. Abused and attacked by his owner in 1848, Scott, with the assistance of antislavery lawyers, brought a suit against his owner for assault and battery. The circuit court of St. Louis ruled in Scott's favor. The ruling was appealed by Emerson to the Supreme Court of the state which reversed the lower court's decision. In the meantime, Emerson sold Scott to a New York citizen named Sandford. Determined and courageous Dred Scott brought suit against

A PUBLIC MEETING

WILL BE HELD ON

THURSDAY EVENING, 2D INSTANT,

at 7½ o'clock, in ISRAEL CHURCH, to consider the atrocious decision of the Supreme Court in the

DRED SCOTT CASE,

and other outrages to which the colored people are subject under the Constitution of the United States.

C. L. REMOND,
ROBERT PURVIS,

and others will be speakers on the occasion. Mrs. MOTT, Mr. M'KIM and B. S. JONES of Ohio, have also accepted invitations to be present. All persons are invited to attend. Admittance free.

Sandford on the grounds that they were citizens of different states. The case reached the Supreme Court of the United States where a decision was made in 1857 that had far-reaching implications. Essentially, the Supreme Court ruled that Scott was not a citizen of Missouri, nor any state, and that as a slave he was only property and that his owner could take property to any place within the jurisdiction of the United States. Ownership of Scott and his family soon passed to a Massachusetts family and he was liberated.

According to the historian and curator Charles L. Blockson, most Africans hated their enslavement and used every means at their disposal to escape. He tells the story of William and Ellen Craft of Macon, Georgia, who escaped in 1848.

The clever William asked his wife, Ellen, who was of a light complexion to dress as a man with a well cut suit and a top hat, and he would be her faithful servant. Blockson says that they contrived a broken arm to conceal her inability to write and a bandage for a toothache to conceal her beardlessness. In this manner the couple traveled in sleeping car quarters to Philadelphia.

The intensity of the antislavery meetings was such that slavery sympathizers attacked those who supported freedom for Africans. Charles Blockson also tells us in his article "The Underground Railroad" which appeared in the *National Geographic* in July 1984, that Lucretia Mott, a Quaker minister and leader, drew angry crowds of whites in Norristown, Pennsylvania, when after a major rally

against slavery she walked out of the meeting arm in arm with the great Frederick Douglass. Cool-headed members of the African American community protected the antislavery leaders from harm.

Freedom's road was often long and arduous for enslaved Africans. Many gained the courage to risk their lives and their loved ones lives to seek freedom. While thousands made it to the "other side of Jordan," others were captured by slave-catchers, betrayed by acquaintances, killed by robbers, and captured and re-enslaved by whites other than their former masters. Enough Africans were successful, however, to etch this as an heroic period in world history.

Blue Adinkra,"The Occasion is Solemn,"
Ghana, Africa

"MY LORD GWINETER TO RAIN DOWN FIRE": THE CIVIL WAR

At the beginning of the Civil War the United States was in the midst of a long, uneasy terror caused by the spirit of the slave system. Sapped of much of its moral and spiritual power, the nation increasingly found itself conflicted in its domestic politics.

Africans had spread to every part of the American nation, as free and as slave, by the 1850s. There were Africans in California, some traveling through the treacherous waters of Cape Horn to reach the West Coast; others traveling on land with whites. The South was preeminently the home of the African population by 1860. North Carolina, Georgia, Virginia, South Carolina, and Alabama accounted for more than seventy-five percent of the total black population.

The southern investment in slaves contrasted with the rising northern investment in machinery; the South tended toward labor intensive agriculture and the North became increasingly industrialized. The differential in development meant a widening of the gap between the treatment of Africans in the South and those in the North. Southern blacks experienced the most brutal slavery between 1830–1860. This was the period of ultimate terror. It was as if white slaveowners, padderrollers, and overseers dreamed of the most horrible means of extracting labor and then used

Africans to test their theories of how long a human could live being driven to work harder and harder under the threat of punishment even unto death. Many died. Those who lived blessed the night and dreaded the morning.

As the slave system in the South tightened its reins on the African population, the northern states, because of the needs of industry, gave the free blacks more liberties. By 1860, most northern states had discontinued slavery and more and more Africans were being incorporated into the labor force of the industrial revolution.

The testimony of the enslaved people themselves is most chilling. The case of Nancy, a daughter of Cordelia Loney, shows the extent of human suffering and humiliation that was experienced. Cordelia had seen several of her children sold from her without ever once being told that they would be sold. When her mistress got it in her head that she would work Nancy (who had been in ill health since birth) to death, Cordelia knew that she was powerless to help her daughter. The overseer and his wife had tried to convince the mistress of Nancy's ill health. The mistress would not hear of it. She told the overseer in a fit of anger one day to "whip her every day, and make her work or kill her."

When a nephew of the mistress visited the plantation, Nancy was sold to him and taken to New Orleans. Her mother, Cordelia, upon escaping to freedom, said that when she learned that her sick child had been sold, she felt wretched. But she said, "I was not at liberty to make my grief known to a single white soul. I wept and couldn't help it." The stain upon the nation's soul called for cleansing.

The Civil War, the most devastating war ever fought on American soil and the most deadly in terms of individuals killed, was like a giant cleansing of the land. Those who opposed slavery, black and white, joined against it for their own reasons and ushered in a new history without the enslaved.

Africans in the Civil War

Africans participated on both sides of the Civil War but it was the overwhelming support that the soldiers gave the Union Army that helped turn the war in support of the North. The population of the Confederacy in 1861, at the beginning of the Civil War, was only 5,220,000 whites and nearly four million Africans. By contrast, the Union states had a population of 22,000,000, and the border states of Maryland, Delaware, Kentucky, and Missouri held 430,000 enslaved Africans, included in the Union numbers. The secessionist states, the Confederacy, mustered in 800,000 soldiers, approximately 15 percent of its white population of 5,220,000, compared with the Union's ability to field 1,600,000, about 7 percent of its white population of 21,570,000.

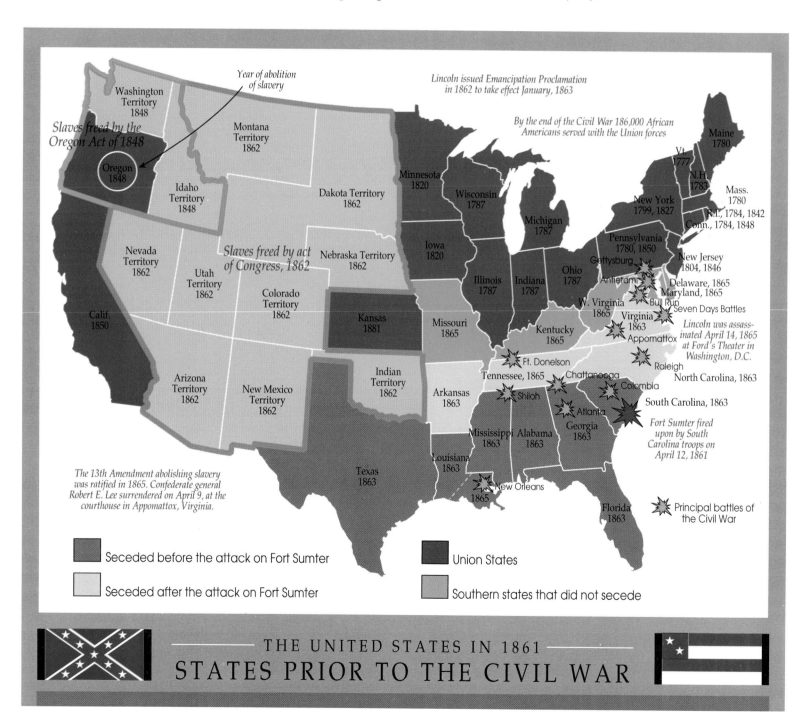

Year of abolition of slavery

Washington Territory 1848

Slaves freed by the Oregon Act of 1848

Oregon 1848

Montana Territory 1862

Idaho Territory 1848

Slaves freed by act of Congress, 1862

Dakota Territory 1862

Lincoln issued Emancipation Proclamation in 1862 to take effect January, 1863

By the end of the Civil War 186,000 African Americans served with the Union forces

Maine 1780

Vt. 1777

N.H. 1783

Minnesota 1820

Wisconsin 1787

Michigan 1787

New York 1799, 1827

Mass. 1780

R.I., 1784, 1842

Conn., 1784, 1848

Nevada Territory 1862

Utah Territory 1862

Nebraska Territory 1862

Iowa 1820

Illinois 1787

Indiana 1787

Ohio 1787

Pennsylvania 1780, 1850

Gettysburg

Antietam

New Jersey 1804, 1846

Calif. 1850

Colorado Territory 1862

Kansas 1881

Missouri 1865

W. Virginia 1865

Bull Run

Delaware, 1865

Maryland, 1865

Seven Days Battles

Kentucky 1865

Virginia 1863

Appomattox

Lincoln was assassinated April 14, 1865 at Ford's Theater in Washington, D.C.

Arizona Territory 1862

New Mexico Territory 1862

Indian Territory 1862

Arkansas 1863

Ft. Donelson

Tennessee, 1865

Chattanooga

Shiloh

Atlanta

Raleigh

North Carolina, 1863

Colombia

South Carolina, 1863

Mississippi 1863

Alabama 1863

Georgia 1863

Fort Sumter fired upon by South Carolina troops on April 12, 1861

Texas 1863

Louisiana 1863

New Orleans 1865

Florida 1863

Principal battles of the Civil War

The 13th Amendment abolishing slavery was ratified in 1865. Confederate general Robert E. Lee surrendered on April 9, at the courthouse in Appomattox, Virginia.

Seceded before the attack on Fort Sumter

Seceded after the attack on Fort Sumter

Union States

Southern states that did not secede

THE UNITED STATES IN 1861

STATES PRIOR TO THE CIVIL WAR

It is generally accepted that the Confederacy was able to fight as long as it did because of the African rear-guard who took care of the factories, the loading docks, the farms, and the fortifications and battery emplacements. Africans were pressed into service in the Confederacy as cooks, servants, and medics. Of course, many Africans took the crisis of the Civil War as an opportunity to run away to the Union side. At first the Union Army refused to accept runaways into Union camps, not recognizing that the African laborers were in fact making it possible for the Confederacy to continue their struggle. President Lincoln had made it clear to all who consulted him that the war was not being fought to free slaves but to preserve the Union. Thus, Union soldiers were forbidden to accept runaways into their ranks. Many Africans were returned to their slave plantations under armed guards of the Union Army. However, most runaways were returned under flags of truce when Confederate soldiers would come into the Union camps looking for Africans. Union generals gladly surrendered any African that was claimed by the southerners.

Soon the Union Army realized that by sending Africans back to the Confederacy they were prolonging the war by giving the South the support it needed for production and maintenance. Furthermore, they understood that if the Union Army kept the Africans, many of whom had come to fight against the Confederacy, they could use them in support of their side. A precedent was set on May 24, 1861 by General Benjamin F. Butler of Virginia when he refused to return three runaways to their owner, a Confederate officer. In fact, Butler's reasoning became the accepted logic and law of the Union. He reasoned that since the runaways were possessions of the enemy who represented a foreign government, as articles of war they had to be confiscated once they came under the control of the Union Army.

Butler called the Africans who had escaped slavery and been confiscated by the Union Army, "contraband." On August 6, 1861, the Congress of the United States passed the first Confiscation Act which allowed the Union Army to confiscate the slaves of those owners who were at war with the Union. Not content to watch the war from afar, thousands of Africans flooded the Union camps to fight against the Confederacy and decide their own destiny.

The Pulitzer Prize-winning playwright, Charles Fuller, has dedicated an entire dramatic series entitled "We" to this important historical situation in the African-American experience. The new situation—Africans prepared to die for their freedom—meant a new response from the North. The new attitude on the part of African soldiers also meant that they wanted to be treated fairly in terms of wages. The situation was to cause the Union Army to act with caution regarding the black troops.

The Union Army did not respond immediately to the flood of African sentiment about fighting against the Confederacy. Rather, at first, Africans were used in much the same way as they had been used in the Confederate Army.

Christian Fleetwood

Nevertheless, the clamor to engage the enemy increased among Africans, particularly in the North. In Pittsburgh, Philadelphia, Cincinnati, Detroit, Washington, New York, and Boston, Africans rented halls and practiced war drills, some even volunteered to pay their expenses to fight against the South. Artisans of every occupation in the African-American community petitioned the government for enlistment. The official policy of the Department of War was that ". . . the Secretary of War has no intention of using colored soldiers." Lincoln's administration wanted to keep the war, as much as possible, "a white man's war" with no reference to Africans. The public knew that this could not be done and prominent Africans such as John Rock and Frederick Douglass increasingly forced the issue. Eventually, northern sentiment was that it wanted a victory and the recruitment of Africans to the Union

MEN OF COLOR, TO ARMS! NOW OR NEVER!

This is our Golden Moment. The Government of the United States calls for every Able-Bodied Colored Man to enter the Army for the THREE YEARS' SERVICE, and join in fighting the Battles of Liberty and the Union. A new era is open to us. For generations we have suffered under the horrors of slavery, outrage and wrong; our manhood has been denied, our citizenship blotted out, our souls seared and burned, our spirits cowed and crushed, and the hopes of the future of our race involved in doubts and darkness. But now the whole aspect of our relations to the white race is changed. Now therefore is our most precious moment. Let us Rush to Arms! **Fail Now and Our Race is Doomed** on this the soil of our birth. We must now awake, arise, or be forever fallen. If we value Liberty, if we wish to be free in this land, if we love our country, if we love our families, our children, our homes, we must strike NOW while the Country calls: must rise up in the dignity of our manhood, and show by our own right arms that we are worthy to be freemen. Our enemies have made the country believe that we are craven cowards, without soul, without manhood, without the spirit of soldiers. Shall we die with this stigma resting on our graves? Shall we leave this inheritance of shame to our children? No! A thousand times No! **We WILL Rise!** The alternative is upon us; let us rather die freemen than live to be slaves. What is life without liberty? We say that we have manhood—now is the time to prove it. A nation or a people that cannot fight may be pitied, but cannot be respected. If we would be regarded *Men*, if we would forever **SILENCE THE TONGUE OF CALUMNY,** of prejudice and hate; let us rise NOW and fly to arms! We have seen what **Valor and Heroism** our brothers displayed at **PORT HUDSON and at MILLIKEN'S BEND;** though they are just from the galling, poisoning grasp of slavery, they have startled the world by the most exalted heroism. If they have proved themselves heroes, can not we prove ourselves men? **ARE FREEMEN LESS BRAVE THAN SLAVES?** More than a Million White Men have left Comfortable Homes and joined the Armies of the Union to save their Country; cannot we leave ours, and swell the hosts of the Union, to save our liberties, vindicate our manhood, and deserve well of our Country?

MEN OF COLOR! All Races of Men—the Englishman, the Irishman, the Frenchman, the German, the American, have been called to assert their claim to freedom and a manly character, by an appeal to the sword. The day that has seen an enslaved race in arms, has, in all history, seen their last trial. We can now see that **OUR LAST OPPORTUNITY HAS COME!** If we are not lower in the scale of humanity than Englishmen, Irishmen, white Americans and other races, we can show it now.

MEN OF COLOR! BROTHERS and FATHERS! WE APPEAL TO YOU! By all your concern for yourselves and your liberties, by all your regard for God and Humanity, by all your desire for Citizenship and Equality before the law, by all your love for the Country, to stop at no subterfuges, listen to nothing that shall deter you from rallying for the Army. Come forward, and at once Enroll your Names for the **Three Years' Service. STRIKE NOW,** and you are henceforth and forever **FREEMEN!**

Army was finally recognized as a key to that victory.

In early 1861, the Louisiana Native Guards had been organized as the first regiment formed by free Africans. This regiment had sided with the Confederacy and marched with the state militia in a parade in New Orleans on November 23, 1861. A principal reason free Africans in New Orleans formed their own regiment was to avoid being forced into the Confederacy ranks as common laborers and servants. Others, of course, had a stake in the Confederacy itself as slave-owning blacks. As for these southern regiments actually firing a shot, there is no established evidence that they were ever called upon to fight against the Union. In fact, as soon as the Union Army gained control over New Orleans, the regiment switched sides and gave its services to the Union.

On the Union side, more than 185,000 Africans eventually fought in the war, setting high marks for valor, courage, and tenacity. Their casualty rate was nearly 37 percent due to the Confederacy's policies of not taking African prisoners. Those who were captured were almost always killed. While the white northerners may have seen the Civil War as a dispute about the integrity of the Union, Africans saw it as their chance to even scores, to liberate themselves, and to prove once and for all that they were prepared to take up arms to defend themselves against those who had exploited their persons and minds. The high casualty rate among African American soldiers was deliberate on the part of the southerners but it also suggested that the northern army used the African troops as vanguard or point troops in dangerous situations.

Recruitment posters went up in all of the major cities of the North. Philadelphia, Boston, New York, and Rochester were particularly involved in recruitment drives. Both women and men recruiters from the ranks of the abolitionists encouraged Africans to strike their blow for liberty.

The opposition to Africans serving in the Union Army had created a strong reaction in the African American community. Joined by their white allies from the abolition movement, Africans petitioned to be able to fight in the war. Considerable agitation existed in the urban communities of the North for arming Africans, afterall, the struggle was about the future of the African in the United States despite the rhetoric about keeping the Union one. William Lloyd Garrison and Wendell Phillips believed that the government was acting in a cruel and unnatural manner by denying Africans the right to demonstrate how much they wanted freedom. Furthermore, northern blacks should have the opportunity to show their southern and enslaved brothers and sisters how much they were willing to give for liberty.

The arguments against Africans fighting came not only from the Lincoln Administration, but from several sources. Many white soldiers did not want to see Africans fighting in the war. They reasoned that the Union uniform should be reserved for those whose claim to citizenship was unquestioned. Some even went so far as to voice their opinion that the war was "a white man's war." The president feared that citizens in the border states would object to the arming of Africans to fight whites. He also believed that this action would erode his support in the North. President Lincoln felt that the sentiment against the African in the North, while different than that in the South, would be against arming blacks with Union weapons. It was not until the spring of 1862 that Lincoln, under pressure from the military leaders who had begun to fear that the southerners were growing stronger, agreed to arm Africans.

Robert Smalls

Robert Smalls was born in Beaufort, South Carolina, April 5, 1839. As all enslaved Africans, he was prevented from doing the things he dreamed of doing. He could not gain an education without

breaking the law of South Carolina. Others could not teach him how to read or write without breaking the law.

In 1851, he was sent to Charleston and began work as a outfitter for ships. This job allowed Smalls to become very familiar with ships and sailing. According to the record of the House of Representatives, Forty-seventh Congress, second session, Report No. 1887, which placed Smalls on the Retired List of the Navy he was entitled to retirement because of his valuable service to the country during the Civil War. By 1861, he had become aware and knowledgeable of the steamer which was later to make him famous.

On May 13, 1862, the Confederate steamboat *Planter* was taken out of the port of Charleston by Smalls and delivered to one of the vessels of the Federal fleet then blockading the port. The day before, May 12, the ship had returned to Charleston from an engagement which included moving guns from Cole's Island to James Island. The officers had gone ashore and slept in the city, leaving on board a crew of eight African men. Among them was Robert Smalls who had earlier been ordered by the Confederates to serve on the naval ship *Planter*. However, on May 13, the brave Smalls, with the contingent of seven other enslaved Africans, decided that he could steer the ship out of Charleston Harbor and surrender it to the Union forces blockading the harbor.

Smalls was called a "wheelman" because the title of "pilot" was reserved for whites. The expertise he demonstrated in directing the ship to the Union forces indicated skill, courage, and intelligence. Consulting with the other Africans, his crew, Smalls discovered that five of them wanted to join him. Two remained behind. According to the House of Representatives Report the design was very hazardous. The boat would have to pass beneath the guns of the forts in the harbor. Lack of courage and steadiness or detection by the Confederates would mean certain death.

Robert Smalls

When the Fort Sumter soldiers discovered that the ship was headed for the Federal fleet they signalled to the Morris Island contingent to stop her. But it was too late. The ship had passed beyond the range of the Morris Island guns and was making its way toward the Union vessels. Robert Smalls knew exactly what he was doing. As the ship approached the Union forces, a white flag was displayed, but because it was not seen at first, the Union steamers stood ready to defend themselves. Just as they were about to fire, they noticed the flag of truce. Smalls became one of the first African American naval heroes. The Union army saluted him as a member of the navy with retirement.

John Brown

John Brown, who was born in Connecticut in 1800, had prepared all of his life to overturn slavery. On October 16, 1859, he seized the arsenal at Harper's Ferry, Virginia. His plan was to make his way into the mountains with his nineteen men and from those fastnesses to sally back and forth to destabilize the slave institutions.

John Brown went to Kansas and joined his five sons in a battle against pro-slavery forces in 1855. On May 24, 1856 he had killed five of his opponents at Pottawatomie Creek, Kansas. The apologists for slavery feared John Brown. He took it upon himself to rid the region of pro-slavery sympathizers. Later in the year, John Brown's forces repelled a strong Missouri invading force intent on introducing slavery into Kansas territory.

In the spring of 1858, Brown met with a group of white and black abolitionists in Chatham, Ontario, to tell them about his plan to establish an antislavery community and stronghold in the mountains of Virginia and Maryland. He proposed, and the convention of people gathered adopted, a provisional constitution and set of ordinances for the people of the United States. He was elected commander-in-

Every precaution was taken by the careful Smalls. Having made the resolution, he planned the action to the smallest detail. Under his command, wood was taken on the ship, steam was put on, and with her valuable cargo of guns and ammunition, intended for a new fortification, Fort Ripley, the *Planter* moved out of the harbor at two o'clock in the morning.

Smalls steered the ship up beyond the North Atlantic wharf, where his wife and two children, and eight other people were waiting to embark. These passengers were taken aboard at 3:25 in the morning, May 13.

The perilous journey had begun. There was no turning back. With nine men, five women, and three children, Robert Smalls passed Fort Johnson and blew the usual salute on the steam-whistle. He proceeded down the bay. When he had reached the area of Fort Sumter, he stood in the pilot-house leaning out of the window as the captain had usually done. He even folded his arms in the same manner and wore the same kind of straw hat. The signal that was required to be given as a ship passed out into the sea was blown as cooly as any other captain would have done. Fort Sumter answered by signal, "all right," and the ship headed toward Morris Island, occupied by a light artillery unit, and then beyond the guns of Fort Sumter.

Kennedy Farm
Rented Kennedy farm in July 1859 where plans for the mission were made and training began

MARYLAND

On Monday, October 11 a large portion of the arms captured at Harper's Ferry were taken to a school house in Maryland.

School House

In total Brown's men killed one marine, three Virginia citizens, and one black railroad employee

Potomac River

Citizens from the surrounding area banded together to attack the engine house. The attack liberated all but the ten most important hostages which had been moved to another part of the building. At this time there were forty hostages under Brown's control.

Potomac Bridge

Washington Farm
Seized Colonal L. W. Washington and several of his slaves and brought them to engine house as hostages.

Attack took place Sunday, October 16, 1859 between 11:00 PM and 12:00 AM. Attacking force consisted of Brown and twenty-one men.

Harper's Ferry, WV

Engine House
Took over engine house and used it for base of operations

Armory

Lee and his troops took the engine house by storm.

Arsenal

Took over the federal armory and arsenal, distributing arms to his men and stealing arms to supply an army of 1,500.

B & O Railroad

Potomac River

Brown's men held rifle works until they were overrun by townspeople and were killed or captured.

All but the seven men with Brown and the group that carried the arms to the school house were killed on Monday.

The government ordered the marines under the command of then colonel Robert E. Lee to resolve the uprising.

Rifle Works

Shenandoah River

Shenandoah Bridge

VIRGINIA

Miles
0   .5

SUNDAY, OCTOBER 16, 1859
JOHN BROWN'S RAID ON HARPER'S FERRY

chief of this provisional government. Gerrit Smith and other prominent Boston abolitionists invited him to Boston to present his plans. They also arranged to provide him with funds. Leading African Americans, Harriet Tubman, and Frederick Douglass, among them, were kept apprised of the movement. Brown had settled in North Elba, New York, an African American community, because he felt comfortable among the exploited and oppressed. Brown's small cadre of revolutionists captured the armory and rounded up about sixty leading citizens as hostages. They were able to hold out during his skirmishes with the local militia, but when a contingent of marines came to the battlefront, Brown had to surrender. He lost two of his sons in the fighting.

Thus, only two days after his seizure of the arsenal in Harper's Ferry, he was wounded, captured, and depressed. Three months later he was hanged for treason, slave insurrection, and murder. His death was a energizing force to the abolitionists. They made memorials to John Brown throughout the land. He was praised as the best America had to offer from the most prestigious pulpits; slave parents taught their children about the deeds of John Brown—he was a hero in his own time.

Some hated him and despised him for standing against slavery. Those who supported the institution of slavery saw John Brown and his spirit as dangerous for the nation. Should the Africans get into their heads that they would follow the pattern set by John Brown there would be difficulty throughout the land. In councils and assemblies in Maryland and Virginia, the slaveowners questioned the extent of John Brown's influence. Others passed judgment on his character and his mental stability, going so far as to say that he had become unhinged because of his love for the African people. Of course, John Brown was neither crazy nor a fool. He had spent months, maybe even years, organizing his plot, assessing the kind of support he would receive from the Africans were he to succeed, consulting with the leading abolitionists, and preparing his sons to fight alongside him.

John Brown

When the war between the states finally began, the Union soldiers used John Brown's name and vision for their own inspiration. He had seen the war coming and had warned that it was impossible to build a nation with one part of it slave and the other part of it free.

Few men have given their lives so freely for the liberation of others. There is perhaps no greater story of sacrifice on the part of a white person during the Great Enslavement than the life story of John Brown, forever enshrined in the best memories of the United States of America.

The Legacy of John Brown

John Brown understood more about the nature of the Civil War (which he never lived to see) than many of those who directed it. President Abraham Lincoln and his cabinet insisted in all of their documents and speeches that the war was not to be fought over the slavery issue.

Lincoln was not John Brown. While Lincoln opposed slavery in a general way, he did not believe in social or political equality for Africans. It was therefore important for him to insist that the war was not over slavery. If he had agreed that the war was over slavery he could have been accused of prosecuting a war against whites in support of blacks. Thus, in his official rhetoric he argued that the war was over Union.

Most African Americans knew that the war was over slavery. The peculiar institution overshadowed all other issues. It stood astride everything. There was no way for the government to avoid slavery as an issue; it would not go away. Lincoln had even thought seriously about colonization as an answer to the issues surrounding the slave question. In 1862, he proposed a gradual emancipation which would have allowed slaveowners to be compensated for enslaved Africans set free under his scheme. The idea was to free Africans and then return them to Africa. Africans in New York, Washington, Baltimore, Boston, and Philadelphia held protest

meetings against this idea and it never saw the light of day as official policy.

It has been argued that Lincoln believed that if he emancipated Africans in the rebel territories, whites would more easily accept the emancipation were the Africans made to leave the country. As it turned out, when the Emancipation Proclamation was issued on January 1, 1863, it did not have much immediate impact. It actually took the Thirteenth Amendment, which was finally ratified in December, 1865, to put teeth in the emancipation.

What the Emancipation Proclamation did was to encourage blacks to enlist in the Union Army. Lincoln had initially rejected pressure to allow Africans to fight in the war but soon relented when the North seemed to lose initiative on the battlefront. Africans had fought in every war before the Civil War but no war was more eagerly fought than this one. When the war was over, African American children gave orations in praise of the spirit of John Brown.

The Battles of Mobile and New Orleans

During the Battles of Mobile and New Orleans in 1812, African troops distinguished themselves by heroic deeds. Under Andrew Jackson's command at Mobile, some white troops were retreating in disarray until an African named Jeffries saved the day by taking lead of the soldiers and rallying them for the battle. At the Battle of New Orleans, Jackson specifically called on the Africans to assist in the struggle against the British. When the battle was over he thanked the fighters in these words: "Soldiers: from the shores of Mobile I collected you to arms. I invited you to share the perils and to divide the glory with your white countrymen. I expected much from you, for I was not uninformed of those qualities which must render you so formidable to an invading force. . . . I knew that you loved the land of your nativity, and that, like ourselves, you had to defend all that is most dear to man. But you have surpassed all my hopes."

Problems after the Civil War

The Civil War came to an end on April 9, 1865, but the misery of Africans did not cease with the end of the enslavement that had lasted nearly 250 years. By December 1865, the Thirteenth Amendment outlawing slavery in any territory and state was made a part of the Constitution, enough states having ratified it. With Abraham Lincoln dead and Andrew Johnson sworn in as president, the four million Africans began to test their new freedom. Thousands wandered the country they had never known looking for lost relatives in counties and states they had only heard about before. The war had dislocated relatives but more freedom gave the African an opportunity to find relatives who had escaped or been sold to different masters prior to emancipation. This was the period of the Great Mourning Treks. They worked for wages where the wages were fair but often refused to be treated like slaves now that they were free.

President Andrew Johnson admitted four states back into the Union seven months after he took office on April 1865. This angered some members of Congress who believed that the President disregarded reality. Leaders of southern states quickly restored their dominance and introduced a group of laws known as Black Codes to control the freed Africans. These codes granted some rights which were denied under the enslavement such as marriage, property ownership, and testimony in court. However, restrictions were included which were meant to insure complete white control over the lives of the freed Africans. The southern courts could take African children who either had parents who could not support them, seemed to be orphaned, or actually were orphaned and assign them to whites. This was a new form of slavery, a way to secure black labor without pay. The Black Codes required Africans to have jobs approved by whites or be arrested, fined, or assigned to jobs with whites who only had to pay whatever fine was assessed against the Africans.

Congress was furious with President Johnson's actions which were seen as lenient to the South. The state of Georgia had even sent the former Vice President of the Confederacy to Congress. In June 1866, Congress passed the Fourteenth Amendment which extended citizenship and civil rights to Africans. The amendment also reversed the Dred Scott decision of 1857 that had taken away African citizenship prior to the Civil War and it prohibited certain confederate officers from holding public office. In February 1866, President Andrew Johnson vetoed a bill passed by Congress to broaden the powers of the Freedmen's Bureau. The bureau of Refugees, Freedmen, and Abandoned Lands had been established on March 3, 1865 for the purpose of resettling and educating rural Africans in the south. However, as early as 1861, four years prior to the end of the Civil War, Lewis Tappan of the American Missionary Association had sent teachers to open the first day school for the freed persons at Hampton, Virginia. By 1864 the American Missionary Association had sent more than 250 northern teachers to the South.

While the missionary efforts of the Baptists, Methodists, Presbyterians, Congregationalists, African Methodists, and Friends were enormous, the Freedmen's Bureau was chiefly responsible for starting schools between 1865 and 1870. During the first year of the Civil War, 4,239 schools were established with 9,307 teachers and nearly 250,000 students. Carter Woodson and Charles Wesley wrote in their book, *The Negro in Our History*, that several white teachers would be remembered when historians write "High upon the roll of honor Negroes inscribe as immortal apostles . . . Corey at Virginia Union, Packard and Giles at Spelman, Cravath at Fisk, Ware at Atlanta, Armstrong at Hampton, Graves at Morehouse, and Tupper at Shaw." Africans and their supporters had found the Freedmen's Bureau to be an indispensable ally in the south. President Andrew Johnson did as much as he could to weaken the agency. Thus, his veto of the bill which should have given the Freedmen's Bureau more powers was followed quickly by other presidential actions. Two months later he vetoed a civil rights bill meant to protect African Americans from the restrictions of the Black Codes. Congress repassed both bills within three months over Johnson's veto. Tennessee, the home state of Andrew Johnson, was the only ex-confederate state to ratify the Fourteenth Amendment. The ten other states, at Johnson's suggestion, voted against the amendment.

Radical Republicans controlled the Congress after the 1866 elections and they dealt severe blows to President Johnson's policies and the ex-confederates. A series of laws were passed that brought southern white control of government to an end in the South. The Military Reconstruction Acts were put into effect by the summer of 1867. Under these acts the governments in the South set up by President Johnson were dissolved. These governments did not permit blacks to vote, imposed a new kind of slavery through the Black Codes, and failed to protect defenseless Africans who were frequently harassed and killed during the two years of southern white government.

The Military Reconstruction Acts affected the ten states still out of the Union. Tennessee had been allowed to reenter. There were five military districts with a union general in charge of each district. 20,000 soldiers were stationed over the districts to provide security and to assist in law enforcement. The generals were responsible for voter registration. Each state was permitted to return to the union if it ratified a new constitution, elected a new government under the constitution, and ratified the Fourteenth Amendment.

Six of the ten states returned to the Union by June 1868. The four remaining

Some of the Significant Civil War Battles
Engaged in by African Regiments

Amite River
Appomattox Court House
Arkansas River
Ash Bayou
Ashepoo River

Ashwood Landing
Athens
Barrancas
Bayou Bidell
Bayou Boeuf

Bayou Macon
Bayou St. Lewis
Bayou Tensas
Bayou Tunica
Bermuda Hundreds

Berwick
Big Creek
Big River
Big Springs
Black Creek

Black River
Boggs' Mill
Boyd's Station
Boykin's Mills
Bradford Spring

Brawley Fork
Brice's Cross Roads
Brigsen Creek
Brush Creek
Bryant's Plantation

Cabin Creek
Cabin Point
Camden
Cedar Keys
Chaffin's Farm

Charleston
Chattanooga
City Point
Clarkesville
Clinton

Coleman's Plantation
Columbia
Concordia Bayou
Cow Creek
Cox's Bridge

Dallas
Dalton
Darbytown Road
David's Bend
Decatur

Deep Bottom
Drewry's Bluff
Deveraux Neck
Dutch Gap
East Pascagoula

Eastport
Fair Oaks
Federal Point
Fillmore
Floyd

Fort Adams
Fort Anderson
Fort Blakely
Fort Brady
Fort Burnham

Fort Donelson
Fort Gaines
Fort Gibson
Fort Jones
Fort Pillow

Fort Pocahontas
Fort Smith
Fort Taylor
Fort Wagner
Franklin

Ghent
Glasgow
Goodrich's Landing
Grand Gulf
Gregory's Farm

Haines' Bluff
Hall Island
Harrodsburg
Hatcher's Run
Helena

Henderson
Holly Springs
Honey Hill
Hopkinsville
Horsehead Creek

Indian BayIndian Town
Indian Village
Island Mound
Island No. 76
Issequena County

Jackson
Jacksonville
James Island
Jenkin's Ferry
John's Island

Johnsonville
Jones' Bridge
Joy's Ford
Lake Providence

Laurence
Little Rock
Liverpool Heights
Madison Station
Magnolia
Marengo

Mariana
Marion
Marion County
Mckay's Point
Meffleton Lodge

Memphis
Milliken's Bend
Milltown Bluff
Mitchell's Creek
Morganzia

Moscow Station
Mound Plantation
Mound Pleasant
Landing
Mud Creek

Murfreesboro
Nashville
Natchez
Natural Bridge
New Kent Court

House
New Market Heights
Olustee
Owensboro
Pass Manchal

Palmetto Ranch
Pettersburg
Pierson's Farm
Pine Barren Creek
Pine Barren Ford

Pine Bluff
Plymouth
Point Lookout
Point of Rocks
Point Pleasant

Poison Springs
Port Hudson
Powhatan
Prairie d' Anne
Pulaski

Raleigh
Rector's Farm
Richland
Ripley
Roache's Plantation

Rolling Fork
Rooseville Creek
Ross Landing
Sabine River
Salkehatchie

Saltville
Sand Mountain
Sandy Swamp
Scottsboro
Sherwood

Shipwith's Landing
Simpsonville
Smithfield
South Tunnel
Spanish Fort

St. John's River
St. Stephens
Steamer *Alliance*
Steamer *Chippewa*
Steamer *City Belle*

Steamer *Louts*
Suffolk
Sugar Loaf Hill
Sulpher Branch
Swift Creek

Taylorsville
Timber Hill
Town Creek
Township
Trestle

Tupelo
Vicksburg
Vidalia
Wallace Ferry
Warsaw

Waterford
Waterloo
Waterproof
White Oak Road
White River

Williamsburg
Wilmington
Wilson's Landing Wharf
Yazoo City
Yazoo Expedition

AFRICANS IN THE UNION ARMY

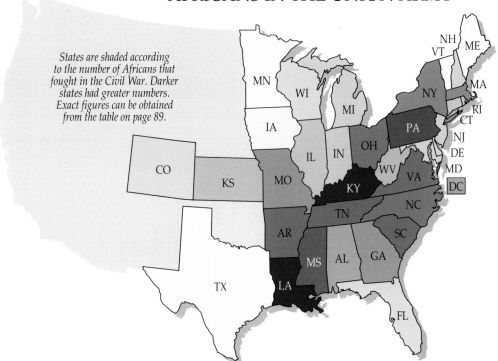

States are shaded according to the number of Africans that fought in the Civil War. Darker states had greater numbers. Exact figures can be obtained from the table on page 89.

states became a part of the Union again in July 1870. The last four states had to ratify the Fifteenth Amendment as well since it passed Congress in 1869 and became a part of the Constitution in March 1870. However, now that the states were back in the Union, it did not signify that there was a change of heart regarding the rights and opportunities to be granted to blacks. The new political arrangement would serve as a shield for a continuation of discrimination against Africans. Just as soon as the Union Army left and the South became acceptable to the Union, the African Americans became desperate.

The Compromise of 1877, which had seen the North capitulate to the South against the will of the African masses, brought about greater emphasis on self help, racial dignity, and pride. The programs of the Reconstruction did not cease—there was still interest in political franchise, civil rights, and representation in political bodies. Nevertheless a greater emphasis on education was being shown.

Increasingly, the African community knew that it had been abandoned. In fact, during the national convention held in Louisville, Kentucky in 1883, the delegates said in part that the laws intended

to secure rights for African Americans were nothing but dead letters.

Africans were angered by the lack of federal support for civil rights. At state and regional conventions throughout the North and South, and especially the South, delegates vowed to use all legal means within their power to secure their rights. They complained about prejudiced judges and juries, short school terms, discrimination in the Republican party, and the convict lease system. In 1885, the people of Baltimore founded the Brotherhood of Liberty with the express purpose of fighting for the just rights of African Americans.

In 1888, more than 350 African Americans met in Georgia to condemn the chain gang, discrimination in public transportation, lynch law, disfranchishment, and general harassment. They supported the temperance issue as well as industrial education.

Two significant conventions were held in 1890. These two conferences represented the best thinking of the time on questions confronting the African American community. T. Thomas Fortune, the newspaper journalist who had become known as an agitator, founded the Afro-American League in Chicago. This was

to become one of the principal agencies for dissemination of African American political ideas. A few months later in Washington, DC, a group of about 500 blacks gathered to establish the American Citizens' Equal Rights Association. J. C. Price was named head of the convention. He served as a leading spokesperson for both organizations until they ceased to function due to internal ideological problems.

Into Battle

Africans have distinguished themselves as soldiers in every war fought by Americans. We shall not recount each campaign but simply convey the extent of the African's nobility and character in military campaigns.

The Boston Massacre occurred on March 5, 1770, when British troops marched down State Street and were confronted by a group of Americans led by Crispus Attucks, a tall, impressive African of ebony complexion. Attucks and three others were killed, the African being the first to die. There is a monument in Boston, the Attucks Monument, to honor the courage of Attucks. Later, at the Battle of Bunker Hill, Peter Salem showed unusual courage by rushing forward and shooting Major Pitcairn of the British Army as he was exulting in his anticipated victory. Also during the Revolutionary War, the man who captured General Prescott was an African named Prince, not the American, General Barton, as often claimed.

Civil War

The examples of Crispus Attucks, Peter Salem, and Salem Poor in the American Revolutionary War would inspire thousands of African soldiers during the Civil War. Africans fought in the Civil War by state and individual enlistment, the latter being enlistment in which a person simply reported to a Union officer and asked to be signed up. Although this was considered by some officers to be irregular, many black soldiers used irregular measures in order to gain entry

African American Servicemen Awarded
The Congressional Medal of Honor

U.S. Army

William Appleton	4th U.S. Colored Troops	September 29, 1864	Cited for gallant conduct at New Market Heights, Virginia.
Private William H. Barnes	38th U.S. Colored Troops		Among the first to enter the confederate works, although wounded, at Chaffin's Farm near Richmond, Virginia.
First Sergeant Powhatan Beaty	5th U.S. Colored Troops	September 29, 1864	Cited for gallantry in action at Chiffin's Farm near Richmond.
First Sergeant James H. Bronson	5th U.S. Colored Troops	September 29, 1864	Cited for gallantry in action at Chiffin's Farm near Richmond.
Sergeant William H. Carney	54th Massachusetts Colored Infantry		The first African American to win the Congressional Medal of Honor. Carney was cited for valor on June 18, 1863, during the Battle of Fort Wagner, South Carolina, in which he carried the colors and led a charge to the parapet after the standard bearer had been killed. He was twice severely wounded during this battle.
Seargent Decatur Dorsey	39th U.S. Colored Troops	July 30, 1864	Cited for valor in the Battle of Petersburg, Virginia. When his regiment was driven back to Union lines, he carried the colors and rallied the men in his unit.
Sergeant-Major Christian A. Fleetwood	4th U.S. Colored Troops		Cited for gallantry in action at Chiffin's Farm near Richmond.
Private James Gardiner	36th U.S. Colored Troops		Cited for gallantry in action at Chiffin's Farm near Richmond.
Sergeant James Harris	38th Colored Troops		Cited for gallantry in action at Chiffin's Farm near Richmond.
Sergeant-Major Thomas Hawkins	6th U.S. Colored Troops	July 21, 1864	Cited for valor in the Battle of Deep Bottom, Virginia. Credited with the rescue of his regimental colors.
Sergeant Alfred B. Hilton	4th U.S. Colored Troops		Cited for gallantry in action at Chiffin's Farm near Richmond.
Sergeant-Major Milton M. Holland	5th U.S. Colored Troops		Cited for gallantry in action at Chiffin's Farm near Richmond.
Corporal Miles James	36th U.S. Colored Troops		Cited for gallantry in action at Chiffin's Farm near Richmond.
First Sergeant Alexander Kelly	6th U.S. Colored Troops		Cited for gallantry in action at Chiffin's Farm near Richmond.
First Sergeant Robert Pinn	5th U.S. Colored Troops		Cited for gallantry in action at Chiffin's Farm near Richmond.
First Sergeant Edward Radcliff	38th U.S. Colored Troops		Cited for gallantry in action at Chiffin's Farm near Richmond.
Private Charles Veal	4th U.S. Colored Troops		Cited for gallantry in action at Chiffin's Farm near Richmond.

U.S. Navy

Aaron Anderson	serving on the gunboat *Wyandank*.	Participated in the clearing of Mattox Creek on March 17, 1865. Cited for carrying out his duties courageously in spite of devastating fire from the enemy.
Robert Blake	serving on the gunboat *Marblehead*	An ex-slave enlisting in the navy after escaping from a Virginia plantation, Blake displayed heroism on the *Marblehead* December 25, 1863.
John Lawson	serving on the gunboat *Hartford*	Cited for bravery in the Battle of Mobile Bay on August 5, 1864. He was knocked unconscious, but when he regained consciousness he continued to perform his duties although four of the men at his station had been killed by enemy fire.
Joachim Pease	serving on the gunboat *Kearsarge*	Cited for gallantry in action in the engagement with the Confederate gunboat *Alabama*.

African American Soldiers Serving in the Civil War	
Alabama	2,969
Arkansas	5,526
Colorado Territory	95
Connecticut	1,765
Delaware	954
District of Columbia	3,269
Florida	1,044
Georgia	3,486
Illinois	1,811
Indiana	1,537
Iowa	440
Kansas	2,080
Kentucky	23,703
Louisiana	24,052
Maine	104
Maryland	8,718
Massachusetts	3,966
Michigan	1,387
Minnesota	104
Mississippi	17,896
Missouri	440
New Hampshire	125
New Jersey	1,185
New York	4,125
North Carolina	5,035
Ohio	5,092
Pennsylvania	8,612
Rhode Island	1,837
South Carolina	5,462
Tennessee	20,133
Texan	47
Vermont	120
Virginia	5,723
West Virginia	196
Wisconsin	104
Not accounted for by a state	5,896
Total Serving	**169,038**
Casualties	**68,178**

into the war. Nearly 170,000 African Americans are accounted for by states as serving in the Civil War, but another 10,000 or so remain unaccounted for in this measure.

The role of African American women in the war was critical to the conduct of the battle on the frontlines. When the contraband (i.e., Africans who walked into the Union army camps and were seized from the slaveowners as spoils of war) came to the towns and cities, the African American women served as social welfare experts and supporters. They gathered food, shelter, and clothing for the contraband and prepared them to function in freedom. Some of the women worked in hospitals and in military camps. They moved into liberated areas in the South to help people find jobs and homes. They became school teachers in communities that had 100 percent illiteracy. They organized study groups to teach women and men from the southern plantations how to take care of themselves. The African American women were as active as the men in their sphere of work. No one seemed to wait for others to work; they all had responsibilities.

Like other wars in other places and times, the Civil War served to further liberate African American women. Most women had some degree of training and could teach others how to serve themselves and the nation in a more effective way. By the end of the war in 1865, 10 percent of the total government troops' strength had been supplied by African Americans. Twenty-five percent of the navy's sailors were Africans.

African troops who enlisted in the army were always placed in "colored" regiments. They were either in light or heavy artillery, cavalry, infantry, or engineers. Most of these regiments were led by white officers. There were occasional black non-commissioned officers. Among the white officers who became well-known for having good commands of African troops were Colonel Robert Gould Shaw of the Fifty-Fourth Massachusetts Regiment, Colonel Thomas

Sergeant W. H. Carney

Wentworth Higginson of the First South Carolina Volunteers, and General N. Banks of the First and Third Louisiana Native Guards.

It should be noted that two regiments of General Butler's Corps d'Afrique were staffed by African Americans. Among the African officers was Captain P. B. S. Pinchback. In addition to Pinchback, who became a politician during the Reconstruction, were Major F. Dumas, Captain H. Ford Douglass, Lieutenant W. D. Matthews, and Major Martin R. Delany. These officers served with dignity and honor. The Civil War may have started out as a white man's war, as some of the white officers had claimed, but in the end it was a war for the liberation of the African—and African men and women participated in it fully.

Adwini Asa, "We Have Exhausted the Possibilities,"
Ghana, Africa

"SWING LOW, SWEET CHARIOT": 8
THE PROMISE OF RECONSTRUCTION

The end of the Civil War brought about an incredible thirst for knowledge and information. Rarely in history have a people longed for education as the freed Africans longed. When the words were spoken, "Freedom has come," thousands of Africans began their search for the fountains of knowledge believing that one of the great differences between them and the whites was knowledge.

The response of the Freedmen's Bureau was massive within the context of the times. Riding upon the limited goodwill of the people of the United States, the Bureau set up 4,000 schools, found 9,000 teachers, and taught 250,000 Africans, young and old, how to read and write. At Emancipation only one out of every ten Africans could read and write. The widespread assistance of the Bureau was necessary to provide safe and secure conditions for the newly freed Africans.

The narratives of freed Africans tell various stories of generosity and eagerness to learn. In some instances, Africans were taught in schools that had been established on the farms where they worked before and after emancipation. Now more than ever, the institutions of higher learning became more popular. Schools such as Lincoln University founded in 1854 in Pennsylvania and Hampton Institute in Virginia attracted large numbers of students from the South.

More and more schools were opened for the business of educating the African American population. With an insatiable desire for knowledge, some African Americans spent years securing rudimentary educations in order to serve others as teachers. "Each one teach one" seemed to have been the motto of the day as those who gained the basic education rushed to teach those who had no education. In some instances teachers were those who had achieved the equivalent of a fifth grade education. Believing that it was possible to secure the American Dream through proper education, African Americans in the South created local organizations and support groups to encourage especially promising students to gain more education. Churches set up educational committees which, in some instances, became the basis for starting schools and colleges. Seldom have so many churches been committed to the social and educational advancement of the African American. With minimal resources they created the conditions, through hard work and diligence, which elevated a downtrodden community. Consistent to the principles of self-help, these churches and institutions recorded some of the most glorious achievements of the African community.

On the whole, African Americans were not welcomed into the white colleges in the nation in the post-war era. Some northern colleges, such as Oberlin, achieved reputations as liberal institutions that welcomed good African American students, but by no means was this welcome universal. Although one would think that the educated community of the South would be opened to the newly freed Africans even if other sectors of the society were not, this was not the case.

African Americans had the support of numerous philanthropic families and institutions from the North. Combined with the support of the African American churches, these supporters made a difference.

Exodus

In May 1879, Africans from throughout the South gathered in Nashville, Tennessee to discuss the continuing violence against their families. In a report adopted by the body at that convention grievances and proposed remedies were set forth. Indeed, the convention encouraged people to emigrate to the North and West in search of better living conditions.

Forty thousand Africans went to Kansas in less than two years. Others left the South for Missouri, Indiana, and Colorado. The entire African population in the South was convinced that the whites of the South defeated during the war would take out their frustrations on the Africans remaining in the South after the Reconstruction Era.

In 1877, the Liberian Exodus Joint Stock Company had been formed in Charleston, South Carolina, and had purchased a ship, the *Azor*. Their aim was to send emigrants to Africa, to bring African products to the United States, and to establish a regular steamship line between Charleston and Monrovia, Liberia. Whites, fearful of losing domestic workers, did everything they could to prevent the company's success. The ship had been repaired in Boston but whites in Charleston induced the custom house officials to pronounce the ship ill-prepared until it was refurbished with a copper bottom. When that was accomplished (at an expensive price), not all of the people who held places on the ship were permitted to sail. Through the con-

nivance of the captains and business interests in Charleston, the ship was hijacked and sold in Liverpool even though it had been legitimately purchased by the combined resources of Baptists and Methodists in South Carolina. The United States Circuit Court in South Carolina refused to even entertain a suit brought by the Africans to reclaim their property.

The turbulent road to freedom was often marked by economic, physical, and legal harrassment, yet the African American community continued to produce men and women who defied the odds. Those who built towns and cities dreamed of the possibility of living in America free of political and social discrimination. So the towns of Langston, Boley, and Mound Bayou became metaphors for the search for peace and tranquility in the midst of the racial hatred which existed in the South. The towns were shelters in the time of storms.

Labor and the Newly Freed African

The labor movement did not greet the free African with open arms. The relationship between the white worker and the black worker was initially one of bitter suspicion. White workers met in 1866 to form the National Labor Union. This was meant to be the representative union of working people. However, African Americans were never accepted on equal basis with whites in the National Labor Union. White workers felt that the Africans, so recently freed from slavery, did not understand the true principles of labor unions.

In response to the reluctance of white unions to admit them as full members, the African American workers met in 1869 to form the National Negro Labor Union with the express purpose of advancing the cause of black workers. It was not until the 1880s that African American workers finally succeeded in having an affiliation

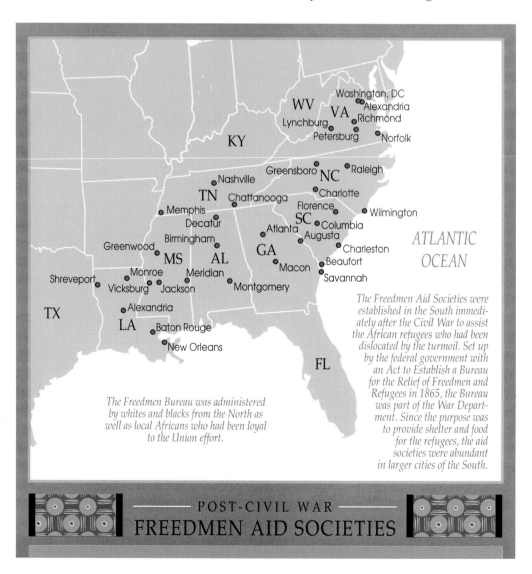

The Freedmen Bureau was administered by whites and blacks from the North as well as local Africans who had been loyal to the Union effort.

The Freedmen Aid Societies were established in the South immediately after the Civil War to assist the African refugees who had been dislocated by the turmoil. Set up by the federal government with an Act to Establish a Bureau for the Relief of Freedmen and Refugees in 1865, the Bureau was part of the War Department. Since the purpose was to provide shelter and food for the refugees, the aid societies were abundant in larger cities of the South.

POST-CIVIL WAR
FREEDMEN AID SOCIETIES

with the National Labor Union. In fact, prior to that time, the National Labor Union looked upon the black workers as strike-breakers, willing to work for lower wages than white workers.

The position of the African American worker in the society was not enviable. Used by manipulative employers the black worker was often forced to work for lower wages in order to have a job at all. Ruthless and unfair bosses fired Africans first and hired Africans last.

African Americans entered every legitimate field of employment in the United States soon after slavery. In Savannah, Georgia, former slaves collected enough money among themselves to capitalize a business for $50,000 which turned out to be of no value. Also in Savannah, Africans tried to run a lumber company in which they had invested $40,000. This business failed as well. In 1865, the black community of Baltimore organized a shipyard, the Chesapeake and Marine Railway and Dry Dock Company, capitalized at $40,000. It went out of existence in 1883. Since the African American community had little expertise in the business world it was prey for many fast-talking white entrepreneurs. The inability to control the economics of the African American community meant the eventual failure of the social vision of Reconstruction.

The Stark Facts on Lynchings

The decade between 1890 and 1900 was the most dangerous time in the post Civil War era for an African man to be alive. Nearly 1,700 persons were lynched in that decade as compared to 921 in the decade between 1900 and 1910; 840 from 1910 to 1920; and nearly 400 between 1920 and 1930. Mob violence against blacks continued into the 1980s. Beyond the numbers which tell their own stories, the aggravated brutality of the murders shouted an irrational hatred of African Americans. The lust for blood and gore, which is not satisfied by the recourse to law or by the normal process of men engaged in warfare, drove the mob to the most heinous types of murders.

Cases of Africans being burned at the stake occurred as far back in American history as the early nineteenth century. But the special brutality of the lynchings of blacks was reserved for the period after the Civil War. In the first part of the twentieth century, between 1918 and 1927, eleven black women were also lynched, three with child at the time. The mobs burned victims to death, hanged them and burned their bodies, mutilated them to death by cutting parts of their bodies, drowned them, or dragged the victims through the streets tied to an automobile.

The states which led in the number of lynchings in the post Civil War period were also the ones that led in the irrational brutality and mutilation of the bodies of the victims. Texas mobs lynched 55 persons during the late nineteenth century, sixteen victims were sadistically murdered. Of thirty-four victims, Arkansas put five people to death during the same period with unusual viciousness. The story is the same for Georgia, Alabama, Mississippi, and Louisiana. Citing figures alone will not give the reader the entire story. Many of the victims were not guilty of the crimes for which they were accused.

The following true story should show a human dimension. Henry Lowry of Nodena, Arkansas, had been held in bondage for a white landowner for more than two years. On Christmas Day, 1920, the African American asked the landlord to pay him his back pay. He was cursed and struck by the landlord and shot by the landlord's son. Lowry drew his own gun and shot and killed the landlord and his daughter. He then escaped to Texas where he was arrested. The Governor of Arkansas guaranteed him a fair trial. He waived his rights to remain in Texas and agreed to return to Arkansas. The two officers who went to Texas to bring him back, took him through Louisiana and Mississippi. At Sardis, Mississippi, a mob, previously arranged, overpowered the officers, and took Lowry from them and held him to be lynched. The newspapers were urged to print the details of time and place of the lynching. The Memphis *Press,* sent a reporter to cover the killing. Ralph Roddy wrote:

More than 500 hundred persons stood by and looked on while the Negro was slowly burned to a crisp. A few women were scattered among the crowd of Arkansas planters, who directed the gruesome work of avenging the death of O. T. Craig and his daughter, Mrs. C. P. Williamson.

Not once did the slayer beg for mercy despite the fact that he suffered one of the most horrible deaths imaginable. With the Negro chained to a log, members of the mob placed a small pile of leaves around his feet. Gasoline was then poured on the leaves, and the carrying out of the death sentence was under way.

Inch by inch the Negro was fairly cooked to death. Every few minutes fresh leaves were tossed on the funeral pyre until the blaze had passed the Negro's waist. Even after the flesh had dropped away from his legs and the flames were leaping toward his face, Lowry retained consciousness. Not once did he whimper or beg for mercy. Once or twice he attempted to pick up the hot ashes in his hands and thrust them into his mouth in order to hasten death. Each time the ashes were kicked out of his reach by a member of the mob.

As the flames were eating away his abdomen, a member of the mob stepped forward and saturated the body with gasoline. It was then only a few minutes until the Negro had been reduced to ashes (White 1969).

Roddy's account was like hundreds in the late nineteenth and early twentieth century. An African was charged with some crime, sometimes on the slightest of evidence, and before he could be brought to trial, a mob had overcome the sheriff, or police, and dragged the victim out to be lynched. So much a part of the reality of the South was lynch law that white families brought their children to see black men lynched. In these moments of deepest pain for the African American community—pain which has never healed—the white mobs found cruel joy. Lynching Africans became a pastime to rival any form of cheap amusement.

It was in times like these that African Americans hated the past and questioned the future. Only faith and hard won character kept alive the possibilities for redress. Neither lynching nor mob violence could

Nobody Knows de Trouble I See

Nobody knows de trouble I see. Nobody knows but Jesus.
Nobody knows de trouble I see. Glory Hallelujah!

Oh! Nobody knows de trouble I see. Nobody knows but Jesus.
Nobody knows de trouble I see. Glory Hallelujah!

Sometimes I'm up. Sometimes I'm down,
Oh, yes, Lord.
Sometimes I'm almos' to de groun'.
Oh, yes, Lord.
Altho' you see me goin' 'long so.
Oh, yes, Lord:
I have my trials here below.
Oh, yes, Lord.

Oh! Nobody knows de trouble I see. Nobody knows but Jesus.
Nobody knows de trouble I see. Glory Hallelujah!

prevent the African American from seeking to secure all of the legal and political rights which were due under law.

The rise of the South, that is, the white South, was based on the disfranchisement of the African American. All of the guarantees made by the Constitutional Amendments were nothing more than high sounding ideal if they could not bear concrete results. It was difficult for the people who had struggled to be free to see how the federal government could protect them from the anger, bitterness, and wanton harrassment of their white neighbors who were intent on trying to prove that they still maintained power over the lives of blacks.

The Ku Klux Klan was the epitome of the violent agents against African American rights. Other groups of whites had organized before the Klan in the South. In Georgia, the Regulators, Black Horse Cavalry, and Jayhawkers were hunting down and shooting blacks in the 1880s. Scores of these organizations appeared all over the South. These were societies with names like the White Line, Knights of the White Camelia, the Pale Faces, White League, Rifle Clubs of South Carolina, and the White Brotherhood. Their aim was to preserve white privilege and re-establish white supremacy in the face of what they saw as the encroachment upon their privileges by African Americans.

Ku Klux Klan

The Ku Klux Klan inherited the mantle of the Knights of the Golden Circle, a secret white organization organized before the Civil War to advance southern interests. Combining the Greek *Ku Klos*, circle, and the English *clan*. The organizers of the Ku Klux Klan met in Pulaski, Tennessee in 1866 to form their secret society.

Soon thereafter, the organization adopted the costumes of an African brotherhood with origins in the Moorish conquest of Spain as their official uniforms, long white robes with hooded caps. The Ku Klux Klan was not a funny organization, it was the vanguard of racial attacks against Africans. Carrying out a campaign of whippings, burnings, bombings, and intimidations, the organization created havoc over the entire South. Since the Klan members generally did its evil at night, it seemed difficult for authorities to capture and convict them for persecuting Africans.

Fourteenth Amendment

Africans had lived in North America for nearly 250 years before significant numbers of whites even came close to wanting the same things that African Americans wanted for themselves. The American Reconstruction Period (1865–1877) was one of the most remarkable periods in the history of an oppressed people. Africans who had mostly worked in agri-

Ku Klux Klan Membership, 1925	
Alabama	115,910
Arizona	5,001
Arkansas	150,000
California	350,000
Colorado	126,930
Connecticut	65,590
Delaware	20,000
District of Columbia	15,133
Florida	391,040
Georgia	156,010
Idaho	30,000
Illinois	300,324
Indiana	200,000
Iowa	350,031
Kansas	150,000
Kentucky	441,560
Louisiana	50,000
Maine	150,041
Maryland	53,190
Massachusetts	130,780
Michigan	875,130
Minnesota	65,000
Mississippi	93,040
Missouri	175,000
Montana	40,000
Nebraska	352,110
Nevada	1,003
New Hampshire	75,000
New Jersey	720,220
New Mexico	53,111
New York	300,429
North Carolina	129,410
North Dakota	50,000
Ohio	400,000
Oklahoma	239,550
Oregon	150,000
Pennsylvania	300,000
Rhode Island	21,321
South Carolina	200,641
South Dakota	54,329
Tennessee	163,980
Texas	450,000
Utah	20,000
Vermont	80,301
Virginia	169,630
Washington	150,000
West Virginia	75,903
Wisconsin	220,850
Wyoming	24989
Total Membership	**8,902,487**

culture also became successful as owners of their own farms; others served in state legislatures and succeeded in passing legislation that guaranteed public education for all children, still others were judges, congressmen, and senators who represented the best interests of their constituents, black as well as white.

The Fourteenth Amendment introduced the word "equal" into the Constitution and the Fifteenth declared that no person should be denied the vote on account of race, color, or previous condition of servitude. This legal foundation for the idea of equality was erected with the full participation of Africans in private and public consultations and assemblies.

However valiant the African-American heroines and heroes were in defense of the just right of Africans to be treated fairly and equally in the American society, they did not succeed during the Reconstruction Period. Indeed, DuBois, the eminent scholar, could write in *The Souls of Black Folk:* "despite compromise, war, and struggle, the Negro is not free."

Vigorous campaigns against injustice and for equality for all have characterized the legendary struggles of Africans in America; always aiming to make the nation more responsive to the moral dimensions of its own grand vision. Reconstruction, nobly conceived by a few and bitterly opposed by the many, was for all practical purposes a failure. The federal government abandoned the recently freed Africans to conditions defined by white southerners; refused to seriously consider granting the freed African "forty acres of land and a mule;" and consigned the defenseless Africans to a life of sharecropping for whites.

While the myth abounds of a radical reconstruction movement led by Africans to take over the South, this is far from the truth. Only in the state of South Carolina during one session of the lower house did Africans form a majority. During the

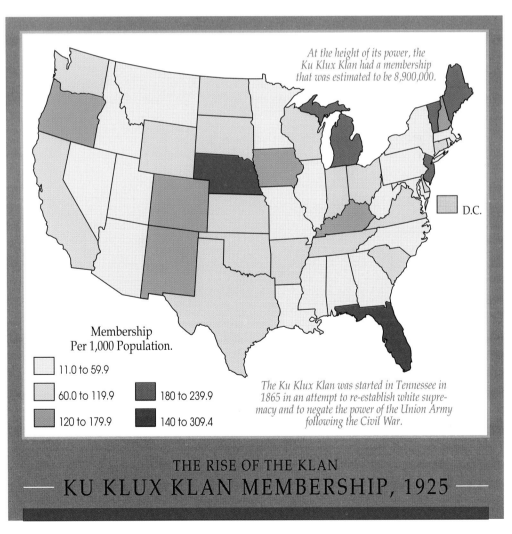

At the height of its power, the Ku Klux Klan had a membership that was estimated to be 8,900,000.

D.C.

Membership Per 1,000 Population.

11.0 to 59.9

60.0 to 119.9

120 to 179.9

180 to 239.9

140 to 309.4

The Ku Klux Klan was started in Tennessee in 1865 in an attempt to re-establish white supremacy and to negate the power of the Union Army following the Civil War.

THE RISE OF THE KLAN
— KU KLUX KLAN MEMBERSHIP, 1925 —

twelve years of Reconstruction there was neither a black governor nor a black majority on any state board governing hospitals, prisons, or universities. In effect, fear and apprehension of Africans were responsible for much of what whites wrote about the Reconstruction Period. In fact, Africans sought to make America what it has always said it wanted to be, but they were not to succeed. The 1877 Compromise was to lead to the withdrawal of the United States Army from the South and the abandonment of the Africans to violent attacks of the Ku Klux Klan. Reconstruction would come to an end and it would be nearly one hundred years before another movement to bring equality would emerge; it would then be called the Civil Rights Movement.

Plessy v. Ferguson

In the famous case of *Plessy v. Ferguson* in 1896 the Supreme Court was asked by Homer Adolph Plessy to decide the constitutionality of Louisiana's Jim Crow law.

Plessy was arrested for riding in the "white" section of the railway coach while on a sixty-mile stretch from New Orleans to Covington, Louisiana. His refusal to sit in the Jim Crow section was illegal under Louisiana law which required "equal but separate accommodations for the white and colored races" in public facilities. The defendant in the case, Ferguson, was the Louisiana judge who conducted the trial on criminal charges. The counsel for Plessy was Albion W. Tourgee, a white lawyer from upstate New York who had been a judge briefly in North Carolina during Reconstruction. In his brief to the Supreme Court, Tourgee said, "Justice is pictured blind and her daughter, the Law, ought at least to be colorblind." The only dissenting justice, John Marshall Harlan, caught this phrase in his dissent and reduced it to "Our Constitution is colorblind."

The United States Supreme Court declared that the action brought by Plessy was under the provision of the Fourteenth Amendment which required, according to the court, only that separate accommodations be equal. The Court had sanctioned

segregation as the law of the land. This law remained in force for fifty-eight years until 1954.

New Governments

The ten occupied southern states registered 700,000 black and 660,000 whites to vote in the elections held in 1867 and 1868. Registration figures indicate that many whites refused to vote although they constituted a majority of the population. Many northerners, whites and some blacks, came south to assist the freed persons. Lawyers, teachers, businessmen, and federal officials, with their carpetbag suitcases, thus the name "carpetbaggers," entered the South to help reconstruct the society. While some opportunists were among them, most were dedicated to improving the educational and economic lot of Africans recently freed.

Among the African Americans elected to office were two who represented the state of Mississippi in the United States Senate. Hiram Revels represented Mississippi for a partial term of 1870–1871 and Blanche Kelso Bruce for a full term of 1875–1881. Twenty blacks were in the U.S. House of Representatives between 1869–1901. Scores of blacks served in state legislatures and as state treasurers, lieutenant governors, and school superintendents and clerks. Lieutenant Governor P. B. S. Pinchback served as Governor of Louisiana for forty-three days when the Governor was removed from office. The only African to serve on a state supreme court was Justice Jonathan Jasper Wright of South Carolina. Although the great majority of Africans were illiterate, those who were elected to high office were usually educated. Senator Revels, for example, had been born free in North Carolina, attended Knox College in Illinois, and had been a school principal in Baltimore before settling in Mississippi. Senator Bruce was born enslaved in Virginia but escaped to Ohio where he attended Oberlin College before settling in Mississippi. He became a planter, sheriff, state legislator, and county school superintendent. Governor Pinchback was the son of a white father

and black mother. Set free by his father, he attended school in Cincinnati but had to withdraw when the white relatives of his father robbed his mother of the property which had been given to her and the ten children she bore for him. Pinchback worked on river boats, enlisted in the Union Army and rose to Captain in the Louisiana Native Guards. Not all of the Africans elected to office had such worldly credentials as these three but they were by no means an illiterate group of politicians as depicted in the highly controversial film "Birth of a Nation."

African Americans went to the polls to vote in elections with tremendous excitement. Having been denied the freedom to vote in democratic elections in a nation that was based upon the idea of democracy, the campaigns and elections were the greatest gifts to a long mistreated people. Savoring their right to vote, many African Americans risked their lives and futures by going to the polls despite threats and harrassments.

Mississippi elected a remarkable group of politicians between 1868 and 1874. The state legislature undertook to construct an economic system that would assist in pulling the state out of an economic crisis of the first order. The state had been virtually wiped out during the Civil War. Perhaps not even Georgia, with General Sherman's March to Savannah, suffered so much physical destruction as Mississippi. The state still lay in waste when the 40 black and 120 white state legislators took control of both houses in 1872. Earlier in 1868, at a constitutional convention, sixteen African Americans and eighty-four whites had worked out a new constitutional document which included provisions against racial discrimination and property qualifications for juries and suffrage.

The achievements of these reform-minded individuals were stunning under the circumstances. They reorganized the University of Mississippi, created a biracial educational system and voted to finance it, established two schools for African Americans, and set up one university for the training of African American professionals.

In this state, one of the most wedded to the slavocracy, public accommodations were opened to all without regard to race or color. So advanced was the state legislature that new facilities for the handicapped were also voted on and funded.

Some of the giants of the Reconstruction Period served here. John K. Lynch served as the speaker of the Mississippi lower house, T. W. Cardozo was superintendent of education, James Hill was secretary of state, and A. K. Davis was lieutenant governor. Only three African Americans have ever served in the United States Senate, two were from Mississippi. When Edward W. Brooke (R., Massachussets) was elected in 1966, he joined the limited company of Hiram Revels and Blanche K. Bruce.

Revels' record and qualifications were superior in his day. He had served in the Union Army, studied in seminary, and rose to the post of presiding elder in the African Methodist Church before he was elected to the Natchez City Council.

On January 20, 1870, the Mississippi legislature agreed, after petitions from the black community to elect Revels to fill the unexpired U.S. Senate term of Confederate President Jefferson Davis. Revels was popular among the African American community and was well liked because of his generous nature. At the age of 42, Revels became the first African American Senator in history. Acceptance by his Senate colleagues was not certain, however.

Pressure from the black community was constant and consistent. Revels was the best person qualified for the post. It took three days of debate over Revels' qualifications to settle the issue. When the election was finally held, the United States Senate voted overwhelmingly to seat the first African American Senator. The public galleries broke out in joyous celebrations as Hiram Revels walked down the aisle for his swearing in ceremony. The date was Friday, February 25, 1870.

Blanche Bruce, Mississippi's second African American U.S. Senator, served from 1875 to 1881. He was well educated and possessed impressive oratorical skills.

Bruce had served in a number of government posts in the state of Mississippi prior to becoming a Senator. He was sergeant-at-arms of the state senate, tax assessor for Bolivar County, and sheriff. He also served as superintendent of public schools. By the time of his 1874 election, Bruce owned a one thousand acre farm.

Bruce was known as a spokesperson for the African American community but also made his mark in the Senate in support of the rights of other oppressed groups. He introduced numerous bills intended to improve the lives of African Americans; he castigated the United States for its treatment of the Native Americans; and he gave speeches against the bill which restricted Chinese immigration. Bruce was one of the most respected members of the Senate. He was proposed for the Vice Presidency in 1880. He withdrew in favor of Chester A. Arthur, who later became the president of the United States. Bruce was eventually appointed registrar of the United States Treasury by President James A. Garfield.

Grandfather Clause

As soon as the Union Army withdrew from the South, the life and liberty of African Americans were at risk. Southern states found ways to render the thirteenth, fourteenth, and fifteenth amendments useless. The Fifteenth Amendment (1870) said "the right . . . to vote" could not be taken away because of "race, color, or previous condition of servitude." However, each of the southern states, led by Mississippi and South Carolina, devised novel responses to African American citizenship and voting rights. Most states employed three devices to eliminate African American voters from the polls: criminal convictions; poll taxes; and literacy tests. The state of Mississippi changed its constitution in 1890 to bar any person "convicted of bribery, burglary, theft, arson, obtaining money or goods under false pretenses, perjury, forgery, embezzlement or bigamy" from voting. To deprive Africans of the right to vote, the white officials often arrested

blacks and convicted them of offenses to remove them from the voting rolls. Whites who actually committed such offenses were overlooked. In addition to the criminal offense device, the states required a poll tax to be paid usually nine months before the election, thus, in Mississippi the tax had to be paid in February and the election was held in November. The voter had to bring the receipt indicating payment to the polling place. Many African Americans were unable to pay the poll tax which was cumulative, that is, if a voter wanted to vote the poll tax for previous years had to be paid as well. Many more individuals, due to living conditions, were unable to keep the receipts for nine months. These receipts were often lost or misplaced between February and November. A potential voter with no criminal record, who had paid the poll tax and kept the receipt still faced an additional test. The person would have to demonstrate that he or she could read and interpret sections of the state constitution. Many educated African Americans were denied the right to vote because the registrar was the sole judge.

Whites who may have lost their right to vote if the same rules were applied to them escaped disfranchisement because of laws the southerners referred to as "grandfather clauses." Louisiana passed such a law in 1898 when it became the third state to change its constitution to keep African Americans from voting.

The Louisiana law read in part: "No male person who was on January 1st, 1867 or at any date prior thereto, entitled to vote . . . and no son or grandson of any such person. . . . shall be denied the right to register and vote." Since blacks could not vote until after March 2, 1867, the law was discriminatory against virtually every African American in the state. Other states passed similar laws.

Sika Futuro, "Gold Dust,"
Ghana, Africa

"NOW AIN'T THEM HARD TRIALS": 9
A NEW REPRESSION COMETH

In reaction to the end of Reconstruction, many southern states enacted repressive legislation with the aim of disfranchising Africans. By 1879, many people felt compelled to leave the South. The years from 1890–1910 became the anvil upon which the rights of Africans were crushed.

Africans had gone through severe political repression and oppression from the very origins of the English settlements. However, free Africans had been able to vote in every one of the thirteen states except Georgia and South Carolina. In 1792, the state of Delaware enacted the first legislation against free Africans voting. This was followed by Maryland, Virginia, and finally Connecticut in 1814, legislated against free Africans voting. By the time of the Civil War, called by some the "Uncivil War," only five states in New England and, under certain limitations, the state of New York, allowed free Africans to vote.

The war brought new realities to the South. Indeed, the consequences were to be found in the Thirteenth Amendment to the Constitution which abolished slavery, the Fourteenth Amendment which gave citizenship to formerly enslaved Africans, and the Fifteenth Amendment which protected the right to vote.

Yet the southern reaction to the Reconstruction, with its mixture of achievements and failures largely due to lack of education, harassment by whites, and inadequate financing, was swift and brutal. All over the South in the decade from 1870–1880, white thefts, assaults, intimidations, suppression of ballot boxes, removal of polls to secret places, false certifications, and lynchings conspired to deny the African the right to vote.

The white northerners became interested in material advantages in the South and left the Africans to the conscience of the white southerner. In little or no time the evil peonage system was put into effect. Peonage meant that an African could be arrested for the smallest offense and in many cases people were arrested for no offense and made to work for white landowners and businessmen. This outgrowth of the convict lease system continued many of the labor traditions of the plantation era.

Share-cropping was introduced to ensnare the labor of Africans who had committed no offenses but who were needed by white landowners to sow and harvest their crops. When Africans became satisfied with their share of the share system and sought to leave the farms, whites enacted new laws to make it technically illegal for an African to

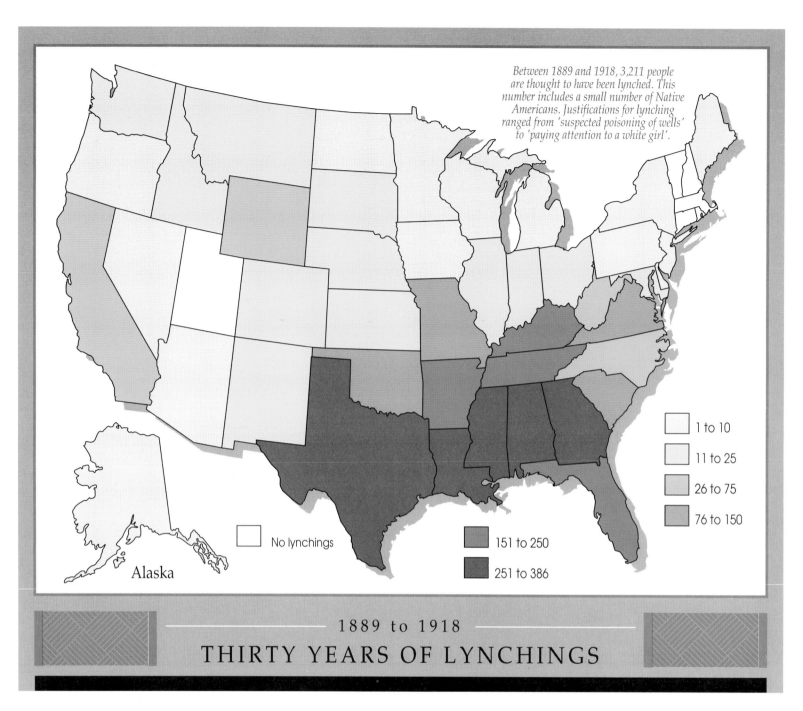

Between 1889 and 1918, 3,211 people are thought to have been lynched. This number includes a small number of Native Americans. Justifications for lynching ranged from 'suspected poisoning of wells' to 'paying attention to a white girl'.

	1 to 10
	11 to 25
	26 to 75
	76 to 150
	151 to 250
	251 to 386

No lynchings

Alaska

1889 to 1918

THIRTY YEARS OF LYNCHINGS

leave the employ of a white. In effect, slavery under the guise of a share system deprived Africans of labor and profits and threatened their lives.

In 1890, Mississippi became the first state after the Civil War to legislate to disfranchise Africans. Five years later, South Carolina amended its constitution with similar effect. However, it was left to Louisiana to invent the "grandfather clause" in 1898. This legislation excused descendants of men who had voted before the Civil War, thereby allowing illiterate whites without property and payment of poll tax to vote. North Caro-

lina in 1900, Virginia and Alabama in 1901, Georgia in 1907, and Oklahoma in 1910 painstakingly disfranchised Africans while skirting the Fifteenth Amendment.

Lynchings

The lynchings of Africans in the South became one of the greatest blots on the American society at the end of the nineteenth and beginning of the twentieth century. In 1872, twelve Africans were lynched, twenty years later in 1892 the number had reached 255. Benjamin Brawley claims that "within a period of thirty-five years not less than 3,200 Negro men

and women were lynched within the boundaries of the United States, and sometimes the burning or mutilation of the victims was savage in its brutality" (Brawley 1924).

Exploitation of African labor could not exist without deprivation of political rights and denial of justice in the courts. Thus, the South promulgated everywhere the idea of African inferiority and established that idea by providing inferior services and wages. Prisons proliferated to "break" the Africans who refused to bow to inferior treatment. In every sector of society—education, economics, and

Lynchings, 1889–1918

Alabama	276
Alaska	4
Arizona	8
Arkansas	214
California	26
Colorado	18
Connecticut	0
Delaware	1
Florida	178
Georgia	386
Idaho	11
Illinois	24
Indiana	19
Iowa	8
Kansas	22
Kentucky	27
Louisiana	313
Maine	1
Maryland	4
Massachusetts	0
Michigan	4
Minnesota	4
Mississippi	373
Missouri	81
Montana	22
Nebraska	17
Nevada	4
New Hampshire	0
New Jersey	3
New Mexico	13
New York	3
North Carolina	22
North Dakota	2
Ohio	12
Oklahoma	96
Oregon	4
Pennsylvania	4
Rhode Island	0
South Carolina	120
South Dakota	13
Tennessee	196
Texas	335
Utah	0
Vermont	0
Virginia	78
Washington	16
West Virginia	11
Wisconsin	4
Wyoming	34

Indiana Lynching, 1920s

Lucy Stone

Lucretia Mott

law—the Africans were given less and treated harshly. Whites became alarmed at the human being their policies had created. Simultaneously, whites feared and envied the freedom, virility, passion, and temperament of the African.

By 1893, white mobs lynched an African a day. Crime against a white woman was the reason most frequently given as to what justified the lynching. However, Brawley says that "this did not figure in more than 30 percent of the cases recorded" over a thirty year period. The most common cause seems to be murder growing out of disputes over wages. Ida B. Wells and Booker T. Washington made the prohibition of lynching one of the most important topics of the early twentieth century.

The situation did not moderate with the entry of the United States in the First World War. When the war was over and African American soldiers came home, they were met with the same segregation and racism they had left behind.

The Crisis Magazine, published by the National Association for the Advancement of Colored People, spoke for the returning soldiers in one of its editorial pages: "This country of ours, despite all its better souls have done and dream, is yet a shameful land. It lynches . . . It disfranchises its own citizens . . . It encourages ignorance . . . It steals from us . . . It insults us . . . We return. We return from fighting. We return fighting. Make way for Democracy! We saved it in France, and by the Great Jehovah, we will save it in the U.S.A., or know the reason why" (Brawley 1924).

Booker T. Washington

Booker T. Washington sat astride African-American education for an entire generation. The ramifications of his achievements were felt in every sector of the American society. Washington was the first "Negro spokesman" after the Reconstruction period. Born in West Virginia during the reign of slavery, he was educated at Hampton Institute and later founded Tuskegee Institute in Alabama. From this past, Booker T. Washington emerged as a national leader with a reputation far beyond the hamlet of his birth.

Washington was greeted by kings, queens, and presidents as the African-American leader. Washington was consulted whenever anyone sought facts or opinions on questions related to African Americans. Consequently, his impact on African-American education was impressive. During the Washingtonian era, it seemed little Tuskegees were being established everywhere, would-be African-American leaders or educators modeled their styles after him, and major philanthropists endowed him with financial support for his institution.

His philosophy, stated in several books and hundreds of speeches, was straightforward: education of the hands and hearts for work and discipline was more important than political or social rights. This philosophy often threw him into conflict with African Americans from the North, such as W. Monroe Trotter and W. E. B. DuBois. They believed that political and civil rights were necessary to assure that whatever economic gains were achieved would be secured. DuBois, for example, contended the right of African Americans to vote was fundamental to a democratic society.

Despite his detractors on many issues, Washington pressed ahead on creating a population of Africans in the South who would be self-sufficient and economically capable. Failure to recognize the intractability of racism in the South and throughout the nation, and to adequately prepare students to resist the intellectual and cultural attacks on Africans may have been his most serious flaw. Nevertheless, African-American education cannot be discussed in any meaningful way without comment on Booker T. Washington, who died in 1915.

Booker T. Washington

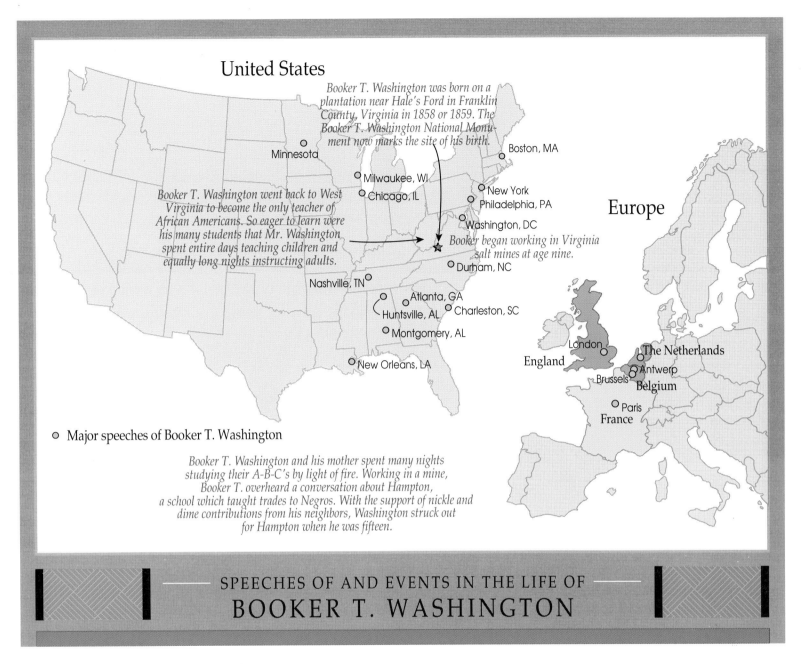

United States

Booker T. Washington was born on a plantation near Hale's Ford in Franklin County, Virginia in 1858 or 1859. The Booker T. Washington National Monument now marks the site of his birth.

Booker T. Washington went back to West Virginia to become the only teacher of African Americans. So eager to learn were his many students that Mr. Washington spent entire days teaching children and equally long nights instructing adults.

Booker began working in Virginia salt mines at age nine.

Minnesota

Boston, MA

Milwaukee, WI

Chicago, IL

New York

Philadelphia, PA

Washington, DC

Durham, NC

Nashville, TN

Atlanta, GA

Huntsville, AL

Charleston, SC

Montgomery, AL

New Orleans, LA

Europe

England

London

The Netherlands

Antwerp

Brussels

Belgium

Paris

France

○ Major speeches of Booker T. Washington

Booker T. Washington and his mother spent many nights studying their A-B-C's by light of fire. Working in a mine, Booker T. overheard a conversation about Hampton, a school which taught trades to Negros. With the support of nickle and dime contributions from his neighbors, Washington struck out for Hampton when he was fifteen.

SPEECHES OF AND EVENTS IN THE LIFE OF

BOOKER T. WASHINGTON

Ida B. Wells Barnett

Born in Holly Springs, Mississippi in 1862, Ida B. Wells began to teach in a country school at the age of 14. Moving to Memphis in 1884, she continued to teach while attending Fisk University in Nashville during the summer. Due to a law suit involving her refusal to give up her seat in a railroad car designated for "whites only," Wells lost her teaching job and subsequently turned to journalism. For a time she wrote for a local Afro-American weekly, *Living Word*, and in 1891 she became co-owner and editor of the Memphis weekly, *Free Speech*. A year later, after she revealed in print who was responsible for the lynching of

three Memphis Afro-Americans, a mob of whites demolished her printing press and office. Wells fled to New York City—where she was hired by an Afro-American weekly—and launched into an antilynching campaign. The antilynching cause took her on lecture tours across the country and to England twice. Later Wells settled in Chicago and in 1895 she married Ferdinand L. Barnett. In Chicago, she contributed to newspapers and periodicals and also founded and headed the Ida B. Wells Club. In 1898, Wells led a delegation to President William McKinley to protest lynchings, and that same year she became the secretary of the national Afro-American

Council. Some ten years later Wells founded the Negro Fellowship League. In 1913, she was appointed adult probation officer in Chicago, and two years later she was elected vice-president of Chicago's Equal Rights League.

The State of Tennessee has recognized Ida B. Wells Barnett as one of its leading historical figures in communication. Few states can boast of someone as bold and brave as Ida B. Wells Barnett. In her prime she fought against all anti-African people, convinced that the African American people needed to defend themselves. She had been blessed with the ability to write and felt that it was her responsibility to take on the challenge of eradicating ignorance

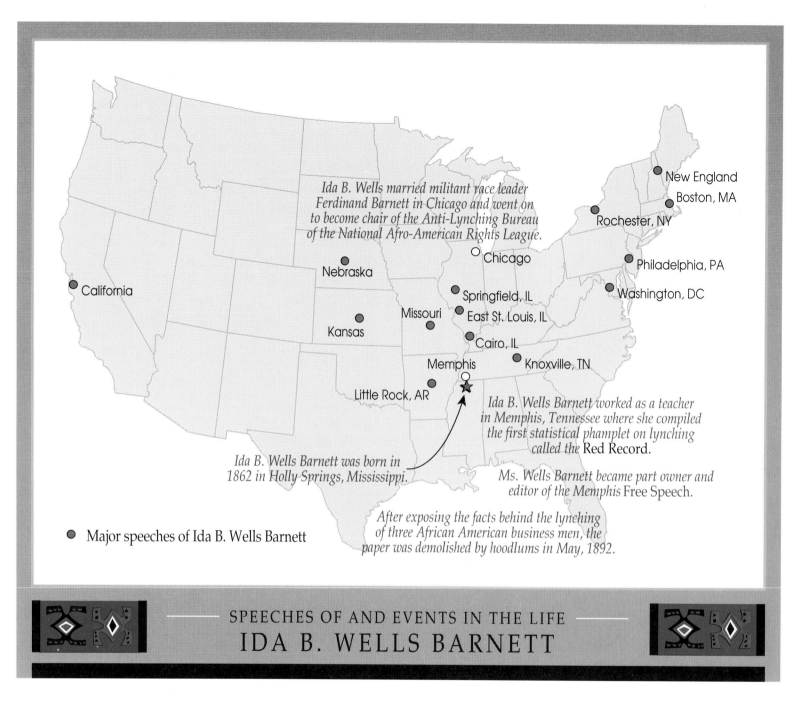

Ida B. Wells married militant race leader Ferdinand Barnett in Chicago and went on to become chair of the Anti-Lynching Bureau of the National Afro-American Rights League.

New England
Boston, MA
Rochester, NY
Chicago
Nebraska
Philadelphia, PA
California
Springfield, IL
Washington, DC
Missouri
East St. Louis, IL
Kansas
Cairo, IL
Memphis
Knoxville, TN
Little Rock, AR

Ida B. Wells Barnett worked as a teacher in Memphis, Tennessee where she compiled the first statistical phamplet on lynching called the Red Record.

Ida B. Wells Barnett was born in 1862 in Holly Springs, Mississippi.

Ms. Wells Barnett became part owner and editor of the Memphis Free Speech.

After exposing the facts behind the lynching of three African American business men, the paper was demolished by hoodlums in May, 1892.

● Major speeches of Ida B. Wells Barnett

SPEECHES OF AND EVENTS IN THE LIFE
IDA B. WELLS BARNETT

but most of all saving the innocent lives of African American people who were lynched as a matter of amusement. Never fearful of her own life (though she was placed in some difficult situations), Barnett could only think of the mutilated bodies of black men and women that she had seen in the South. These sights alone were enough to give her all of the courage and boldness she needed.

The combination of the enterprising and courageous Ida B. Wells Barnett and Booker T. Washington was a powerful union of spirit and purpose. They both worked to get an antilynching bill

passed. The difficulty this bill met in the United States Congress demonstrated the plight of the African American. With no one really defending the rights of the African, the antilynch law was certain never to see the light of day during the height of lynch law in the South. The lobby against the law was very strong and numerous attempts were made to force the Congress to abandon discussion of it. By now the Klan had grown to an organization of more than 100,000 white-hooded knights. They had made more than 200 appearances and seemed to flourish in the South and North Cen-

tral States. Booker T. Washington took strong exceptions to the Klan and joined Ida B. Wells Barnett in supporting the antilynch legislation.

The African American people have been tremendously tested by the circumstances of living in the United States. Yet in every generation there have been men and women who have taken up the task of fighting against injustices. The Grimké family was famous for its commitment to truth. Strong convictions led Angela Grimké to write poetry and Charlotte Forten Grimké to write essays. The Grimkés were stalwarts against any kind

Ida B. Wells Barnett

of discrimination. An important aspect of the sense of eventual victory over segregation was the African American's vital belief that conditions can get better. With this faith the justice pioneers could go from victory to victory with confidence.

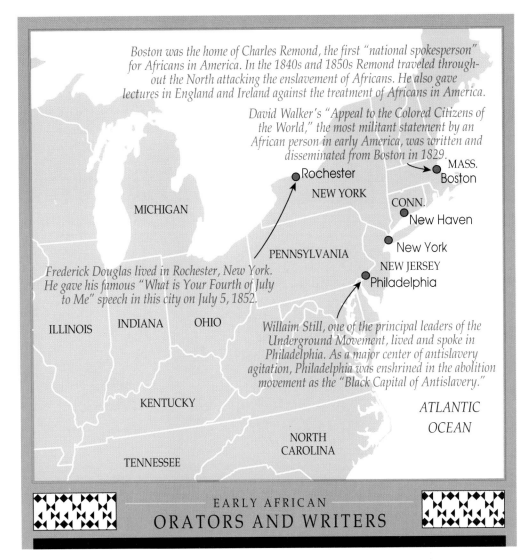

Boston was the home of Charles Remond, the first "national spokesperson" for Africans in America. In the 1840s and 1850s Remond traveled throughout the North attacking the enslavement of Africans. He also gave lectures in England and Ireland against the treatment of Africans in America.

David Walker's "Appeal to the Colored Citizens of the World," the most militant statement by an African person in early America, was written and disseminated from Boston in 1829.

Frederick Douglas lived in Rochester, New York. He gave his famous "What is Your Fourth of July to Me" speech in this city on July 5, 1852.

Willaim Still, one of the principal leaders of the Underground Movement, lived and spoke in Philadelphia. As a major center of antislavery agitation, Philadelphia was enshrined in the abolition movement as the "Black Capital of Antislavery."

EARLY AFRICAN
ORATORS AND WRITERS

Charlotte L. Forten Grimké

A. H. Grimké

F. J. Grimké

Akyeapim, "A Thousand Shields Will Protect Me,"
Ghana, Africa

"I'M GOING TO STAND THERE": IN DEFIANCE OF SEGREGATION 10

The achievements of African Americans in the arts, education, science, business, religion, and industry have been extraordinary within the context of the historical realities. Up from the valley of despair, African Americans have erected the banners of hope and human will in many different arenas. What is America without the names and accomplishments of Paul Robeson, Katherine Dunham, John Biggers, Elizabeth Catlett, Billie Holiday, Max Roach, Wynton Marsalis, John Coltrane, Duke Ellington, Sammy Davis, Jr., Josephine Baker, Alvin Ailey, Pearl Primus, Michael Jackson, Miles Davis, Stevie Wonder, Ira Aldridge, Bill Cosby, Sidney Poitier, and Harry Belafonte? It is impossible to think seriously about literature without considering the significant works of Ralph Ellison, Toni Morrison, Langston Hughes, Alice Walker, Sonja Sanchez, Charles Fuller, Toni Cade Bambara, Gloria Naylor, Rita Dove, Mari Evans, Gwendolyn Brooks, August Wilson, Ed Bullins, James Baldwin, Richard Wright, Paul Laurence Dunbar, Carlton Molette, Sterling Brown, Zora Neale Hurston, Langston Hughes, John Edgar Wideman, and Imamu Baraka.

In every field of human endeavor, African Americans have made lasting impressions. The stand taken by scholars, artists, writers, and educators has been based upon the social and political order in America. As Martin Luther King, Jr. reminded his African American audiences, "We are in America, and we are in America to stay." King was giving voice to the generally accepted belief that the vast majority of African Americans will always be domiciled in the United States. In taking a stand to participate in the American arena, African Americans have fought in all of the wars, made contributions in every sphere, and sought to make the dream of equality a reality within the American society.

Faced with enormous challenges to the human spirit, Africans have often thought it impossible to realize the dream in America. No intellectual, social, or political idea has escaped the thinking of the best minds of the population regarding the plight and condition of African Americans.

The personalities who have given their intellectual resources to the problems confronting African Americans are a veritable panoply of brilliant and articulate leaders: Charles Remond, David Walker, Frederick Douglass, Anna Julia Cooper, Henry Highland Garnet, T. Timothy Fortune, R. C. Benjamin, George T. Downing, Ida B. Wells, Mary Ann Shadd, Marcus Garvey, A. Philip Randolph, Roy Wilkins, Mary McLeod Bethune, W. E. B.

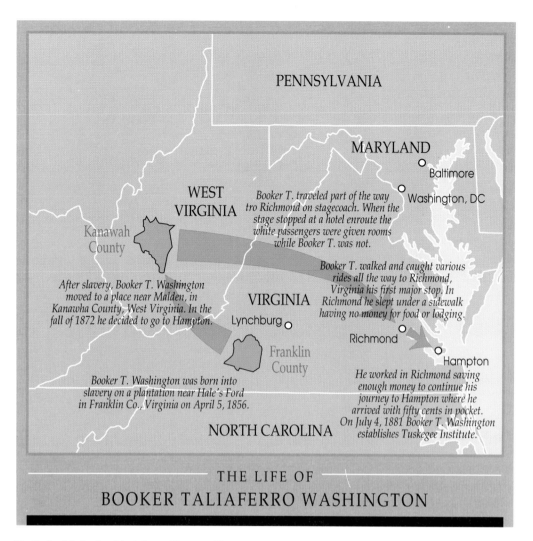

PENNSYLVANIA

MARYLAND

○ Baltimore

WEST VIRGINIA

Booker T. traveled part of the way tro Richmond on stagecoach. When the stage stopped at a hotel enroute the white passengers were given rooms while Booker T. was not.

○ Washington, DC

Kanawah County

After slavery, Booker T. Washington moved to a place near Malden, in Kanawha County, West Virginia. In the fall of 1872 he decided to go to Hampton.

Booker T. walked and caught various rides all the way to Richmond, Virginia his first major stop. In Richmond he slept under a sidewalk having no money for food or lodging.

VIRGINIA

Lynchburg ○

Richmond ○

○ Hampton

Franklin County

Booker T. Washington was born into slavery on a plantation near Hale's Ford in Franklin Co., Virginia on April 5, 1856.

He worked in Richmond saving enough money to continue his journey to Hampton where he arrived with fifty cents in pocket. On July 4, 1881 Booker T. Washington establishes Tuskegee Institute.

NORTH CAROLINA

THE LIFE OF
BOOKER TALIAFERRO WASHINGTON

DuBois, Malcolm X, Adam Clayton Powell, are just a few of the courageous men and women who have sought to make America responsive to the needs of the African American population.

The two social and political champions of the twentieth century were supported by the growing disenchantment among Africans in the urban areas of the North. Thus, Marcus Garvey and W. E. B. DuBois found the source of their inspiration among the northern communities, each finding a different group of northerners for his power base. On the other hand, Booker T. Washington had already established himself as the agrarian apostle, believing that it was better for African Americans to perfect the working with hands in order to control industry and agriculture.

Garvey arrived in the United States in 1916, a year after Washington's death. He had admired him from afar and hoped to appeal to the same common

people as Washington. DuBois, college educated and erudite, found that he could best serve by continuing the line of thinking he had embarked on during Washington's lifetime.

Moving On Up

The generation of African Americans who lived in the first quarter of the twentieth century experienced a period of severe discrimination and injustice. With hardly any support from the federal government, they struggled to maintain homes and institutions under extreme conditions. White control of the South, sanctioned by the federal government, meant that Africans were not legally protected from the most overt kinds of racism. Any white person could insult any black person with impunity. By the turn of the century, the segregation mode introduced as custom in the South had attained legal status almost everywhere in the region. Africans suf-

fered most from the inequities of the justice system.

The fact that the South had lost the war created a strong residual element of irrational hatred for Africans. Since the whites could not punish the federal government, they could certainly punish African Americans at will and dare the federal government to interfere with their states' rights to treat Africans any way they pleased. Furthermore, having lost the free African labor, the whites resented the fact that they now had to pay Africans for work that was once done by enslaved Africans. So the justice system was the stage for southern victories over northern sentiments.

For instance, even though the Supreme Court ruled that blacks had to be allowed on juries; in practice, it almost never occurred.

The structure of racial segregation did not develop immediately after Reconstruction but it was gradually put in place by a series of complicated laws and maneuvers that had the effect of totally reducing the African to a slave within the framework of law. Much like the South African apartheid system was to become, the segregation system of the South made everything legal. Prohibition against the African community was sanctioned by the law of the city or state. In this manner, segregation was made legal. It was illegal for Africans to sleep in the same house with whites. It was illegal for Africans to attend theatres with whites, and so forth. Severe penalties would be exacted from Africans who violated the laws that had been set up to enforce segregation; many Africans paid the penalty of death for dignity.

In 1901, Congressman George White delivered his farewell address to Congress by saying that it was in behalf "of an outraged, heart-broken, bruised and bleeding, but God-fearing people, faithful, industrious, loyal people—rising people, full of force." It would be more than a quarter of a century before an African would again serve in the Congress. Oscar De Priest, a Republican, would be elected congressman from Chicago in 1928, the first African American to be elected from a northern state.

Conditions became so desperate in the early part of the twentieth century that white philanthropists held several meetings of leading Africans to discuss the problems confronting the community. In 1904, John D. Rockefeller began donating large sums to train teachers for the African American community. During the next year, Andrew Carnegie called a meeting of black leaders which included Booker T. Washington and W. E. B. DuBois.

The proposals from that conference included a resolution to press for absolute civil, political, and public equality. DuBois was clearly in conflict with Washington's more conciliatory method. Thus, when the Niagara Movement was formed in 1905 with a representation that included twenty-nine militant African American intellectuals from fourteen states, it was in clear opposition to Booker T. Washington. When members of this group later formed the National Association for the Advancement of Colored People in 1909, Washington voiced his opposition.

The NAACP charter was signed by several prominent individuals including DuBois, Jane Addams, John Dewey, Willam Dean Howells, and Lincoln Steffens. Signers of the NAACP charter understood the fragile nature of the African's life in the United States. They knew that despite the political rights that Africans were supposed to have in the North, these rights were often unavailable. Some states did not permit Africans to vote in the same manner as whites until the Fifteenth Amendment had been passed. Now in the twentieth century there were rights which had to be reinforced and tried on a regular basis before they became acceptable to white northerners. Political rights, shaky as they may have been in some northern states, were not quite as difficult to at-

W. E. B. DuBois

tain as civil rights. Segregated riding coaches persisted into the twentieth century in some northern communities; residential segregation was still practiced; and Africans could often be discriminated against in public accommodations in northern cities. As soon as African Americans began to hold posts in city governments and on the judiciary in the north, political rights led to some limited

protection for civil rights. What the mass of Africans discovered was that laws on the books did not necessarily mean better living conditions. Outright public hostility toward Africans often carried more weight than the law. If white citizens rose up against the granting of some right to Africans, many times the right was rescinded.

Economically, the African American

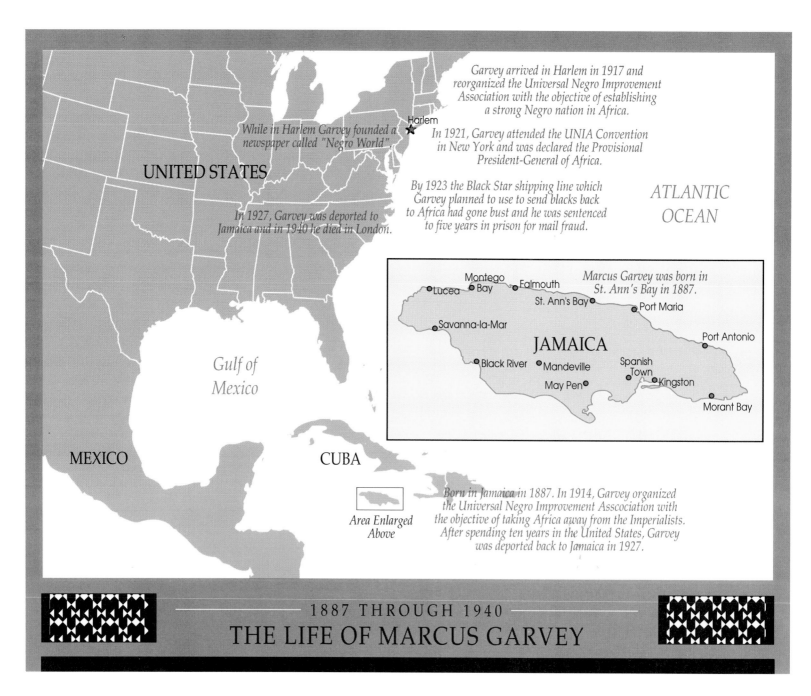

Garvey arrived in Harlem in 1917 and reorganized the Universal Negro Improvement Association with the objective of establishing a strong Negro nation in Africa.

While in Harlem Garvey founded a newspaper called "Negro World".

In 1921, Garvey attended the UNIA Convention in New York and was declared the Provisional President-General of Africa.

In 1927, Garvey was deported to Jamaica and in 1940 he died in London.

By 1923 the Black Star shipping line which Garvey planned to use to send blacks back to Africa had gone bust and he was sentenced to five years in prison for mail fraud.

UNITED STATES

ATLANTIC OCEAN

Gulf of Mexico

MEXICO

CUBA

Marcus Garvey was born in St. Ann's Bay in 1887.

JAMAICA

Montego Bay · Lucea · Falmouth · St. Ann's Bay · Port Maria · Savanna-la-Mar · Port Antonio · Black River · Mandeville · Spanish Town · Kingston · May Pen · Morant Bay

Area Enlarged Above

Born in Jamaica in 1887. In 1914, Garvey organized the Universal Negro Improvement Asscociation with the objective of taking Africa away from the Imperialists. After spending ten years in the United States, Garvey was deported back to Jamaica in 1927.

1887 THROUGH 1940
THE LIFE OF MARCUS GARVEY

worker at the turn of the century was inheriting the whirlwind generated by the anti-African hostility of the post Reconstruction Period. Industrial employers in both the North and the South were discriminatory. Labor unions were hardly any different at the time. Africans were either not hired or if hired given the worst jobs in terms of conditions and pay. Many of the craft unions exercised exclusionistic principles which kept blacks from good paying positions. Instead of protecting all workers, the early unions protected positions for white men only. Actually, the hostility toward African workers was one of the chief reasons for the decline in the number of skilled Africans in the crafts. During the Great Enslavement, the majority of craftsmen in many areas were African. The blacksmiths, carpenters, plasterers, and other tradespeople during the enslavement were most often Africans. This did not change drastically until the post-Reconstruction period, when many immigrants from Europe began to arrive and take the skilled jobs blacks had held.

W. E. B. DuBois

DuBois' name is synonymous with the best in African-American scholarship. No intellectual of his day ranks with him although giants lived among the people: Woodson, Locke, Hurston, Brawley, Frazier. His intellectual life stretches from 1889 to 1963 and covered some of the most momentous times of our history.

Great Barrington, Massachusetts is rather inauspicious in African-American history except for the fact that it is the birthplace of DuBois. That alone has distinguished this tiny village in Massachusetts. From Great Barrington, DuBois traveled to Fisk, Harvard, and Berlin for his education. Fisk infused the young DuBois with the love of learning and gave him a lifetime commitment to the uplift of his people. Harvard and Berlin introduced him to the great minds of the European world and showed him how to secure his own place. When he received his doctorate in 1897, he had established himself as a scholar. His dissertation, "The Suppression of the African Slave Trade" is one of the most widely known dissertations in history.

DuBois left African Americans with legacies of intellect, activism, and devotion of cause. He wrote more than two thousand documents including books, articles, pamphlets, plays, poetry, manifestoes, and protest essays. Like Imhotepian in the breadth of his interests, DuBois' intellectual output established him as a twentieth century leader in history, sociology, and political science. An activist from his student days, he remained committed to erasing color discrimination until his death in Ghana in August 1963. As one of the founders of the National Association for the Advancement of Colored People (NAACP) he promoted the campaign against racial discrimination for nearly fifty years as an active editor for the organization's *Crisis Magazine*.

DuBois taught at Wilberforce University in Ohio and Atlanta University and was a visiting professor at dozens of universities around the world. No major American university ever offered him a permanent post. The University of Pennsylvania made him an assistant (not assistant professor) while he wrote the monumental *The Philadelphia Negro*. Undaunted by racism, DuBois kept the flame of his activism burning against all forms of discrimination. His devotion to cause meant that he applied discipline to every activity in the interest of African-American rights.

Depression

The economic collapse that hammered the United States during the 1930s struck the African-American community with the most brutal blow. Already at the lowest rung of the American economic ladder, the African-American un-

Marcus Garvey

employment figures escalated far beyond their already high percentages. Being the last worker to be hired and the first to be fired, the African-American could count on being out in the cold as the Great Depression bore down on the land.

In 1931, the nation followed the famous Scottsboro trial in the newspapers and on the radio. Nine African American youths were framed in Alabama. They were accused of attacking two white female hoboes. They were fi-

Joe Louis

nally freed. By 1933, Franklin Delano Roosevelt had felt the outrage of the African-American community and moved to hire several people, including the great Mary McLeod Bethune, as a "Black cabinet." Events which would remain in the annals of American history, such as Arthur Mitchell's election to Congress from Chicago as the first African-American Democratic congressman in 1934; Joe Louis' defeat of Braddock in 1937; William Hastie's appointment as a federal judge in the same year; and Marian Anderson's appearance before 75,000 at the Lincoln Memorial could only add to the drama of the era. By 1935, one-sixth of the people on relief were African Americans who constituted about one-tenth of the total United States population.

President Roosevelt skillfully negotiated the social and economic interests of the African-American community. The alphabet soup agencies—W.P.A., Works Progress Administration; C.C.C., Civilian Conservation Corps; and N.Y.A., National Youth Administration—were strongly urged to hire African Americans as consultants and advisors. Wage

A. Philip Randolph

Lena Horne

Paul Robeson

Langston Hughes

differentials based on race were forbidden and the Administration pursued a generally sensitive policy toward African Americans. The masses of the African population became Roosevelt New Deal Democrats and ended the dominance of the Republicans in African-American politics.

Harlem Renaissance

An incredible aura of confidence and creativity occurred in the northern cities as African Americans journeyed to the urban areas during the 1920s. In New York City, the black population produced artists, writers, musicians, orators, dramatists, and entertainers of such great talents and with so much authenticity that the period was called the Harlem Renaissance. In fact, this period in American history was not only significant for the African American community but for the regeneration and rejuvenation of the entire scope of American art and entertainment. Lasting into the 1940s, the Harlem Renaissance was localized in New York but its impact was far-ranging. Displaying the cultural and creative abilities of the African American

Billie Holiday

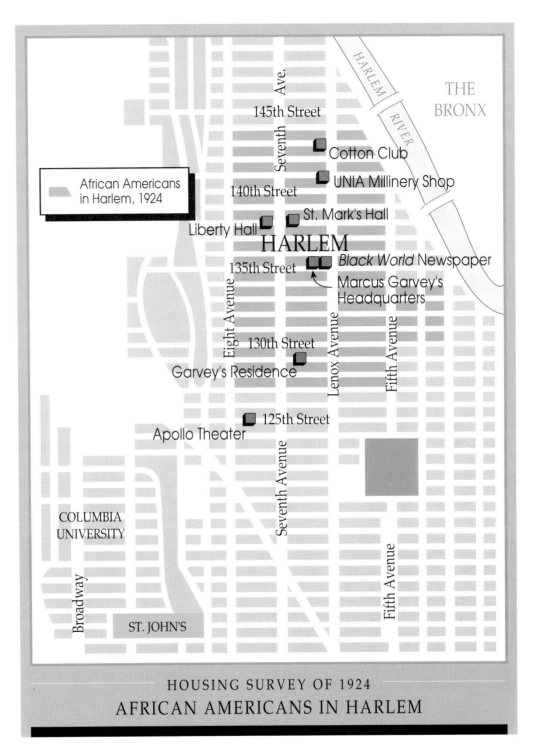

HOUSING SURVEY OF 1924
AFRICAN AMERICANS IN HARLEM

community, writers and artists from various parts of the nation descended upon Harlem. Indeed, the name of the community was synonymous with all that was best in the African American population. Small communities in many cities identified themselves as Harlem. There were Harlem cookies, Harlem books, Harlem behaviors, and Harlem attitudes. Harlem was in vogue. Around the world, people heard the name of Harlem and it was no longer the Dutch city that

people thought of, but the American community made famous from the richness of its culture.

The best of the poets, the jazz and blues classicists, the choreographers and dancers with something new to demonstrate, and the plastic artists and dramatists who wanted to show the world what the African American had achieved in the art world since the Emancipation, came to this community by the droves. This was an upbeat time, the people were optimistic, the rhetoric was visionary, and the streets were lively. The literature of the period was varied and diverse. Langston Hughes and Zora Neal Hurston would be the king and queen of the parade of excellence and their dynamic voices would inspire numerous other poets and writers. Arna Bontemps, Sterling Brown, Robert Hayden, Owen Dodson, Margaret Walker, and Melvin Tolson would enter this chapter of the creative genius of the African Americans either as members of the Harlem community or contributors to its intellectual power. They drew their inspiration from earlier writers such as Countee Cullen, Claude McKay, James Weldon Johnson, Alain Locke, and Benjamin Brawley.

Although the Harlem Renaissance has been discussed in relationship to the influence it had on many white patrons and indeed their influence on the artists and writers of this period, most scholars believe that the Harlem cultural revolution was the single most important movement in the African American art community before the Black Power Sixties. Numerous books have appeared

since the Harlem Renaissance that attest to the making of the critical and creative movement that pushed African American art to the forefront of the American cultural stage.

Among the names that should be on

Percy Julian

the tongues of every American child and certainly names that should be known by all African people are Paul Laurence Dunbar, one of the greatest dialect poets of all time, and Gwendolyn Brooks, the first African American poet to receive a Pulit-

Ruby Dee

Pearl Primus

Richard Wright

Count Basie

Jackson State University, 1952
From top left: Arna Bontemp, Melvin Tolson, Jacob Reddick, Owen Dodson, Robert Hayden. From bottom left: Sterling Brown, Zora Cole Hurston, Margaret Walker, Langston Hughes.

zer Prize for Poetry. They framed the Harlem Renaissance, Dunbar coming just before it, and Brooks coming just after it.

The character of a people is often reflected in the work of their writers. Arna Bontemps was a poet, novelist, and short story writer, whose career spanned the Harlem Renaissance and the early years of the Black Arts Movement. In 1925 he wrote *Golgotha is a Mountain* and received the Alexander Pushkin Award for the poem. Two years later he received the first honors in the *Crisis Magazine* contest for his *Nocturnes at Bethesda*. Among his novels are *Black Thunder, God Sends Sunday*, and *Drums at Dusk*.

Maya Angelou was born in St. Louis in 1928. She has lived in Acrra, Ghana and London, England. She studied African dance with Pearl Primus in the 1950s. Angelou is a multi-talented writer whose works (which were inspired by her own personal history) have created an entirely new biographical genre. Her international fame rests on her major work, *I Know Why the Caged Bird Sings*.

Zora Neale Hurston is by all accounts one of the most important figures in African American letters. She was born in 1903 in Eatonville, Florida. Hurston is the most dominant female figure in the Harlem Renaissance Era. Her legacy is seen today in the writing of Toni Morrison, Alice Walker, Toni Cade Bambara, Kristin Hunter, Gloria Naylor, and Marita Golden. The elements of the Harlem Renaissance period which opened the way for a new interpretation of the African American reality were a commitment to understanding the historical and cultural values which had produced resilience, practical expression of the poetic and narrative qualities of the culture, and a full recognition of the emotional and rational attributes of a people who had raised themselves above the conditions of oppression. It was a self-assertive age. A time of concrete response to the many dimensions of life in the urban communities of the North. But this response, dynamic and spontaneous at first, became in the lengthening years of the Renaissance a more deliberate response. One reason for this type of response had to do with the popularity of the earlier voices, such as Countee Cullen, Claude McKay, Alain Locke.

They made it possible for the voices of Langston Hughes, Arna Bontemps, and Zora Neale Hurston to be more deliberate in their creative responses to the circumstances they encountered later. Commercial success had a lot to do with this inasmuch as they also had sponsors who were capable of giving them money to produce shows, read poetry, write books, or go on trips to investigate cultural and historical phenomena related to African people. Thus, the elements which were responsible in the first place for the outbursts of intellectual and creative energies which were dubbed the Harlem Renaissance were essentially supersede by the new circumstances. This did not mean that the Renaissance had lost its character; it only meant that the writers of the era were becoming more capable of determining what needed to be said to different audiences. Quite frankly, the Harlem Renaissance prepared the way for other movements in the African diaspora, such as the Negritude Movement in France, the Indigenist Movement of Haiti, and Abdias do Nascimento's Negro Theatre Movement of Rio de Janeiro, and the Afro-Cuban Movement of Nicolas Guillen.

The Great Wars of the Twentieth Century

More than 700,000 African Americans registered for the Armed Forces on July 5, 1917. Before the end of the World War I more than 2,290,500 men and women had enlisted; 400,000 of those had been called into active service. According to John Hope Franklin, the eminent historian, 32 percent of blacks who registered were accepted while only 26 percent of whites were accepted due to discrimination against blacks in the matter of exemptions.

One of the sharpest blows to the African American population was the retirement of the highest ranking black officer, Colonel Charles Young, due to high blood pressure. Colonel Young rode his horse from Ohio to Washington, DC to demonstrate his health, but to no avail. The retirement board was not convinced that he was physically fit and did not rescind his retirement. African Americans took up the challenge of commissioned officers as a civil rights campaign. Congress created schools to train white officers but not black officers. A delegation of distinguished citizens led by Joel Spingarn appealed to the military authorities to make the training of African American officers one of their priorities. The military establishment was unconvinced. Subsequently agitation grew at Fisk, Howard, Tuskegee, Atlanta, and Lincoln as well as some other colleges. Soon thereafter, General Leonard Wood met with Joel Spingarn and asked him to secure the names of 200 African Americans of college status willing to become officers. The Central Committee of Negro College Men was established at Howard University and within ten days it had gotten the names of 1,500 men who wanted to become army officers. A sustained campaign, supported by the NAACP and other organizations, was mounted to get Congress to act. Finally, the camp, segregated from the white training camps and isolated from the black communities, was established in Fort Des Moines, Iowa. On October 15, 1917, 639 men received their commissions.

To further combat German propaganda circulating in the United States about America's alleged plan to use black soldiers as cannon fodder, Emmett J. Scott, who had been Booker T. Washington's secretary for eighteen years, was made special assistant to the U.S. Secretary of War, Newton Baker.

Nevertheless, during the first Great European War (World War I) no African Americans served in the Marine Corps and served only in the most menial Navy jobs. The Army permitted African Americans in every section except aviation. All of the other units were open such as engineers, infantry, cavalry, signal corps, hospital corps, field artillery, intelligence, adjutants, chaplains, and mechanics. The Army of the early twentieth century was segregated and the positions opened to blacks were limited; yet the resistance to discrimination in the Army was sustained and persistent.

African Americans serving in the Armed Forces faced daily threats, insults, and harassments. In Charlotte, North Carolina where 10,000 African Americans were stationed, only a table outside a Y. M. C. A. frequented by white soldiers was available for African Americans to use to write letters. The Military Police attacked African-American soldiers at will and white officers assigned them to the most difficult, hazardous labor battalions although they had qualified for posts requiring higher skills. Under such circumstances it was difficult to keep up morale for fighting for one's country. However, convinced that it was necessary in order to demonstrate once more the African's persistence, few men gave up under the oppressive conditions.

In September 1917, some of the men of the 24th Infantry became embroiled in a general riot with whites in Houston, Texas. Numerous and repeated insults were hurled at the African American soldiers by the white civilians. The commanding officer disarmed the soldiers, fearing that they might be provoked into using their weapons to defend themselves. The soldiers refused to provide

opportunity for the citizenry to attack them with civilian weapons and managed to retain some weapons of their own. Seventeen whites were killed in the ensuing battle. Thirteen soldiers were hanged for murder and mutiny and forty-one sentenced to life in prison. With no pretense of a fair trial, the government came down on the side of white racism and against the honest self defense of its own African soldiers. The trial and case linger in the African-American psyche as one of the greatest examples of injustice in the history of American injustice. The thirteen soldiers have never been forgotten and now they are martyrs to the cause of dignity. The Pulitzer-Prize winning dramatist Charles Fuller captures the poignancy of these issues in his powerful play *The Brownsville Raid*. In 1973, Representative Augustus F. Hawkins, Democrat from California, sponsored a bill in the U.S. Congress directing the Secretary of Defense to rescind the effect of the dishonorable discharges of the Brownsville Soldiers. Meanwhile, the Army Secretary Robert Froehlke ordered the charges dropped and the dishonorable discharges changed to honorable discharges.

When the opportunity came to distinguish themselves on the war front, the African Americans did not wane. The 369th United States Infantry arrived in France in early 1918. By April of the same year, they had moved to the front lines of the fighting, exactly one year to the day after the American government had declared war on Germany.

Few men have fought any braver. They took Champagne and for a few months held almost 20 percent of the territory occupied by American forces. The 369th was then moved into the direct path of the German offensive at Minaucourt and bore the heaviest part of the offensive. But they did not budge. By the end of the war they had received numerous firsts, awards, and recognitions. They had been the first allied unit to reach the Rhine River. They had never lost a man to capture. They had never lost a trench. They had never lost a foot of territory. Furthermore, the historic 369th Regiment served in active combat as a unit of a foreign army longer than any other American unit in battle; the brave men fought for 191 continuous days on the front line. The Germans called them the "Hell Fighters" and the entire regiment won the French Government's Croix the Guerre. One hundred seventy-one individuals were cited with the Croix de Guerre and Legion of Honor for exceptional gallantry.

In addition to the Hell Fighters of the 369th, the Eighth Illinois Infantry, renamed the 370th United States Infantry when it reached France, the 371st Infantry which was organized at Camp Jackson, South Carolina, the 372nd Infantry composed of African American national guardsmen all fought in France. The 370th, equipped with French weapons, served in Mihiel and the Argonne Forest by September 1918. The 270th had begun a campaign from the area around Mont de Tombes and Les Tueries to pursue the Germans out of France and into Belgium. Twenty-one men received the Distinguished Service Cross, one received the Distinguished Service Medal, and sixty-eight were awarded some grade of the Croix de Guerre. The 370th was involved in the last battle of the war, attacking and capturing fifty German supply wagons and their crews a half an hour after the armistice went into effect.

The 371st Infantry Regiment arrived in France in April 1918. It was attached to the French 157th Division, the famous "Red Hand." The 371st held the front at Avocourt and later at Verriores for three months. In the September offensive, the 371st took several German posts near Monthois. They captured German prisoners, weapons, a munitions depot, and several railroad cars. For this brave action the entire regiment was decorated by the French government. Three officers won the Legion of Honor, 123 won the Croix de Guerre, and 26 won the Distinguished Service Cross.

The 372nd was a combination of national guardsmen from several states and the District of Columbia. It also reached France in April 1918. In May, this regiment took over the defense of the West Argonne sector. For three months the 372nd came under intense shelling, but by September the regiment was in hot pursuit of the enemy. The French General Moreau decorated the regiment's colors after German surrender in November.

Every African American fighting unit paid a heavy price. The Germans dropped leaflets on the soldiers of the 92nd Division stating that the United States was a racist nation that would never give Africans equal opportunity or justice even if they fought for the Americans. Not one African American deserted to the German side although every African American recognized the social and political situation in the United States.

America presented the African American soldier with racism, discrimination, and indignity. Yet most of the military men and women recognized and subscribed to the eventual overthrow of American injustice. They were fighting men and women whose purpose was to demonstrate the commitment and loyalty of the African American to the United States. The persistent failure of the American society to reward the heroism of African Americans after the first World War became a sad reminder of the truth in the German propaganda. Of course, as time would prove the African Americans understood much more about the nature of racism than the Germans thought. When World War II started and the German racism against Jews, the Rom, and Africans became clear, the German actions were validation of the suspicions of the African American soldiers of World War I.

Many African Americans distinguished themselves in every war fought by the United States. A few reached high positions in the military during the World Wars. Others achieved fame during the Korean and Vietnam wars. The names of the heroes of battle are like diamonds studded in the center of every page of American warfare: Peter Salem, Salem Poor, Christian Fleetwood, Dorie Miller, Benjamin O. Davis, Chappie James, Colin Powell, and hundreds of others.

General Benjamin O. Davis

General "Chappie" James

Black Fathia, "No Man Governs Alone,"
Ghana, Africa

"GREAT DAY, GREAT DAY, THE RIGHTEOUS MARCHING": THE ERA OF DEMONSTRATIVE PROTEST

Martin Luther King, Jr. epitomized the decade of the Civil Rights Movement. Two events may be said to have contextualized the decade. One event, *Brown v. Topeka Board of Education*, occurred in 1954 as a decision by the Supreme Court; the other, the Civil Rights Act of 1964, was an action of the Congress of the United States.

The electric nature of the protests and demonstrations led by King and his Southern Christian Leadership Conference colleagues stole much of the limelight from the aging National Association for the Advancement of Colored People and the Urban League which had been content to rely on legal solutions and economic answers to the problems confronting African Americans. King's movement had the moral authority of the Christian Church and the labor leaders and the international community behind it. He transcended the narrow legal confines of the American judiciary and raised a higher level of questions about the possibilities of human beings living together in a free and open society. Out of this movement came new coalitions, new arguments for justice, new approaches to racism, and new methods for negotiating with recalcitrant administrations. Released at this time also were energies which led to more militant and insistent calls for

revolution and change in the way the nation conducted social and political business. The voices of Huey P. Newton, Maulana Karenga, Bobby Seale, Stokely Carmichael, Eldridge Cleaver, and Angela Davis were raised in new lines of argument. They were young voices, the children of Malcolm X, who would be heard in the corridors of power and whose words would be repeated in the pulpits.

Malcolm X, like Martin Luther King, Jr., was a pivotal figure in the movement for equal rights and opportunities for African Americans. Malcolm X was as much an authentic hero as Martin Luther King, Jr. He was as responsible for the Black Power Movement as anyone because he was the spiritual force behind it. Stokely Carmichael, the national chairperson of the Student Non-Violent Coordinating Committee (SNCC), may have shouted the words "Black Power" in 1966 which he had heard in Adam Clayton Powell's speech at Howard University but it was Malcolm X's day.

The Black Power Movement was not a sudden departure from the Civil Rights Movement but rather it was a carefully developed strategy that had its roots in the philosophy of the cultural nationalists. Chief among these individuals was Malcolm X, a follower of the

Seattle #67

Portland #62

Grand Rapids #61
#3 Milwaukee
#16 Lansing
Flint #53
Detroit #1

Boston #11
#13 Springfield
Buffalo #23
Hartford #14
New Haven #40
Bridgeport #41
#76 Patterson
#21 Jersey City
#25 Newark
New York
#7 Harlem
#7c Brooklyn
#7b Corona
#7d Bronx

#72 Richmond
#73 Sacramento
Pittsburg #59
Oakland #77
#26 San Francisco

#2 Chicago
#17 Joliet
#49 Kankakee
South Bend #31
Gary #33
Cleveland #18
Youngstown #9
#37 Akron
#44 Trenton
#12 Philadelphia
Camden #20
Pittsburgh #22
Wilmington #35
Atlantic City #10

Fresno #39

#51 Denver

#43 Columbus
Springfield #71
Dayton #19
#6 Baltimore
Washington D.C. #4

#74 Indianapolis
Cincinnati #5

Kansas City Mo. #30
#68 Kansas City Kan.
#28 St. Louis

#24 Richmond
Norfolk #57
Portsmouth #57b

Bakersfield #39b
Las Vegas #75

#56 Winston Salem
Durham #34

#27 Los Angeles
Compton #54
#42 Long Beach

Nashville #60
Charlotte #36

#8 San Diego

Oklahoma City #50
#63 Little Rock
Memphis #55

Columbia #38

Phoenix #32

Atlanta #15, 15b

Birmingham #69

#52 Fort Worth
Dallas #48
#70 Tyler

Jackson #78

Jacksonville #66

#65 Baton Rouge
#58 Prichard
Austin #64
#45 Houston
#46 New Orleans

Tampa #47

#29 Miami

———— MAJOR MOSQUES ————
NATION OF ISLAM

Honorable Elijah Muhammad of the Nation of Islam. It was the nationalists' philosophies of self help, self interested policies, no-nonsense politics, and strong cultural values that made the call for "Black Power" so natural during the l960s. It expressed faith in the ability of African Americans to act for themselves. The refrain was interpreted by many Americans as a separatist call. White groups that had given support to the Civil Rights organizations began to question whether they should continue to do so. Some dropped their support and criticized black leadership for not

calling for sanctions against Carmichael and the Black Power leaders. Maulana Karenga of the US movement and Huey Newton of the Black Panthers occupied central places in the evolution of ideas that were found in both King's and Malcolm X's doctrines.

Martin Luther King, Jr. symbolized an entire era of civil protest in the United States. Valiant and eloquent, he was the consummate field marshall on the battlefield of justice. African Americans saw in King the long-awaited promise of the deliverer who would put before the courts and officials the numerous

grievances of an oppressed, segregated, and passionate people.

There were several events that propelled King to the forefront of the Civil Rights Movement. In the first instance, the 1954 Supreme Court decision found that segregated schools were inherently unequal and reversed a half century of tradition and law that had begun with *Plessy v. Ferguson*. This prepared the way for numerous challenges to *segregation*, the practice of separating the races and giving African Americans the least desirable part of the separation. In 1955, Rosa Parks refused to get up from her seat on a Montgomery bus because she was tired, and initiated the Montgomery Bus Boycott. Martin Luther King, Jr. became the chief spokesperson and leading strategist of the boycott. Alongside Fred Gray, then a young attorney, King developed a civil rights mode of operation that would culminate in many successors.

Throughout the South, segregation was confronted as never before. It was the age of heroes and heroines. Young and courageous African-American elementary and high school students marched into hostile educational institutions with only their faith that justice would be victorious on their side. President Dwight Eisenhower ordered United States troops into Little Rock, Arkansas to enforce court-ordered desegregation in 1957. Three years later, four North Carolina college students began a lunch counter sit-in at a department store. The movement swept across the entire nation as African Americans demanded to be served as any other citizens would be served.

King mounted hundreds of protests in small and large cities; freedom riders tested desegregation laws and were mobbed in 1961 by groups in Birmingham, Alabama; James Meredith was guarded by U.S. marshalls as he became the first African to enroll at the University of Mississippi in 1962. By 1963, civil rights protests had reached their peak and thousands of people had been arrested and jailed and scores of people murdered in the quest for freedom. The 1963 March on Washington brought more than 200,000 people together at the Lincoln memorial to demand jobs and civil rights legislation. It was Martin Luther King, Jr.'s and the Civil Rights Movement's finest hour.

August 28, 1963 was memorable because of King's eloquent "I Have a Dream" speech and the unity of the movement. This was the high point of national consciousness about racial inequality. From this time forward, legislators began a campaign to place civil rights on the legislative agenda of the United States. King emerged from this speech as the moral voice of a nation. The United States would never be the same and the meaning of America would be stretched to include more people.

Malcolm X

Malcolm X did not attend the March on Washington. He was at the height of his personal charisma as a national leader and stood out as the only visible African American leader who refused to meet President John Kennedy. Malcolm X believed that the president was not doing enough to advance the rights of Africans. He expressed the belief that the United States should have protected working class Africans in the South from the Ku Klux Klan. His positions on issues had been formed by the discipline of the Nation of Islam.

Malcolm X had been born Malcolm Little in Omaha, Nebraska. He had lived in Detroit, Boston, and New York. He converted to the Islamic teachings of the Honorable Elijah Muhammad while in prison. When he came out of prison he became the most ardent follower and the leading evangelist for the Nation of Islam. In 1964, Malcolm X broke with the Nation of Islam and Elijah Muhammad to form his own organization, the Organization of Afro-American Unity.

The strength of Malcolm X's appeal was his simple, staccato logic. Few

Martin Luther King, Jr. and Ralph Abernathy

speakers could match his control of the idioms and tropes which represented the culture of the African American people in the urban communities. Ossie Davis said of Malcolm X, "He was our manhood." He spoke the words that were on the minds and in the hearts of thousands of downtrodden and exploited Africans. His eloquence was not the eloquence that comes from reading high-sounding books or studying the figures and metaphors of the ancient writers and speakers, but Malcolm X's rhetoric was solidly based in the folkways and cultural styles of the people to whom he addressed his message.

There was something real about his message that made people feel that he was genuinely concerned about the issues to which he gave voice. Malcolm X could not be questioned on ethical and moral grounds without responding with precise arguments. He understood the nature of his leadership role and acted it out with tremendous fidelity to his movement.

Malcolm X understood what many of the professors analyzing his words and writings did not understand. He knew that the principal struggle was for the minds of the African American people. Few scholars and writers accepted his analysis while he was alive. In fact,

Huey Newton

Archie Epps, questioned whether Malcolm X understood that it was irrelevant that Africans had civilizations hundreds of years ago. What one sees is that Malcolm X was far beyond his detractors in his analysis of the conditions of blacks in

Bobby Seale

America. What he was saying in his speeches was that the conquest of the mind is necessary before you can have the proper conquest of material conditions. His life was committed to substance in the midst of a society committed to sym-

Maulana Karenga

Malcolm X

Kawame Toure (Stokely Carmichael)

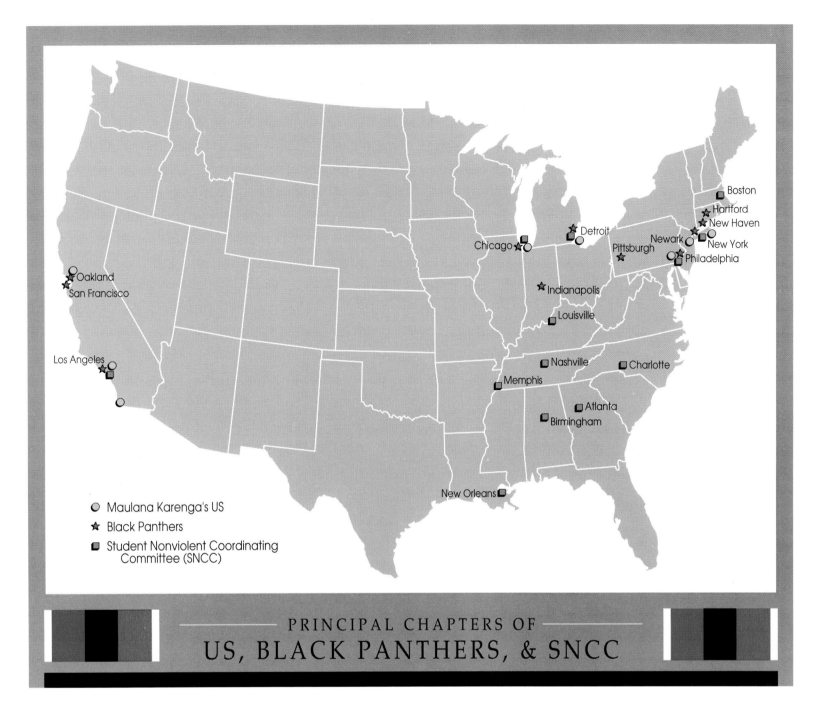

○ Maulana Karenga's US

★ Black Panthers

■ Student Nonviolent Coordinating Committee (SNCC)

PRINCIPAL CHAPTERS OF
US, BLACK PANTHERS, & SNCC

bol. There was no empty rhetoric in his soul, no carnal imagination, no evil spirit, just simple, direct, committed logic in support of the best values and traditions of a society founded upon revolution and change. This meant that he had to attack the false signs and images which paraded as justice and righteousness. His intent was to love in a cleansing manner. He erected no great monuments to piety but he played in the same arena of civil and human relations as the great thinkers of any age.

His chief gift to the nation was the appropriateness of his oratory. He

understood propriety at a time when others were dealing in platitudes. He spoke not to some unknown audience, but to his own audience. In the best traditions of oratory and rhetorical theory, Malcolm X was a master because when he spoke his audiences felt that they could have given the same speech had they the ability and the courage.

Coupled with this unusual gift of oratory was his sincerity. There has rarely been an African American leader who conveyed more authentic sincerity than Malcolm X. Those who heard him knew exactly what he meant because in the

manner of his speaking he told them what he meant. The philosopher Maulana Karenga created the Kwanzaa holiday as a celebration of joy in 1966. The seven principles of familyhood—umoja, unity; kujichagulia, self-determination; ujima, collective work and responsibility; ujamaa, cooperative economics; nia, purpose; kuumba, creativity; and imani, faith—are the centerpiece of the celebration. Kwanzaa begins on December 26 and lasts for seven days. A candle is lit on each of the seven days and one of the principles is discussed. Among the items necessary for the

POLITICAL PRISONERS OF USA FASCISM

Kwanzaa celebration are the kinara, candleholders; mkeke, mat; kikombe, the cup; and various hand-made gifts.

The Kawaida (custom and tradition) philosophy of the US movement gave birth to numerous student groups around the nation. During the 1960s the US movement maintained a consistent policy of teaching African American cultural values. Maulana Karenga was a doctoral student at the University of California, Los Angeles, when he conceived of the organization US for the liberation of the minds of African Americans. He believed that it was impossible to discuss political or economic liberation until there had been psychological liberation. Karenga's movement included the writers Imamu Baraka and Haki Madhubuti, both of whom estab-

lished institutions based on the Kawaida philosophy. Kawaida's appeal was both intellectual and political.

Huey P. Newton and Bobby Seale were the co-founders of the Black Panther Party in Oakland, California. The Party had a ten point program which included the freeing of all political prisoners, the feeding of school children, and the removal of the police from the African American community. A key component of the Black Panther Party was self-defense for the African community. They argued that it was as American as the Constitution for a person to defend him or herself. The young people in the Student Non-Violent Coordinating Committee were led by Stokely Carmichael and H. Rap Brown. Both Carmichael and Brown were outstand-

ing orators, capable of speaking without notes for hours. In this quality they shared with Newton, Seale, Karenga, and Malcolm the gift of the African American culture. Julian Bond and John Lewis also played central roles in the early development of SNCC.

The Growth of Islam

Islam's greatest growth among African Americans was generated in the twentieth century by six charismatic readers: Noble Drew Ali, Master Wallace Fard Muhammad, Honorable Elijah Muhammad, Malcolm X, Wallace D. Muhammad, and Louis Farrakhan. Each leader attracted new adherents and taught Islam as an alternative to the Christian religion. Noble Drew Ali came to Newark, New Jersey from North Carolina and founded the Moorish Science Temple in 1913. He established temples in Philadelphia, New York, Baltimore, Boston, and Chicago. In 1929, Ali died in Chicago while still trying to institutionalize the Moorish Science Temple. His success had been encouraging and soon after his death, W. D. Fard or Master Wallace Fard Muhammad appeared in Detroit as the reincarnation of Noble Drew Ali. He set up temples of Islam in Detroit and Chicago, attracting many followers from the Garvey Movement as well as Noble Drew Ali's Moorish Science Movement. Serving as a lieutenant to Master Wallace Ford Muhammad, a young Georgian, Elijah Poole, studied Islam and African American nationalism and became the heir to the movement when Master Wallace Fard Muhammad mysteriously disappeared in 1934. As Elijah Muhammad he became sole leader of The Nation of Islam and began to build the organization into a national presence. Elijah Muhammad's son Wallace D. Muhammad and Louis Farrakhan were to emerge as inheritors of Elijah's legacy. Malcolm X, assassinated in February 1965, had been the most eloquent and skillful orator for The Nation of Islam prior to being censored and suspended

Lorraine Hansberry

of her lifetime she made dramatic history becoming the first African American dramatist to win the New York Drama Critics Circle Award in 1959.

Her play, *A Raisin in the Sun*, became an international success. It was the first major play by an African American to appear on Broadway. Hansberry, originally from Chicago, had written the play while she lived in New York. A second play, *The Sign in Sidney Brustein's Window*, was about the western intellectual's preoccupation with reflection rather than action.

Walter White

Walter White was the secretary of the NAACP during its most courageous period. Born in 1893, White died in 1955 after being one of the most stalwart champions of African American rights. He published several books against lynching. His most famous work was *Rope and Faggot: A Biography of Judge Lynch*. He also wrote two earlier novels, *Fire in the Flint* and *Flight*. The NAACP awarded him the coveted Spingarn Award in 1937.

Thurgood Marshall

Thurgood Marshall, Supreme Court Justice, was born on July 2, 1908, in Baltimore, Maryland. He attended Lincoln University and Howard University Law School. Marshall graduated from Howard at the top of his 1933 class. His career as an attorney was to span the civil rights era. His career with the

in November 1963 by Elijah Muhammad for saying after President John Kennedy's death that "The chicken had come home to roost," by which he later explained he meant that the climate of violence had led to the killing of the President.

The Nation of Islam started as a nationalist organization but evolved into a religious organization. With mosques around the country, the religion attracted many young men who saw it as the most active force in the nation. The Nation of Islam's appeal seemed to be in the directness of its message, the discipline of its followers, and the political consciousness of its adherents. This is different from the organization under the leadership of Elijah Muhammad. Under his leadership, the organization disavowed any political ambitions or involvement in religion. The Honorable Elijah Muhammad taught that the government of the United States should have nothing to do with the Nation of Islam and that the Nation of Islam should have nothing to do with the United States of America.

Lorraine Hansberry

Lorraine Hansberry was born in 1930 and died in 1965. Within the short span

Thurgood Marshall

Walter F. White

Constance Baker Motley

sions requiring the admission of qualified African Americans to the University of Texas Law School and the right of Texas blacks to vote in the Democratic primaries. In 1961 he served on the federal bench as circuit judge for the Second Circuit.

The pinnacle of his distinguished career in law came in 1967 when he was asked by President Lyndon B. Johnson to serve on the Supreme Court. Thurgood Marshall has always had strong sentiments in support of human rights and justice. He once criticized the nation for not understanding the role blacks played in expanding justice.

Gwendolyn Brooks

Gwendolyn Brooks received the Pulitzer Prize for Poetry in 1950 for her book *Annie Allen*. She was born in 1912 in Topeka, Kansas. Her family moved to Chicago when she was still very young. In 1945, she completed a book called *A Street in Bronzeville*. This book brought her to the attention of the country as *Mademoiselle* named her as one of the ten outstanding American women. Brooks has received numerous awards includ-

NAACP was the most distinguished in its legal history. He was named national special counsel in 1938 and handled all cases that dealt with the constitutionality of African American rights. He was appointed to the job of director-counsel

of the Legal Defense and Educational Fund in 1950. In this position, he played a key role with a team of lawyers in arguing the now famous Supreme Court case on school desegregation.

Marshall also figured in the deci-

Gwendolyn Brooks

Whitney M. Young, Jr.

Roy Wilkins

ing being the national poet laureate at the Library of Congress. Her name is synonymous with the best tradition of African American letters.

Her books include *Bronzeville Boys* and *Girls, Maud Martha, The Bean Eaters, In the Mecca, Riot, Family Pictures, Beckonings, Aloneness, Primer for Blacks*, and *To Disembark*. She has written many other books and articles and is the major African American poet since Langston Hughes.

She has been a keen supporter of young writers, giving them advice and criticism. Brooks represents the bridge between the Harlem Renaissance generations and the Black Arts Movement, becoming in her own poetry and style the embodiment of the best traditions of both. In her judgment, the 1960s had much more promise for the liberation of art than did the Harlem Renaissance.

Whitney Young

Whitney Young was the executive director of the National Urban League from 1961 to 1971. He was born in Kentucky in 1922 and drowned while swimming in Lagos, Nigeria in 1971. An indefatigable worker and a serious campaigner for African American rights in the field of economics and housing, Whitney Young was one of the major civil rights leaders during the 1960s.

He served as Dean of the School of Social Work at Atlanta University from 1954 to 1961. He wrote several books on racism including *To Be Equal* and *Beyond Racism*. While serving as Dean of Social Work at Atlanta University, he was elected to the post of president of the National Association of Social Workers. He was called upon to serve on seven presidential commissions as well as the boards of some major American corporations and foundations. His work in the urban communities also enabled him to be involved with organizations such as the Urban Coalition, Urban Institute, and the Rockefeller Foundation.

Constance Baker Motley

Constance Baker Motley became the first African American female federal judge in 1966 when she was appointed to the U.S. District Court for Southern New York by President Lyndon Johnson. Motley worked for the NAACP while she was still a student at Columbia. She

had argued nine successful cases before the Supreme Court before she left her position with the NAACP. In 1982, she was named chief judge of the Federal Court that covers New York City.

Jackie Robinson

Jackie Robinson was born in Cairo, Georgia on January 31, 1919. He was raised in Pasadena, California, and attended college at UCLA. After a stint in the army as a lieutenant during World War II, Robinson returned to the states hoping to become a physical education teacher. He chose to play baseball with the Black Baseball League in order to sharpen his skills. In 1945, Branch Rickey of the Brooklyn Dodgers assigned him to the Montreal Royals to be groomed for the major league. At the time Robinson was playing for the Kansas City Monarchs.

On April 10, 1947, the Brooklyn team announced that it had purchased Robinson's contract. A day later Jackie Robinson began his career in the major leagues. He retired in 1956 after compiling an outstanding record as a hitter, base stealer, and fielder. He had been cited for being

Jackie Robinson

Carl Rowan

the Most Valuable Player in 1949, had played on one world championship team, and had stole home base 19 times, once during a world series game.

When Jackie Robinson died in 1972 in Stamford, Connecticut, he had become a legend in his own time.

Ella Fitzgerald

Ella Fitzgerald has been called the greatest female jazz artist. She was born in 1918, discovered in 1934 after an amateur contest, and made her first recording in 1935. Since that time Ella Fitzgerald's name has become synonymous with with jazz interpretation. Musicians honor her for her ability to use her voice as an instrument. She has improvised with the greatest of ease in the midst of all kinds of tunes. Few jazz artists are so universally acclaimed.

Carl Rowan

Carl Rowan held two important posts in the United States government. He was ambassador to Finland in 1963 and later he was the Director of the United States Information Agency. He was born in Ravenscroft, Tennessee on

August ll, 1925 and at the age of nineteen became one of the first fifteen African Americans commissioned by the navy. Rowan attended the Tennessee State University, Oberlin College, and the University of Minnesota where he he majored in journalism.

Carl Rowan became a much sought after feature writer and journalist once he entered the profession. Along the way he wrote several books, including *South of Freedom*, *Go South in Sorrow*, *The Pitiful and the Proud*, *Wait Till Next Year*, and others.

Elliot Percival Skinner

Elliot Percival Skinner, like Carl Rowan, was an appointee under the Johnson Administration, to a government post. Skinner, the leading scholar on the Mossi culture of Burkina Faso (Upper Volta) was appointed to the ambassadorship because of his expert knowledge of the history and culture of the Mossi people. Dr. Skinner is the Franz Boas Professor of Anthropology at Columbia University. He has been one of the principal Africanists, writing and teaching on Africa, for the past thirty years.

Ralph Ellison

Kariamu Welsh Asante

Kariamu Welsh Asante, the winner of numerous creative arts awards from the national Endowment of the Arts and the New York State Council of the Arts during the 1970s, was invited by Prime Minister Rob-

Ella Fitzgerald

Charles Fuller

James Brown

Ray Charles

Muhammad Ali

ert Mugabe of Zimbabwe in 1981 to organize the national Dance Company of Zimbabwe. As one of the first African Americans to live in post-independence Zimbabwe, she made the national Dance Company one of the most internationally successful companies on the continent. The Umfundalai dance technique, which she created to identify African dance steps, is now used throughout the African dance community.

The singular brilliance of the expressive culture of African Americans is seen in the dance, such as the umfundalai technique of Kariamu Welsh Asante or the interpretative style of Ray Charles' music. The dramatist Charles Fuller's concentration on what African American historical experiences are and ought to have been is of the same fabric with Ellison's insights into the nature of being among African Americans. Muhammad Ali was the audacious presentation of the soul. There is, in every aspect of the American society, the presence and voice of the African, thinking, working, creating, inventing, performing, expressing all of the pathos and hope of a unique historical experience.

Madame C. J. Walker

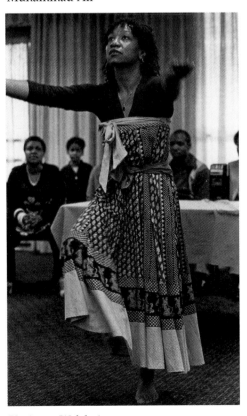

Kariamu Welsh Asante

Afoakwa Mpua Nkron, "Nine Tufts of Hair,"
Ghana, Africa

"BEFORE THIS TIME ANOTHER YEAR": THE TRANSFORMING OF AMERICA

The social and economic condition of African Americans has never been in parity to the state of the American nation. Indeed, the quest of the African in America from the beginning until now has been the acquisition of a similar social and economic status as Americans of European descent. The unequal origin of these populations one white and free and the other black and enslaved has made this quest elusive.

During the past twenty years, numerous achievements have been made in politics but the economic and social conditions of African Americans have remained constant. While it is possible to boast of hundreds of elected officials at the municipal, state, and national level, the shift in the American economy that has caused numerous industrial manufacturing jobs to leave the urban north has added severe pressures on African American families. The number of African Americans in corporate positions is far greater now than twenty years ago, yet the intense poverty faced by the masses of African Americans has been unrelenting. Facts such as these demonstrate the seemingly intractable nature of the depressed social and economic situation.

If social and economic conditions have presented the nation with frustratingly difficult problems, the passage of the Civil Rights Restoration Act of 1988 over a presidential veto, the passage of enforcement amendments to the Fair Housing Act of 1968, and the two candidacies of Jesse Jackson for nomination to the highest office in the land have kept alive the spirit of struggle and the vision for a more equitable society. With more than 6,000 elected officials, African Americans are in a much better position than ever to make a difference in the moral and political climate of the nation. In 1990, David Richardson, Pennsylvania State Representative and a national leader of African American state representatives said, "the social and economic conditions will only get better as the ethical climate gets better. That is one of the main jobs for state legislators and other national leaders." All major indicators of the economic, social, and political climate in the nation suggest that unless Americans collectively remove the stones from the path of progress; the nation will never live up to its noblest aspirations.

The National Urban League has called for Parity 2000, a vision that by the year 2000 the private and public sectors of the American society achieve equity in education, training, hiring, health, and housing. Judging from the statistical information reported in this volume, such a goal is useful as a point of departure for a vision of the future, but it will take concrete

African American Colleges and Universities

		Location	Highest Degree Conferred	Control	Percent African	1989 Enrollment
1	Olive-Harvey College	Chicago, IL	Associate	Private	96	8,314
2	Lincoln University	Lincoln, PA	Master's	Public	98	1,250
3	Cheyney State College	Cheyney, PA	Master's	Private	95	1,666
4	Coppin State College	Baltimore, MD	Master's	Public	86	2,448
	Morgan State University	Baltimore, MD	Doctorate	Public	92	3,982
5	Delaware State College	Dover, DE	Baccalaureate	Public	55	2,389
6	Bowie State College	Bowie, MD	Master's	Private	72	3,074
7	University of District of Columbia	Washington, DC	Baccalaureate	Private	81	11,869
	Howard University	Washington, DC	First Professional/Doctorate	Private	85	10,756
8	University of Maryland—Eastern Shore	Princess Anne, MD	Master's	Public	72	1,316
9	Central State University	Wilberforce, OH	Baccalaureate	Public	84	2,779
	Wilberforce University	Wilberforce, OH	Baccalaureate	Private	99	739
10	Rio Grande College	Rio Grande, OH	Baccalaureate	Private	88	1,709
11	Virginia Union University	Richmond, VA	First Professional	Private	98	1,200
12	Hampton Institute	Hampton ,VA	Master's	Private	92	5,147

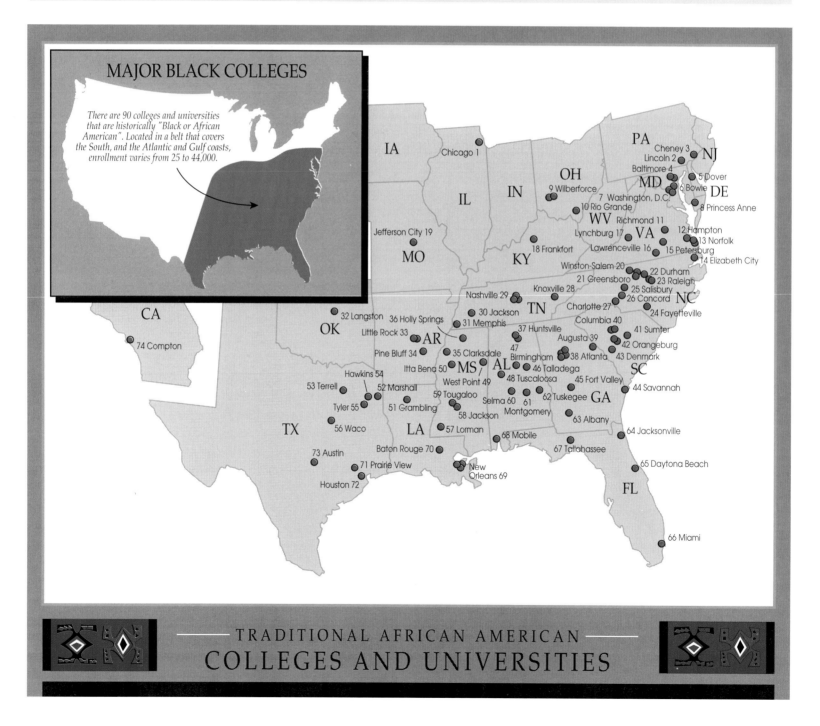

MAJOR BLACK COLLEGES

There are 90 colleges and universities that are historically "Black or African American". Located in a belt that covers the South, and the Atlantic and Gulf coasts, enrollment varies from 25 to 44,000.

TRADITIONAL AFRICAN AMERICAN
COLLEGES AND UNIVERSITIES

African American Colleges and Universities (continued)

#	Name	Location	Highest Degree Conferred	Control	Percent African	1989 Enrollment
13	Norfolk State College	Norfolk, VA	Master's	Private	88	7,721
14	Elizabeth City State University	Elizabeth City, NC	Baccalaureate	Private	80	1,583
15	Virginia State College	Petersburg, VA	Master's	Public	92	3,891
16	Saint Paul's College	Lawrenceville, VA	Baccalaureate	Private	97	736
17	Virginia Seminary	Lynchburg, VA	Master of Divinity	Private	95	50
18	Kentucky State University	Frankfort, KY	Baccalaureate	Public	42	2,105
19	Lincoln University	Jefferson City, MO	Baccalaureate	Public	26	2,478
20	Winston-Salem State University	Winston-Salem, NC	Baccalaureate	Public	82	2,358
21	Bennet College	Greensboro, NC	Baccalaureate	Private	98	549
	North Carolina Agricultural & Technical State University	Greensboro, NC	Master's	Public	90	5,991
22	North Carolina Central University	Durham, NC	Master's/First Professional	Public	83	4,552
23	Saint Augustine's College	Raleigh, NC	Baccalaureate	Private	98	1,671
	Shaw University	Raleigh, NC	Baccalaureate	Private	98	1,473
24	Fayetteville State University	Fayetteville ,NC	Baccalaureate	Private	74	2,679
25	Livingstone College	Salisbury, NC	Baccalaureate/First Professional	Private	98	642
26	Barber-Scotia College	Concord, NC	Baccalaureate	Private	98	441
27	Johnson C. Smith University	Charlotte, NC	Baccalaureate	Private	99	1,165
28	Knoxville College	Knoxville, TN	Baccalaureate	Private	98	680
29	Fisk University	Nashville, TN	Master's	Private	98	650
	Meharry Medical College	Nashville, TN	First Professional/Doctorate	Private	76	751
	Tennessee State University	Nashville, TN	Master's	Public	62	7,012
30	Lane College	Jackson, TN	Baccalaureate	Private	99	1,310
31	LeMoyne-Owen College	Memphis, TN	Baccalaureate	Private	98	906
62	Langston University	Langston, OK	Baccalaureate	Private	75	2,532
33	Philander Smith College	Little Rock, AR	Baccalaureate	Private	89	582
	Shorter College	Little Rock, AR	Two Years	Private	80	100
34	University of Arkansas — Pine Bluff	Pine Bluff, AR	Baccalaureate	Public	83	3,531
35	Coahoma Junior College	Clarksdale, MS	Two Years	Public	98	614
36	Rust College	Holly Springs, MS	Baccalaureate	Private	98	919
37	Alabama Agricultural & Mechanical University	Huntsville, AL	Master's	Public	85	3,800
	Oakwood College	Huntsville, AL	Baccalaureate	Private	99	1,075
38	Atlanta University/Clark College	Alanta, GA	Doctorate	Private	93	3,292
	Morehouse College	Alanta, GA	Baccalaureate	Private	99	2,387
	Morris Brown College	Alanta, GA	Baccalaureate	Private	90	1,300
	Spelman College	Alanta, GA	Baccalaureate	Private	99	1,757
39	Paine College	Augusta, GA	Master's	Private	90	708
40	Allen University	Columbia, SC	Master's	Private	99	25
	Benedict College	Columbia, SC	Baccalaureate	Private	99	1,616
41	Morris College	Sumter, SC	Baccalaureate	Private	99	796
42	Claflin College	Orangeburg, SC	Baccalaureate	Private	99	791
	South Carolina State College	Orangeburg, SC	Baccalaureate	Public	92	4,781
43	Voorhees College	Denmark, SC	Master's	Private	98	616
44	Savannah State College	Savannah, GA	Master's	Public	79	1,824
45	The Fort Valley State College	Fort Valley, GA	Master's	Public	89	1,735
46	Talladega College	Talladega, AL	Baccalaureate	Private	98	560
47	Miles College	Birmingham, AL	Baccalaureate	Private	99	680
48	Stillman College	Tuscaloosa, AL	Baccalaureate	Private	98	791
49	Mary Holmes College	West Point, MS	Two Years	Private	99	622
50	Mississippi Valley State University	Itta Bena, MS	Master's	Public	98	2,396
51	Grambling State College	Grambling, LA	Master's	Public	89	6,205
52	Wiley College	Marshall, TX	Baccalaureate	Private	98	417
53	Southwestern Christian College	Terrell, TX	Two Years	Private	92	240
54	Jarvis Christian College	Hawkins, TX	Baccalaureate	Private	98	466
55	Texas College	Tyler, TX	Baccalaureate	Private	98	450
56	Paul-Quinn College	Waco, TX	Baccalaureate	Private	93	509
57	Alcorn State University	Lorman, MS	Master's	Public	96	2,600
58	Jackson State University	Jackson, MS	Master's	Public	95	6,030
59	Tougaloo College	Tougaloo, MS	Baccalaureate	Private	93	7,988
60	Selma University	Selma, AL	Baccalaureate	Private	98	220
61	Alabama State University	Montgomery AL	Master's	Public	98	44,000
62	Tuskegee Institute	Tuskegee, AL	Master's/First Professional	Private	82	3,095
63	Albany State College	Albany, GA	Baccalaureate	Public	85	1,893
64	Edward Waters College	Jacksonville, FL	Baccalaureate	Private	96	671
65	Bethune-Cookman College	Daytona Beach, FL	Baccalaureate	Private	96	1,888
66	Florida Memorial College	Miami, FL	Baccalaureate	Private	81	2,321
67	Florida Agricultural & Mechanical University	Tallahassee, FL	Master's	Public	81	5,949
68	S. D. Bishop State Junior College	Mobile, AL	Two Years	Public	67	1,857
69	Dillard University	New Orleans, LA	Baccalaureate	Private	94	1,340
	Southern University in New Orleans	New Orleans, LA	Baccalaureate	Public	95	2,729
	Xavier University of Louisiana	New Orleans, LA	Master's	Private	88	2,207
70	Southern University and Agricultural & Mechanical College	Baton Rouge, LA	Master's/First Professional	Public	96	9,811
71	Prairie View Agricultural & Mechanical University	Prairie View, TX	Master's	Public	81	57
72	Texas Southern University	Houston, TX	First Professional/Doctorate	Public	93	7,447
73	Huston-Tillotson College	Austin, TX	Baccalaureate	Private	90	50
74	Compton Community College	Compton, CA	Associate	Public	89	4,700

Lincoln College, 1857

moral and financial commitments to correct the wrongs perpetrated on the African American population that began with the Great Enslavement.

Two hundred and fifty-eight years after the establishment of the Virginia Colony, Africans were finally emancipated from bondage. During this period white Americans had every advantage afforded to them by the laws of the country. The two hundred and forty-four years Africans worked for free, from 1619 to 1865, were years in which the wealth accumulated by the white population grew at an enormous rate. Cities were built, fortunes were made, property acquired while Africans waited for the day when America would pay its great debt of freedom and prosperity.

Black Colleges

The primary educational delivery capability of the historically black colleges and universities was underscored in 1990 when Walter Annenberg donated $50 million to The United Negro College Fund. Since the middle of the nineteenth century, when Lincoln and Cheyney were established, the Historically Black Colleges and Universities (HBCU) have had

a profound impact on the quality of the African-American professional classes. From 1852 to 1954, these colleges essentially kept African Americans in the professional ballgame. Without them the condition of blacks in America would have been even more dismal. But the HBCU produced an educated cadre committed to service and the uplift of the masses. Out of this commitment came lawyers, doctors, teachers, engineers, and preachers who would keep the condition of the race uppermost in their minds.

Initially, Lincoln and Hampton were founded to serve both Native Americans and African Americans. The Native Americans who attended both these schools often came from homes and communities closely related to the African population.

Although these HBCUs play a decreasing role in educating the black population, the better institutions continue to attract high quality students from throughout the African world. More than eighty percent of all African Americans in higher education are at predominantly white institutions. Some of these institutions such as Wayne State, Temple Uni-

versity, City College, and California State University, Dominguez Hills have percentages of African American students above the percentage of blacks in the national population. In some instances, major urban institutions have populations of African American students beyond the total numbers for some historically black colleges in their region. For example, the population of African American students at Temple University is larger than that of Cheyney and Lincoln universities combined. The African American student population at Wayne State University in Detroit, is larger than all of the HBCUs with the exception of Southern, Howard, Texas Southern, Tennessee State, and Tuskegee.

Nevertheless, the reputations for quality remain strong at Tuskegee, Lincoln, Hampton, Morehouse, Howard, and Spelman. These schools have experienced a resurgence in student interest during the past decade. What this means is that the African American community has found a tremendous need for these colleges. Bill and Camille Cosby donated $20 million to Spelman College in 1988. Lincoln University in Pennsylvania is reported to have inherited art worth more than one-half billion. Born in separatism forced by segregation, these colleges have achieved their prestige because of the commitment to teaching, humanity, and progress.

Graduate Programs

Eight universities in the United States offer graduate degrees in African American Studies either through interdepartmental programs or in departments. Temple University in Philadelphia offers the only comprehensive African American Studies program in the nation. With three degrees—B.A., M.A., and Ph.D.—Temple is the leading educational center for students studying for the graduate degree in African American Studies. Established in 1988, the doctoral program and the Masters degree program enrolled forty-seven and twenty five-students, respectively.

In addition to Temple, there are M.A. degree programs in African American Studies at three other departments in the nation: Ohio State University, Cornell University, and the State University of New York at Albany. Yale University, University of California—Los Angeles, the University of California—Berkeley, and the University of Wisconsin, Madison, offer interdisciplinary and interdepartmental programs.

More than two hundred universities and colleges offer degrees at the B.A. level. Among the most significant departments, in addition to those that offer graduate programs, are the University of Wisconsin-Milwaukee, Brown University, Indiana University, California State University—Long Beach, California State University—Northridge, and Kent State University. These schools offer strong curricula and have consistently had dedicated faculty and students. They serve large and diverse constituencies.

The departments and programs in African American Studies are direct outgrowths of the pioneering work of educators such as Carter G. Woodson, W. E. B. DuBois, Charles Johnson, Alain Locke, and Mary McLeod Bethune.

Carter G. Woodson

The "Father of African American History" is what many of his peers called Carter G. Woodson. He did more than anyone to institutionalize the teaching and study of the history of African Americans. Although W. E. B. DuBois is considered by many to be the greatest intellectual of his time, Woodson was undoubtedly the most unswervingly committed historian.

Woodson was born in New Canton, Virginia in 1875, and educated at Berea College, the University of Chicago, Harvard, and the Sorbonne. His major achievements include the creation of the

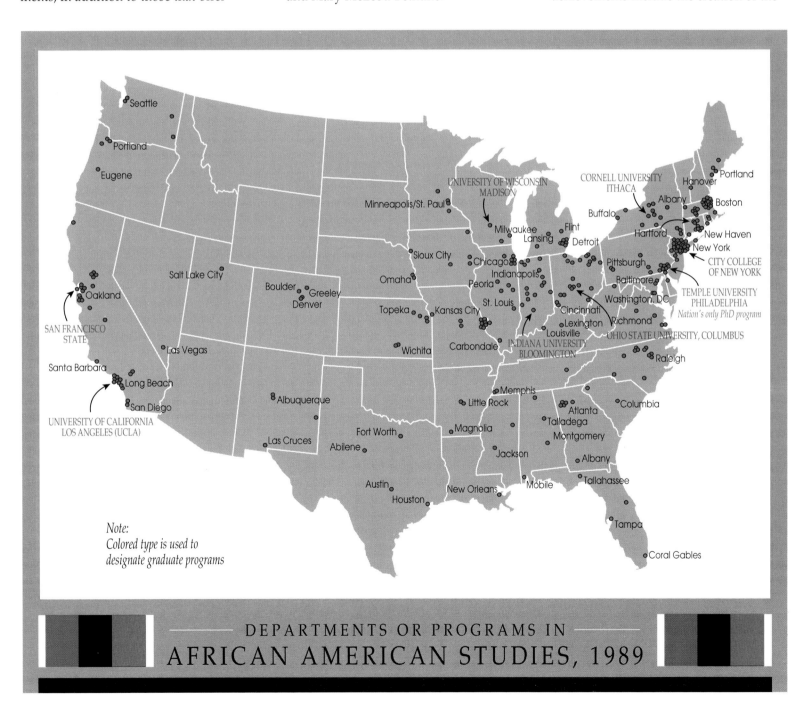

Note:
Colored type is used to designate graduate programs

DEPARTMENTS OR PROGRAMS IN
AFRICAN AMERICAN STUDIES, 1989

Carter Woodson

Association for the Study of Negro Life and History in 1915, the *Journal of Negro History* in 1916, the Associated Publishers in 1921, and the book, the *Miseducation of the Negro*. African American history, which is a part of African American Studies, owes a great debt to Woodson.

Medicine

The people of Africa brought to America much of the accumulated medicine of the continent. Indeed, African medicine at the time of the European slave trade was equal to if not superior to medicine in Europe. Many healers knew the medicinal value and curative properties of numerous herbs, minerals, and plants as well as surgical and rehabilitative procedures inherited from thousands of years of practical experience.

Root medicine became a prominent aspect of African American life during and after slavery. Practitioners, whether of the conjuring, the herbalist, or the spiritualist tradition, occupied prominent places in the community. Various therapies utilized in Africa were used in America. For example, the vaccination of smallpox was introduced into the Ameri-

can colonies by an African named Oneissimus. In 1740, an African who had escaped was identified as being able "to bleed and draw teeth." In 1751, another African, Cesar, was credited with discovering a cure for rattlesnake bite. Santomee was trained in Holland and practiced medicine among the Africans, Dutch, and English in New York.

James Derham was the first trained physician. During the 1780s he established one of the largest followings in New Orleans. Derham was an astute observer of the traditional African healers and took this tradition into consideration in some of his own practices. Among the physicians of the nineteenth century were James Still, David Ruggles, William Wells Brown, and Martin Delaney. Eight African physicians served the Army medical corps in the Civil War: John V. DeGrasse, C. B. Purvis, A. Tucker, William Powell, John Rapier, William Ellis, A. R. Abbott, and A. T. Augusta. The famous African nationalist John S. Rock was a lawyer but also a physician.

Medical schools were opened at Howard and Meharry in 1872. Six other medical schools opened but soon closed due to lack of finance, inadequate equipment and supplies, and local resistance. The three principal medical colleges established by African Americans are Howard University Medical School, Meharry Medical College, and Morehouse College of Medicine. Despite the fact that these colleges have been chronically underfunded, they have continued to produce the greatest number of African American physicians and medical scientists.

At the beginning of the twentieth century, four African American physicians were considered the outstanding medical innovators: Daniel Hale Williams, who performed the first open heart surgery in history; George Cleveland Hall, surgeon who developed diagnostic techniques that were used by his peers; Nathan F. Mossell, founder of the Frederick Douglass Hospital in Philadelphia; and Auston M. Curtis, a colleague and protégée of Dr. Williams

in Chicago. In the later part of the twentieth century, the names of Louis T. Wright, antibiotic aureomycin; William Hinton, Hinton test for syphilis; Jane Cook Wright-Jones, chemotherapy; Ulysses Grant Dailey, International College of Surgeons founder-fellow; Charles Drew, blood plasma; W. Montague Cobb, anatomist; Arthur Lee, cardiac surgery; Louis Sullivan, U.S. Secretary for Health, and numerous others must be added to the list.

Charles Richard Drew

Charles R. Drew, M.D. was born in Washington, DC on June 3, 1904. He attended and graduated from Dunbar High School, lettering in four sports. An athletic

Charles Drew

scholarship and part-time work as a waiter assisted him through Amherst College in Massachusetts. At Amherst College, Drew, an outstanding athlete, won letters and an award for excellence in five sports.

He graduated from Amherst in 1926, and entered McGill University School of Medicine two years later. In Montreal he rapidly demonstrated his brilliance as a student. Because of his discipline and enthusiasm for science, he was invited to work as an assistant on a blood research project. Although he trained in surgery, he never lost sight of his first love: blood research. His persistence in this field of research led to the significant discovery of the techniques for separating and preserving blood and advancing work with blood plasma. This discovery would revolutionize the storage of blood, blood transfusions, and make it possible to establish a blood bank. Thus, when Drew completed his research, established and opened the first blood bank, he became one of the most distinguished scientists of his day. Already holding the M.D., in 1940 he became the first African American to earn the Doctor of Science in Surgery.

The importance of Charles Drew's research was underscored by the fact that Europe was at war and thousands of soldiers who would have been considered mortally wounded prior to Dr. Drew's discoveries, were saved. In 1941, the American Red Cross appointed Drew director of its first Blood Bank. When Pearl Harbor was attacked by the Japanese, Drew was able to provide blood plasma for Americans who were wounded during the surprise attack.

However, the American Red Cross decided to use only blood from white donors for wounded members of the military, insisting that they did not want to mix the blood of African Americans with white blood. Drew was enraged. He resigned from his position over the unscientific position of the American Red Cross saying, "The blood of individual human beings may differ by blood type groupings, but there is absolutely no scientific basis to indicate any difference according to race."

Fortunately, he was named head of the Department of Surgery, Chief Surgeon at Freedman's Hospital, now Howard University Hospital in Washington, DC. He continued to distinguish himself as a practical scientist. On April 1, 1950, he was fatally injured in a car accident in North Carolina, two months before his forty-sixth birthday. It was reported that

Drew bled to death because the "white" hospital would not admit him. Ironically, the surgeon, scientist, scholar, whose life's work was devoted to saving others was denied access to the methods and procedures he invented to save his own life.

Necessity and Freedom

African Americans found two important factors as contributors to inventions: necessity and freedom. The selected inventions found in this section represent a few of the practical inventions created by African Americans. Freedom meant that creative individuals could have their works patented. During the Great Enslavement any objects invented by an enslaved person was owned by the enslaver. How many inventions were developed by blacks but credited to white inventors during the Great Enslavement, no one knows. Just by examining the profusion of inventions patented by Africans in the period 1871–1900, one gets the idea that this creativity did not start with the emancipation.

More than three hundred patents were recorded during the twenty-nine year period mentioned above. Many of these patents were being developed during the Great Enslavement and were only revealed when slavery had ended. Artisans and tool-makers were often allowed to tinker in their owners' work sheds. Blacksmiths particularly were responsible for fashioning new inventions in order to make the work on the farms easier. Sometimes one enslaved person would take an idea to a blacksmith and ask him if he could create something to perform a certain task. When they were able to accomplish these creative feats to lessen the drudgery of their work, they felt some satisfaction.

The inventive spirit which poured forth after the Civil War and during the era of Reconstruction must be considered remarkable for a number of reasons. For the most part, the African American population was illiterate, few men or women could read or write. Yet within a few years inventors were capa-

ble of seeking their own patents. Many of the inventors used others to secure their patents for them. In some cases, unscrupulous lawyers and friends took advantage of the ignorance of the African American inventors and claimed the inventions as their own. Incidents such as this occurred often enough to make inventors cautious about their ideas. In fact, many African Americans instead of securing the patents for themselves sold the patents to entrepreneuring whites—who then made money on the inventions of Africans. The case of Garrett A. Morgan is one of the most celebrated examples of an African selling his invention or idea to whites who went on to reap great financial benefits from the idea. Morgan was born in 1877 and lived until 1963. He was an exceptionally bright inventor, creating several products of benefit to society.

Morgan's gas inhalator was shown to be effective against smoke when he rescued several men in Cleveland while wearing the inhalator. Hundreds of orders came in for the inhalator from fire companies throughout the United States. When southerners found out that the inventor was an African, they often cancelled their orders. In the First World War, the gas inhalator was transformed into a gas mask.

Unwilling to take a chance that prejudice against his race would thwart his aims to market his most famous technological invention, Garrett A. Morgan sold his automatic traffic light invention to the General Electric Company for $40,000.

Artists

When the word is spoken in the context of African Americans it arouses excitement and promise. From the performing arts to the plastic arts, the number of African Americans that can be classified as artists or who classify themselves as such is staggering given the population. Painters, poets, entertainers, dancers, choreographers, musicians, comedians, sculptors, actors, and composers are gathered in the African American popu-

Selected Inventions
by African Americans, 1871–1900

Inventor	Invention	Date
Ashbourne, A. P.	Biscuit cutter	November 30, 1875
Bailey, L. C.	Folding bed	July 18, 1899
Beard, A. J.	Rotary Engine	July 5, 1892
Beard, A. J.	Car-coupler	November 23, 1897
Becket, G. E.	Letter Box	October 4, 1892
Bell, L.	Locomotive smoke stack	May 23, 1871
Benjamin, M. E.	Gong and signal chairs for hotels	July 17, 1888
Binga, M. W.	Street sprinkling apparatus	July 22, 1879
Blackburn, A. B.	Railway signal	January 10, 1888
Blair, Henry	Corn planter	October 14, 1834
Blair, Henry	Cotton planter	August 31, 1836
Boone, Sarah	Ironing board	April 26, 1892
Brooks, C. B.	Street-sweepers	March 17, 1896
Brown, O. E.	Horseshoe	August 23, 1892
Burr, J. A.	Lawn mower	May 9, 1899
Butts, J. W.	Luggage carrier	October 10, 1899
Carter, W. C.	Umbrella stand	August 4, 1885
Church, T. S.	Carpet beating machine	July 29, 1884
Cook, G.	Automatic fishing device	May 10, 1899
Cooper, J.	Elevator device	April 2, 1895
Cornwall, P. W.	Draft Regulator	February 7, 1893
Cralle, A. L.	Ice-cream mold	February 2, 1897
Davis, W. R., Jr.	Library table	September 24, 1878
Dorticus, C. J.	Machine for embossing photo	April 16, 1895
Elkins, T.	Refrigerating apparatus	November 4, 1879
Flemming, F., Jr.	Guitar (variation)	March 3, 1886
Grant, G. F.	Golf tee	December 12, 1899
Gregory, J.	Motor	April 26, 1887
Headen, M.	Foot power hammer	October 5, 1886
Jackson, B. F.	Gas burner	April 4, 1899
Latimer and Nichols	Electric lamp	September 13, 1881
Marshall, T. J.	Fire extinguisher (variation)	May 26, 1872
McCoy, E.	Lubricator for steam engines	July 2, 1872
Spears, H.	Portable shield for infantry	December 27, 1870
Sutton, E. H.	Cotton cultivator	April 7, 1878
Woods, G. T.	Electromechanical brake	August 16, 1887
Woods, G. T.	Railway telegraphy	November 15, 1887
Woods, G. T.	Induction telegraph system	November 29, 1887
Woods, G. T.	Overhead conducting system for electric railway	May 29, 1888
Woods, G. T.	Electromotive railway system	June 26, 1888
Woods, G. T.	Railway telegraphy	August 28, 1888

lation at a higher percentage of the work force than in the general population. There is a belief that the person who brings joy and happiness to others sits closest to heaven.

Avery Brooks, the actor of stage and film, once spoke about his gift in terms of it being an attribute that comes with the territory of his family and his culture. He did not go to school to learn to sing; he sings. Music and dance, always part of the African culture, have remained the chief components in the drama of the African American artists. This is true whether an artist conceptualizes movies as Spike Lee does or paints as John Biggers paints. Dance and music are the elementary bases of the cultural approach. Thus, the poets and choreographers and sculptors deal with the complexities of the music and dance idioms in the African American culture. From the earliest days of the African Company in 1821 and Henry Brown's African Grove in the 1825 to the current time, African Americans have provided America with some of the most memorable occasions in entertainment. This expertise has not only known in the United States but all over the world, even in Africa itself. Pearl Primus established the National Dance Company of Liberia and Kariamu Welsh Asante established the National Dance Company of Zimbabwe. Other African American choreographers and artists have introduced African American culture and art to international audiences. This is particularly true with musicians.

Henry Ossawa Tanner

Henry Ossawa Tanner was born in Pittsburgh in 1859. He chose painting as a career during a time when it was difficult for an African American to make a living as an artist. After he attended the Pennsylvania Academy of Fine Arts, he discovered that he could not make a living unless he taught art and took photographs on the side.

Tanner's most famous work is called *The Banjo Lesson* (1890). Unable to make the kind of impact he wanted to make in the art field in the United States, Tanner went to France in 1891, where he concentrated on religious themes. At the time of his death in 1937 he had attained the stature of being the most respected black artist of his day.

Edmonia Lewis

Edmonia Lewis was the first African American woman to be considered an artist. She was also the first woman in America to be recognized as a sculptor.

She was born in 1845 in upstate New York. She was educated at Oberlin College in Ohio which was the first college to admit women on a nonsegregated basis. Edmonia Lewis was extremely interested in European classical subjects while at Oberlin. As soon as she left school she moved to Boston where she did a bust of Robert Gould Shaw, the commander of the first African American regiment from the state of Massachusetts during the Civil War. Lewis left the United States for Rome in 1865. She became a leading artist in Italy and when she returned to the states she was commissioned to do many works. She died in Rome in 1890.

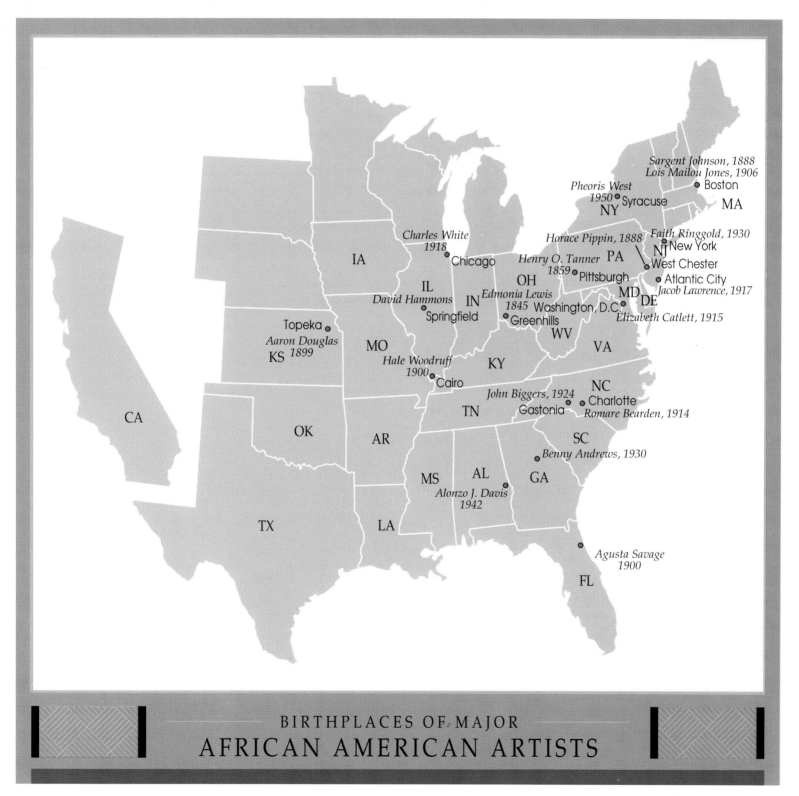

BIRTHPLACES OF MAJOR
AFRICAN AMERICAN ARTISTS

Lois Mailou Jones

Lois Mailou Jones is one of the greatest African American artists of the twentieth century. Born in 1905 in Boston, Jones was educated at the Boston Museum School of Fine Arts and Designers School.

She has become famous for the diversity of her art. She started as a fashion artist with award winning textile and design illustrations. In 1930, she became a professor at Howard University, teaching courses in design and watercolor painting. Jones interprets the African world from the background of her experiences in many cultures. She explores with sensitivity the depth and power of the compelling forces of color and shapes in the African American world view.

Sammy Davis, Jr.

Sammy Davis, Jr., "the world's greatest entertainer," died in 1990. Davis was born in New York City on December 8, 1925. He began appearing on stage at the age of four. His uncle, Will Mastin, had a trio which included Sammy Davis, Sr. and Sammy Davis, Jr.

During World War II, Davis joined the army and wrote and directed plays for the entertainment of the troops. When he returned to civilian life, he was able to secure an engagement in Hollywood. Davis became popular across the nation after his Hollywood stint. He recorded numerous hit tunes and was famous for his many talents as a singer, actor, dancer, mimic, and musician. Sammy Davis, Jr. was the complete entertainer.

Aretha Franklin

Aretha Franklin was born in 1942. She im-

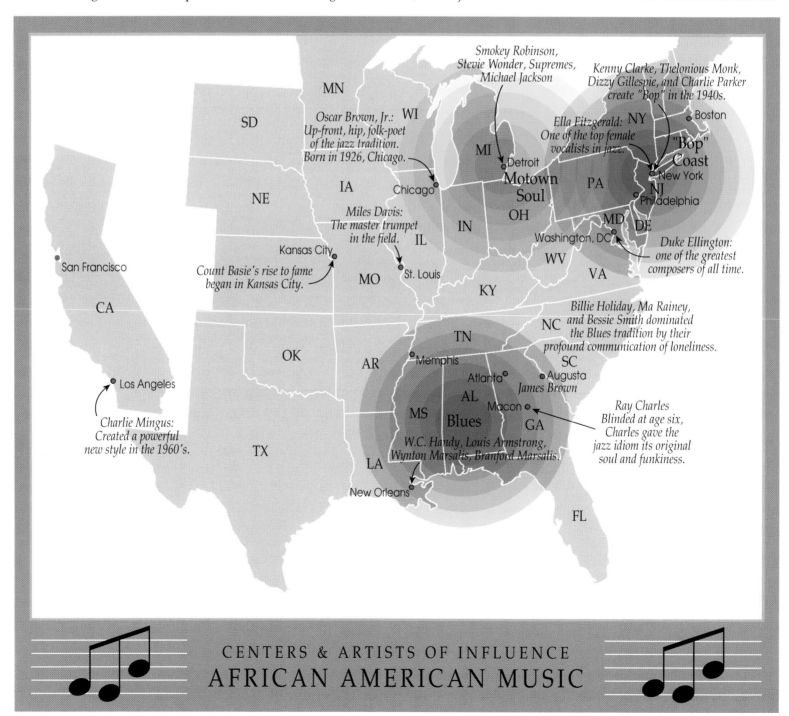

Smokey Robinson, Stevie Wonder, Supremes, Michael Jackson

Kenny Clarke, Thelonious Monk, Dizzy Gillespie, and Charlie Parker create "Bop" in the 1940s.

Oscar Brown, Jr.: Up-front, hip, folk-poet of the jazz tradition. Born in 1926, Chicago.

Ella Fitzgerald: One of the top female vocalists in jazz.

"Bop" Coast

Motown Soul

Miles Davis: The master trumpet in the field.

Duke Ellington: one of the greatest composers of all time.

Count Basie's rise to fame began in Kansas City.

Billie Holiday, Ma Rainey, and Bessie Smith dominated the Blues tradition by their profound communication of loneliness.

James Brown

Charlie Mingus: Created a powerful new style in the 1960's.

Ray Charles Blinded at age six, Charles gave the jazz idiom its original soul and funkiness.

Blues

W.C. Handy, Louis Armstrong, Wynton Marsalis, Branford Marsalis.

CENTERS & ARTISTS OF INFLUENCE
AFRICAN AMERICAN MUSIC

Duke Ellington

Mahalia Jackson

mersed herself in the spirituals and gospels that were popular in her father's church in Detroit. By the time she signed a contract with Atlantic Records, she had already become a major figure in the gospel singing world. But it was not until she started singing rhythm and blues that she became a superstar. Her albums have sold millions of copies around the world with her special blend of gospel sounds and blues cadences. She has appeared in film, entertained in Europe and Asia, and launched several artistic ventures of her own. Called by her contemporaries, "the modern queen of soul," Aretha Franklin is a musician of superior ability.

Davis and Franklin are two examples of a host of talented African American musicians. The list is endless: Paul Robe-son, Grace Bumbry, Ray Charles, Samuel Coleridge-Taylor, Margaret Bonds, Duke Ellington, Count Basie, Leontyne Price, Martina Arroyo, Ted McDaniel, Frank Foster, David Baker, Marian Anderson, Michael Jackson, Stevie Wonder, and Andre Watts.

Duke Ellington

Duke Ellington is believed to be the single most impressive figure in modern American music. Unquestionably he contributed more to jazz than any other composer. He is responsible for writing more than five hundred compositions, some of them standards in the field.

He was born in 1899 in Washington, DC to a well-to-do family. Because of his artistic gifts, he was given a scholarship to the Pratt Institute of Fine Arts in New York. However, he decided to play local music engagements instead. To support himself between engagements he painted signs and houses. Soon he was doing well enough with music to forego his painting. Some people believe that he would have become a fairly successful artist had he continued in that genre. As it turned out, Ellington did not do so badly in music.

Gaining fame from his tours with such greats as Fats Waller and Sonny Greer,

Michael Jackson

Duke Ellington worked to establish the jazz discipline. A five year stint at the Cotton Club from 1927 to 1932 cemented his talents and his reputation in the field of African American music. He made many records from the Cotton Club and became a prominent figure in the jazz world. Other bandleaders used Ellington as their lodestone. His genius was so vast and so creative that he moved the world of jazz in any way he wanted. While other musicians and bandleaders may have been satisfied with remaining a fixture at the Cotton Club, the Duke took his show on the road and found more success than he had ever dreamed possible. His collaborations with Cootie Williams, Barney Bigard, and Johnny Hodges established the style of jazz orchestrations for the next twenty-five years. Among his contributions to the field of jazz were practical, as well as theoretical items. For example, Ellington was the first musician to gain more than the three minute limit on the length of commercial records. He was also the first to use scatting as a jazz instrument. The

Dizzy Gillespie

best musicians of the time played with his band. Oscar Peterson, Ben Webster, Ray Nance, and Harry Carney were just a few of the giants of the business who played with Duke's band.

Dizzy Gillespie and Charlie Parker

The co-founders of the innovative jazz movement known as Be Bop were Dizzy Gillespie and Charlie Parker. The creations of these two musical geniuses continues to direct the field of jazz. Gillespie was an arranger and writer as well as a master trumpeter. Charlie Parker was a gifted saxophonist. The combination of Gillespie and Parker was electric for the jazz field. After the death of Charlie Parker in 1955, Dizzy Gillespie went on to become the major interpreter of the Be Bop school of jazz.

Gillespie was born in 1917 in North Carolina. He moved to Philadelphia and later joined with Fletcher Henderson and others in small orchestras. By the time he joined with Cab Calloway and Mercer Ellington he had perfected his Be Bop experimentation and his name was sealed in history.

John Coltrane

John Coltrane left his mark on the tenor saxophone in such a way that it is impossible to discuss the instrument without reference to him. Coltrane spent many years developing his style and technique in Philadelphia. His early work in the jazz idiom was with Miles Davis, Thelonius Monk, and Dizzy Gillespie.

Coltrane was the epitome of tenor saxophone innovators. His music was often considered harsh and different but it became the standard by which younger saxophonists judged themselves. No presence in jazz saxophone was as dominating as that of John Coltrane during his short life. His experimentation, particularly alongside Thelonius Monk, has been compared with the innovation of Gillespie and Parker. At his death in 1967, Coltrane was already a historical figure.

Louis Armstrong

Louis Armstrong was born on July 4,

1900. By the time of his death in 1971, he had become one of the best loved people on earth. As a child of fourteen, Armstrong was arrested in New Orleans for firing a pistol. He was sent away to the boys' home where he learned to play the cornet. When he was released from the home, Armstrong knew what he wanted to do for a living.

King Oliver, who had played in the Kid Ory Band, left for Chicago in 1919 and Louis Armstrong was given his place in the band. When he went to Chicago in 1922 to join King Oliver, he was well on his way to international fame. Oliver and Armstrong perfected duets which engaged them in counterpoint with each other. The audiences loved their performances. Armstrong also worked with Fletcher Henderson and Erskine Tate. Through all of his engagements he continued to exhibit tremendous charisma as a performer. He traveled the world as an ambassador of jazz.

When he performed solo, as he did on many occasions, he elevated jazz in the minds of many listeners because of his skill and his ability to engage the audiences. Louis "Satchmo" Armstrong was one of the greatest performers to have lived in the twentieth century. He performed in films, plays, and as a soloist. In the 1930s he toured Europe with Bing Crosby to rave reviews for his artistry. He died in his sleep in 1971.

B. B. King

B. B. King's influence in the blues world is without comparison. In the 1960s and 1970s he became the most celebrated blues musician of all time. No other blues artist has sold as many records as B.B. King. He was born in Indianola, Mississippi in 1925. From the humble beginnings of a black child in Mississippi during the period of Mississippi's worst outbreak of violence against blacks, B. B. King rose to become the most famous name in blues.

B.B. King gained international recognition after he made a tour of Europe and appeared on a number of television shows.

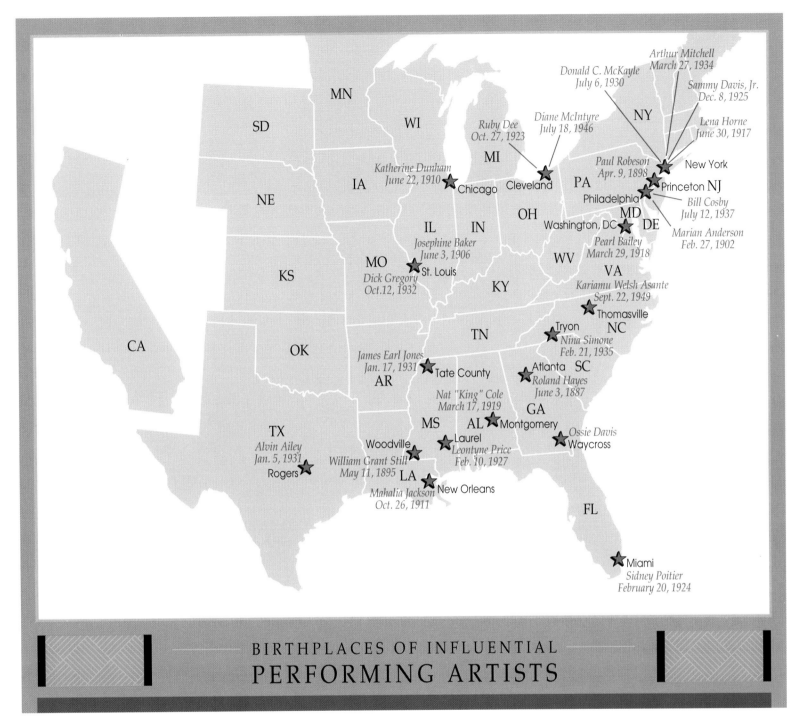

Neither Billie Holiday, Big Bill Broonzy, Bessie Smith, nor Leadbelly ever came close to the popularity of the versatile guitarist B.B. King.

Billie Holiday

Billie Holiday dominated the vocal tradition in blues in ways that neither Bessie Smith nor Ma Rainey were ever able to do. She was referred to by Lester Young, as "Lady Day" because of style and charisma. Born in Baltimore in 1915, Holiday moved to New York when she was still a young girl. In Harlem she began to sing at various nightclubs to the thrill of her audiences. In 1934, she made her first recording with Benny Goodman.

Billie Holiday's most famous records were "Strange Fruit" and "God Bless the Child." In both of these classic recordings she conveyed the universal sense of loneliness that has become so much a part of the African American's ethos—a deep, personal, and collective longing for a place, some place, far away from here.

The Movie Industry

The portrayal of African Americans in the popular media in the United States has always been caught on the cross of expediency. White filmmakers and producers have not seen the African American audience as primary in the presentation of images and symbols. Therefore, the images of the African American that appear in the movie are more often than not images that are comfortable to whites. Inherent in the presentation of images of Africans that are comfortable to whites is the contradiction that they will not be positive, real, or utilitarian images to blacks.

The movie industry has had this problem since 1915, when *The Birth of a Nation*, was presented to the public. D. W. Griffith, the filmmaker, was considered among the most innovative filmmakers of the period and he is still revered as one of the great minds of the film industry. He established the pattern that was to be followed by successive filmmakers and producers in Hollywood.

The movie was a hit with white audiences, but it was negative about Africans. Blacks in this film were portrayed by whites in blackface. The image Griffith presented of the African American was of a scared, laughing, clowning, benevolent fool. Furthermore, African Americans during the Reconstruction were shown as corrupt, vile, licientious villains. It is not difficult to see how these images could be rejected by blacks. While whites may have gained laughter from the portrayals, blacks saw them as one more attempt to destroy the self-esteem of African Americans. Thus, the complexity of the expediency question was thrown into relief for succeeding generations of white movie makers. Griffith made another film, *One Exciting Night* in 1922 which further underscored his negative portrayal of Africans. Apologists for Griffith often cite the film *Intolerance* as his attempt to counter the stereotypes he had created about the African. At the height of the southern attacks on Africans the presentation of these negative images simply added fuel to fires of hatred already burning.

The image of Africans as savages and barbarians was presented in other movies. Thus, early movies such as *Hallelujah* and *Hearts in Dixie* served to create the most appalling images of African Americans. It is true that these images were found in the literature and popular culture of the society but the movie industry gave a legitimacy to them which has continued to the present time.

Sidney Poitier

Black exploitation films popular in the 1970s as a reaction to the interest in African images were almost universally sadistic, macho, and violent. However, blacks flocked to these films because Hollywood was providing images of blacks, while not flattering, were action oriented and full of popular culture. When the industry regained its financial footing, the making of movies with a specifically black interest again disappeared. The movies of the seventies exploited the African American audience but provided no real substance in terms of the concerns and interests of the black community. The films of this period were financially successful until the audience grew weary of the same formula of beautiful women and men who were sexy savages, killing each other for drugs.

The rise of Spike Lee as a filmmaker in the 1980s created a stir in Hollywood because for the first time a filmmaker seemed to have the heart and soul of his black audience in mind as he made his films. Spike Lee spoke of his work as Afrocentric in the sense of the African American being a subject rather than a

marginal object. Such a revelation may well continue to activate the best filmmakers in African American culture.

Sidney Poitier

Sidney Poitier was the most dominant African American film actor for a generation. He was born in Miami on February 20, 1927. His family raised him in the Bahamas until he was fifteen years old. At that time he returned to Miami and finally caught a freight train to New York. Once he arrived in New York he secured employment at a restaurant washing dishes. When the war came, Poitier enlisted and served for four years.

As soon as he got out of the army he headed for New York again. This time he auditioned for the American Negro Theatre Company. He was eventually allowed to work for the company but had to take acting and diction lessons.

His first film was the 1950 film, *No Way Out*. In succession he made about ten films during the decade of the 1950s. He starred in *A Raisin in the Sun* both on Broadway and in the film version. In 1965 Sidney Poitier received the Oscar for his performance in *Lilies of the Field*, the first African American to receive the award for a starring role. He had been nominated earlier for the award for his performance in *The Defiant Ones*.

Paul Robeson

Paul Robeson was born in Princeton, New Jersey, on April 9, 1898. Robeson rose to become one of the best known African Americans in history. He went to Rutgers University on a football scholarship and won letters in every sport in which he participated, establishing a record for the university. He was not only a world-class athlete but he also gained Phi Beta Kappa honors for his academic achievements.

Because of his thirst for knowledge he enrolled in Columbia Law School and obtained a law degree in 1923. He made his professional debut as an actor in 1922 in *Taboo*. His most famous roles were in *Emperor Jones* and *Othello*.

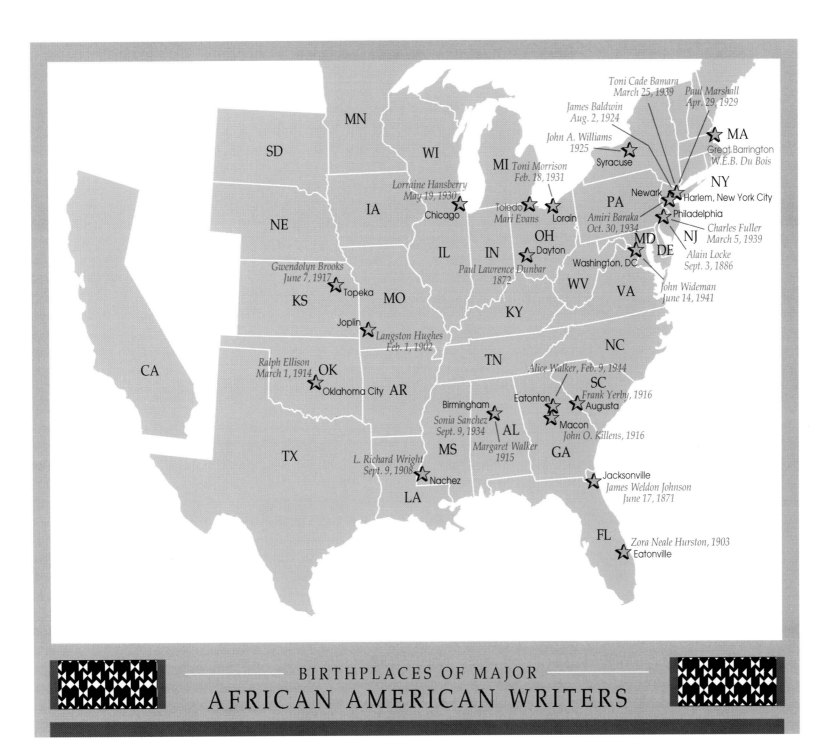

Toni Cade Bamara
March 25, 1939

Paul Marshall
Apr. 29, 1929

James Baldwin
Aug. 2, 1924

John A. Williams
1925

MA
Great Barrington
W.E.B. Du Bois

Syracuse

MN

SD

WI

MI Toni Morrison
Feb. 18, 1931

Lorraine Hansberry
May 19, 1930

NY

Newark

Harlem, New York City

IA

NE

Chicago

Toledo
Mari Evans

Lorain

PA

Amiri Baraka
Oct. 30, 1934

Philadelphia

IL

IN

OH
Dayton

MD

DE

NJ

Charles Fuller
March 5, 1939

Gwendolyn Brooks
June 7, 1917

Paul Lawrence Dunbar
1872

Washington, DC

Alain Locke
Sept. 3, 1886

Topeka

MO

WV

VA

John Wideman
June 14, 1941

KS

Joplin

KY

CA

Langston Hughes
Feb. 1, 1902

NC

Ralph Ellison
March 1, 1914

OK

TN

Alice Walker, Feb. 9, 1944

SC

Oklahoma City

AR

Birmingham

Eatonton

Frank Yerby, 1916

Augusta

Sonia Sanchez
Sept. 9, 1934

AL

Macon
John O. Killens, 1916

TX

MS

Margaret Walker
1915

GA

L. Richard Wright
Sept. 9, 1908

Nachez

LA

Jacksonville
James Weldon Johnson
June 17, 1871

FL

Zora Neale Hurston, 1903
Eatonville

BIRTHPLACES OF MAJOR
AFRICAN AMERICAN WRITERS

Paul Robeson was a living legend. He traveled to many countries, singing and acting and demonstrating the versatility and depth of African American culture. He spoke Spanish, French, German, Russian, Chinese, and Gaelic. He was a political activist as well as a scholar and actor. Wherever he saw oppression and human exploitation, he spoke out against it. His career suffered as a result, but Robeson was true to his commitments in support of human rights.

African American Writers

African American writers have become major interpreters of the contemporary and historical scene. The most important American writers of this era cannot be named without the naming of African Americans. Toni Morrison is one of the most significant novelists at the onset of the 1990s. Her works continue to thrust her into the forefront of the genre. By the same token, she is joined by Paule Marshall, Alice Walker, and Gloria Naylor as major figures in the literature

of the novel. In drama, the playwrights Charles Fuller and August Wilson must be considered two of the best of the last two decades. Other writers include John A. Williams, Mari Evans, John Edgar Wideman, Sonia Sanchez, Ntozake Shange, Ismael Reed, David Bradley, and Marita Golden.

Margaret Walker

Margaret Walker was born on July 7, 1915 in Birmingham, Alabama. She published her famous poem, *For My People*, in 1942.

She received a fellowship to study at the University of Iowa. Her most famous novel is *Jubilee*. She has written several other works including an intellectual and analytical biography of Richard Wright.

John A. Williams

John A. Williams was born in Jackson, Mississippi in 1925. He is considered one of the best contemporary novelists. Williams has consistently made innovations in the novel form while maintaining a strong identification with his audience. Convinced that he should write for his audience, his most famous works are *The Angry Ones*, *The Man Who Cried I Am*, *Click Song*, *Sissie*, and *Sons of Darkness*.

Richard Wright

Richard Wright was the first major African American novelist to gain wide acceptance for his work. His work is still seen as the measure of many other writers. He had a significant influence on the manner in which Ralph Ellison and James Baldwin articulated their views of the African American reality. Wright's major works were *Native Son* and *Black Boy*.

Zora Neale Hurston

Zora Neale Hurston was a consummate writer who used her experiences and those of her people as the materials for her novels and essays. Her most famous novel which is now considered a classic is *Their Eyes were Watching God*. She also wrote anthropological essays and folklore as well as an autobiography.

Allensworth: The Philosopher's Town

Having shown extraordinary industry in overcoming the deficiencies of the previous condition of servitude, Africans at the turn of the twentieth century felt the stings of discrimination and prejudice meant to force them into political, economic, and social subjugation through segregation laws. Numerous individuals—determined to establish new possibilities—built schools, institutions, businesses, and towns. One of the most remarkable characters in this period was Colonel Allen Allensworth, the founder of Allensworth, the only African Ameri-

James Baldwin

Richard Wright

Alice Walker

Sonia Sanchez

Toni Cade Bambara

can town ever built in California.

Allen Allensworth was born in Louisville, Kentucky on April 7, 1842. He showed early evidence of resistance to a system that would not allow him to learn to read. At the age of twelve he was sold for teaching himself to read and write. His slaveowner thought he would become uncontrollable and create dissension among other Africans. As soon as he was twenty-one years of age, Allensworth fled slavery and became a member of the United States Army. His experience in the Union Army served as a basic lesson in the future of America.

After the Civil War, Allensworth worked in the commissary of the St. Louis Navy Yard until he could save money for a business. In 1867, he entered the restaurant business with his brother. Always eager to better his living conditions, he took advantage of the Eli Normal School's program to improve his education. This led him to the study of the Bible and the ministry. By 1871, Allensworth was an ordained preacher for the Fifth St. Baptist Church. Six years later he married the talented pianist Josephine Leavell who was also a school teacher. They had two daughters, Nellie and Eva.

The United States Army had four black regiments in the 1880s and none of them had a black chaplain. Allensworth appealed to President Grover Cleveland to appoint him chaplain for the African soldiers. This request was granted on April 1, 1886 and Allensworth was made chaplain of the 14th Infantry with the rank of captain. He later reached the rank of lieutenant colonel. He served the Army until 1906 and upon his retirement took his family to settle in Los Angeles.

Since Allensworth had become a leading orator for self-help programs of economic empowerment, he was ready in 1908 to put his philosophy to practice.

William Payne, a young teacher, was to become Allensworth's chief supporter when the colonel proposed a race colony. Payne had received some education at Denison University in Granville, Ohio, and was a gifted teacher. Unable to acquire a job in public education in Pasadena, Payne combined his talents and resources with those of Allensworth. They persuaded several others to join their efforts to establish a colony. Dr. Peck, an African Methodist Episcopal minister; Mr. Palmer, a Nevada miner; and Mr. Mitchell, a Los Angeles realtor joined to form the California Colonization and Home Promotion Association.

The organization selected an area around a depot connecting Los Angeles and San Francisco on the Santa Fe rail line. The depot, called Solito, was renamed Allensworth. It began a thriving community of farmers, artisans, and teachers. Allensworth had its own post office, school, drug store, livery stable, machine shop, and hotel. Plans to build a vocational school on the philosophy of Booker T. Washington were developed but the state legislature refused to support the idea.

Amiri Baraka

Zora Neale Hurston

Larry Neal

Toni Morrison

The Allensworth Progressive Association was the governing body of the town. The officers were elected and held town meetings to foster full participation by all residents. The town became a school district in 1912, incorporating thirty-three square miles. In 1914, the town was made a judicial district and two residents, Oscar Overr and William H. Dotson, became the first black men in California history to hold elected offices as justice of the peace and constable, respectively. Colonel Allensworth was killed in Los Angeles in 1914 when he stepped off a streetcar and was struck by a motorcyclist.

Despite the lack of water and constant legal battles with the Pacific Farming Company, (the land development company responsible for delivering water to the town), Allensworth survived until 1966 when suspiciously high levels of arsenic were found in the town's well water. The town became a state historical site on May 14, 1976.

Toni Morrison

Toni Morrison emerged in the 1970s and 1980s as an authoritative African American novelist. Born in Lorain, Ohio, on February 19, 1931, Morrison's influence has grown with each novel. Among the novels which have gained her international recognition are *The Bluest Eye* (1970), *Sula* (1973), *Song of Solomon* (1977), *Tar Baby* (1981) and *Beloved* (1987) for which she won the Pulitzer Prize. She has explored childhood madness, the estrangement of friends, fables of eroticism, discovery and power, enslavement, and the supernatural. Toni Morrison is recognized as one of the most influential writers of the twentieth century.

Frances Ellen Harper

Born of free parents in 1825 in Baltimore, Frances Ellen Harper was educated in

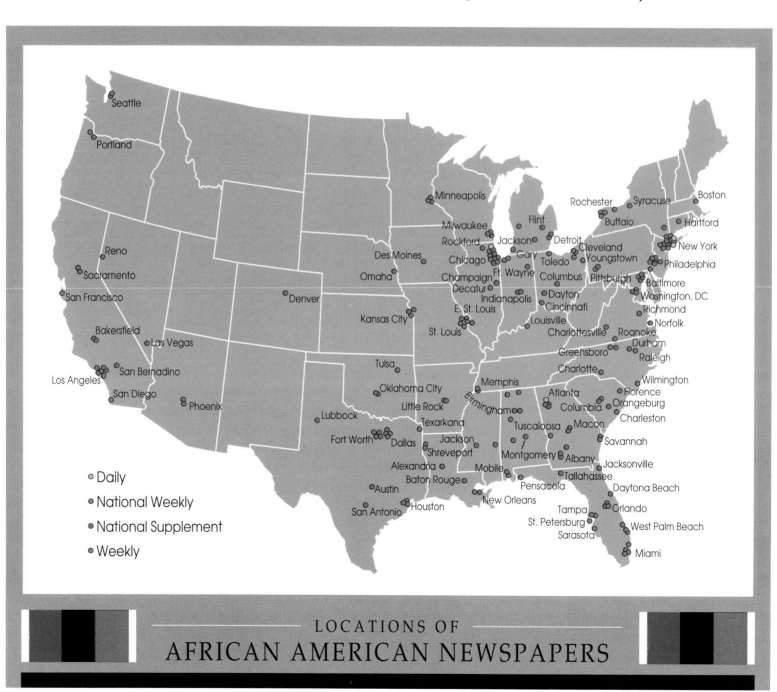

LOCATIONS OF
AFRICAN AMERICAN NEWSPAPERS

Baltimore at a school run by her uncle. Born Frances Watkins, she married Fenton Harper in 1860. A volume of her verse, *Poems on Miscellaneous Subjects* (1857), sold 10,000 copies in the first five years following publication. Her other works include *Sketches of Southern Life* (1872) and *Moses: A Story of the Nile* (1869). The most popular black poet of her time, she raised the question of whether Afro-American authors should dwell on their own racial problems or address such wider issues as temperance.

Music and Dance

Olaudah Equiano wrote in *The Interesting Narrative of the Life of Olaudah Equiano* (London 1789) that in Africa "every great event . . . is celebrated in public dances, which are accompanied with songs and music suited to the occasion." Among African Americans the dance remains a principal medium of expression. The exclamation, "Let's party!" is synonymous with "Let's dance!" This compound expressive modality, combining party and dance, has precedents in Africa with the words "music" and "dance." In many West African languages, to say music is to mean dancing as well. Thus, to conceive of music without the dance is almost impossible.

The Spirituals represent the most fundamental epic of the African American people. Collectively, the more than one thousand songs growing from the deepest emotional wellsprings of a patient, optimistic, persistent, long-suffering, strong, joyous, hard-working, clever, religious, creative, sorrowful, happy people, are the intense testaments of nobility.

They are the noble statements of a gifted people, infused with dignity and strength under duress, these songs voice the majestic grandeur of victory over oppression. They possess an exalted

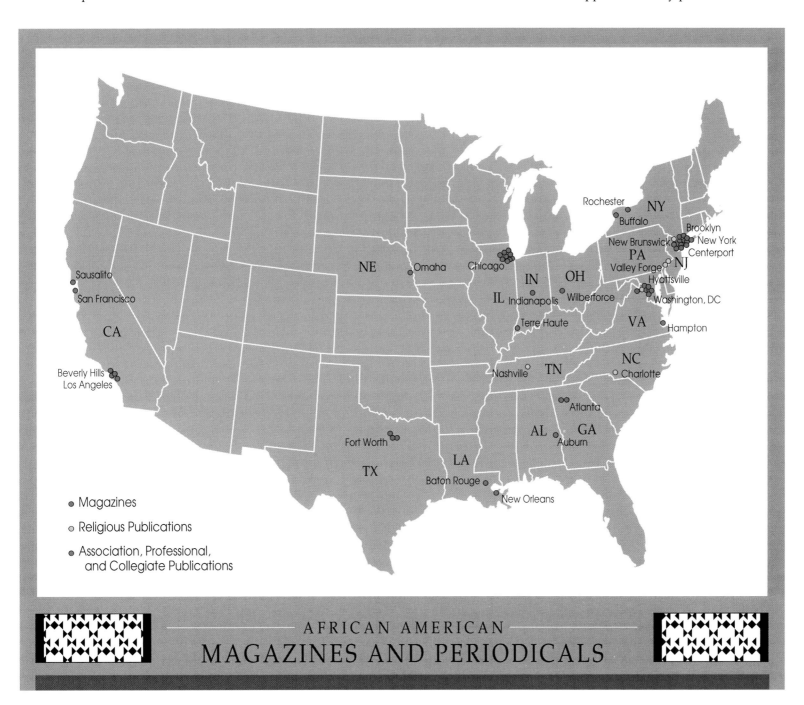

AFRICAN AMERICAN
MAGAZINES AND PERIODICALS

sentiment that never falls below the line of greatness. Whether you hear "Go Down Moses" or "Walk Together, Children," you will feel the same sense of grandeur.

Those who created these Master Songs did so despite the fact that they had come from various parts of the continent of Africa. In the crucible of slavery were Yoruba, Ibo, Hausa, Fulani, Akan, Ewe, Ga, Wolof, Touculeur, Mande, Sherbro, Luba, Kuba, Dan, Douala, Ibidio, Edo, and more than one hundred other ethnic groups.

Over a 250 year period these songs constituted the most elegant statement of a people's relationship to the universe and one another. In the music of the Spiritual one finds the total embodiment of the African soul in response to the alien conditions of a new land, a new language, and a new religion.

Indeed, the Spirituals serve as calling cards to the world, a signature attesting to the uniqueness of African Americans' historical experiences in America.

*"Go down Moses, way down yonder
in Egypt's land, tell ole
Pharaoh to let my people go"*

With a limited knowledge of Africa and a rich imagination applied to the stories from the Jewish Bible, African Americans translated so much of the Judeo-Christian legacy into specific situations.

*You got to walk that lonesome valley.
You got to do there by yourself.
Ain't nobody here can go there for you.*

The instruction was definite; the commitment personal. Ultimately, each person had to go through whatever "valley" of life alone. Often when parents would witness their children sold away from the

AFRICAN AMERICAN
RADIO STATIONS

plantation where they had been born, they would retire to their shacks and sing in the most mournful tones "You got to walk that lonesome valley."

These songs make the African American's spiritual world. They frame the mythical ideas that inform the epic journey of the people in a strange land. What the early Africans attempted to do in the cotton and tobacco fields with these songs was to record, if not on paper with pen, in the hearts of the people with pathos, the meaning of the enslavement and the emancipation from it. The songs grew out of religious sentiment, perhaps in some instances incomplete Christian references, but certain and meaningful African religious ideas and patterns of living. Thus, they held the African's commitment to family, to children, to mother, to the earth, to the water, particularly the river, and to hope. In fact, hope as faith was the central element in many of the earlier songs. The Africans could not live under the Great Enslavement without some hope, some possibility of liberation, some balance in God's system of justice.

DuBois, in his wisdom, called these master songs the sorrow songs because they recorded the sufferings and pains of an enslaved people. Always, however, these songs introduced an element of victory over despair. The people danced.

The Law

The condition of Africans in America has always been consecrated by law, regardless of the political era. Thus, under enslavement the federal and state laws defined the limits of African freedom. Despite the social, theological, and economic reasons given for enslavement, the ultimate grounds of the American case against Africans were the system of laws effected to define the African's place.

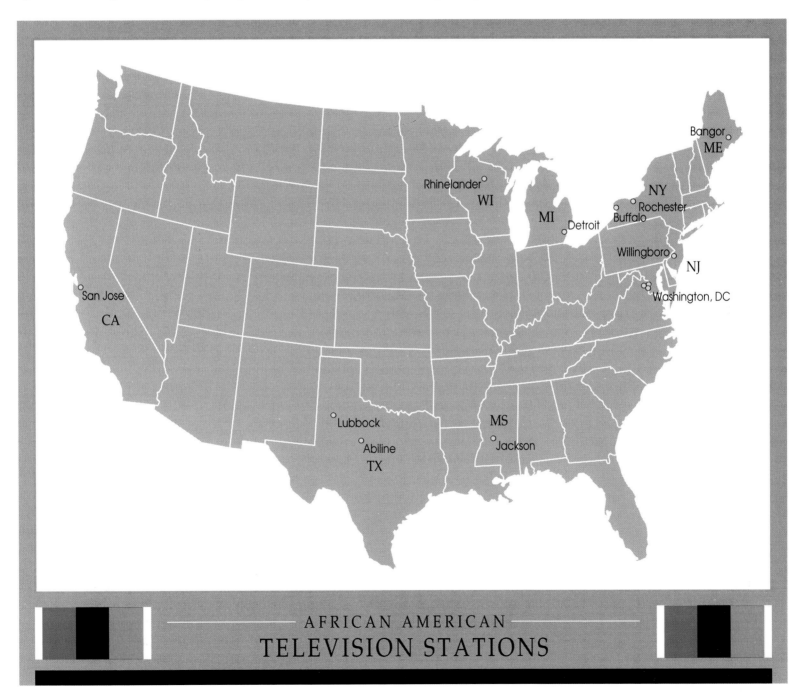

AFRICAN AMERICAN
TELEVISION STATIONS

Much like the situation of blacks in South Africa during most of the twentieth century, Africans in America experienced legal imprisonment.

Many issues were raised during Enslavement which had to be adjudicated by law. In fact, the draconian system of laws often created ambiguity even in the minds of the enslaved. The Dred Scott case and the subsequent decision of 1857, ostensibly nullified the power of Congress to prohibit slavery in the territories. The Supreme Court, under Chief Justice Roger B. Taney, followed the lead of many lower courts on African rights. Indeed, in 1849 the Massachusetts Supreme Court had upheld Boston's right to keep schools segregated. Although this was later struck down by the Massachusetts legislature, the Boston case would be cited in many subsequent court cases.

It would take the Civil Rights era to usher in the new dispensation. Lawyers such as Thurgood Marshall and Fred Gray made legal history. Gray, a young attorney in Montgomery, was considered alongside Martin Luther King, Jr., a leader of the Montgomery Bus Boycott movement. A skillful attorney, Gray, like King, was in his twenties when the boycott was introduced. A graduate of Case Western Reserve School of Law in Cleveland, Ohio, Fred Gray's ambition had always been to provide legal services for those who could least afford them. Montgomery gave him service and national prominence. Influenced by the courage and genius of the NAACP's lawyers, particularly Thurgood Marshall, Gray was a southern example, much like Medgar Evers, of the will to challenge racism and segregation in their own chambers.

With reference to the wrongs inflicted and injuries received by the African American community in Montgomery and other cities in Alabama and the South, the young lawyers of the Southern Christian Leadership Conference preached a religion of equality, civil rights, justice, and peace. They gained political insight, educational experiences, and practical skills which were to be used in many venues during the Civil Rights Movement. These local attorneys assisted the legal battle for civil rights by defending demonstrators in court.

Civil Rights/Unionism

By 1963, more than 100 of the then 130 affiliate chapters of the AFL-CIO had pledged to abolish racially segregated chapters, accept all eligible applicants regardless of race, color or creed, and work for non-discrimination agreements in all contracts made with management. This did not mean that all of the local affiliates were successful in transforming themselves.

Segregation was a matter of practice and custom in the United States federal government and often agencies found themselves searching out their own racial contradictions. Through all of this, the African American community kept up its campaign to desegregate American society beginning with the government.

Nearly 300,000 African Americans worked for the U.S. Government in 1963, representing a total of approximately 13 percent of all government employees. Most of these employees were in blue

Julian Bond

collar jobs and those in white collar jobs were concentrated in the four lowest grades. Nevertheless, some African Americans pointed to the percentage of the government labor force as indicative of achievement during a time when African Americans were only 11 percent of the national population.

As in other periods of American history, so it was in the 1950s and early 1960s, the bulk of the black population was untouched by the government hiring statistics. For example, in 1963, the year of the March on Washington, 12 percent of the African American population was unemployed as compared to 5.6 percent unemployment for the whole population.

The 1960s were to be turbulent and dynamic years. The condition of African Americans at the top of the 1960s was severe to say the least. Segregated housing was still the custom of the land. This meant an intensification of all of the social problems that come with high density enforced by the iron hand of practice: overcrowded schools, poor health, high insurance rates, deterioration of housing stock, and juvenile delinquency.

Protests and petitions were developed and executed in an effort to force real estate firms and banks to discontinue discriminatory practices. The more than 1,400,000 African Americans who had migrated to the North in the 1950s served a catalytic role in many of the protests in the North. Thus, North and South, the movement for freedom and justice was joined and in the 1960s the nation was one massive cauldron of shifting ideologies and structural transformations.

The National Association for the Advancement of Colored People had introduced a wide range of lawsuits contesting discrimination on the basis of race in every public sector. Rivalry between leaders of the civil rights organizations produced attacks on segregation on the economic, legal, and social fronts. Leaders of the NAACP, the Congress of Racial Equality, and the Urban League, were joined by the Southern Christian Leadership Conference and the Student

Nonviolent Coordinating Committee as the Big Five of the Civil Rights Movement. Supported by the labor movement they produced the dramatic 1963 March on Washington.

James Weldon Johnson

By the 1950s, the NAACP had demonstrated its ability to attract some of the most intelligent activists of the century. Alongside DuBois and Walter White, James Weldon Johnson was a stalwart in every campaign for respect and dignity. He joined the staff of the NAACP in 1916, two years before Walter White, and established himself as one of the leading promoters of the organization. Johnson, along with his brother Rosamond, wrote the "Negro National Anthem" which begins "Lift Every Voice and Sing." Johnson's place in the annals of African American history is singularly enshrined in protest against injustice and in the defense of freedom.

The Age of Glory

Martin Luther King, Jr. gave his famous "I Have a Dream" speech at the Lincoln Monument in Washington, DC, on August 28, 1963. Four young African American girls were bombed to death in a Birmingham, Alabama church during the same year. The battle lines were clearly drawn and segregationists intensified their campaign to enforce the laws of violence and terror. They were met with the tenacity and courage of scores of young leaders. Julian Bond, Robert Moses, James Forman, Charles Blackwell, Dona Richards, Fannie Lou Hamer, Cornelia Gray, and an army of volunteers. The movement was larger than anyone. It could not be stopped because the moral outrage was so vast and monumental that the society was carried toward a new destiny. As the Yoruba say, "Eshu was having his own way and that was that."

James Chaney, Michael Schwerner, and Andrew Goodman were murdered in Philadelphia, Mississippi, in 1964. The federal government arrested nineteen whites for various charges but not mur-

James Weldon Johnson

der. Among those arrested were the sheriff and deputy sheriff of Neshoba County. Robert Moses emerged as one of the chief organizers of the Student Nonviolent Coordinating Committee. He helped to fashion a regional network linking the civil rights workers with resources and volunteers. James Forman assumed a leadership role in the struggle by asserting a militant stand against Christians who support segregation. Julian Bond led the demonstrations against segregated lunch counters in Atlanta, Georgia. Dona Richards left the University of Chicago and went south during the summer of 1964. She registered voters under the freedom registration program. The Freedom Democratic Party was firmly established and founded upon voter's strength. Fannie Lou Hamer, Cornelia Gray, and other local people traveled to Atlantic City to the Democratic National Convention of 1964. The case of the party was placed before the Credentials Committee of the Democratic Party. Hamer refused to accept a compromise and is projected into history because of her eloquent defense of principle and morality. Her tone was

firm because it was based upon the concrete work she had done with the organizers of the Freedom Democratic Party.

The names of the martyrs were read in churches: Medgar Evers, Jimmie Lee Jackson, Viola Liuzzo, James Reeb, Chaney, Schwerner, and Goodman. Organizations worked around the clock to defeat the racists who attempted to block the movement through fear tactics.

James Farmer of the Congress of Racial Equality (Core) became a visible symbol of leadership, breaking with the more moderate position of the leadership of other civil rights organizations to join with the Southern Christian Leadership Conference and the Student NonViolent Coordinating Committee for more direct action. CORE became a dynamic ally of the civil rights movement, helping to shape and direct its course. The leadership of the NAACP and Urban League were supportive but noncommittal on the value of direct action to achieve effective progress for the African American community. Nevertheless they were supportive of the general aims of the movement.

Roy Wilkins, the leader of the NAACP, and Whitney Young, leader of the Urban League, had always seen themselves as the legitimate heirs to the protest tradition. They had become suspect to the leaders of SNCC, CORE, and VISTA because of the slowness with which they moved for legitimate redress of grievances. Both were stalwarts of the struggle in much the same way as A. Philip Randolph, the Father of the Modern Protest, had been during his active days. They believed that legal remedies were permanent remedies.

Like the rest of the nation, the civil rights community was stunned by the creativity, courage, and boldness of the students in the movement. The Freedom Riders and volunteers for the freedom registration campaigns had focused the national attention so keenly on the grievances of the African American people that it was only a matter of time before racial segregation as a system crumbled.

Blue Fathia,
Ghana Africa

"DIDN'T MY LORD DELIVER DANIEL": SOCIAL AND ECONOMIC REALITIES

African Americans were predominantly a rural and southern people until the Great Urban Migration of the World War II era. Thousands of African Americans moved to the major northern urban centers to seek better jobs and more equitable living conditions, free from racial prejudice.

The great cities of the North that had attracted escaped Africans during the Great Enslavement now provided opportunities for southern blacks to begin life anew. Cities such as Chicago, New York, Philadelphia, and Detroit became magnets for entire southern communities. In some instances, family members would gain employment and then send for other family members, relatives, and friends.

What attracted African Americans most was the freedom from anti-African sentiment. This was translated in practical terms as the ability for people to secure employment without regard to race. The lure of economic prosperity, political enfranchisement, and social mobility overpowered the young men and women. The elderly were often left on the farms, as the young people went off to the North to work and perhaps send for their parents and grandparents once they were firmly established.

The North did not hold all good fortune. In fact, residential segregation in the North was frequently the pattern. Much like the African-American commu-

nities in the South, the segregated northern communities were centers of commerce and culture. Harlem in New York, South Street in Philadelphia, Woodlawn in Detroit, Southside in Chicago, and Hough in Cleveland were written into the African-American imagination as places of high style, fashion, music, art, culture, religion, and commerce. The evolution of the African-American communities from southern and rural to northern and urban has occurred since 1945.

According to the last census, the largest populations of African Americans are found in New York (2.1 million), Chicago (1.4 million), Detroit (800,000), Philadelphia (700,000), and Los Angeles (600,000). Washington, Houston, Baltimore, New Orleans, and Memphis also have populations of African Americans in the hundreds of thousands.

The five cities with populations over 300,000 with the greatest percentages of African Americans are Washington (70%), Atlanta (67%), Detroit (65%), New Orleans (55%), and Memphis (40%). For cities under 100,000, East St. Louis, Illinois (96%) is the leader.

While the top four cities with the largest populations of African Americans are in the North, the cities with the highest percentages of African Americans include only one northern city (Detroit). Southern urban centers remain more heavily African American than northern cities.

Seven states have African-American populations of more than 20 percent. These states are southern and predominantly rural. Among these states are: Mississippi (35%), South Carolina (30%), Louisiana (29%), Georgia (27%), Alabama (26%), Maryland (23%), and North Carolina (22%).

The 1990 population of African Americans is estimated to be 35 million. In addition to the population domiciled in the United States, there are an additional one million African Americans abroad, mainly in cities in Africa and Europe. The African-American population continues to grow at a rate faster than the national average.

The African-American Population

Distribution of the African population in the United States is historically and economically based. Indeed, the reasons are interrelated in all cases. The states with the highest percentages of their total population being African American are all former slave-holding states. Three of those states: Mississippi, South Carolina,

Urban African American Population, 1980
(order based on total population)

		Percent			Percent
1.	New York, NY	25.2	26.	Nashville, TN	23.3
2.	Los Angeles, CA	17.0	27.	Austin, TX	12.2
3.	Chicago, IL	39.8	28.	Oklahoma City, OK	14.6
4.	Houston, TX	27.6	29.	Kansas City, MO	27.4
5.	Philadelphia, PA	37.8	30.	Fort Worth, TX	22.8
6.	Detroit, MI	63.1	31.	St. Louis, MO	45.6
7.	San Diego, CA	8.9	32.	Atlanta, GA	66.6
8.	Dallas, TX	29.4	33.	Long Beach, CA	11.3
9.	San Antonio, TX	7.3	34.	Portland, OR	7.6
10.	Phoenix, AZ	4.8	35.	Pittsburgh, PA	24.0
11.	Baltimore, MD	54.8	36.	Miami, FL	25.1
12.	San Francisco, CA	12.7	37.	Tulsa, OK	11.8
13.	Indianapolis, IN	21.8	38.	Honolulu, HI	1.2
14.	San Jose, CA	4.6	39.	Cincinnati, OH	33.8
15.	Memphis, TN	47.6	40.	Albuquerque, NM	2.5
16.	Washington, DC	70.3	41.	Tucson, AZ	3.7
17.	Jacksonville, FL	25.4	42.	Oakland, CA	46.9
18.	Milwaukee, WI	23.1	43.	Minneapolis, MN	7.7
19.	Boston, MA	22.4	44.	Charlotte, NC	31.0
20.	Columbus, OH	22.1	45.	Omaha, NE	12.0
21.	New Orleans, LA	55.3	46.	Toledo, OH	17.4
22.	Cleveland, OH	43.8	47.	Virginia Beach, VA	10.0
23.	Denver, CO	12.0	48.	Buffalo, NY	26.6
24.	El Paso, TX	3.2	49.	Sacramento, CA	13.4
25.	Seattle, WA	9.5	50.	Newark, NJ	58.2

AFRICAN AMERICAN POPULATION, 1990

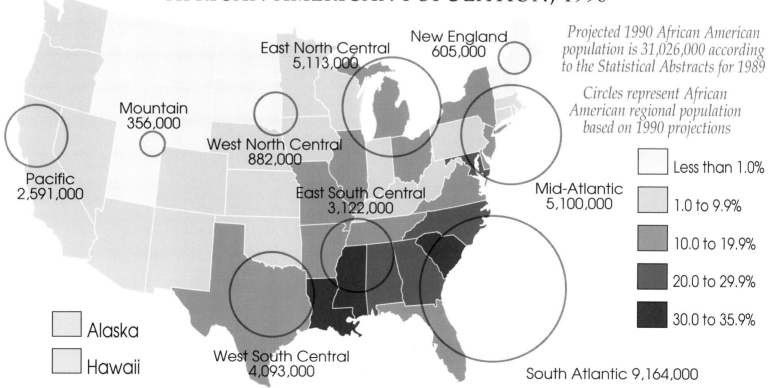

Projected 1990 African American population is 31,026,000 according to the Statistical Abstracts for 1989

Circles represent African American regional population based on 1990 projections

New England 605,000
East North Central 5,113,000
Mountain 356,000
West North Central 882,000
Pacific 2,591,000
East South Central 3,122,000
Mid-Atlantic 5,100,000
West South Central 4,093,000
South Atlantic 9,164,000

Alaska
Hawaii

Less than 1.0%
1.0 to 9.9%
10.0 to 19.9%
20.0 to 29.9%
30.0 to 35.9%

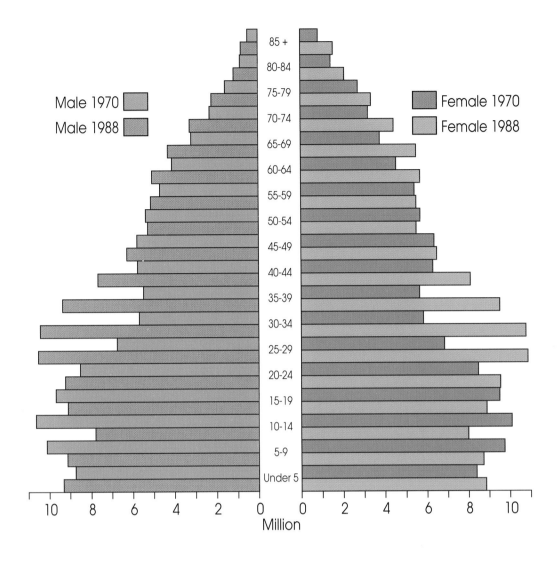

Male 1970
Male 1988

Female 1970
Female 1988

85 +
80-84
75-79
70-74
65-69
60-64
55-59
50-54
45-49
40-44
35-39
30-34
25-29
20-24
15-19
10-14
5-9
Under 5

10   8   6   4   2   0   0   2   4   6   8   10
Million

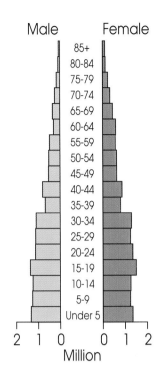

Male   Female

85+
80-84
75-79
70-74
65-69
60-64
55-59
50-54
45-49
40-44
35-39
30-34
25-29
20-24
15-19
10-14
5-9
Under 5

2   1   0   0   1   2
Million

MEDIAN AGE FOR AMERICANS

Age

40

Female

Both sexes

30

Male

Female

20

Both sexes

Male

——— African American
——— White

10

1950   1960   1970   1980   1987

and Louisiana have percentages of 35, 30, and 29 respectively. Along with Georgia (27%), Alabama (26%), Maryland (23%), North Carolina (22%), and Virginia (18%) these states constitute the heart of the region of the slavery economy.

States with the lowest percentages and lowest numbers of Africans have had less economic attraction and less historical connection with the African-American labor pool. Therefore, Vermont, Montana, Maine, Idaho, South Dakota, and North Dakota have limited populations of Africans. Another reason it seems obvious that the situation is due to history and economics rather than to climatic factors or distance away from the population centers of the South is the relatively strong showing of the state of Alaska which has a larger percentage of African Americans than states such as Minnesota, Oregon, New Mexico, Washington, Arizona, Rhode Island, Nebraska, and West Virginia. While the total number of Africans in the Alaskan population is not large, only about 14,000, the figure constitutes a larger percentage of

AFRICAN–AMERICAN POPULATION TRENDS, 1985
BY CITY

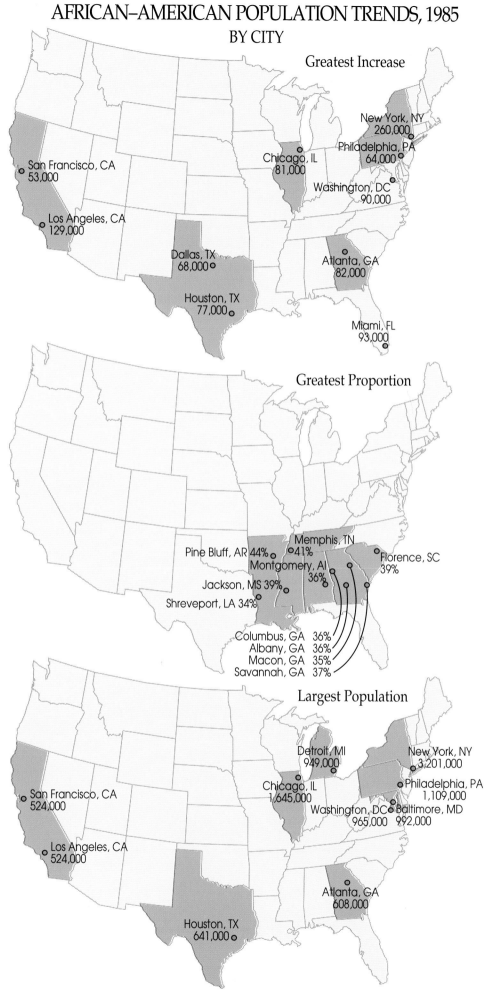

Greatest Increase

New York, NY
260,000

Philadelphia, PA
64,000

Chicago, IL
81,000

Washington, DC
90,000

San Francisco, CA
53,000

Los Angeles, CA
129,000

Dallas, TX
68,000

Atlanta, GA
82,000

Houston, TX
77,000

Miami, FL
93,000

Greatest Proportion

Pine Bluff, AR 44%

Memphis, TN
41%

Montgomery, Al
36%

Florence, SC
39%

Jackson, MS 39%

Shreveport, LA 34%

Columbus, GA   36%
Albany, GA   36%
Macon, GA   35%
Savannah, GA   37%

Largest Population

Detroit, MI
949,000

New York, NY
3,201,000

Chicago, IL
1,645,000

Philadelphia, PA
1,109,000

San Francisco, CA
524,000

Washington, DC   Baltimore, MD
965,000   992,000

Los Angeles, CA
524,000

Atlanta, GA
608,000

Houston, TX
641,000

that state's total population than nineteen other states including Hawaii. Rather than climate or proximity, economics and the promise of independence and opportunity have been the factors that lured African Americans to Alaska. Many families experience Alaska first as military employees and then remain as permanent residents.

Washington, DC is more than 70 percent African American. African Americans often refer to the city as Bannekerville, in honor of Benjamin Banneker one of the surveyors who laid out the city. The history of Washington's concentrated African-American population can be traced to the Emancipation Proclamation and the African's response to the Union government. Africans, literate and non-literate, converged on Washington and became home buyers and civil servants. Most African Americans in Washington are employees of the federal agencies or the District's government. This fact led the great Arkansas Blues singer to write a song popular in the 1940s and 1950s which said "Washington, DC is a bourgeois town." With a larger percentage of Africans than any major metropolitan area, Washington, DC contains all of the cultural achievements, social dislocations, intellectual dynamism, and political action to be seen elsewhere in the African-American community.

Population Trends

Not only is the African-American population a young community, it is profoundly urban. Only 3,901,009 African Americans are classified as rural while 22,594,061 are classified as urban. Most of the rural population is concentrated in the South with its longer history of enslavement of Africans for agricultural work. Family farms not confiscated from Africans after the fall of Reconstruction now account for a greater proportion of African Americans in the rural areas than remnants of share-cropping. Owning property during the slave period was impossible for most Africans, but for free persons it was possible although extremely difficult because of the unusually high prices asked from free persons for farm land. Farms purchased from whites during the late nineteenth and early twentieth century gave southern and mostly rural African Americans a stake in the productive sector with which they were most familiar.

Migration from the South

Ku Klux Klan attacks on African-American property owners and voters in the South at the beginning of the twentieth century drove thousands of farm families away from the South and their property was often lost to whites. Failure of the United States government to protect African Americans during the Reconstruction meant that many people were beaten, harassed, and killed. Those able to retain their property often fled to the North and left family members as caretakers. Nevertheless, the heavier concentration of rural African Americans in the South has a historical basis in the preeminently agrarian nature of the enslavement of Africans.

Population Change

The African population of the United States will increase by 1 percent as the white population decreases by 5 percent by 2010. This means that the United States population will become increasingly colored although it will remain overwhelmingly white. In 1980, "other" as a category made up 2 percent of the population. By 2010 that figure will be 5 percent.

Interestingly, the African population growth will derive from birth rate while growth in the "other" category will largely be a result of immigration. Immigration from Africa to the United States is negligible in the statistics, accounting for less than 1 percent of all immigrants to the United States. Actually, the African-American population has had less ethnic infusion than most groups in the American society. Having originated in the seventeenth century with more than 90 percent of its families able to

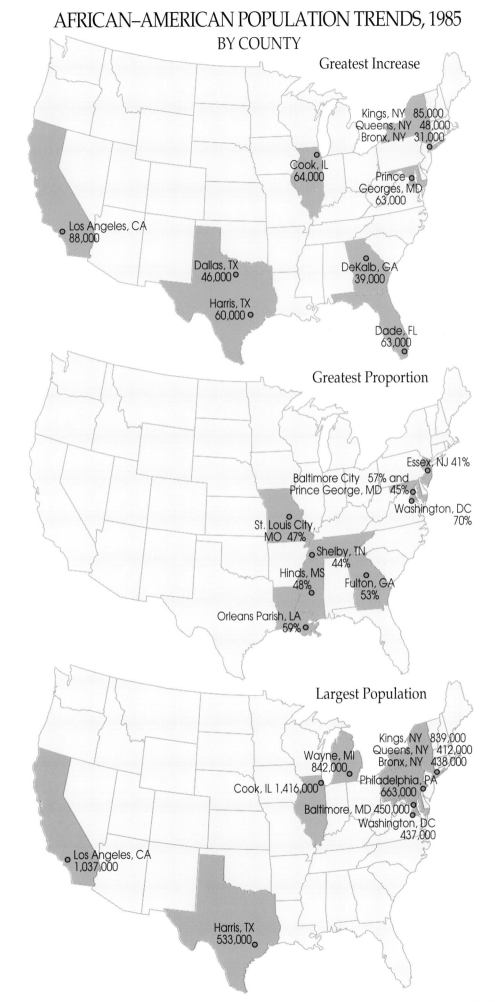

AFRICAN–AMERICAN POPULATION TRENDS, 1985
BY COUNTY

Greatest Increase

Kings, NY 85,000
Queens, NY 48,000
Bronx, NY 31,000

Cook, IL
64,000

Prince
Georges, MD
63,000

Los Angeles, CA
88,000

Dallas, TX
46,000

DeKalb, GA
39,000

Harris, TX
60,000

Dade, FL
63,000

Greatest Proportion

Essex, NJ 41%

Baltimore City 57% and
Prince George, MD 45%

Washington, DC
70%

St. Louis City,
MO 47%

Shelby, TN
44%

Hinds, MS
48%

Fulton, GA
53%

Orleans Parish, LA
59%

Largest Population

Kings, NY 839,000
Queens, NY 412,000
Bronx, NY 438,000

Wayne, MI
842,000

Philadelphia, PA
663,000

Cook, IL 1,416,000

Baltimore, MD 450,000

Washington, DC
437,000

Los Angeles, CA
1,037,000

Harris, TX
533,000

AFRICAN–AMERICAN POPULATION

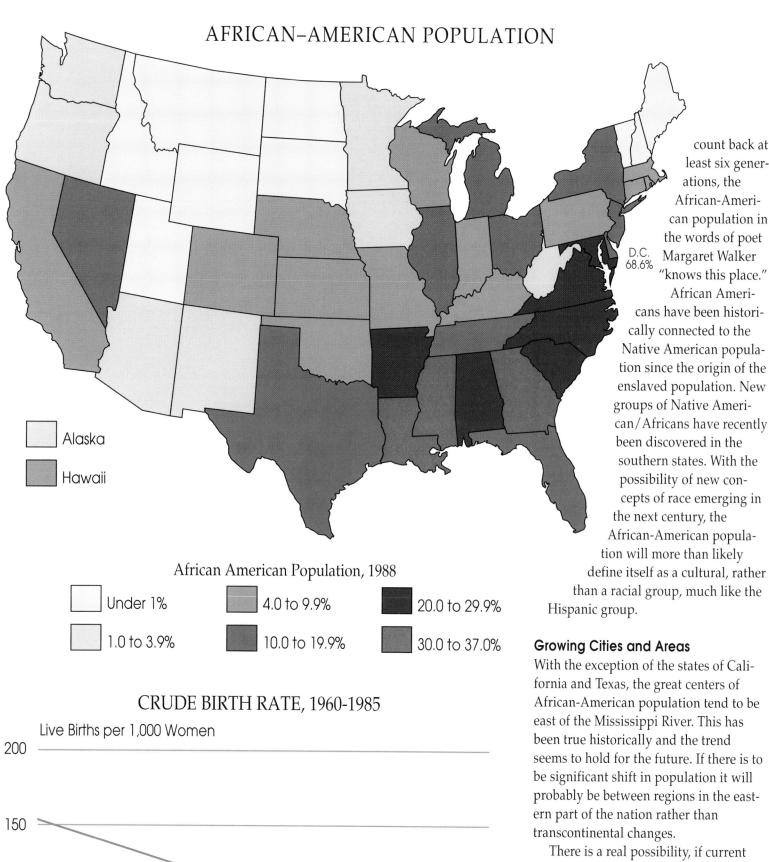

D.C.
68.6%

African American Population, 1988

Under 1%	4.0 to 9.9%	20.0 to 29.9%
1.0 to 3.9%	10.0 to 19.9%	30.0 to 37.0%

Alaska

Hawaii

CRUDE BIRTH RATE, 1960-1985

Live Births per 1,000 Women

200

150

African American

100

US

White

50

1960   1970   1980   1985

count back at least six generations, the African-American population in the words of poet Margaret Walker "knows this place." African Americans have been historically connected to the Native American population since the origin of the enslaved population. New groups of Native American/Africans have recently been discovered in the southern states. With the possibility of new concepts of race emerging in the next century, the African-American population will more than likely define itself as a cultural, rather than a racial group, much like the Hispanic group.

Growing Cities and Areas

With the exception of the states of California and Texas, the great centers of African-American population tend to be east of the Mississippi River. This has been true historically and the trend seems to hold for the future. If there is to be significant shift in population it will probably be between regions in the eastern part of the nation rather than transcontinental changes.

There is a real possibility, if current trends continue, that the population will flow from the northern urban communities back to the southern small towns. During the past fifty years there was a decidedly one way flow of migration from the South to the North. This trend started in the 1970s and seems to be con-

AFRICAN–AMERICAN CRUDE DEATH RATE

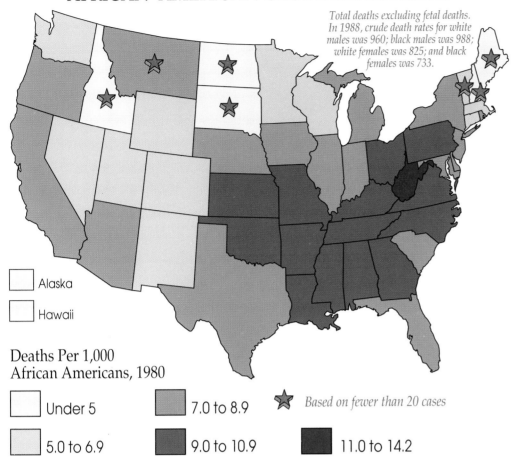

Total deaths excluding fetal deaths. In 1988, crude death rates for white males was 960; black males was 988; white females was 825; and black females was 733.

| | Alaska |
| | Hawaii |

Deaths Per 1,000 African Americans, 1980

| | Under 5 | | 7.0 to 8.9 | ⭐ *Based on fewer than 20 cases* |
| | 5.0 to 6.9 | | 9.0 to 10.9 | | 11.0 to 14.2 |

BIRTHS TO SINGLE AFRICAN–AMERICAN PARENTS

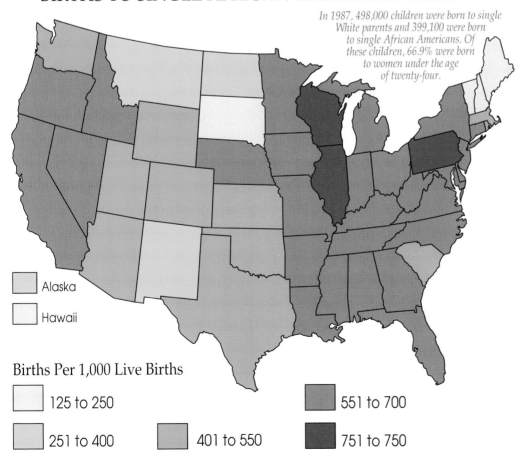

In 1987, 498,000 children were born to single White parents and 399,100 were born to single African Americans. Of these children, 66.9% were born to women under the age of twenty-four.

| | Alaska |
| | Hawaii |

Births Per 1,000 Live Births

| | 125 to 250 | | 551 to 700 |
| | 251 to 400 | | 401 to 550 | | 751 to 750 |

tinuing at the present time because of the elimination of most discrimination.

Crude Birth Rate

While the data show that the African-American birth rate has declined since 1960, it remains higher than the U. S. average and the white average. However, the rate of births for the African-American community appears to be headed in the direction of the national average. As one can see, the crude birth rate dropped from more than 150 live births per 1,000 women to well below 100 live births per 1,000 women in a twenty-five year span.

The implications of this dramatic shift in the birth rate for African-American women are not easy to determine. It seems certain that the trend toward having fewer children will continue into the near future with uncertain consequences. While the white live birth rate also declined during the twenty-five year span, the rate of decline was less dramatic than that for African-American women. This could mean that more African-American women and men are using some form of contraceptives than in previous years.

Crude Death Rate

West Virginia has the highest crude death rate in the nation. In a state with only 65,051 Africans Americans, 923 died according to the 1980 census. This represents 1.4 percent of the population. By contrast, Hawaii, with a population of 17,364, recorded only 2 deaths in 1980.

A number of factors may account for the high death rate in West Virginia. The most obvious has to do with the age of the population. While Hawaii tends to attract younger African Americans (i.e., those who remain in Hawaii after serving in the military), West Virginia has a higher percentage of older African Americans. In general, West Virginia may hold a hazard for the population due to cases of the black lung disease. The age of West Virginia's African-American population is not inconsequential in the determination of the health of the community.

THE GROWTH OF THE AFRICAN–AMERICAN POPULATION

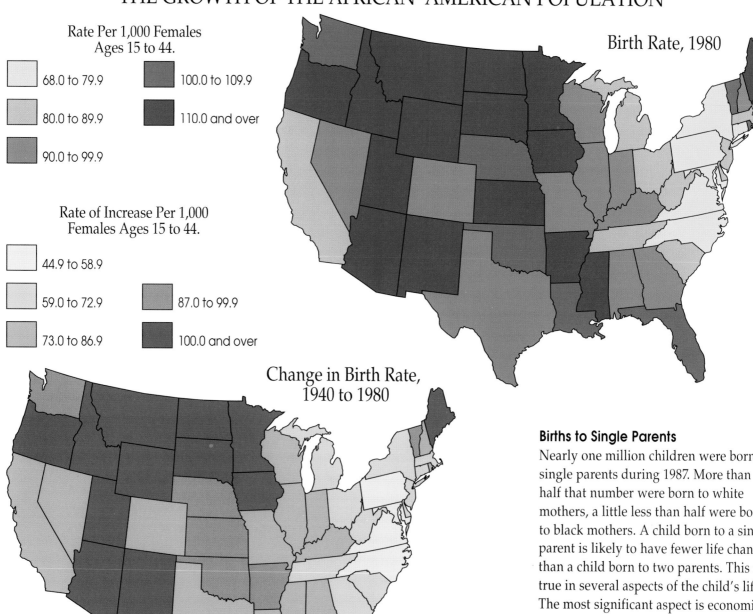

Rate Per 1,000 Females
Ages 15 to 44.

- 68.0 to 79.9
- 80.0 to 89.9
- 90.0 to 99.9
- 100.0 to 109.9
- 110.0 and over

Birth Rate, 1980

Rate of Increase Per 1,000
Females Ages 15 to 44.

- 44.9 to 58.9
- 59.0 to 72.9
- 73.0 to 86.9
- 87.0 to 99.9
- 100.0 and over

Change in Birth Rate,
1940 to 1980

PROJECTED AFRICAN–AMERICAN POPULATION

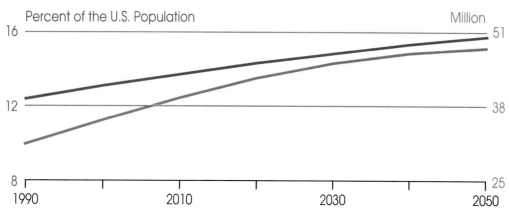

Percent of the U.S. Population

Million

16

51

12

38

8

25

1990   2010   2030   2050

Births to Single Parents

Nearly one million children were born to single parents during 1987. More than half that number were born to white mothers, a little less than half were born to black mothers. A child born to a single parent is likely to have fewer life chances than a child born to two parents. This is true in several aspects of the child's life. The most significant aspect is economic support. A child born to a two parent family will most likely have the financial support needed to do well in school, compete in team or group activities, take vacations, and find amusement. On the other hand, a child born in a single parent family will find it more difficult to find the resources necessary for effective learning opportunities. This is not to say that a child will not learn or succeed in a single parent family; obviously this cannot be true since we have thousands of examples where people do succeed. It is essentially the advantage that having a two parent family may give a child. Among the other benefits are the visitations to the school or to the sports arena or to the dance studio, and so forth that are more likely to occur if the child

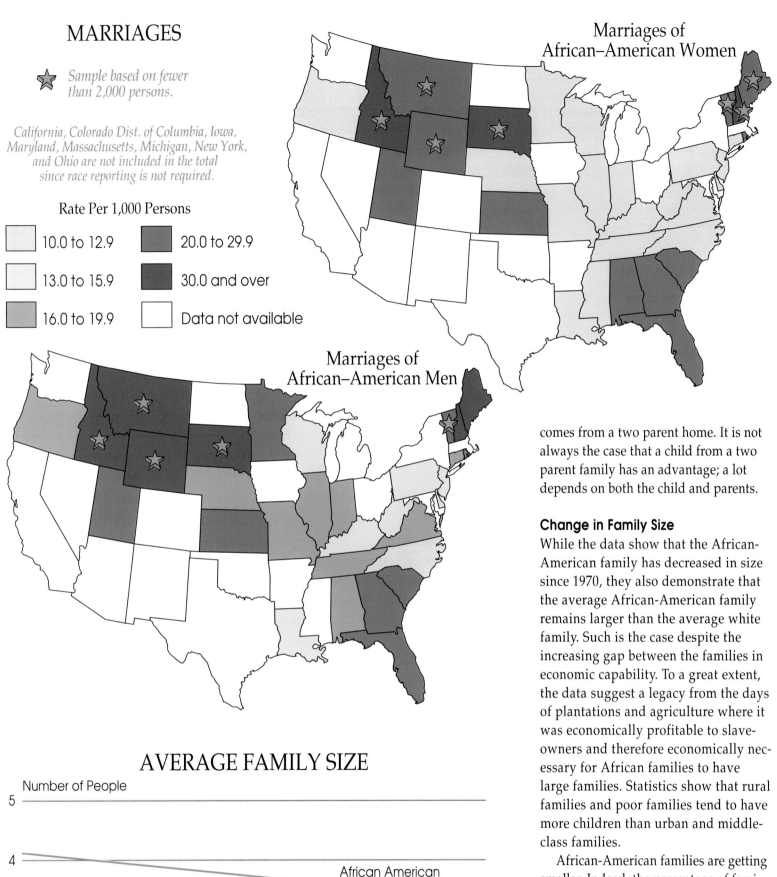

MARRIAGES

★ *Sample based on fewer than 2,000 persons.*

California, Colorado Dist. of Columbia, Iowa, Maryland, Massachusetts, Michigan, New York, and Ohio are not included in the total since race reporting is not required.

Rate Per 1,000 Persons

☐ 10.0 to 12.9		☐ 20.0 to 29.9	
☐ 13.0 to 15.9		☐ 30.0 and over	
☐ 16.0 to 19.9		☐ Data not available	

Marriages of African–American Women

Marriages of African–American Men

AVERAGE FAMILY SIZE

Number of People

5

4 — African American

All

White

3

2

1970   1975   1980   1985 1987

comes from a two parent home. It is not always the case that a child from a two parent family has an advantage; a lot depends on both the child and parents.

Change in Family Size

While the data show that the African-American family has decreased in size since 1970, they also demonstrate that the average African-American family remains larger than the average white family. Such is the case despite the increasing gap between the families in economic capability. To a great extent, the data suggest a legacy from the days of plantations and agriculture where it was economically profitable to slave-owners and therefore economically necessary for African families to have large families. Statistics show that rural families and poor families tend to have more children than urban and middle-class families.

African-American families are getting smaller. Indeed, the percentage of families with no children grew in 1987 to reach more than 40 percent for the first time in 1970. In addition, families with one or two children increased while families with three and four children decreased. The decreasing numbers of

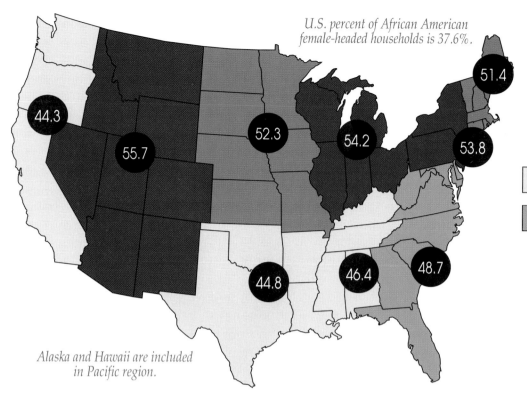

U.S. percent of African American female-headed households is 37.6%.

Alaska and Hawaii are included in Pacific region.

AFRICAN–AMERICAN FEMALE HEADS OF HOUSEHOLDS

Percent of Household That Have Females As Heads in 1988

44.0 to 47.9%	50.0 to 52.9%
48.0 to 49.9%	53.0 to 56.0%

Data show that the decline in family size is steady within the African-American family. As late as 1970, the average household had more than four people; now this is down to about three and a half. Economic pressures on the family unit have played important roles in convincing families to reduce the number of children. Economic vulnerabilities created by the lack of protection for health emergencies or accidents or other calamities are only a few of the reasons given for minimizing the risk to the family by limiting its size. The relative risks of economic catastrophe impact on the way adults view their family possibilities. Thus, the family size is most often related to aspirations.

children in the African-American family is probably linked to the rise of the two-job families. Parents are finding it more difficult to fulfill the responsibility of their professions or jobs and to raise families at the same time. With more women entering the workplace and the men already working out of the home, there is no one left to mind the children.

Family Characteristics

African-American women and men marry at about the same rate across the nation. However, in a few states the rate is slightly different for both sexes. The highest rate of marriage for both women and men is found in the southeastern United States and the mountain states. On the average there are more than thirty marriages per 1,000 persons in those two regions. This may be the result of strong religious sentiments or social traditions. Women tend to marry more often in Alabama than men. Men tend to marry at a higher rate than women in Oregon. In other regions of the country the rate of marriage for men and women tends to be nearly equal.

Change in Family Structure

While the data show that the African-American family has decreased in size, it has also taken on other characteristics. There is a growing trend of females heading households. While most families are still maintained by males, the increase in female-headed families is of concern because of the economic implications of such a structure. Women who work tend to make less money than men who work and therefore the family will normally be economically penalized for having a female head.

WAGE EARNERS IN AFRICAN–AMERICAN FAMILIES
1980–1989

Total Families with Earners	19.5%
Married-couple Families	3.9%
One Earner	-15.2%
Husband	-23.4%
Wife	3.5%
Two or More Earners	17.6%
Husband and Wife	23.9%
Families Maintained by Females	43.3%
Families Maintained by Males	65.9%

MEDIAN FAMILY INCOME, 1988

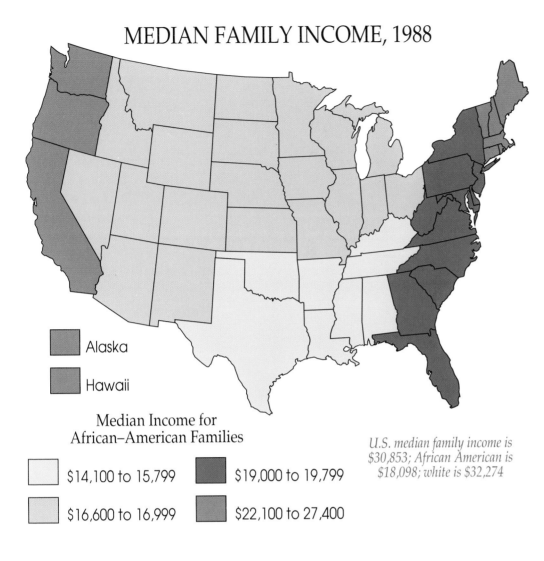

Alaska

Hawaii

Median Income for African–American Families

	$14,100 to 15,799		$19,000 to 19,799
	$16,600 to 16,999		$22,100 to 27,400

U.S. median family income is $30,853; African American is $18,098; white is $32,274

AFRICAN–AMERICAN
FAMILIES IN POVERTY, 1988

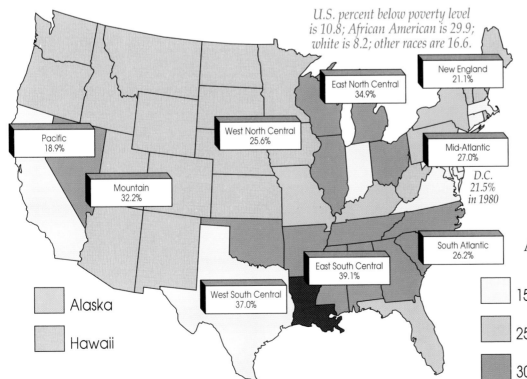

U.S. percent below poverty level is 10.8; African American is 29.9; white is 8.2; other races are 16.6.

New England
21.1%

East North Central
34.9%

West North Central
25.6%

Mid-Atlantic
27.0%

D.C.
21.5%
in 1980

Pacific
18.9%

Mountain
32.2%

South Atlantic
26.2%

East South Central
39.1%

West South Central
37.0%

Alaska

Hawaii

African–American Families Below Poverty Level

	15.0 to 24.9%		40.0 to 49.9%
	25.0 to 29.9%		50.0 to 52.0%
	30.0 to 39.9%		Sample too small

Whether or not these women have informal support systems will determine to what extent children in such families suffer from the lack of care and concern. Informal support networks such as mutual help linkages with other women are often well-developed over a period of years. These households may not be as isolated as one may think. Relatives and close family friends often provide the backbone of the network. Such informal networks have strong implications for the practical and material comfort of the family. These networks may provide food, shelter, money, and services.

Some women have also found these networks useful for child care if they have to run errands or go somewhere. In addition to reciprocal child care, the women often exchange commodities. An informal sisterhood is usually formed where services and goods are given to each other on an ask-and-give basis. Informal networks such as this can help to overcome economic insecurity and social vulnerability. One other benefit of these informal linkages is psychological and affective. Women are able to share with each other their problems and gain support in the raising of their children. These spiritual bonds are central to many of the informal networks.

Income

Nowhere in the United States is the median African-American family income equal to that of the white family. In most cases the comparison highlights the vast economic gap that has existed between Africans and whites since the founding of the nation. The Midwest and Northeast have the greatest distinctions. In the Midwest, for example, whites have a median

INFANT MORTALITY

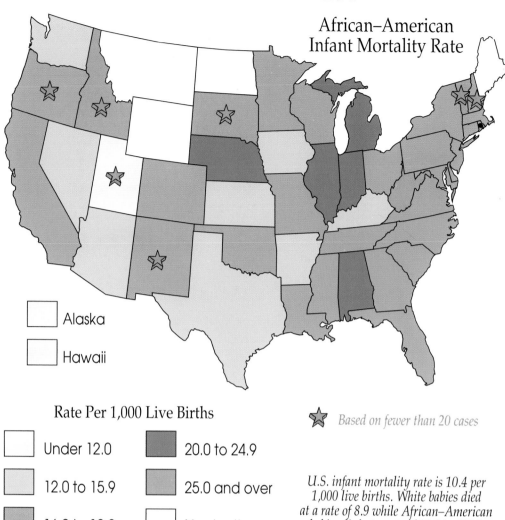

African–American Infant Mortality Rate

Alaska

Hawaii

Rate Per 1,000 Live Births

☐ Under 12.0	■ 20.0 to 24.9
☐ 12.0 to 15.9	■ 25.0 and over
☐ 16.0 to 19.9	☐ No deaths

⭐ *Based on fewer than 20 cases*

U.S. infant mortality rate is 10.4 per 1,000 live births. White babies died at a rate of 8.9 while African–American babies died at a rate of 18.0 in 1986.

income of $32,149 while African Americans in the region have a median income of $16,755. Whites in the Northeast have a median income of $35,262 compared to the African-American family median of $20,678. The income gaps in the Midwest and Northeast are $15,394 and $14,584.

According to the Urban League report for 1989, African-American incomes are substantially below the incomes of whites in every region of the United States. Consequently, the purchasing power of the average African-American family is well below that of the white family. In addition to the income gap is the estate wealth gap which makes the white family income more elastic than the African-American family income. Two families, one African-American and the other white, with the same salary cannot be equated when the white family's accumulated wealth in stocks, bonds, land, etc., far exceeds that of the African-American family.

Families in Poverty

African Americans living in Louisiana and Mississippi are more likely to be below the poverty level than African Americans living in other states. Almost every index of the quality of living is worse in Louisiana and Mississippi. Therefore, it is not surprising that these two states also have the largest percentages of their African Americans in poverty. Both states are agriculturally based and have limited diversification in their industrial bases.

These two states are not alone in large populations of poor blacks. While poverty is more pronounced in those states, no state where there is a sizable population of African Americans can speak with confidence about the character of the economic status enjoyed by its black citizens.

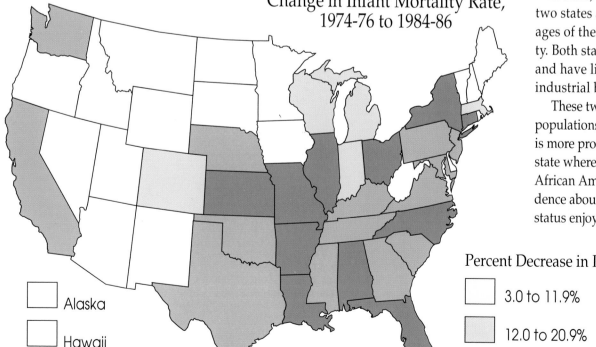

Change in Infant Mortality Rate, 1974-76 to 1984-86

Alaska

Hawaii

Percent Decrease in Infant Mortality Rate

☐ 3.0 to 11.9%	■ 29.0 to 36.9%
☐ 12.0 to 20.9%	☐ 37.0 to 43.4%
☐ 21.0 to 28.9%	☐ Unreliable data

Death Rates for Selected Causes, 1986 (per 100,000 population)

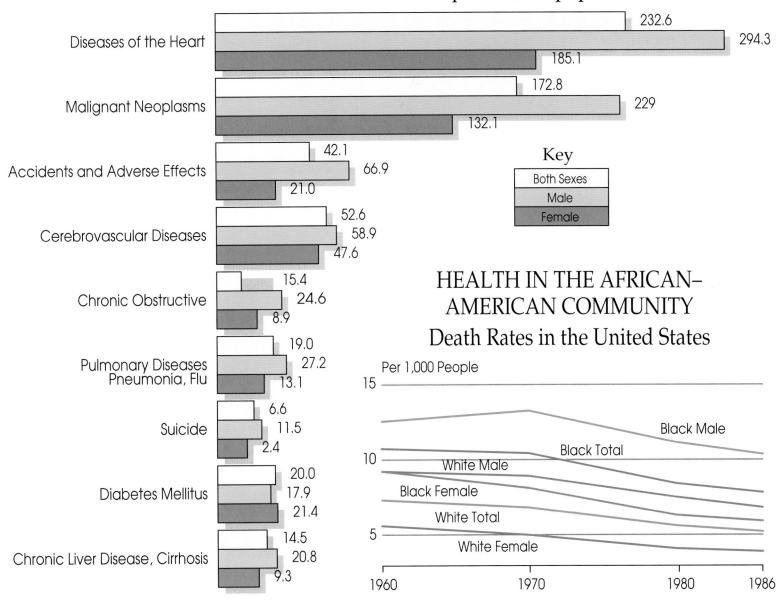

Diseases of the Heart
232.6
294.3
185.1

Malignant Neoplasms
172.8
229
132.1

Accidents and Adverse Effects
42.1
66.9
21.0

Key

| Both Sexes |
| Male |
| Female |

Cerebrovascular Diseases
52.6
58.9
47.6

Chronic Obstructive
15.4
24.6
8.9

Pulmonary Diseases Pneumonia, Flu
19.0
27.2
13.1

Suicide
6.6
11.5
2.4

Diabetes Mellitus
20.0
17.9
21.4

Chronic Liver Disease, Cirrhosis
14.5
20.8
9.3

HEALTH IN THE AFRICAN–AMERICAN COMMUNITY
Death Rates in the United States

Per 1,000 People

15

Black Male

Black Total

10
White Male

Black Female

White Total

5
White Female

1960   1970   1980   1986

Infant Mortality

Infant mortality is one of the standard measures for determining the health of a community or nation. The infant mortality rate in the United States remains higher than that in other industrial countries. The rate for African Americans is more than twice what it is for the white population.

The death rate of black children in infancy approaches that of underdeveloped nations. Large urban cities have become the tombs of many African-American infants.

States such as Illinois (23.3) and Michigan (23.7) represent giant industrial states, relatively rich regions of the country yet they have an infant mortality rate that is like that of a poor southern state. This is due to poor health care in the large, poor urban communities.

Health

While the data show that the African-American family is decreasing in size, the state of African-American health seems to be increasingly jeopardized. From the time of the Great Enslavement, when the health of the enslaved person was looked at only in terms of economic considerations, to the present time, where the cost of health care has placed most medical care beyond the reach of the great majority of African

Americans, health is a serious but costly business in the black community.

African Americans still have one of the highest mortality rates of any ethnic or cultural group in the United States. As socioeconomic levels decline, mortality rates increase. The condition of African-American health is directly related to poverty factors such as the lack of medical care for children and poor nutrition. Added to these factors are the unequal access to medical care and discriminatory delivery of the care when it is available.

Unquestionably there has been a gradual improvement in the health of African Americans since the Great Enslavement.

AFRICAN–AMERICAN EDUCATION

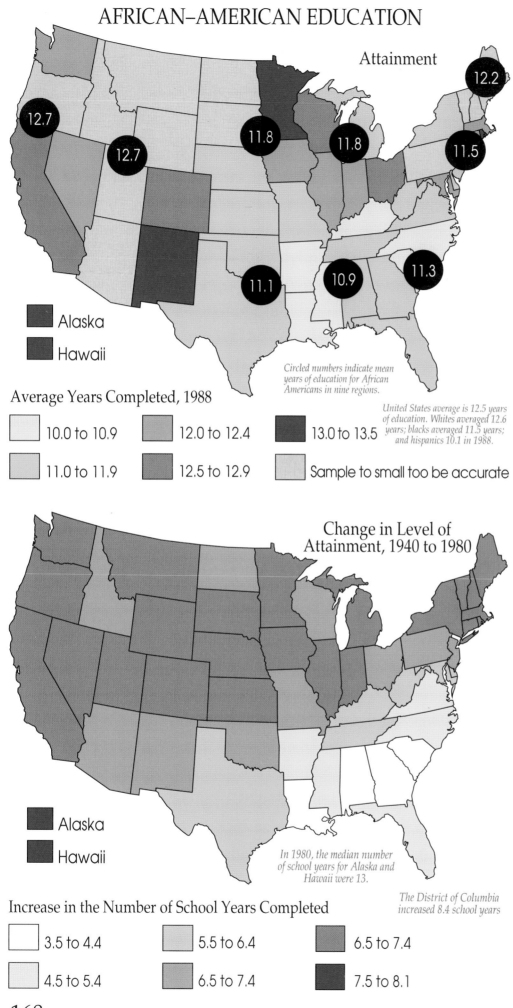

Attainment

Circled numbers indicate mean years of education for African Americans in nine regions.

Average Years Completed, 1988

United States average is 12.5 years of education. Whites averaged 12.6 years; blacks averaged 11.5 years; and hispanics 10.1 in 1988.

- 10.0 to 10.9
- 11.0 to 11.9
- 12.0 to 12.4
- 12.5 to 12.9
- 13.0 to 13.5
- Sample to small too be accurate

Alaska
Hawaii

Change in Level of Attainment, 1940 to 1980

In 1980, the median number of school years for Alaska and Hawaii were 13.

Alaska
Hawaii

The District of Columbia increased 8.4 school years

Increase in the Number of School Years Completed

- 3.5 to 4.4
- 4.5 to 5.4
- 5.5 to 6.4
- 6.5 to 7.4
- 6.5 to 7.4
- 7.5 to 8.1

During this same period, the health of black women has improved over that of black men. Actually it is possible to speak of a convergence in the life expectancies of African-American women and white women in the twentieth century. The picture is bleaker for African-American men.

Mortality and Morbidity

Like the infant mortality rate, the death rate for African-American men is the highest in the United States. A significant portion of the statistics regarding the high death rate of black males is based upon intentional injury statistics. The rate at which African-American males kill each other in violent confrontations has alarmed all health workers.

The risks associated with violent death seem to be psychological and cultural. A young African-American male with poor self-esteem and from the lowest socio-economic level is much more likely to be at risk than any other member of the black community. Add to these factors the lack of information and knowledge about African cultural values and the chances are very great that the person will end up in a violent confrontation that might mean his death or the death of someone else. Homicide remains the leading cause of death for black males between the ages of 15 and 34.

Other leading causes of death in the African-American community are heart disease, malignant neoplasms, cerebrovascular disease, chronic obstruction, and pulmonary diseases. Within the past ten years AIDS has spread within the African-American community. There is no effective vaccine or cure for the disease; yet enough information is available about the disease that it can be prevented. Most African Americans tend to get infected through the sharing of needles used for the injection of illicit drugs. Women may pass the disease to their children through pregnancy. Substance abuse constitutes an enormous health care problem as well.

School Enrollment, 1980

Fifty Largest SMSAs	Rank by Population	African (thousands)	Total (thousands)
1. New York–N. New Jersey–Long Island	1	651	2,401
2. Los Angeles–Anaheim–Riverside	2	368	2,219
3. Chicago–Gary–Lake County	3	498	2,041
4. Philadelphia–Wilmington–Trenton	4	271	1,253
5. San Francisco–Oakland–San Jose	5	125	918
6. Detroit–Ann Arbor	6	285	1,175
7. Boston–Lawrence–Salem	7	55	645
8. Washington, DC	8	313	944
9. Houston–Galveston–Brazoria	9	159	813
10. Dallas–Fort Worth	10	138	839
11. Cleveland–Akron–Lorain	11	108	525
12. Miami–Ft.Lauderdale	12	81	372
13. Pittsburgh–Beaver Valley	13	54	561
14. St. Louis	14	143	599
15. Baltimore	15	162	605
16. Atlanta	16	173	560
17. Minneapolis–St.Paul	17	16	605
18. Seattle–Tacoma	18	23	467
19. San Diego	19	40	547
20. Cincinnati–Hamilton	20	44	331
21. Denver–Boulder	21	25	436
22. Tampa–St.Petersburg	22	51	335
23. Milwaukee–Racine	23	54	383
24. Phoenix	24	14	396
25. Kansas City	25	61	371
26. Portland–Vancouver	26	11	344
27. New Orleans	27	149	325
28. Columbus	28	48	306
29. Buffalo–Niagara	29	42	339
30. Indianapolis	30	51	343
31. Norfolk–Virginia Beach–Newport News	31	68	210
32. Sacramento	32	27	342
33. Providence–Pawtucket–Fall River	33	3	140
34. San Antonio	34	24	305
35. Hartford–New Britain–Middletown	35	18	149
36. Charlotte–Gastonia–Rock Hill	36	50	191
37. Rochester	37	29	209
38. Louisville	38	44	181
39. Dayton–Springfield	39	45	254
40. Memphis	40	106	232
41. Salt Lake City–Ogden	41	4	283
42. Birmingham	42	71	224
43. Oklahoma City	43	28	207
44. Greensboro–Winston Salem–High Point	44	60	192
45. Nashville	45	44	230
46. Albany–Schenectady–Troy	46	10	218
47. Honolulu	47	9	241
48. Richmond–Petersburg	48	61	181
49. Jacksonville	49	54	209
50. Orlando	50	33	209

Education

Although there has been a continuous rise in the number of school years completed by African Americans since the end of the World War II, the number of school years completed still lags behind the general population. In effect, the legacy of slavery, discrimination, and poverty affects the opportunities and motivation of African Americans even though there remains a strong education ethic within the community. Between 1940 and 1986 there was almost a nine-fold increase in the number of African Americans completing four or more years of high school. This phenomenal rate of increase had a lot to do with the

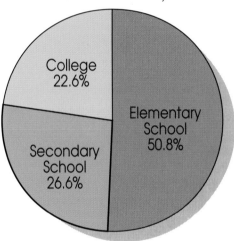

Total Enrollment Except African–American, 1980

College 22.6%
Elementary School 50.8%
Secondary School 26.6%

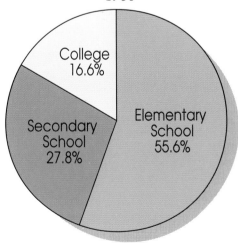

African–American Enrollment, 1980

College 16.6%
Elementary School 55.6%
Secondary School 27.8%

more open societies in the North during the war years and the substantial reliance of African-American parents on education to secure children an opportunity for blunting racism.

College attendance also increased over this period of time: from 1.3 percent having completed four or more years of college in 1940 to 10.9 percent by 1986. The biggest gains were made between 1940 and 1970 when the political and social mood of the nation encouraged the admission of African Americans into predominantly white colleges. Heretofore, the one hundred or so African-American colleges had educated more than 90 percent of the African-American population. With the Civil Rights Movement of the 1950s and 1960s the expansion of educational opportunity emerged as a cardinal component of social progress. Autherine Lucy's integration of the University of Alabama, James Meredith's integration of the University of Mississippi, and

Charlayne Hunter's integration of the University of Georgia meant that the walls of segregation were breached in the deepest parts of the American South. College became more accessible to individuals living at home or in close proximity to major colleges. African Americans took full advantage of these opportunities in the 1960s and 1970s.

Among the issues concerning education that confronted African Americans during the past twenty years are fairness in testing, equity in opportunity, curricula changes, and Afrocentric models and examples at every grade level in public schools and in colleges. These issues will continue to be discussed.

Between 1972 and 1982 numbers of African-American students attending higher education institutions increased. This increase was felt by most major institutions, although the historically black colleges and universities continued to be the main educators of profession-

als. Both graduate and undergraduate enrollment were up during the decade. A slowing of the trend is expected when the data for the period 1982–1992 are finally compiled and analyzed.

During the years of President Ronald Reagan's administration, many programs to support students were cut back. An assessment of the Reagan Doctrine on the education of African Americans will reveal that despite the fact that 16.6 percent of black students continued their studies in college, the figure should have been much higher.

Illiteracy

Although there has been a continuous rise in the number of school years completed by African Americans, there is still a large population of functionally illiterate individuals. This means that they are unable to read the newspaper, to read captions on the television, to answer mail, to read street signs, and to sign checks.

AMERICANS AND FUNCTIONAL ILLITERACY, 1986

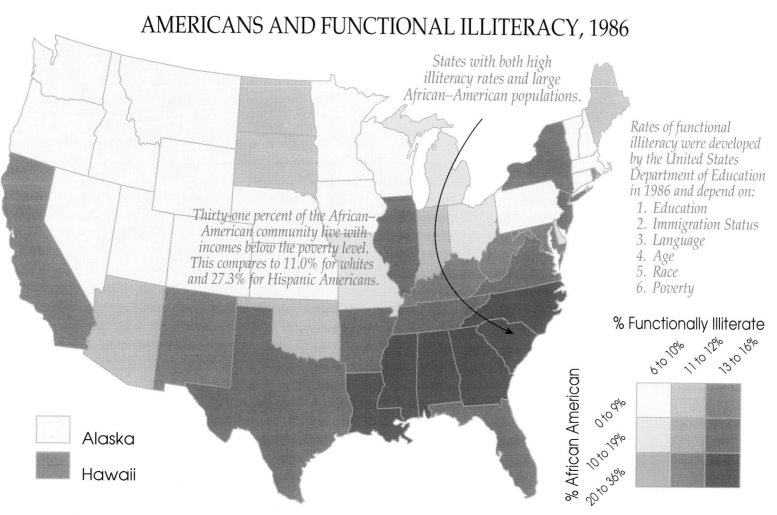

States with both high illiteracy rates and large African–American populations.

Rates of functional illiteracy were developed by the United States Department of Education in 1986 and depend on:
1. *Education*
2. *Immigration Status*
3. *Language*
4. *Age*
5. *Race*
6. *Poverty*

Thirty-one percent of the African–American community live with incomes below the poverty level. This compares to 11.0% for whites and 27.3% for Hispanic Americans.

Alaska

Hawaii

% Functionally Illiterate
6 to 10% 11 to 12% 13 to 16%

% African American
0 to 9%
10 to 19%
20 to 36%

AFRICAN–AMERICAN VOTING AND VOTER REGISTRATION

Percent of Total State Voting Age Population That is African American

- 3.6 to 10.9%
- 11.0 to 17.9%
- 18.0 to 24.9%
- 25.0 to 32.5%
- Not reported

Percent of State African–American Voting Age Population That is Registered to Vote

- 45.0 to 54.4%
- 55.0 to 64.4%
- 65.0 to 74.4%
- 75.0 to 82.6%
- Not reported

African–American Voters That Voted in 1988

- 21.0 to 33.4%
- 33.5 to 45.9%
- 46.0 to 58.4%
- 58.5 to 71.9%
- Not reported

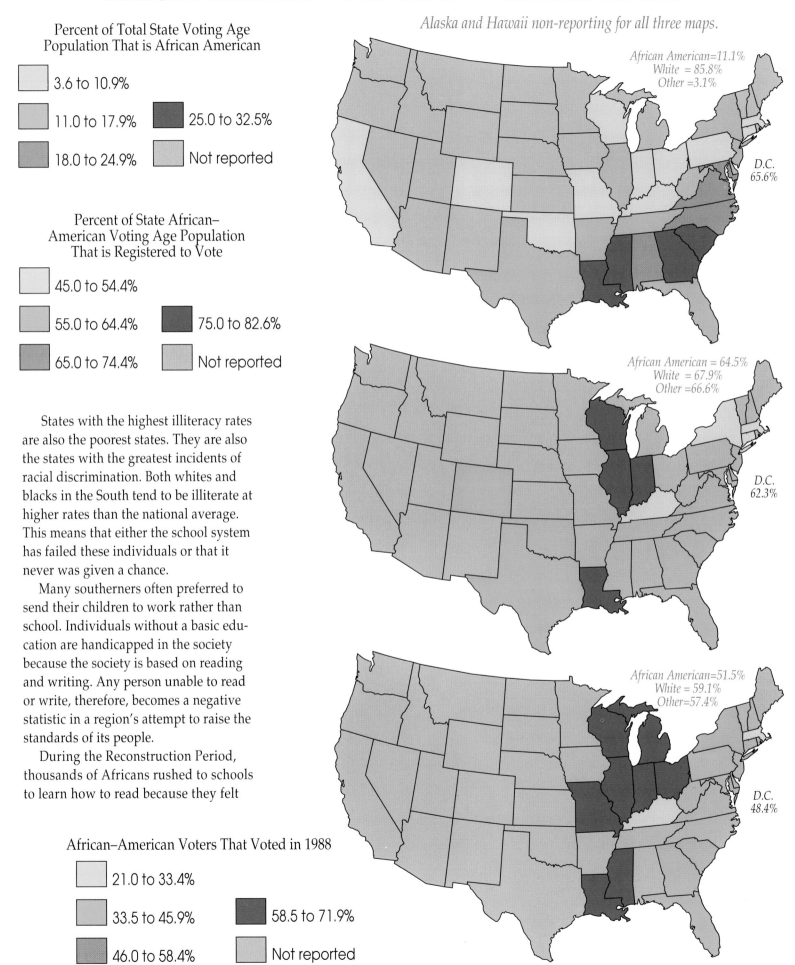

Alaska and Hawaii non-reporting for all three maps.

African American=11.1%
White = 85.8%
Other =3.1%

D.C.
65.6%

African American = 64.5%
White = 67.9%
Other =66.6%

D.C.
62.3%

African American=51.5%
White = 59.1%
Other=57.4%

D.C.
48.4%

States with the highest illiteracy rates are also the poorest states. They are also the states with the greatest incidents of racial discrimination. Both whites and blacks in the South tend to be illiterate at higher rates than the national average. This means that either the school system has failed these individuals or that it never was given a chance.

Many southerners often preferred to send their children to work rather than school. Individuals without a basic education are handicapped in the society because the society is based on reading and writing. Any person unable to read or write, therefore, becomes a negative statistic in a region's attempt to raise the standards of its people.

During the Reconstruction Period, thousands of Africans rushed to schools to learn how to read because they felt

AFRICAN AMERICANS AS
PERCENT OF THE LABOR FORCE, 1988

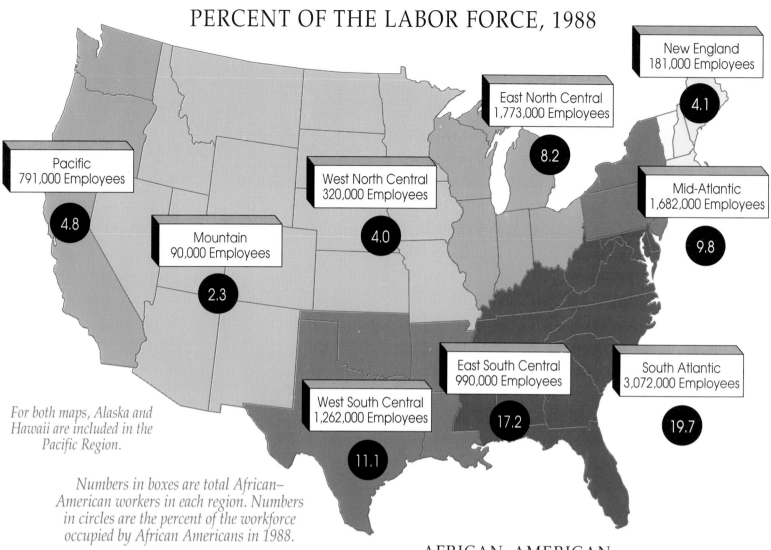

New England
181,000 Employees
4.1

East North Central
1,773,000 Employees
8.2

Pacific
791,000 Employees
4.8

West North Central
320,000 Employees
4.0

Mid-Atlantic
1,682,000 Employees
9.8

Mountain
90,000 Employees
2.3

East South Central
990,000 Employees
17.2

South Atlantic
3,072,000 Employees
19.7

West South Central
1,262,000 Employees
11.1

For both maps, Alaska and Hawaii are included in the Pacific Region.

Numbers in boxes are total African–American workers in each region. Numbers in circles are the percent of the workforce occupied by African Americans in 1988.

AFRICAN–AMERICAN
WOMEN IN THE WORKPLACE, 1988

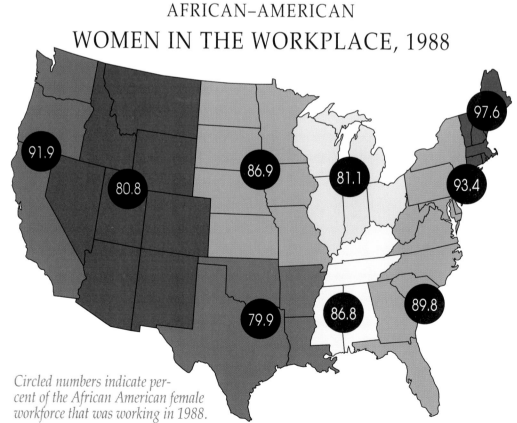

91.9

80.8

86.9

81.1

97.6

93.4

79.9

86.8

89.8

Circled numbers indicate percent of the African American female workforce that was working in 1988.

that they could not be proper citizens without the ability to read and interpret the basic documents of the society.

Illiteracy among African Americans in large urban states approaches the rates in the southern states but there is a difference. The African Americans who live in the central cities of New York, Chicago, Detroit, and Philadelphia are at the greatest risk. They tend to have more functional illiteracy than African Americans who live in the Plains States or the West.

Voting

By 1989, there were more than 7,000 African-American elected officials, covering every state with the exceptions of Idaho, Montana, and North Dakota. Predictably, the states with the highest per-

AFRICAN–AMERICAN
MALES IN THE WORKPLACE, 1988

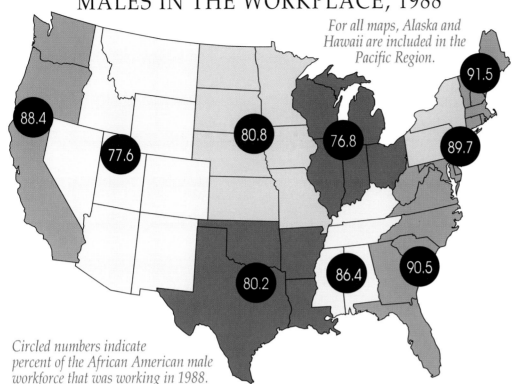

For all maps, Alaska and Hawaii are included in the Pacific Region.

Circled numbers indicate percent of the African American male workforce that was working in 1988.

data represented in the following illustrations show African Americans, whites, and others employed in certain sectors. The charts illustrate the percentage of African-American or white workers employed in a particular economic sector; they do not illustrate the percentage of African Americans in the total economic sector itself. Therefore, taking the African-American population as a whole, you will discover the percentage employed in agriculture, banking, entertainment, and so forth.

Clearly, while African Americans share in some of the same employment interests as whites, the percentages of the African-American population engaged in certain economic sectors differ greatly from white interests. For example, a larger percentage of the African-American population is

centages of African Americans of voting age population tended to have the largest numbers of African-American elected officials. The District of Columbia, with 65.6 percent of African Americans of the voting age population, had 244 African-American elected officials as of 1988. The fact that the District is a city, with limited opportunities compared to a state (e.g., there is no District legislature), suggests that were the District to become a state, the number of African Americans elected would be larger than any of the present states.

Without the District of Columbia, the largest number of African-American elected officials are predictably found in Mississippi with 578, Louisiana with 524, Georgia with 458, Illinois with 443, Alabama with 442, and North Carolina with 428.

African-American Employment

Employment percentages in various sectors have always been different for African Americans than for whites in the United States. The patterns of employment are determined historically. The

AFRICAN–AMERICAN EMPLOYMENT BY AGE

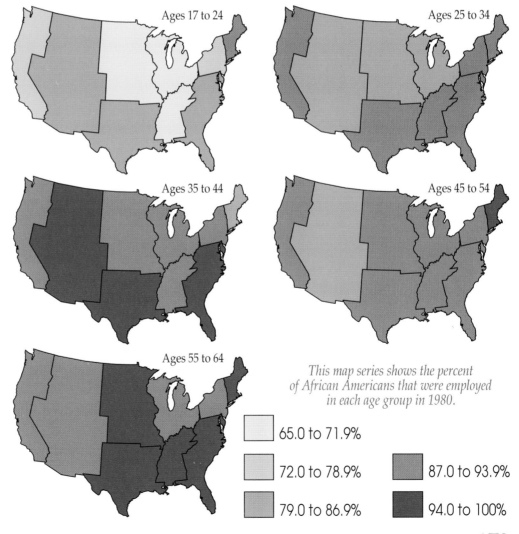

This map series shows the percent of African Americans that were employed in each age group in 1980.

65.0 to 71.9%	
72.0 to 78.9%	87.0 to 93.9%
79.0 to 86.9%	94.0 to 100%

employed in the professional public administration sector than whites. More than a quarter of all African Americans who are employed are in the professions or public administration sector. By contrast, the largest percentage of employed whites is in the wholesale and retail sector. The employed African Americans are much more likely, therefore, to be employed as directors, managers, teachers, educators, lawyers, medical practitioners, and institutional administrators than as business persons. The predominant employer in the professional/public administration is the federal government. A considerable number of African Americans have been employed by major municipal governments since the 1960s.

The southeastern United States has the highest percentage of African Americans in the labor force. Nineteen percent of the work force in that area is black. Out of more than sixteen million laborers in the region, just over three

Percent of Total African Americans in Each Occupation

	1957	1970	1980
White-Collar Workers	**12.7**	**27.9**	**38.2**
Professionals: Technical & Kindred	3.6	9.1	12.4
Medical and Other Health Professionals	0.6	1.6	4.2
Teachers (exc. college)	1.3	2.9	2.8
Other Professionals and Technicians	1.7	4.7	5.4
Managers, Officials, and Proprietors	2.1	3.5	5.1
Clerical Workers	6.0	13.2	17.9
Stenographers, Typists, and Secretaries	1.2	2.3	3.8
Other Clerical	4.8	10.9	14.1
Sales Workers	1.0	2.1	2.8
Retail Trade	0.8	1.6	1.5
Other Sales Workers	0.2	0.5	1.3
Blue-Collar Workers	**41.7**	**42.2**	**42.2**
Crafters and Supervisors	5.6	8.2	16.9
Carpenters	0.5	0.7	9.3
Construction Crafters (exc. carpenters)	1.4	1.7	1.3
Mechanics and Repairers	1.8	2.6	2.4
Metal Crafters (exc. mechanics)	0.5	0.8	0.4
Other Crafters & Kindred Workers	1.1	1.5	2.3
Supervisors	0.3	0.9	1.2
Operatives	21.1	23.7	18.6
Drivers and Deliverers	4.6	4.1	4.7
Other Operatives	16.5	19.6	13.9
Nonfarm Laborers	4.5	10.3	6.7
Service Industry Workers	**32.0**	**26.0**	**17.9**
Private Household Workers	14.9	7.7	0.3
Service Workers (exc. private households)	17.1	18.3	17.6
Protective Service Workers	0.5	0.9	1.1
Waiters, Cooks, Bartenders	3.6	3.4	5.4
Other Service Workers	13.0	14.0	11.1
Farmworkers	**13.5**	**3.9**	**1.7**
Farmers and Farm Managers	4.2	1.0	0.3
Farm Laborers and Supervisors	9.3	2.9	1.4
Paid Workers	6.6	2.6	1.3
Unpaid Family Workers	2.7	0.3	0.1
African American Workers	**100.0**	**100.0**	**100.0**

OCCUPATIONS OF AMERICANS

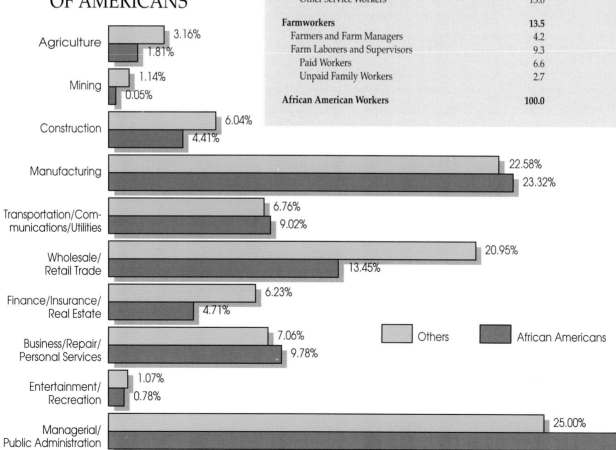

	Others	African Americans
Agriculture	3.16%	1.81%
Mining	1.14%	0.05%
Construction	6.04%	4.41%
Manufacturing	22.58%	23.32%
Transportation/Communications/Utilities	6.76%	9.02%
Wholesale/Retail Trade	20.95%	13.45%
Finance/Insurance/Real Estate	6.23%	4.71%
Business/Repair/Personal Services	7.06%	9.78%
Entertainment/Recreation	1.07%	0.78%
Managerial/Public Administration	25.00%	32.25%

million are African Americans. Due to the great disparity in wages between blacks and whites, African Americans do not share nineteen percent of the income of the region.

As demonstrated in the map on page 172, the West North Central, Mountain, New England, and East North Central states have the lowest percentages of African Americans in the labor force. Those regions also have the lowest percentages of blacks in the population.

Historically the South Atlantic region has always led in the percentage of African Americans in the labor force. Because of the higher concentration of enslaved Africans in the region before emancipation, the result is a more intensive black labor force in the region.

During the 1950s the Honorable Elijah Muhammad, a nationalist leader, argued that the southern states should become a new African-American nation because of the heavy presence of African Americans. However, the strong concentration of African Americans in the labor force in the region is not one of diversity. The vast majority of the laborers are in agricultural and light manufacturing. The high technology fields of space science, information processing, biomedicals, and telecommunications often found in the "sunbelt" do not now employ a large percentage of African Americans. This is a situation which is likely to change as the available white labor force becomes smaller due to low birth rate. Already acute shortages of skilled persons in the high technology fields are threatening the United States' position as a world leader in technological innovation. The African-American labor pool in the southern region will have to be trained for the new roles in this field.

African-American males are employed at a higher percentage of the potential labor force in the West South Central states—notably Texas, Oklahoma, Louisiana, and Arkansas—than in any other region. Ninety-one percent of the African-American males in the labor force were employed in 1980. Lowest percentages of employed males were

recorded in the East North Central and West North Central regions, respectively. This contrasts with the African-American female employment figures where the East South Central, and East North Central had the lowest and second lowest percentages.

Black males have historically found employment as ranchers, oil-riggers, and farm hands in the Southwest. Females have not found the area to be as attractive for their employment. On the other hand, females do exceptionally well in the Mountain region, New England, Pacific, and West South Central regions. The Mountain region posted 94 percent of its African-American females as employed—out of a labor force of thirty-eight persons, thirty-six women were working.

Labor force represents only those individuals who are eligible and seeking jobs. Persons may not be counted in the labor force for various reasons, (e.g., military, prison, or medical disabilities). Thus, to say that 91 percent of African-American males in the labor force in the West South Central region are employed is not the same as saying 91 percent of the African-American males in the region are employed.

African Americans in Industries

The distortions of racial history in the United States are evidenced in the employment of African Americans in various sectors. Cleavages of race have affected the patterns of employment in the United States. The percentage of African Americans employed in the professions and public administration is higher than the percentage of other Americans employed in that sector. Lawyers, accountants, and managers constitute a large part of this sector. Only in the East South Central region does the percentage of whites and others employed in the professions and public administration approach the figures for African Americans.

Most of the African-American growth in this sector occurred during the Civil Rights era and represented the federal

government's response to increased demands for integration of African Americans into the society. In the 1950s and 1960s the employment for African-American graduates in the professions was limited due to racial discrimination. The federal government and its various agencies hired many of the college graduates who were blocked from entering the corporate world. Thus, during the 1960s the U.S. government became the largest employer of African-American lawyers. In some ways, the U.S. government relieved the pressure building among professionals who could not find employment in the private sector by increasing African-American employment in the public sector.

In the South, while a large percentage of whites were also employed in the public sector, their employment was initially more state related than federal. By 1980 however, African Americans had entered many of the state jobs in the South as a result of the voting rights laws. Although whites still dominate the professions and public administration in the South, the percentage of the white population employed in that sector has decreased during the past decade, while African-American employment in the sector has increased.

Outside of the South, African-American professionals participate in the professions and public administration at an even higher percentage of the working population. In New England, nearly 36 percent of the African Americans working are employed in the professions or public administration sector. This compares with 25 percent of the working whites in the region who are employed in the professions and public administration.

Only in the South, with its historical concentration of African Americans, is there a sizable wholesale and retail work force. Yet in no region of the South does the percentage of regional employment of African Americans in wholesale and retail trade top 15 percent. Largely because of the businesses established in the African-American community to cater to personal service needs of the community, the percentage of employment in retail and wholesale trade is greater than in any other region.

Most of the African-American businesses in the South are located in the urban centers of Atlanta, New Orleans, Houston, San Antonio, Memphis, Little Rock, Nashville, Louisville, Birmingham, and Dallas. Smaller cities such as Macon, Charleston, Augusta, Chattanooga, Jackson, and Montgomery, as well as scores of other communities, have basic businesses such as grocery stores, funeral homes, restaurants, and beauty and barber shops. Some agricultural regions have wholesale businesses engaged in selling farm produce (e.g., pecans, vegetables, livestock).

The percentage of African-American employment in transportation, communication, and utilities (TCU) is generally higher than the percentage for whites and others. This is not the case, however, in the East South Central and the South Atlantic regions. In both of those regions whites have a slightly higher percentage of employed people working in the TCU sector. In the East South Central region, 7.4 percent of whites and others are employed in the TCU sector while only 6.0 percent of African Americans are so employed. The figures are slightly different in the South Atlantic region where the percentage is 7.4 for whites and others and 7.2 for African Americans.

Most African Americans who work in this sector are found in warehousing, the U.S. Postal Service, services incidental to transportation, and sanitary services. While African Americans can also be found as pilots for major and minor airlines, radio and television broadcasters, and utility engineers, numbers are comparatively small.

The percentage of African Americans employed in the manufacturing sector is generally less than whites and other Americans employed in that sector. Out of nine national regions, African Americans are employed in a greater percentage of the working population in manu-

facturing in only two regions, the Mid-Atlantic and West North Central. In one other region, the South Atlantic, the percentage of African Americans working in manufacturing is about the same as that for whites and other Americans. Actually, in the Mid-Atlantic region there is a larger percentage of the African-American population working in manufacturing (20.4%) than whites and others (18.3%). Likewise, in the West North Central region the African-American percentage of the population in manufacturing is 22.9 and the percentage of whites and others 20.3; however, in the South Atlantic region the African-American percentage is 23.7 and the white and others is 24.7.

The other six regions show a much higher percentage of white and other workers who are employed in the manufacturing sector. African Americans are employed in higher percentages of the working population in those areas of the country where textile mill products are made. Thus, the area from Georgia to Virginia constitutes the textile belt but it is also the tobacco region. Since textile workers and tobacco workers are usually on the low end of the pay-scale, employers in the textile or tobacco manufacturing area tend to employ persons from the area of the product. This is particularly true in the South where the workforce, black or white, is not necessarily highly educated. Furthermore, the pattern of giving African Americans low-paying jobs means that a larger concentration of African-American workers might be found in manufacturing in these regions.

The greatest disparity in terms of percentage of workers by region and race is in the Mountain region where 28.0% of the white and other population is employed in manufacturing while only 6.1% of African Americans in that region are employed in manufacturing. Whites in the Mountain region have a long history of work in logging and millwork. African Americans in that region are much more likely to be in other employment sectors such as the professions and

public administration.

In no region of the country does the percentage of African-American workers in the finance, insurance, and real estate sector exceed 10 percent of the working population. Nevertheless, the percentage of African Americans working in finance, insurance, and real estate is nearly the same as it is for white and other workers. However, unlike the whites working in finance, insurance, and real estate, the positions filled by African Americans are more likely to be in the lower echelons of the sector. For example, the numbers of African Americans in this sector reflect the large numbers of African Americans who work as bank tellers and clerks as well as the numbers who are insurance salespersons. One is less likely to find African Americans in the management levels of finance, insurance, and real estate.

The South Atlantic and East South Central regions—the traditional Deep South—has the lowest percentages of African Americans employed in the finance, insurance, and real estate sector. This pattern, illustrated where the percentage of African Americans employed in this sector in the South Atlantic (2.9%) and East South Central (2.7%), is related to the history of discrimination against African Americans in employment in such areas as banking, credit agencies, saving and loan associations, and investment companies. As late as the 1950s in Georgia, Alabama, and South Carolina, African Americans were employed in banking institutions only as messengers and maintenance workers. The 1980 census data indicate that the South remains the area least likely to employ African Americans in finance and banking.

Agriculture and Africans were bound together in America for nearly 250 years. Indeed, from 1619 to 1865 the African was the principal instrument in the development of American agriculture. In every aspect of the industry, from clearing the forests, plowing the land, tilling the soil, planting the seeds, harvesting the crops, and taking them to market, the African was nearly indispensable. Even after Emancipation Proclamation, Africans were sharecroppers on land throughout the southern states. The migration to the North, the Great Flight, depleted the farms of African-American workers beginning in the 1940s. Even the recent reversal of African-American migration has not meant a return to agriculture.

The percentage of white and other workers in agriculture is larger than that for employed African-American workers in every region. The region with the largest percentage of employed African Americans in agriculture remains the South Atlantic region of the country. Despite the fact that this region is the farm belt for the African-American population, only 3.8 percent of African Americans were employed in the agriculture sector according to the 1980 census. The percentage of white and other workers employed in the agriculture sector is also relatively small, with the exception of the 7.9% in the West North Central region, the percentage of all Americans in agriculture has steadily decreased over the past four decades.

Nearly a quarter (22%) of the employed African Americans in the Mountain region are in business, repair, and personal service. This percentage represents the largest percentage of African Americans in this sector for any region. The African-American population in the Mountain region is both a newly-established and independent one. Therefore, a higher percentage of that relatively small population has found it necessary to find business or personal service employment. In every region of the nation, however, the percentage of African Americans employed in the business, repair, and personal service sector is higher than that for whites and others. The lowest percentage (6.7%) of African Americans employed in this sector is located in the East North Central region, but only 5.9% of whites and others in that region are employed in the sector.

Although African Americans are more represented than whites and others in this sector it does not mean that the benefits of business have accrued to African Americans. Many of the jobs in this sector occupied by African Americans are the menial and lower-paying positions. Furthermore, the sector comprises those working for themselves and those working for others.

Only in the West South Central region does the percentage of employed African Americans represent about the same as that of whites and others in the construction sector. The New England region has the lowest percentage (1.8%) of African Americans in the construction sector. The history of African Americans in the construction industry begins in the earliest urban areas of the country where laborers were used to build houses, stores, and government buildings. Furthermore, as the Chinese laborers became famous for their heroic work on the railroads of the West, the African Americans had lent manual labor to the construction of the rail system in the Eastern half of the continent. John Henry, the "steel drivin' man," gained his reputation from the participation of African Americans in constructing the railways of the East.

Trade guilds and unions often control entry into the construction sector. Thus, unless African Americans have workers who will apprentice them they may never gain access to the trades. Construction remains one of the most financially rewarding fields for those without college or high school certification. Of the total white working population in the South Atlantic region, 8.6% are employed in the construction industry as compared with 6.7% of the African-American working population. Most of the whites employed in the construction industry in this region, like the African Americans, are not college graduates.

The percentage of the African-American population engaged in the entertainment and recreation sector is largest in the mountain region. The 3.7% of the African-American working population employed in the entertainment and recre-

ation sector in the Mountain region is directly linked to the Nevada entertainment industry which includes Reno–Lake Tahoe–Las Vegas. In those areas, the high percentage shows the historic presence of African Americans in entertainment. In fact, the percentage of African Americans employed in this sector is the highest of any region for African Americans or whites. The only other region where the percentage of African Americans in entertainment exceeds that of whites and others is the West North Central region (African Americans 1.4%; whites, 0.6%) where the city of Chicago anchors a strong African-American presence in entertainment and recreation. There is a comparable percentage of African-American and white populations employed in entertainment and recreation in the East South Central region. In both cases, only 0.6% of the populations are so employed.

Included in the percentages for African Americans and whites are the professional athletes. Although the numbers are relatively small, athletes represent a sizable proportion of the African Americans in entertainment and recreation. While African Americans employed in this sector are highly visible because of media exposure and public appearances, they do not constitute a major segment of the employed African-American population. Indeed, the percentages of African Americans employed in every other sector, with the exception of mining, are larger than the percentage in entertainment and recreation.

Only in the westernmost states does the percentage of African Americans employed in the mining industry exceed or equal that of whites and others. The percentages of African Americans and whites in mining are equal in the Pacific region where percentages of employed persons in the sector are 0 .4% for each group. The percentage of employed African Americans (7.3%) compared to whites and others (3.7%) in the mining sector represents available opportunities for African Americans. Of course, in absolute terms there are far more whites in the

AFRICAN–AMERICAN INCOME

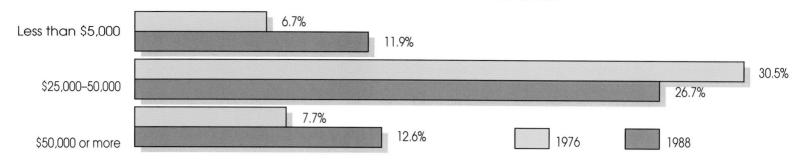

Less than $5,000	6.7%
	11.9%
$25,000–50,000	30.5%
	26.7%
$50,000 or more	7.7%
	12.6%

1976   1988

AVERAGE REGIONAL WAGES, 1988

All Americans

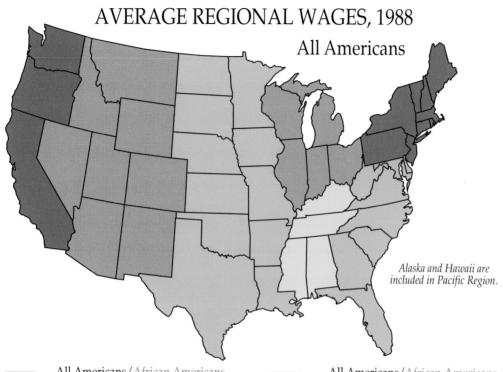

Alaska and Hawaii are included in Pacific Region.

All Americans/African Americans	All Americans/African Americans
$19,000 to 20,000/ $15,000 to 16,000	$21,600 to 24,000/ $17,600 to 20,000
$20,100 to 21,500/ $16,100 to 17,500	$24,100 to 24,250/ $20,100 to 22,000

African Americans

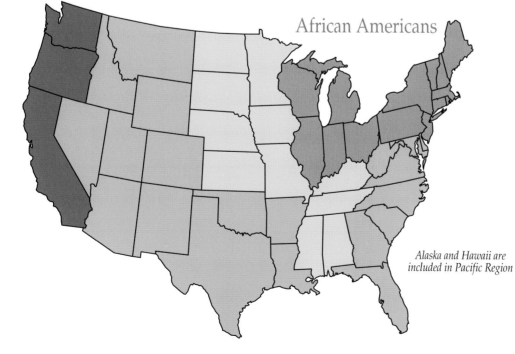

Alaska and Hawaii are included in Pacific Region

mining industry than African Americans. In the other regions, the white and others percentages are at least double the percentages of African Americans employed in the sector. Since the numbers of African Americans living in the Mountain region is very small, the overall percentage of African Americans working in mining is exceptionally minuscule.

African-American Professionals

The percentage of African Americans in managerial occupations is smaller than the national percentage of workers in similar positions. In no region of the nation is the percentage of African Americans in managerial positions more than 7 percent of the population of African-American workers. By contrast, the percentage of managers among the general population is not less than 8 percent in any region. Indeed, 11 percent of all workers in the Pacific region are managers. Only 6.8 percent of African Americans are managers in the same region. The Pacific region boasts the largest percentage of African-American managers vís-a-vís the labor force.

The East South Central and the West South Central regions have the lowest percentages of African-American managers, 2.7% and 3.7% respectively. This contrasts with the overall percentages in the East South Central with 8.1% and the West South Central with 9.2%.

There are several ways to explain the situation faced by the African-American worker; however, each explanation is rooted ultimately in the legacy of racial discrimination. African Americans were generally denied access to mentoring, refused entry into certain training programs, and hired at entry level positions.

The "revolution" of the 1960s changed many of the discriminatory practices of the past preparing the way for more access. However, the residual effects of historical discrimination continue to the present day and account for the low percentage of African Americans in managerial positions.

The separation of African Americans and whites in the workplace was common a few years ago. In those days, professional African Americans had few jobs in the North and fewer in the South. Learning to live with black professionals was one of the most difficult lessons whites had to learn in order to change their attitudes about African Americans. The lessons have not been fully learned in some quarters even now, but the situation is far different and more equitable than it has ever been.

The exclusion of African-American professionals from many companies was demanded by white workers. This had been the pattern since the early twentieth century when white unionists struck several companies to prevent them from hiring black workers. At another level, many white professionals let it be known that they would not work with black professionals. The fear and hatred of the black worker was often irrational. There was, in fact, no basis for their apprehension about working with black workers. However, the stereotypes they had received from education, parents, peers, and friends, prepared them for the most horrible experience should they be required to work with African Americans.

This problem did not escape the federal government. Hundreds of white workers protested when President Truman sought to change the racist nature of the workplace at the federal government. Some whites resigned rather than work with Africans. Truman had also attacked racism in the armed forces. He appointed two commissions to study racial matters. This was the first time that a president had taken (what was considered at the

time) such a bold step. The President's Committee on Civil Rights denounced racial discrimination and called for the elimination of segregation in American life. In 1950, three years after the first committee, Truman appointed another committee on Equality of Treatment and Opportunity in the Armed Forces. They named their report Freedom to Serve, taking a cue from the first committee's document "In Search of These Rights."

One committee's report gave the government the reasons it needed to attack racism on all fronts. Truman gave the first Presidential Speech on Civil Rights in the history of the nation in February, 1948. It was after that speech that he decided to go with the second committee and to eventually bring down the barriers to black army personnel.

These were not easy battles to fight, neither for African Americans nor for the president. How must one feel when a colleague feels such great revulsion in working with you that, before he would allow himself to work with you, he would quit his job? Nothing could be so compelling in its correctness than the end to racial discrimination, color prejudice, and religious intolerance.

Wages for African-American Workers

The gap between the white worker and the African-American-worker steadily increases in terms of wages. The gap between whites and blacks has become an ocean of difference in terms of the estate wealth of the white family and the African-American family.

Since the 1960s it is true that the wages between different classes within the black community have shown a severe split between those who "can" and those who "cannot." Incomes grew fast in the 1960s, but then the 1970s brought a slow-down. Reductions in poverty rates slowed, and African Americans were the victims of the slow-down. In fact, nearly one-third of black families remained below the poverty line when Reagan instituted his policies. A number of scholars such as Joseph Feagin and

Sidney Wilhelm have argued that the conditions of blacks got worse in the 1980s precisely because of the policies of the Reagan administration.

Whatever the case, the concrete fact is that the wages of the black worker began to drop more and more behind that of the white worker. Earnings inequality has certainly increased in the past two decades. Forty percent of blacks and 20 percent of whites earn less than $10,000. Nearly half of the black male population earned less than $10,000 in 1984. The percentage of black families with incomes less than $10,000 increased from 26.8 to 30.2 percent between 1970 and 1984.

Twenty-two percent of white men earn more than $50,000. The number of black men earning more than $50,000 is 8.8 percent. The white community has been making steady progress on widening the gap between it and African Americans.

There is a divergent experience among upwardly mobile blacks and those who are drop- or drug-outs. While middle class blacks are much better off than blacks of lower social class status, neither group approaches the white group in terms of earnings. In fact, middle- and upper-class blacks have never been able to maintain wage parity with middle- and upper-class whites.

Black college graduates did manage to see a rise in their earnings percentage relative to those of whites by about 6 percent over wages in 1979. Despite the gains that African Americans have made at the middle-class levels, the level remains far behind that of whites. The most well-heeled African Americans had a hard time meeting the standards of the Bureau of Labor Statistics for income needed to maintain middle-class living standards for a family of four. About 24 percent of African-American families were considered middle class in 1979 as compared with 50 percent of white families. By 1988, this figure had climbed to 30 percent for blacks and more than 61 percent for whites.

Wage disparity will probably remain a factor in the economic underdevelopment of the African-American community for the forseeable future. Manning Marable has based his book, *How Capitalism Underdeveloped Black America*, on the premise that African Americans are controlled through structural economic conditions, that is, in terms of the structural elements of the overall American economy.

Employment/Unemployment

The Bureau of Census has been keeping employment and unemployment records since 1940. A person is said to be in the workforce when that person is either employed or unemployed but has sought a position within the past six months. The employment rate is the ratio of people employed to the total number of people in the workforce. The unemployment figure for African-American males ages 17 to 24 is 26.1%, a staggering figure. With such a high unemployment rate, there are many young men who remain idle, and therefore susceptible to the street life. In addition, to the economic disaster unemployment brings to the African-American community, such a high rate of unemployment also brings an awesome social price. This means that these young men have no money coming in from a legitimate job. They are therefore available for jobs which may be anti-social, anti-community, even anti-themselves. Young females are not far behind the males. With 22.7% unemployment among teenage and young adult women, it is

Mean Annual Wage, 1980

	African American	All Other Americans	White	Others
Executive, Administrative, and Managerial Occupations	14,052	18,537	20,698	16,377
Professional Specialty Occupations	1,2626	17,159	16,062	18,257
Technical, Sales, and Administrative Support	9,431	9,983	10,763	9,203
Service Occupations	6,210	6,403	6,580	6,226
Farming, Fishing, and Forestry	5,563	6,257	7,270	5,244
Precision Production, Craft, and Repair Occupations	12,081	14,056	15,835	12,278
Operators, Fabricators, and Laborers	9,923	10,232	11,515	8,948

MEDIAN WEEKLY EARNINGS, 1988

In current dollars of typical weekly earnings

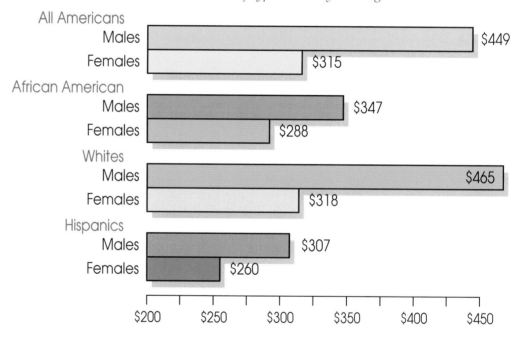

All Americans
Males $449
Females $315

African American
Males $347
Females $288

Whites
Males $465
Females $318

Hispanics
Males $307
Females $260

$200 $250 $300 $350 $400 $450

AVERAGE WAGES FOR AFRICAN AMERICANS, 1988

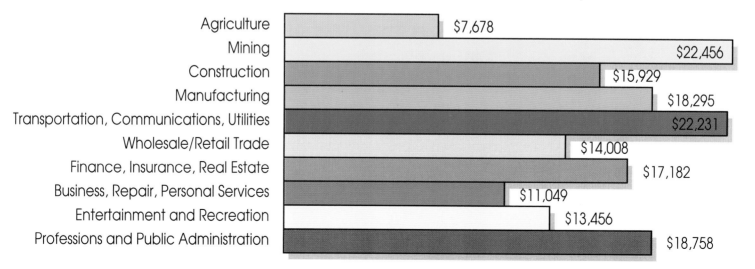

Agriculture	$7,678
Mining	$22,456
Construction	$15,929
Manufacturing	$18,295
Transportation, Communications, Utilities	$22,231
Wholesale/Retail Trade	$14,008
Finance, Insurance, Real Estate	$17,182
Business, Repair, Personal Services	$11,049
Entertainment and Recreation	$13,456
Professions and Public Administration	$18,758

AFRICAN AMERICAN UNEMPLOYMENT BY AGE, 1980

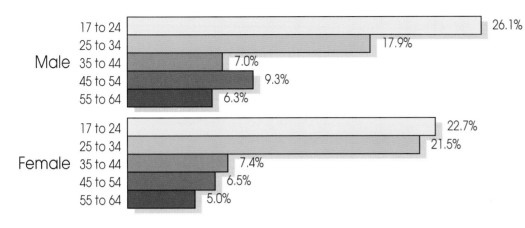

Male	17 to 24	26.1%
	25 to 34	17.9%
	35 to 44	7.0%
	45 to 54	9.3%
	55 to 64	6.3%
Female	17 to 24	22.7%
	25 to 34	21.5%
	35 to 44	7.4%
	45 to 54	6.5%
	55 to 64	5.0%

AMERICAN UNEMPLOYMENT

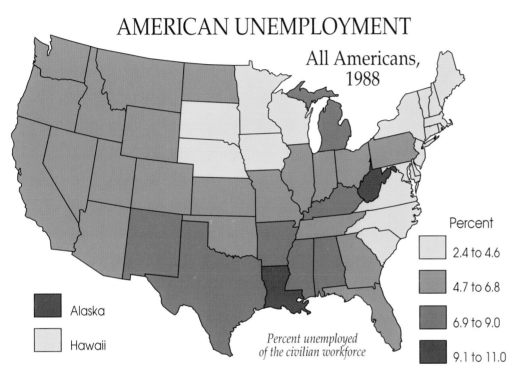

All Americans, 1988

Alaska
Hawaii

Percent unemployed of the civilian workforce

Percent
- 2.4 to 4.6
- 4.7 to 6.8
- 6.9 to 9.0
- 9.1 to 11.0

African Americans, 1984

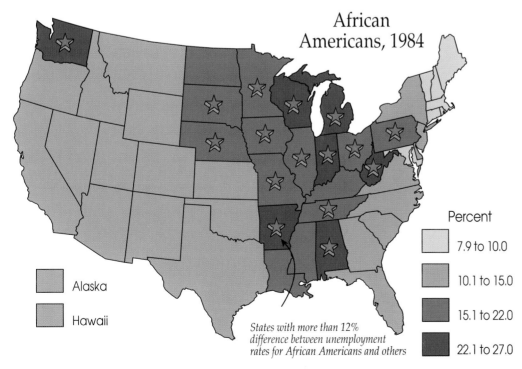

Alaska
Hawaii

States with more than 12% difference between unemployment rates for African Americans and others

Percent
- 7.9 to 10.0
- 10.1 to 15.0
- 15.1 to 22.0
- 22.1 to 27.0

not difficult to see how pregnancy becomes an alternative to the idle lifestyle.

African Americans have always worked. Slavery was full employment. But it is not just work or a job that inspires human beings, people need work that fulfills their human spirits. During World War II, almost 9 out of 10 men aged 25 to 54 had good, solid jobs. This was true whether they were black or white. In the last few years, however, the situation has grown very ominous because blacks are not employed at the previous rates. Quite a number of individuals have totally dropped out of the work world. They have neither interest nor motivation to work. The proportion of African-American men and women who work has fallen to one of the lowest points in history. Normally we could speak of black women doing better than the black man, but not in this case. Unemployment among women and men together show the cruel truth of the African-American condition in America. Unemployment has hovered around twice what it is for the white population.

The highest percentages of black unemployment seem to be in the states of Louisiana and West Virginia. Both of these states have lost some of their industrial bases in recent years. Louisiana and West Virginia are also relatively poor states in the union. West Virginia uses the coal mines as its principal resource. Since many of the coal mines have closed down, the miners are out of work. In Louisiana, the oil boom was to place the state on the top of the oil world. Money was to be bountiful. Under those conditions the state would find jobs for whites as well as hire African Americans in the surplus jobs. The collapse of the oil market sent the state tumbling. It was not a rich state to begin with and the fact that it had to recover losses in other budgets meant that there was no money for encouraging the hiring of African Americans. Among African-American men in

Louisiana the most drastic decline in the number of jobs has come since the decline in the oil market. A combination of factors contributed to this state of affairs. In the first place, nonparticipation in the workforce is a relatively new phenomenon; it has often been referred to as the "Underclass" amongst other things. By this name, the writers intend to suggest that the people so named do not fit neatly into a little category in the economics books. Most of the people in this category have been men. But women have begun to get their share of the headaches and problems that come with being alone, destitute, and illiterate.

Historically, African-American women have held more jobs than white women. From the days of slavery, the African-American woman was given a job. Yet by the 1980s white women had surpassed the black women in numbers of women hired at the top levels of certain companies and agencies.

A word about the special plight of African-American men is necessary for contextualizing the problem. The nature of the plight of unemployed and unemployable Africans is so urgent that it threatens to stop everything else.

Military Service
The Revolutionary War, 1775–1781
Throughout the history of the United States, African Americans have been employed in military service. Currently, 22.2 percent of the approximately 1.8 million enlisted personnel are African American. African Americans total 6.7 percent of the 300,000 military officers.

Historically, Africans participated in the most famous battles of the American Revolution: Ticonderoga, Lexington, Concord, and Bunker Hill. Five thousand Africans fought in every service of the colonial military. Often the memory of these brave soldiers died quickly with normality. Barred from the regular forces and militias of states in the new nation, Africans were rarely seen as a part of the early history of American forces. Yet in the naval war with France

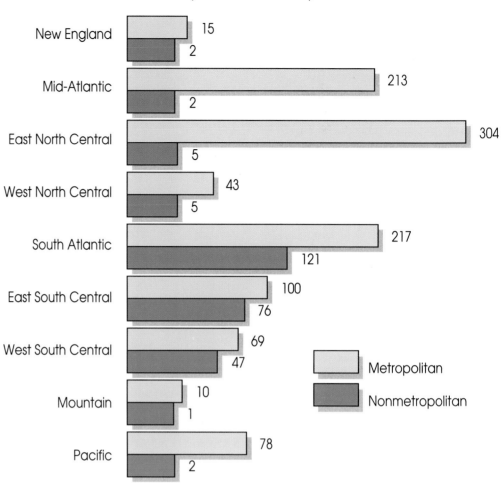

AFRICAN AMERICAN UNEMPLOYMENT
(in thousands)

New England — Metropolitan 15, Nonmetropolitan 2
Mid-Atlantic — Metropolitan 213, Nonmetropolitan 2
East North Central — Metropolitan 304, Nonmetropolitan 5
West North Central — Metropolitan 43, Nonmetropolitan 5
South Atlantic — Metropolitan 217, Nonmetropolitan 121
East South Central — Metropolitan 100, Nonmetropolitan 76
West South Central — Metropolitan 69, Nonmetropolitan 47
Mountain — Metropolitan 10, Nonmetropolitan 1
Pacific — Metropolitan 78, Nonmetropolitan 2

Metropolitan
Nonmetropolitan

African American Professionals, 1980

	Percent of All Professionals	Percent of African American Professionals
Engineers, Architects, and Surveyors	3.3	5.4
Math and Computer Sciencists	5.2	1.7
Natural Scientists	2.6	1.0
Health Diagnosis	2.2	1.6
Health Assessment and Treating	7.1	14.5
Teachers, Postsecondary	6.9	4.6
Teachers, Except Postsecondary	9.1	43.5
Librarians, Archivists, and Curators	8.2	2.2
Social Scientists and Urban Planners	7.7	2.0
Social, Recreation and Religious Workers	13.5	13.7
Lawyers and Judges	2.2	1.4
Writers, Artists, and Entertainers	4.5	6.3
Public Relations Specialists	4.3	0.7
Announcers	6.3	0.3
Athletes	14.5	1.0
All Professions	6.9	100.0

and the War of 1812, Africans figured in all of the battles. Fifty years later, the Civil War was to be the great testing ground of the American policy of excluding Africans from the military.

Three Africans distinguished themselves in this conflict although hundreds fought against the British. Crispus Attucks was one of the first martyrs to American independence. Peter Salem and Salem Poor were cited for gallantry.

War of 1812
When the war ended, one of every six sailors in the U.S. Navy was African. William Brown was cited for courageous service.

Battle of New Orleans (1815)
British were defeated by two battalions which included Africans. Several African soldiers cited for gallant actions.

Civil War
Africans fought in 200 battles and won 20 medals of honor.

Spanish American War
Four African units went to Cuba under the command of Major Charles Young, the highest ranking African-American officer.

World War I
More than 400,000 African soldiers served in the U.S. Army during this war. Needham Young and Henry Johnson of the 93rd Infantry 369th Regiment became the first Americans to receive the French Croix de Guerre.

World War II
Dorie Miller was the first hero at Pearl Harbor on December 7, 1941 when he shot down six Japanese Zeros with a machine gun he had never used before. He was awarded the Navy Cross. Before the end of the war, three other Africans had won the Navy Cross. More than one million Africans entered the United States armed forces. Seven thousand served as officers; four commanded merchant marine ships and Colonel Benjamin O. Davis flew sixty missions.

Korean War
In 1950, the U.S. Army was racially integrated and the eighty-one year old all-African 24th Infantry was the first to be integrated. Two African Americans received the Congressional Medal of Honor.

Vietnam War
Fifty-nine blacks were awarded the Congressional Medal of Honor by 1969; nineteen of them awarded during the Vietnam War.

General Colin Powell was appointed Chairman, Joint Chief of Staff by President George Bush in 1989, becoming the first American of African origin to hold that title. In his position, General Powell is the top military leader in the nation.

VETERANS OF MILITARY SERVICE

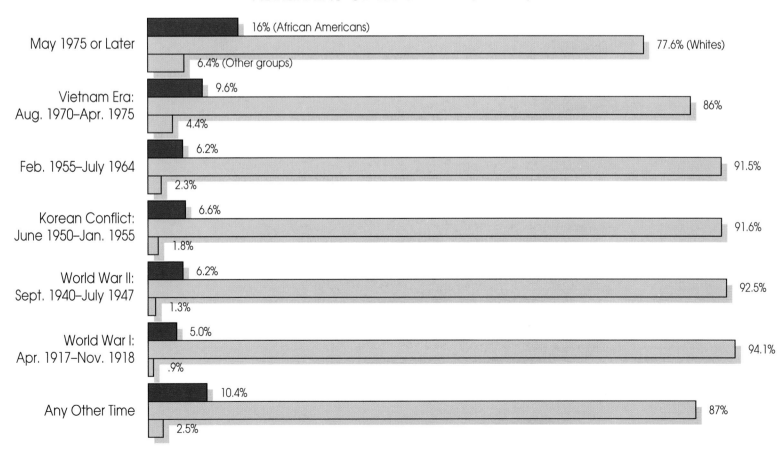

May 1975 or Later
- 16% (African Americans)
- 77.6% (Whites)
- 6.4% (Other groups)

Vietnam Era: Aug. 1970–Apr. 1975
- 9.6%
- 86%
- 4.4%

Feb. 1955–July 1964
- 6.2%
- 91.5%
- 2.3%

Korean Conflict: June 1950–Jan. 1955
- 6.6%
- 91.6%
- 1.8%

World War II: Sept. 1940–July 1947
- 6.2%
- 92.5%
- 1.3%

World War I: Apr. 1917–Nov. 1918
- 5.0%
- 94.1%
- .9%

Any Other Time
- 10.4%
- 87%
- 2.5%

ARCTIC
OCEAN

NORTH AMERICA

1st Kansas Colored Infantry
-October 28, 1862
-Island Mound near Buter, S.C.

EURO

25th Infantry (consolidation of
39th and 40th)
-Fought along the Rio Grande
and Dakotas
-1900; spent 2 years in
Alaska with 1 company of
the 24th Infantry

54th Massachusetts Volunteers
-June 1863
-Fort Wagner on Morris Island,
South Carolina

10th Cavalry
-Assignments in Southwest
-Entered Mexico in 1876
-Campaign in 1885-1886
-Colonel Benjamen Greirson

United States

1st South Carolina Colored Volunteers
-November 1862
-Raids along the Atlantic Coast from
Georgia to Florida

24th Infantry (consolidation of
38th and 41st after 1869)
-Outposts from Louisiana to
New Mexico

Cuba

Mexico

Puerto Rico

1st and 3rd Louisiana Regiments
-May 1863
-Port Hudson (lower Mississippi)

9th Cavalry
-Assignments in Southwest
-Largest campaign in 1880
-Colonel Edward Hatch

6th Massachusetts Volunteer Infantry
-July 3, 1898
-Puerto Rico skirmishes

10th Cavalry
-March 16, 1916
-South across Rio Grande
towards Santa Cruz

ATLANTIC
OCEAN

PACIFIC
OCEAN

24th Infantry
-July 1, 1898
-San Juan and Kettle Hill

SOUTH AMERICA

9th Cavalry
-June 24, 1898-July 1, 1898
-San Juan Hill and Kettle Hill

92nd Infantry Division
-August 1944 in Naples, Italy
-October 1944 fortified hill north
Florence-La Spezia on Italy's we
coast to Pesaro on the Atlantic

10th Cavalry
-June 24, 1898-July 1, 1898
-Los Guasimas and San Juan Hill

99th Fighter Squadron
-June 2, 1943 mission over island
Pantelerain in the Mediterraned
-January 27 & 28, 1944 in Anzio
Beachhead
-By May 1945, Black 332nd Fighte
Group (99th, 100th, 301st, 302nd
Squadrons) were escorting
bombers deep into Germany

25th Infantry
-July 1, 1898
-El Caney, Cuba

1st Volunteer Cavalry
-San Juan Hill and Kettle Hill

AFRICAN AMERICAN UNITS

ASIA

24th Infantry
-July 1950
-as of October 30, 1954, all black units abolished

Korea

PACIFIC OCEAN

25th Division
-May 1945 Garrison troops in Saipan, Tinan, and Marianas Islands

Philippines

1st Battalion of 24th Infantry
-March 11, 1944
-Bouganville Island beat off a Japanese counter attack

RICA

92nd Division
-September 10, 1918
-Served with French during Muese-Argonne Offensive

93rd Division
-372nd and 379th
-September and October 1918
-Muese-Argonne Offensive

369th Division "Men of Bronze"
-July through November 11,1918
-Trench warfare on western front
-Component army of French

370th Division
-September 15-November 16, 1918
-Olsne-Aisne Offensive

Company C 614th Tank Destroyer Battalion
-In 1944, drove off German force which monitored the advances of the 411th Infantry as it approached the town of Climbach

761st Tank Battalion
-Fought its way from France through Germany into Austria

969th Tank Battalion
-Defense of Bastogne in Belgium

452nd Antiaircraft Artillery Battalion
-August 1944 drove across France
-1945 drove inside Germany

INDIAN OCEAN

West Irian

Territory of New Guinea

25th Infantry
-March 28, 1944

25th, 368th, and 369th
-Biak, Morotai, and Mindanao Islands

AUSTRALIA

Civil War 1861-1865
Indian Wars 1869-1890
Spanish American War 1898-1901
Mexican Expedition
World War I
World War II
Korean War 1950-1953

'ARCTICA

LITARY CAMPAIGNS AND WARS

DATES TO REMEMBER IN AFRICAN AMERICAN HISTORY AND CULTURE

1619 Twenty Africans arrive at Jamestown, Virginia aboard a Dutch ship

1645 First American slave ship, the *Rainbowe*, sails

1663 First major African revolt against slavery, Gloucester, Virginia

1688 Quakers in Philadelphia make first formal protest against slavery

1712 African revolt against slavery in New York City

1712 Pennsylvania passes law preventing importation of Africans

1739 Major African revolt in Stono, South Carolina

1741 African revolt in New York City

1760 Jupiter Hammons is first African to publish poetry

1770 Crispus Attucks is first to die in the Boston Massacre

1771 Phyllis Wheatley is first African woman to have poems published

1775 African soldiers in battles of Bunker Hill, Concord, and Lexington

1777 Vermont becomes first state to abolish slavery

1787 Northwest Ordinance prohibits slavery in the Northwest Territories

1787 Constitution approved and extends slavery for twenty years

1800 Africans in Philadelphia petition Congress to end slavery

1804 Ohio enacts "Black Laws" preventing movement of Africans

1807 British Parliament abolishes British slave trade

1807 United States prohibits importation of Africans for slavery

1811 Africans revolt in Louisiana

1816 American colonization society formed to repatriate Africans

1817 Philadelphia's free blacks oppose American Colonization Society

1822 Denmark Vesey leads African revolt in Charleston, South Carolina

1827 John Russwurm and Samuel Cornish publish *Freedom's Journal*

1829 David Walker writes *Appeal to the Colored Citizens of the World*

1831 Nat Turner leads African revolt in Southampton County, Virginia

1834 Henry Blair is first African to receive a patent; invents corn planter

1839 Cinque leads African revolt aboard the ship, *Amistad*

1841 Africans revolt aboard the ship, *Creole*, and flee to Bahamas

1843 Henry Highland Garnet calls for enslaved Africans to revolt

1843 Sojourner Truth starts her travels speaking against slavery

1847 Frederick Douglass publishes his paper, *North Star*

1849 Harriet Tubman escapes from slavery in Maryland

1852 Institute for Colored Youth founded; forerunner of Cheyney University

1854 Ashmun Institute, first African college, is formed; renamed Lincoln University in 1866.

1856 Wilberforce University is founded

1857 Dred Scott decision denies African rights by law

1859 John Brown attacks Harper Ferry, Virginia, now in West Virginia

1859 The last slaver, *Clothilde*, brings Africans to Mobile, Alabama

1860 South Carolina secedes from the Union, followed by Florida, Alabama, Louisiana, and Texas

1861 Confederates attack Fort Sumter, South Carolina; Civil War begins

1863 President Abraham Lincoln signs the Emancipation Proclamation

1863 Robert Gould Shaw leads one of the Civil War's first all-black fighting units, the 54th Regiment of Massachusetts, on a suicide mission to attack Fort Wagner in Charleston, South Carolina.

1864 *New Orleans Tribune* is first black daily newspaper in the South

1865 Freedmen's Bureau established to aid freed Africans

1865 Robert E. Lee surrenders

1865 Nathan B. Forrest organizes the Ku Klux Klan

1865 Thirteenth Amendment abolishes slavery

1866 Fisk University opens

1867 Congress divides the Confederacy into military districts and requires the Confederate states to ratify the right of Africans to vote

1867 Howard, Morehouse, and Talladega are established

1868 Fourteenth Amendment is ratified

1869 Ebenezer Don Carlos Bassett is first African American diplomat, minister to Haiti

1870 Hiram Revels succeeds Jefferson Davis as U.S. Senator from Mississippi, becoming the first African in U.S. Congress

1870 Fifteenth Amendment is ratified

1870 Philadelphian Richard Greener is first black Harvard University graduate

1872 Charlotte E. Ray becomes first African American woman lawyer, graduating from Howard University

1872 Pinckney B. S. Pinchback becomes acting governor of Louisiana upon the impeachment of the incumbent

1874 Reverend Patrick Healy becomes President of Georgetown University

1876 Edward A. Bouchet, obtains a doctorate in physics from Yale becoming the first African American to receive a terminal degree from an American university; he is elected to Phi Beta Kappa

1877 President Rutherford B. Hayes withdraws federal soldiers from the South

1877 Frederick Douglass becomes marshall of the District of Columbia

1877 Henry Flipper graduates from West Point Military Academy

1878 Lewis Latimer works with Hiram Maxim on invention of the incandescent electric light

1879 Many Africans began trek from the South to Kansas and Oklahoma

1881 Booker T. Washington opens Tuskegee Institute

1883 Spelman College is opened

1884 *Philadelphia Tribune* is founded

1892 Ida B. Wells campaigns against lynching

1893 Daniel Hale Williams performs the first open heart surgery in Chicago

1895 W. E. B. DuBois becomes the first African American to obtain a doctorate at Harvard University

1896 Supreme Court upholds "separate but equal" doctrine in *Plessy v. Ferguson*

1903 DuBois publishes *Souls of Black Folks*

1905 The Niagara Movement is organized by African American intellectuals

1905 Robert Sengstacke Abbott starts the *Chicago Defender*

1907 Alain Locke of Philadelphia, a Harvard graduate, becomes first African American Rhodes Scholar

1909 DuBois and others found the National Association for the Advancement of Colored People on the 100th Anniversary of the birth of Abraham Lincoln

1909 Matthew Henson becomes the first man to reach the North Pole

1910 Jack Johnson becomes the heavyweight champion of the world

1915 Carter G. Woodson institutes the Association for the Study of Negro Life and History

1917 United States enters the Great European War; 300,000 African Americans serve

1919 Eighty-three African Americans lynched during the "Red Summer of Hate" as the Ku Klux Klan holds 200 public meetings

1920 Marcus Garvey convenes an international gathering of Africans in Harlem under the banner of the Universal Negro Improvement Association and African Communities League

1921 Harlem Renaissance

1921 Sadie Tanner Mossell Alexander earns a doctorate at the University of Pennsylvania

1922 Dyer Antilynching Bill is passed in U.S. House of Representatives but is defeated in the Senate

1923 George Washington Carver receives the Spingarn Medal for distinguished research

1923 Garrett A. Morgan invents the traffic light

1925 A. Philip Randolph organizes the Brotherhood of Sleeping Car Porters Union

1931 Elijah Muhammad founds the Nation of Islam

1935 Mary McLeod Bethune forms the National Council of Negro Women

1936 Jesse Owens wins four gold medals at the Berlin Olympics

1937 Joe Louis becomes the world boxing heavyweight champion

1937 William H. Hastie is the first African American to be appointed federal judge

1938 Crystal Bird Fauset is the first African American female legislator; she is elected to the Pennsylvania House of Representatives

1939 Eleanor Roosevelt resigns from the Daughters of the American Revolution when it prevents contralto Marian Anderson from singing at Constitution Hall

1940 Richard Wright's *Native Son* published

1940 Benjamin O. Davis, Sr. becomes the first African American army general

1941 Scientist Charles Drew develops techniques to separate and preserve blood. He organizes the first blood bank

1944 Adam Clayton Powell is Harlem's representative to the U.S. Congress

1945 John Johnson establishes *Ebony* magazine

1945 More than one million African Americans are inducted into the armed forces by the end of World War II

1947 Jackie Robinson joins the Brooklyn Dodgers

1949 Wesley Brown becomes the first African American to graduate from the Naval Academy at Annapolis

1953 Father Divine acquires the Woodmont Estate on the mainline outside of Philadelphia for his Peace Mission Society

1954 United States Supreme Court decision in the *Brown v. Topeka Board of Education* case says separate but equal doctrine is invalid in education

1955 Emmett Till, 14, is kidnapped and lynched in Mississippi

1955 Rosa Parks is arrested for refusing to give up her seat to a white man on a Montgomery, Alabama bus

1957 Dr. Martin Luther King, Jr. organizes the Southern Christian Leadership Conference

1958 Lorraine Hansberry's *A Raisin in the Sun* is the first play by an African American woman to be produced on Broadway

1960 Students at North Carolina A&T University stage the first sit-ins

1960 Wilma Rudolph wins gold medals in the 100 meter run, 200 meter run, and 400 meter relay at the Rome Olympics

1962 James Meredith fights to enter the University of Mississippi; federal troops are ordered to protect him

1963 Medgar Evers is assassinated

1963 W. E. B. DuBois dies in Ghana

1963 More than 250,000 march on Washington and hear Martin Luther King, Jr.'s "I Have a Dream" speech

1964 Dr. King wins Nobel Prize for Peace

1964 Civil Rights Act of 1964 is passed

1965 Malcolm X assassinated in Harlem

1965 Uprising in Watts, California, kills thirty-five people

1966 Huey Newton and Bobby Seale found Black Panther Party in Oakland, California

1966 Robert Weaver becomes the first African American to be appointed to the Presidential Cabinet when he is made head of the Department of Housing and Urban Development

1966 Stokely Carmichael is elected head of the Student Nonviolent Coordinating Committee

1966 Edward Brooke, a Massachusetts Republican, becomes the first African American elected to the Senate since the Reconstruction

1966 Maulana Karenga founds US organization on the basis of kawaida principles and it becomes the first human rights organization to recognize the need for cultural reconstruction of the African American people

1967 Thurgood Marshall is appointed to the Supreme Court and becomes the first African American elevated to that office

1968 Dr. Martin Luther King, Jr. is assassinated in Memphis, Tennessee

1968 Shirley Chisholm becomes the first African American female member of the House of Representatives

1969 Molefi Asante and Robert Singleton found the *Journal of Black Studies* at UCLA; Asante is editor and Singleton head of the advisory board. *Journal* is later published by Sage Publications.

1969 Students at Cornell University seize student center to protest harassment of African American females and the burning of a cross on campus

1971 George Jackson, author of *Soledad Brother*, is killed at San Quentin Prison in California

1972 Angela Davis is acquitted on charges of murder, kidnapping, and conspiracy

1972 National Black Political Convention takes place in Gary, Indiana

1972 Barbara Jordan and Andrew Young of Texas and Georgia, respectively, become the first representatives in the U.S. Congress elected from the South since 1901

1972 Shirley Chisholm campaigns for the presidency of the United States.

1973 Coleman Young is elected mayor of Detroit

1974 Henry Aaron of the Atlanta Braves hits home run, number 715, establishing a record

1975 Arthur Ashe wins Wimbledon Tennis Championship

1975 General Daniel C. James of the Air Force becomes the first African American four star general

1977 ABC's television adaptation of Alex Haley's book *Roots* draws the largest television audience of any program in history

1978 Muhammad Ali becomes the first person to win the heavyweight boxing championship three times

1979 Franklin Thomas is named Ford Foundation president, the first black to head a major foundation

1979 Nobel Prize for Economics awarded to Arthur Lewis

1982 Bryant Gumbel is named anchor of NBC's *Today Show*

1982 Playwright-Educator Charles Fuller wins Pulitzer Prize for Drama for *A Soldier's Play*

1982 Michael Jackson records *Thriller*, the biggest selling record of all time

1983 Lt. Colonel Guion Bluford becomes first African from the United States in space; the Afro-Cuban, Arnaldo Tamayo, had preceded him

1983 Alice Walker, author of *The Color Purple*, becomes the first African American woman to win the Pulitzer Prize for fiction

1984 Jesse Jackson, head of Operation Push, makes a serious bid to become the Democratic nominee for President

1985 Eddie Robinson, the football coach of Grambling University, becomes the winningest football coach in history

1986 Dr. Martin Luther King, Jr.'s birthday becomes a national holiday in the United States

1986 Astronaut Ronald McNair is killed in the explosion of space shuttle *Challenger* that also claimed six other lives

1987 Mae Carol Jemison becomes the first African American female astronaut in training

1988 Toni Morrison wins the Pulitzer Prize for fiction with her novel *Beloved*

1988 Temple University in Philadelphia becomes the first university to offer the doctorate degree in African American Studies; thirty-five students enroll in the first class

1989 Douglas Wilder of Virginia becomes the first African American elected to a governorship

1989 David Dinkins becomes the first African American elected mayor of New York City

1989 Representative William Gray III named House Majority Whip

1989 Ronald H. Brown elected chairperson, Democratic National Committee

1990 Eight African Americans, led by Abiyi Ford and Sheila Walker, are invited to Ouagadougou, Burkina Faso to join 130 delegates from Africa, North America, South America, Europe, and the Caribbean to found the first comprehensive international African think-tank, the Institute of the Black Peoples.

SELECTED REFERENCES

General Reference Books

The Arts and Civilization of Black and African Peoples. Lagos, Nigeria: Centre for Black and African Arts and Civilization, 1986.

The Black Resource Guide, 1988–89. Washington, DC: R. Benjamin Johnson and Jacqueline L. Johnson, 1989.

Bogle, Donald. *Blacks in American Films and Television: An Encyclopedia.* New York: Garland Publishing, 1988.

Davis, Marianna. *Contributions of Black Women to America.* Columbia, South Carolina: Kenday Press, 1982.

U.S. Department of Justice. *Bureau of Labor Statistics, Report to the Nation on Crime.* 2nd ed. Washington, DC: Government Printing Office, 1988.

Ebony: Pictorial History of Black America. Nashville: Ebony, 1971.

Evans, Mari (ed.) *Black Women Writers (1950–1980): A Critical Evaluation.* Garden City, New York: Doubleday, 1984.

Harris, Middleton. *The Black Book.* New York: Random House, 1974.

Hughes, Langston and Milton Melzer. *A Pictorial History of the Negro.* New York: Crown Publishers, 1956.

Josey, E. J. and Ann Allen Shockley (eds.) *Handbook of Black Librarianship.* Littleton, CO: Libraries Unlimited, 1977.

Josey, E. J. and Marva L. DeLoach (eds.) *Ethnic Collections in Libraries.* New York: Neal Schuman Publishers, 1983.

Kellner, Bruce (ed.) *The Harlem Renaissance: A Historical Dictionary for the Era.* Westport, CT: Greenwood Press, 1984.

Low, W. Augustus and Virgil Clift (eds.) *Encyclopedia of Black America.* New York: Neal Schuman Publishers, 1983.

Miller, Randall M. and John David Smith (eds.) *Dictionary of Afro-American Slavery.* New York: Greenwood Press, 1988.

Morrison, Donald G., *Black Africa: A Comparative Handbook.* 2nd ed. New York: Paragon House, 1989.

Nunez, Benjamin. *Dictionary of Afro-Latin American Civilization.* Westport, Connecticut: Greenwood Press, 1980.

Ploski, Harry and James Williams, A. *The Negro Almanac: A Reference Work on the Afro-American.* 4th ed. New York, Wiley, 1983.

Rollock, Barbara. *Black Authors and Illustrators of Children's Books: A Biographical Directory.* New York: Garland Publishing, 1988.

Shockley, Allen. *Afro-American Women Writers, 1746–1933: An Anthology and Critical Guide.* Boston: G.K. Hall, 1989.

Smith, Jessie Carney (ed.) *Images of Blacks in American Culture: A Reference Guide to Information Sources.* New York: Greenwood Press, 1984.

Smythe, Mabel M. (ed.) *The Black American Reference Book.* Englewood Cliffs, NJ: Prentice-Hall, 1976.

Van Chi–Bonnardel, Regine. *The Atlas of Africa.* New York: The Free Press, 1973.

The State of Black America, 1989. New York: National Urban League, 1989.

U.S. Bureau of the Census. *County and City Data Book, 1983.* 10th ed. Washington, DC: Government Printing Office, 1983.

U.S. Bureau of the Census. *State and Metropolitan Area Data Book, 1982: A Statistical Abstract Supplement.* Washington, DC: Government Printing Office, 1982.

U.S. Bureau of the Census. *Statistical Abstract of the United States.* Washington, DC: Government Printing Office, 1879–1990, annual.

Bibliographies and Indexes

Allen, Walter R. (ed.) *Black American Families, 1965–1984: A Classified, Selectively Annotated Bibliography.* Westport, CT: Greenwood Press, 1986.

Brignano, Russell. *Black Americans in Autobiography: An Annotated Bibliography of Autobiographies and Autobiographical Books Written Since the Civil War.* Revised. Durham: Duke University Press, 1984.

Campbell, Dorothy W. *Index to Black American Writers in Collective Biographies.* Littleton, CO: Libraries Unlimited, 1983.

Center for Afroamerican and African Studies, The University of Michigan. *Black Immigration and Ethnicity in the United States: An Annotated Bibliography.* Westport, CT: Greenwood Press, 1985.

Chapman, Dorothy Hilton. *Index to Poetry by Black American Women.* New York: Greenwood Press, 1986.

Davis, Lenwood G. *The Black Family in the United States: A Revised, Updated Selectively Annotated Bibliography.* New York: Greenwood Press, 1986.

Davis, Lenwood G. and George Hill. *A Bibliographical Guide to Black Studies Programs in the United States: An Annotated Bibliography.* Westport, CT: Greenwood Press, 1985.

Davis, Lenwood G. and George Hill. *Blacks in American Armed Forces 1776–1983.* Westport, CT: Greenwood Press, 1985.

Davis, Nathaniel. *Afro-American Reference: An Annotated Bibliography of Selected Resources.* Westport, CT: Greenwood Press, 1984.

de Lerma, Dominique-Rene. *A Bibliography of Black Music*. vols. 1–4. Westport, CT: Greenwood Press, 1981–1984.

Herod, Agustina and Charles C. Herod. *Afro-American Nationalsim: An Annotated Bibliography of Militant Separatist and Nationalist Literature*. New York: Garland, 1986.

Hill, George H. *Black Business and Economics A Selected Bibliography*. New York: Garland, 1985.

Hyatt, Marshall. *The Afro-American Cinematic Experience: An Annotated Bibliography*. Wilmington, DE: Scholarly Resources, 1983.

Johnson, Frank J. *Who's Who of Black Millionaires*. Fresno, CA: 1984.

Joyce, Donald. *Blacks in the Humanities, 1750–1984, A Selected Annotated Bibliography*. Westport, CT: Greenwood Press, 1985.

Matney, William C. (ed.) *Who's Who Among Black Americans*. 5th ed. Northbook, IL: 1988.

McPherson, James M. (ed.) *Blacks in America: Bibliographical Essays*. Garden City, NY: Doubleday, 1971.

Michael, Colette V. *Negritude: An Annotated Bibliography*. West Cornwall, CT: Locust Hill Press, 1988.

Momemi, Jamshid A. *Demography of the Black Population in the United States: An Annotated Bibliography with a Review Essay*. Westport, CT: Greenwood Press, 1983.

Momemi, Jamshid A. *Housing and Racial/Ethnic Minority Status in the United States: An Annotated Bibliography with a Review Essay*. Westport, CT: Greenwood Press, 1987.

Newman, Richard. *Black Access: A Bibliography of Afro-American Bibliographies*. Westport, CT: Greenwood Press, 1984.

Page, James A. and Jae Min Roh. *Selected Black American, African and Caribbean Authors: A Bio-Bibliography*. Littleton, CO: Libraries Unlimited, 1985.

Perry, Margaret. *The Harlem Renaissance: An Annotated Bibliography and Commentary*. New York: Garland, 1982.

Sims, Janet. *The Progress of Afro-American Women: A Selected Bibliography and Resource Guide*. Westport, CT: Greenwood Press, 1980.

Skowronski, JoAnn. *Black Music in America: A Bibliography*. Metuchen, NJ: Scarecrow Press, 1981.

Smith, Dwight L. (ed.) *Afro-American History, A Bibliography*. Santa Barbara, CA: ABC CLIO Press. vol.1, 1974; vol. 2, 1981.

Stevenson, Rosemary M. *Index to Afro-American Reference Sources*. New York: Greenwood Press, 1988.

Weinberberg, Meyer (ed.) *The Education of Poor and Minority Children: A World Bibliography*. Westport, CT: Greenwood Press, 1981.

Willis-Thomas, Deborah. *An Illustrated Bio-Bibliography of Black Photographers, 1940–1980*. New York: Garland, 1989.

Individual Biography

Davis, Lenwood G. *A Paul Robeson Research Guide: A Selected Annotated Bibliography*. Westport, CT: Greenwood Press, 1982.

Davis, Lenwood G. and Janet L. Sims, *Marcus Garvey: An Annotated Bibliography*. Westport, CT: Greenwood Press, 1980.

Duffy, Susan. *Shirley Chisholm: A Bibliography of Writings by and about Her*. Metuchen, NJ: Scarecrow Press, 1988.

Johnson, Timothy V. *Malcolm X: A Comprehensive Annotated Bibliography*. New York: Garland, 1986.

Kinnamon, Kenneth. *A Richard Wright Bibliography: Fifty Years of Criticism and Commentary, 1933–1982*. New York: Greenwood Press, 1982.

Newman, Richard. *Lemuel Haynes: A Bio-Bibliography*. New York: Lambeth Press, 1984.

Pratt, Louis H. and Darnell D. Pratt. *Alice Malsenior Walker: An Annotated Bibliography 1968–1986*, Westport, CT: Meckler, 1988.

Pyatt, Sherman. *Martin Luther King, Jr.: An Annotated Bibliogrpahy*. New York: Greenwood Press, 1986.

Robinson, William H. *Phillis Wheatley: A Bio-Bibliography*. Westport, CT: Greenwood Press, 1981.

Scally, Sister Anthony. *Carter G. Woodson: A Bio-Bibliography*. Westport, CT: Greenwood Press, 1985.

Settle, Elizabeth A. *Ishmael Reed: A Primary and Secondary Bibliography*. Boston: G.K. Hall, 1982.

Collective Biography

Black Writers: A Selection of Sketches from Contemporary Authors. Detroit: Gale Research, 1989.

Dance, Daryl Cumber. *Fifty Caribbean Writers: A Bio-Bibliographical Critical Sourcebook*. Westport, CT: Greenwood Press, 1986.

Davis, Thadious M. and Trudier Harris (eds.) *Afro-American Fiction Writers after 1955*. Detroit: Gale, 1984. (Dictionary of Literary Biography, vol. 33).

Davis, Thadious M. and Trudier Harris (eds.) *Afro-American Poets since 1955*. Detroit: Gale, 1985. (Dictionary of Literary Biography, vol. 41).

Davis, Thadious M. and Trudier Harris (eds.) *Afro-American Writers after 1955: Dramatists and Prose Writers*. Detroit: Gale Research, 1985. (Dictionary of Literary Biography, vol. 38).

Davis, Thadious M. and Trudier Harris (eds.) *Afro-American Writers before the Harlem Renaissance*. Detroit: Gale. 1987. (Dictionary of Literary Biography, vol. 54).

Davis, Thadious M. and Trudier Harris (eds.) *Afro-American Writers, 1940–1955*. Detroit: Gale Research, 1988. (Dictionary of Literacy Biography, vol. 76).

Joint Center Political Studies. *Black Elected Officials: A National Roster*. New York: Unipub, 1986.

Logan, Rayford W. and Michael R. Winston. *Dictionary of American Negro Biography*. New York: Norton, 1982.

Southern, Eileen. *Biographical Dictionary of Afro-American and African Musicians*. Westport, CT: Greenwood Press, 1982.

Spradling, Mary Mace. *Black and White: A Guide to Magazine Articles, Newspaper Articles, and Books Concerning more than 6,000 Black Individuals and Groups*. Detroit: Gale, 1980. Supplement, 1985.

Van Sertima, Ivan (ed.) *Great Black Leaders: Ancient and Modern*. New Brunswick, NJ: Journal of African Civilizations, Ltd., 1988.

Histories and Critical Analyses

Brawley, Benjamin. *A Short History of the American Negro*. New York: Macmillan, 1924.

Diop, Cheikh Anta. *The African Origin of Civilization*. New York: Lawrence Hill, 1974.

Dunn, Ross. *The Adventures of Ibn Battuta*. Berkeley: University of California Press, 1986.

DuBois, W. E. B. *The Souls of Black*. New York: Fawcett, 1961.

Gibbs. H. A. R. *The Travels of Ibn Battuta A.D. 1325–1354*. Cambridge: Cambridge University Press, 1971.

Harding, Vincent. *There is a River*. New York: Harcourt, Brace, and Jovanovich, 1981.

Keto, C. Tsehloane. *The Africa-Centered Perspective of History*. Blackwood, NJ: K A. Publications, 1989.

Omari, Ibn al. *Masalik il Absar fir Mamalik el Amsar*. Tr. Gaudefroy, Paris, 1927.

Randall, Dudley, *The Black Poets*. New York: Bantam, 1972.

Van Sertima, Ivan. *They Came Before Columbus*. New York: Random House, 1976.

White, Walter. *Rope and Faggot*. New York: Arno Press, 1969.

SOURCES FOR GRAPHICS

Page 29
Rawley, James. *The Transatlantic Slave Trade*. New York: W. W. Norton and Co., 1981.

Page 49
Jones, Katharine M. *The Plantation South*. Indianapolis, IN: Bobbs-Merril, Co., 1957.

Page 57
Drewy, Sidney William. *The Southampton Insurrection*. Washington, DC: The Neale Company, 1900. Reprint. Murfreesboro, NC: Johnson Publishing Co., 1968.

Page 83
Libby, Jean. *Black Voices from Harper's Ferry: Osbourne Anderson and the John Brown Raid*. Palo Alto, CA: Libby, 1979.

Stavis, Varrie. *John Brown: The Sword and the Word*. Cranbury, NJ: A. S. Barnes, 1970.

Pages 86, 88, and 89
May, Joe H. *Black Americans and Their Contributions Toward Union Victory in the American Civil War*. New York: University Press of America, 1984.

Page 87
Foner, Jack D. *Blacks and the Military in American History: A New Perspective*. New York: Praeger, 1974.

Nalty, Bernard C. *Strength for a Fight: A History of Black Americans in the Military*. New York: Free Press, 1986.

Page 62
Payne, Daniel A. *History of the African Methodist Episcopal Church*. The Basic Afro-American Reprint Library, vols. 1 and 2. New York: Johnson Reprint Co., 1968.

Page 73
Blockson, Charles. "Escape from Slavery: Undergound Railroad," *National Geographic Magazine* 166(1).

Buckmaster, Henreitta. *Let My People Go: The Story of the Underground Railroad and the Growth of the Abolition Movement*. New York: Harper and Brothers, 1941.

Page 95
The Washington Post. November 2, 1930: 14.

Page 103
Washington, Booker T. *The Story of My Life and Work*. New York: Negro Universities Press, 1969.

Bureau of the Census. *Current Population Reports, 1970*. Washington, DC: GPO, 1977.

Page 110
Black, Clinton. *History of Jamaica*. London: Collins Educational, 1983.

Pages 148, 149, 150, 151
Ploski, Harry A. and James Williams, eds., *The Negro Almanac A Reference Work on The Afro-American*, 4th ed. New York: Bellwether Publishing Co., 1983.

Chapter 13
Bureau of the Census. *Census of the Population, 1950, 1970, 1980*. Washington, DC: GPO, 1952, 1973, 1983.

Bureau of the Census. *Historical Statistics of the United States, Colonial Times to 1970*. Washington, DC: GPO, 1975.

Bureau of the Census. *Sixteenth Census Report, Population*. Washington, DC: GPO, 1945.

Bureau of the Census. *Negro Population 1790–1915*. Washington, DC: GPO, 1918.

Bureau of the Census. *Statistical Abstract of the United States*. Washington, DC: GPO, 1928, 1989.

Bureau of Labor Statistics. *Employment and Earnings*. Washington, DC: GPO, December 1969 and 1980, January 1981.

National Center for Health Statistics. *Vital Statistics of the United States, 1960, 1970, 1980, 1985, 1986*. Washington, DC: GPO, 1964, 1974, 1985, 1987, 1988.

Cesar, 136
Chaney, James, 153
Charles, Ray, 129
Charleston, South Carolina, 37, 48, 61, 62
Charles V, King of Portugal, 29
Charlotte, North Carolina, 156
Chastang, Peter, 63
Chesapeake and Marine Railway and Dry Dock Company, 93
Cheyney College, 134
Chicago, Illinois, 155, 156, 158
Chicago Equal Rights League, 71
Child, Lydia Maria, 66, 67
Children:
  birth rates, 160–162
  female-headed households and, 164–165
  infant mortality, 166, 167
  number per family, 163–164
Choreographers, 138
Christianity, 41–42, 47, 48
Chronic obstruction, deaths from, 167, 168
Church, T. S., 138
Churches:
  Baptist, 48, 49, 52
  Methodist, 48, 49, 52, 62
  post-Civil War education and, 91
  post-Civil War membership, 52
  resistance to slavery by, 48–50
  Roman Catholic, 24, 25, 29–30, 52
Cincinnati, Ohio, 80, 156
Cinque, 55–56
Cirrhosis, deaths from, 167
Cities, population in, 155–156
City College, 134
Civil rights:
  in early twentieth century, 109
  post-Civil War, 87
Civil Rights Act of 1964, 119
Civil Rights Movement, 119–124, 152–153, 170
Civil Rights Restoration Act of 1988, 131
Civil War, 77–89
  Africans in, 78–82, 84–86, 89, 183
  battles of, 78, 86
  "colored" regiments in, 89
  problems after, 85, 87
  states prior to, 78
  women in, 89
Clarke, Kenny, 140
Cleaver, Eldridge, 119
Cleveland, Grover, 147
Cleveland, Ohio, 156
Climate, African, 2
Cobb, W. Montague, 136
Coffin, Levi, 72
Coker, Daniel, 48
College enrollment, 169, 170
Colleges, 91–92, 132–135
Collins, George, 48
Colonial Africa, 10–13, 32–33
Colorado, 92, 95, 101
Colorado Territory, 89
Colored Convention of 1817, 11–12
Coltrane, John, 9, 107, 142
Columbus, Georgia, 158
Columbus, Ohio, 156
Communications industry:
  wages from employment in, 180
  worker distribution in, 174, 176
Compromise of 1850, 69
Compromise of 1877, 87, 96
Conestoga wagons, 20–21
Confederacy, 78–79, 81
Confiscation Act of 1861, 79

Congo (Zaire) Rain Forest, 11
Congress, 85, 87, 96, 104, 116
Congressional Medal of Honor, 88, 183
Congressmen, 96, 97, 109, 112
Congress of Racial Equality, 152–153
Connecticut, 89, 95, 99, 101
Constitutional Convention of 1787, 35–37, 42, 43
Construction industry:
  wages from employment in, 180
  worker distribution in, 174, 177
Convict lease system, 99
Cook, G., 138
Cooper, Anna J., 69, 107
Cooper, Mary, 69
Copper, J., 138
Cornell University, 135
Cornwall, P. W., 138
Coronado, Francisco Vasques de, 17, 18
Cortes, Hernando, 16
Cosby, Bill, 107, 134
Cosby, Camille, 134
Cotton Club, 142
Cotton gin, 42, 43
Cotton production, 43, 49
Covey, James, 55
Cowboys, 19–21
Craft, Ellen, 69, 75
Craft, William, 75
Craig, O. T., 93
Craille, A. L., 138
Crisis Magazine, The, 102
Croix de Guerre, 117
Crude birth rates, 160, 161
Crude death rates, 161
Cuffe, Paul, 39–40
Cullen, Countee, 114, 115
Cultural renaissance, 113–115
Cultural resistance, 47–48
Cultural Unity of Black Africa (Diop), 23
Curtis, Auston M., 136

D

Daily, Ulysses Grant, 136
Dallas, Texas, 156, 158, 176
Dana, Richard Henry, Jr., 56
Dance, 47, 129, 138, 149
Dance Company of Zimbabwe, 129
Danish slave trade, 29
Dart, Isom, 19, 64
Davidson, Basil, 12
Davis. A. K., 97
Davis, Angela, 119
Davis, Benjamin O., 183
Davis, Miles, 107, 142
Davis, Nelson, 72
Davis, Ossie, 122
Davis, Sammy, Jr., 107, 140
Davis, W. R., Jr., 138
Daytona Educational and Industrial School for Negro Girls, 70
Death rates, 161, 166–168
Declaration of Independence, 37
Dee, Ruby, 9, 114
DeGrasse, John V., 136
Delaney, Martin S., 89, 136
Delaware, 78, 89, 95, 99, 101
Denver, Colorado, 156
Depression, 111–113
De Priest, Oscar, 109
Derham, James, 136
Desoto, Hernando, 17, 18

Detroit, Michigan, 80, 155, 156, 158
Devine, Annie, 127
Dewey, John, 109
Diabetes mellitus, deaths from, 167
Diaz, Bartholomew, 19
Diop, Cheikh Anta, 6, 23
Discrimination:
  in the Armed Forces, 116, 179
  in the early twentieth century, 108–110
  in employment, 110, 179
  Jim Crow law, 96
  in voting rights, 97
  in wages, 179–180
Disfranchisement, 97, 99, 100
District of Columbia. See Washington, DC
Dodson, Owen, 114, 115
Dorantes de Carranca, Andres, 16
Dorsey, Decatur, 88
Dorticus, C. J., 138
Dotson, Jacob, 17, 18
Dotson, William H., 148
Douglas, Anna, 69
Douglas, Steven A., 69
Douglass, Frederick, 61, 66–68, 75, 80, 83, 107
Douglass, H. Ford, 89
Douglass' Paper, 67
Dove, Rita, 107
Downing, George T., 107
Doyle, Henry, 58
Doyle, Trajan, 59
Dred Scott decision, 74–75, 85, 152
Dresser, Amos, 68
Drew, Charles Richard, 53, 136–137
Drewry, Edwin, 59
DuBois, W. E. B., 95, 102, 107–111, 135, 151
Dumas, F., 89
Dunbar, Paul Laurence, 107, 114
Dunham, Katherine, 107
Du Sable, Jean Baptiste, 65
Dutch slave trade, 25, 26, 28, 29
Dutch West India Company, 26

E

East Africa, emergence of humans in, 2
East St. Louis, Illinois, 155
Ebony Pictorial History of Black America, 30
Education, 85, 91–92, 131–136, 169–172
Educational attainment, 168
Edwards, Peter, 59
Egypt, ancient, 3, 6
Egyptian explorers, 15
Eisenhower, Dwight D., 121
Elementary school enrollment, 169
Elkins, T., 138
Ellington, Duke, 107, 142
Ellis, Charles M., 56
Ellis, William, 136
Ellison, Ralph, 107, 128, 146
El Paso, Texas, 156
Emancipation Proclamation, 84
Employment:
  by age, 173
  during the depression, 111–113
  by industry, 174–179
  occupation distribution, 173–175
  post-Civil War, 92–93, 99, 100
  rate of, 180
  regional distribution of labor, 172, 175
  at the turn-of-the-century, 110
  wages by industry, 180
Entertainment industry:

wages from employment in, 180
worker distribution in, 174, 177
Epps, Archie, 122
Equiano, Olaudah, 149
Estevanico (Estevan de Dorantes), 16–19
Europeans:
  colonization of Africa by, 10–13
  slave trade and. See Slave trade, European
Evans, Mari, 9, 107, 145
Evers, Medgar, 153
Explorers, 15–21

F

Fagg, Bernard, 13
Fair Housing Act of 1968, 131
Families in poverty, 165, 166
Family characteristics, 164
Family earners, 164
Family income, 165–166
Family size, 163–165
Fango, Gobo, 20
Farmer, James, 153
Farmworkers, 51, 174, 176–177
Farrakhan, Louis, 124
Al-Fazari, 26
Feagin, Joseph, 179
Female-headed households, 164–165
Female population, 157
Fifteenth Amendment, 87, 95, 97, 99
Finance industry:
  wages from employment in, 180
  worker distribution in, 174, 176
Fire, early use of, 2
Fitzgerald, Ella, 128
Fitzpatrick, Tom, 64
Fleetwood, Christian A., 79, 88
Flemming, F., Jr., 138
Flipper, Henry O., 65
Florence, South Carolina, 158
Florida, 89, 92, 95, 101
Forman, James, 153
Forten, James, 52
Fortune, T. Thomas, 87
Fortune, T. Timothy, 107
Fort Worth, Texas, 156
Fourteenth Amendment, 85, 94–96, 99
France:
  Haitian Revolution and, 43–44
  Louisiana territory and, 44
  New World commercial activity of, 32
  slave trade of, 23, 25, 26, 29
Francis, Nathaniel, 58
Francis, Salathiel, 57
Francis, Wiley, 58
Franklin, Aretha, 9, 140–141
Franklin, Benjamin, 42
Franklin, John Hope, 26, 48, 62, 116
Frazier, Susan, 69
Free Africans:
  categories of, 51
  in Civil War, 78, 81
  in New Orleans, 45, 48, 61, 62, 81
  in the North, 48–51, 61
  population in 1790, 61
  population in 1860, 61, 62
  restrictions on, 62–63
  in the South, 48, 61–63
  in urban areas, 61, 62
Free African Society, 48, 52
Freedmen's Bureau, 85, 91, 92
Freedom Democratic Party, 153